Secrecy and Community in 21st-Century Fiction

Secrecy and Community in 21st-Century Fiction

Edited by María J. López and Pilar Villar-Argáiz

BLOOMSBURY ACADEMIC
NEW YORK • LONDON • OXFORD • NEW DELHI • SYDNEY

BLOOMSBURY ACADEMIC
Bloomsbury Publishing Inc
1385 Broadway, New York, NY 10018, USA
50 Bedford Square, London, WC1B 3DP, UK
29 Earlsfort Terrace, Dublin 2, Ireland

BLOOMSBURY, BLOOMSBURY ACADEMIC and the Diana logo are trademarks
of Bloomsbury Publishing Plc

First published in the United States of America 2021
This paperback edition published 2022

Volume Editor's Part of the Work © María J. López and Pilar Villar-Argáiz, 2021
Each chapter © of Contributors, 2021

Cover image © Getty Images

For legal purposes the Acknowledgements on p. xv constitute an extension
of this copyright page.

All rights reserved. No part of this publication may be reproduced or transmitted
in any form or by any means, electronic or mechanical, including photocopying,
recording, or any information storage or retrieval system, without
prior permission in writing from the publishers.

Bloomsbury Publishing Inc does not have any control over, or responsibility for, any
third-party websites referred to or in this book. All internet addresses given in this
book were correct at the time of going to press. The author and publisher regret
any inconvenience caused if addresses have changed or sites have ceased to
exist, but can accept no responsibility for any such changes.

Library of Congress Cataloging-in-Publication Data
Names: López Sánchez-Vizcaíno, María Jesús, editor. | Villar-Argaiz, Pilar, editor.
Title: Secrecy and community in 21st-century fiction /
edited by María J. López and Pilar Villar-Argáiz.
Other titles: Secrecy and community in twenty-first-century fiction
Description: New York : Bloomsbury Academic, 2021. | Includes bibliographical
references and index.
Identifiers: LCCN 2020036642 (print) | LCCN 2020036643 (ebook) |
ISBN 9781501365539 (hardback) | ISBN 9781501365546 (epub) |
ISBN 9781501365553 (pdf)
Subjects: LCSH: English fiction–21st century–History and criticism. |
Secrecy in literature. | Communities in literature.
Classification: LCC PR890.S423 S43 2021 (print) | LCC PR890.S423 (ebook) |
DDC 823/.9209—dc23
LC record available at https://lccn.loc.gov/2020036642
LC ebook record available at https://lccn.loc.gov/2020036643

ISBN: HB: 978-1-5013-6553-9
PB: 978-1-5013-7219-3
ePDF: 978-1-5013-6555-3
eBook: 978-1-5013-6554-6

Typeset by RefineCatch Limited, Bungay, Suffolk

To find out more about our authors and books visit www.bloomsbury.com
and sign up for our newsletters.

In Loving Memory of
Pilar Argáiz González

Contents

Notes on contributors	ix
Foreword *Joseph Hillis Miller*	xiii
Acknowledgements	xv

Introduction: Secrecy and community in twenty-first-century fiction *María J. López* 1

Part One Secrecy, literary form and the community of readers

1. Secrecy and community in ergodic texts: Derrida, Ali Smith and the experience of form *Derek Attridge* 23

2. Protective mimicry: Reflections on the novel today *Nicholas Royle* 37

3. 'Where all is known and nothing understood': Narrative sequence and textual secrets in Toni Morrison's *Love* *Paula Martín-Salván* 55

4. Challenging stereotypes of femininity through secrets in Alice Munro's fiction *Mercedes Díaz Dueñas* 71

5. Zoë Wicomb and the secrets of the canon *Liani Lochner* 87

Part Two Communities of secrecy

6. Cryptaesthetic resistance and community in Jhumpa Lahiri's *The Lowland* *María Luisa Pascual Garrido* 107

7. Queering the Māori crypt: Community and secrecy in Witi Ihimaera's *The Uncle's Story* *Gerardo Rodríguez-Salas* 123

8. Secrecy, invisibility and community in Jeanette Winterson's *The Daylight Gate* *Juan L. Pérez-de-Luque* 139

9. Novel mediums: The art of not speaking in (and of) Hilary Mantel's *Beyond Black* *Hannu Poutiainen* 155

Part Three Secrecy, postcolonialism and democracy

10 Shame and the idea of community in Ian Holding's *Of Beasts and Beings* and *What Happened to Us* Mike Marais 173

11 'Whilst our souls negotiate': Secrets and secrecy in Jonathan Franzen's *Purity* Jesús Blanco Hidalga 189

12 Conversing with spectres: Secrets and ghosts in Viet Thanh Nguyen's *The Refugees* Kim L. Worthington 207

Index 225

Contributors

Derek Attridge is Emeritus Professor in the Department of English and Related Literature at the University of York (UK), and a fellow of the British Academy. His publications include *Peculiar Language: Literature as Difference from the Renaissance to James Joyce* (1988), *Joyce Effects: On Language, Theory, and History* (2000), *The Singularity of Literature* (2004, 2017), *Reading and Responsibility: Deconstruction's Traces* (2010), *The Work of Literature* (2015), *The Experience of Poetry: From Homer's Listeners to Shakespeare's Readers* (2019), and, as editor or co-editor, *Post-Structuralism and the Question of History* (1987), Jacques Derrida's *Acts of Literature* (1992) and *Theory after 'Theory'* (2011).

Mercedes Díaz Dueñas is a lecturer in the English department at the University of Granada (Spain). Her research interests focus on contemporary Canadian fiction in English. She is also interested in communitarian theory, comparative literature, translation studies and discourse analysis. Her most recent essays have appeared with Versita, Palgrave Macmillan and Routledge.

María Luisa Pascual Garrido is a senior lecturer at the University of Córdoba (Spain) in the Department of English Studies. Her research interests focus on theories related to community and secrecy in literature, contemporary and modern literature in English, gender studies and women's writing, and literary translation and its reception. She has published articles and book chapters on those areas and several Spanish editions and translations of English-speaking authors. Her most recent book is *Mary Astell. Escritos Feministas* (2013).

Jesús Blanco Hidalga teaches in the English department at the University of Córdoba (Spain). His research interests are modern and contemporary fiction in English, critical theory and political thought. He is the author of *Jonathan Franzen and the Romance of Community: Narratives of Salvation* (2017).

Liani Lochner is Associate Professor of Anglophone Postcolonial Literature at Université Laval (Canada). Educated in South Africa and England, her research interests are in critical theory and world literature, and she has published related essays on the works of Zoë Wicomb, J. M. Coetzee, Kazuo Ishiguro, Milan Kundera, Salman Rushdie and Aravind Adiga. Her current projects include a monograph on Wicomb's writing and a book chapter, 'Ishiguro and Colonialism', for *The Cambridge Companion to Kazuo Ishiguro* (edited by Andrew Bennett).

María J. López is a senior lecturer in the English department at the University of Córdoba (Spain). She is the author of *Acts of Visitation: The Narrative of J. M. Coetzee*

(2011) and co-editor of *J. M. Coetzee and the Non-English Literary Traditions* (2016) and *New Perspectives on Community and the Modernist Subject* (2017). Her work has also appeared in the *Journal of Southern African Studies*, the *Journal of Commonwealth Literature*, the *Journal of Literary Studies*, *English in Africa*, *English Studies* and the *Journal of Postcolonial Writing*.

Mike Marais teaches literary studies at Rhodes University (South Africa). He is the author of *Secretary of the Invisible: The Idea of Hospitality in the Fiction of J. M. Coetzee* (2009). His research interests include the intersection between ethics and aesthetics in modern fiction.

Paula Martín-Salván is a senior lecturer in English and American Literature at the University of Córdoba (Spain). Her research focuses on the representation of communities in modernist and postmodernist fiction, and on contemporary critical theory. She has co-edited the volumes *Community in Twentieth-Century Fiction* (2013) and *New Perspectives on Community and the Modernist Subject* (2017), and is the author of the monograph *The Language of Ethics and Community in Graham Greene's Fiction* (2015).

Juan L. Pérez-de-Luque is a senior lecturer at the University of Córdoba (Spain) in the Department of English and German Studies. His research interests focus mainly on popular fiction, particularly in horror literature and science fiction. He is also interested in witchcraft studies. He has published chapters in collective books such as *Sci-Fi: A Companion* (2019) and *The Lovecraftian Poe: Essays on Influence, Reception, Interpretation and Transformation* (2017).

Hannu Poutiainen is a postdoctoral researcher at Tampere University (Finland). Having recently concluded a research project on the relationship between magic and modern literature, he is currently preparing a monograph on deconstruction and the metaphysics of substitution. His articles have been published in a variety of journals, including *Derrida Today*, the *Oxford Literary Review*, and, most recently, *Correspondences*. In addition to his academic work, he has translated writings by M. R. James, Arthur Machen, William James and John Ruskin.

Gerardo Rodríguez-Salas is a senior lecturer in English literature at the University of Granada (Spain). He holds an MA in Women's and Gender Studies from Oxford University. His research interests focus on gender studies and community theory in modernist and contemporary fiction, with a particular focus on New Zealand and Australian literature. He is the author of three books on Katherine Mansfield and has recently co-edited the volumes *Community in Twentieth-Century Fiction* (2013) and *New Perspectives on Community and the Modernist Subject* (2018). His latest articles have appeared in the *Journal of Language, Literature and Culture*, *Australian Literary Studies*, *Antipodes*, *FEMSPEC*, *JASAL* and *Meanjin*.

Nicholas Royle is Professor of English at the University of Sussex (UK). His books include *Telepathy and Literature* (1991), *E.M. Forster* (1999), *The Uncanny* (2003), *Jacques Derrida* (2003), *How to Read Shakespeare* (2005), *In Memory of Jacques Derrida* (2009), *Veering: A Theory of Literature* (2011), *Hélène Cixous: Dreamer, Realist, Analyst, Writing* (2020) and (with Andrew Bennett) *An Introduction to Literature, Criticism and Theory* (5th edition, 2016). He is also author of two novels, *Quilt* (2010) and *An English Guide to Birdwatching* (2017). His most recent publication is *Mother: A Memoir* (2020).

Pilar Villar-Argáiz is a senior lecturer in British and Irish literatures at the University of Granada (Spain) and the general editor of the major series 'Studies in Irish Literature, Cinema and Culture' by Edward Everett Root Publishers. She is the author of two books on the Irish poet Eavan Boland (2007, 2008). Villar-Argáiz has published extensively on contemporary Irish poetry and fiction, in relation to questions of gender, race, migration, interculturality and community. Her edited collections include *Literary Visions of Multicultural Ireland: The Immigrant in Contemporary Irish Literature* (2014) and *Irishness on the Margins: Minority and Dissident Identities* (2018). Villar-Argáiz is currently the Chairperson of the Spanish Association for Irish Studies and a Member of the Executive Board of the European Federation of Associations and Centres of Irish Studies.

Kim L. Worthington is a senior lecturer in English literature at Massey University (New Zealand). She is the author of *Self as Narrative: Subjectivity and Community in Contemporary Fiction* (1996). Publications in journals such as *Borderlands* (2016), *Australian Literary Studies* (2013) and *Comparative Literature* (2011), and chapters, in books such as *Mapping the Ethical Turn* (2001), *A Companion to the Works of J. M. Coetzee* (2011), *Rethinking Narrative Identity* (2013) and *The Routledge Companion to Pakistani Anglophone Writing* (2018), evidence her longstanding interest in questions to do with community, identity and (literary) ethics.

Foreword

Joseph Hillis Miller

Most people know much about the semantic range of the words 'secrecy' and 'community' as they might be used in a book title such as this one. 'Community' names a group of people who share many assumptions and experiences, such as the collectivity of those who have always lived in Sedgwick, Maine, where I am now writing this. My neighbours know and take for granted a lot of things I, as an outsider, can never know. 'Secrecy', among other uses, can be employed to name things known only to those who live in a given 'close-knit' community. This is often a scandalous closely guarded fact. The truly problematic term in this title, however, is the little word 'and'. 'And' in what sense? As indicating mere adjacency? 'And', 'and', 'and' in a list? Or does 'and' in this case indicate some closer bond between things that *must* go together, as in 'stars and stripes forever'? If the 'and' in this case does indicate a closer bond, just what is it? Among many other accomplishments, this book brilliantly investigates the power of 'and'.

Acknowledgements

This book is part of a research project funded by the Spanish Ministry of Economy and Competitiveness (ref. FFI2016-75589-P), whose support is gratefully acknowledged.

Introduction

Secrecy and community in twenty-first-century fiction

María J. López

As readers of literature, we continually experience secrecy as a fundamental dimension of our relationship to literary texts. In the specific case of fiction, we often encounter it in its most basic form: as a mystery in the story that eventually gets solved or as the lack of information we initially have about a character or another fictional element, which is progressively given to us. A logic of concealment and revelation, then, as Bennett and Royle suggest, traverses the very basic motivation that makes us readers of novels and short stories: 'It is precisely because there are things that remain hidden from us, and because we want to know what these things are, that we continue to read' (2004, 241).

Full revelation and disclosure, however, do not always take place. Thus, we frequently experience what can be frustrating for some readers but exhilarating and delightful for others: the encounter with secrets and hidden things that the literary work actually never reveals. This is because literature, unlike other discourses, often remains silent on the very questions it raises and the very enigmas it creates. As J. Hillis Miller has put it, 'literature keeps its secrets' (2002a, 39).

The different dimensions and understandings of literary secrecy constitute a main concern in this study. We hope to highlight the key role that secrets may play in the formal construction of the literary text, specifically in the construction of narrative sequence, manifested – as pointed out by Calinescu – in the way 'narrative information is withheld, hidden, retracted, and finally revealed (or, in more modern writing, *not* revealed)' (1994, 448; emphasis in the original). Secrets, furthermore, are to be found as part of the story itself: secrets that usually concern the characters of the fictional world in question and around which the whole action of the novel or story may revolve (454). The text that Calinescu aptly chooses to illustrate his ideas of secrecy in fiction is Nathaniel Hawthorne's *The Scarlet Letter* (1850), one of the novels in the Western literary tradition that best exemplifies the fundamental ways in which secrets may work as the driving force of the narrative, while simultaneously depicting a fictional world in which secrecy is presented as the essence of both the human condition and human relationships.

The question of personal relationships and the way they are presented in fiction brings us to the concept of community, which critics have turned to in order to address the novel as a literary genre fundamentally concerned with intersubjectivity and with the knowledge that we may – or may not – have of others. That is the case of Raymond Williams's well-known formulation in *The Country and the City*: 'Most novels are in some sense knowable communities. It is part of a traditional method ... that the novelist offers to show people and their relationships in essentially knowable and communicable ways' (1973, 165).[1] As Miller argues in *Communities in Fiction*, Williams's conception of community is based on the assumption of community as a group of people in which the individual is completely identified with his social placement and in which individuals fully know each other (2015, 4–5).[2] We hope to show in this book how the consideration of secrecy in literature invites us to think of community in alternative terms,[3] as novels and short stories continually offer examples of what we also wish to call 'community', a community, however, not based on knowledge of the other, but rather on the absence of it. As Jiménez Heffernan has argued, Williams's approach to community – together with other well-known communitarian articulations, such as Benedict Anderson's concept of 'imagined communities' (1983) – entail 'a constructed enclave of semiotic immanence inside which human beings obtain selfhood, social credit and a sense of embeddedness' (2013, 31). As we aim to show, communities depicted in literary works, on the contrary, often entail the dissolution of selfhood, social embeddedness and semiotic certainty, as it is through the self's exposure to otherness and finitude, to secrecy and unknowingness, that community paradoxically emerges.

In our concern with what we will call communities of secrecy, we are fundamentally indebted to the thoughts of Jean-Luc Nancy, Maurice Blanchot and Jacques Derrida, who have pointed to the fallacies and dangers of identitarian and excluding communities, arguing for collective forms characterized by irreducible singularity, secrecy and otherness. It is in particular Derridean thought that runs as a common thread throughout the book, working as the nexus between our concern with the secret in relation to literary form and with the role of secrecy in the configuration of communities depicted in fiction. For Derrida – as he argues in *A Taste for the Secret* – the secret certainly signifies the rejection of a totalizing and exclusionary community space, as he associates it with 'not-belonging' (Derrida and Ferraris 2001, 59) and with 'the sharing of what is not shared: we know in common that we have nothing in common' (58). Secrecy stands for singularity and alterity, for 'consensus on the fact that the singular is singular, that the other is other, that *tout autre est tout autre*' (58; emphasis in the original). Giving up one's secrets, on the contrary, implies the relinquishing of

---

[1] According to Williams, these 'knowable communities' are to be found in a very specific historical context – that of pre-capitalist, rural England. With the growth of cities and the expansion of capitalism, 'any assumption of a knowable community ... became harder and harder to sustain' (1973, 165).

[2] In *Communities in Fiction* (2015), Miller argues that community has always been presented in fiction as fractured and precarious. In *The Conflagration of Community*, dealing with fiction before and after Auschwitz, Miller shows how literary texts may bear witness to a community that has been 'dissolved', 'consumed, burned up' (2011, 6).

[3] See also Martín-Salván, Rodríguez-Salas and Jiménez Heffernan (2013) and Rodríguez-Salas, Martín-Salván and López (2018), for similar approaches to community in fiction.

one's singularity in the face of a 'totalitarian space' (59) that demands homogeneity and sameness. In his defence of a socio-political space tolerant of secrecy, then, Derrida is implicitly advocating a community perpetually open to otherness and difference: a 'community without community', 'an open-quasi community' (Caputo 1997, 106, 121). It is in this sense – Caputo argues – that we must understand Derrida's repeated appeal in different writings to what he calls 'the democracy to come': as a defence of a community that is 'a porous, permeable, open-ended affirmation of the other' (122).

Derrida's defence of the secret is, then, linked with his commitment to 'the democracy to come', which in turn leads us to Derrida's understanding of literature as an institution in the West,[4] given the repeated connection that Derrida establishes between these concepts. One of the texts in which Derrida most acutely explores this interrelation between secrets, democracy and literature is 'Passions: "An Oblique Offering"', where he makes the following widely discussed assertion: 'No democracy without literature; no literature without democracy' (1995a, 28).[5] For Derrida, literature as a Western institution is inseparable from the idea of democracy, since both of them are linked to 'a certain noncensure' (ibid.), to freedom of speech, understood as 'the power to say everything ... an authorization to say everything' (Derrida and Attridge 1992, 33).[6]

But this 'right to say everything' – Derrida argues in 'Literature in Secret' – also paradoxically 'implies *in principle* the right ... to hide everything' (2008, 156; emphasis in the original), that is, the right to secrecy. This conception of literary secrecy is one that Derrida develops by making an opposition between literature and 'authorities' such as religion, philosophy, morality, politics or the law, which only tolerate 'conditional secrets', secrets that can and must be made known under certain circumstances (1995a, 25). These authorities 'ask for accounts, that is, responses, from those with accepted responsibilities' (ibid.). The author of a literary work, on the contrary, has 'a right to absolute nonresponse' (29), and this is so because literature is the only institution that tolerates the unconditional or absolute secret: a secret that 'cannot be unveiled' and that 'remains inviolable' (26).

This Derridean conception of 'the secret *of* literature and secrecy *in* literature' (2008, 121; emphasis in the original) has important critical implications. One has to do with the relationship between writers and their political, social and historical context, as they must be free to say and write everything they want while remaining safe from any type of censorship (Derrida and Attridge 1992, 37). Writers are not accountable to established powers, authorities or the ideological body, having 'the unlimited right to ask

---

[4] As Attridge emphasizes, in the elucidation of Derrida's understanding of literature and of his writing on literary texts, it is fundamental to bear in mind Derrida's approach to literature 'as an *institution*: it is not given in nature or the brain but brought into being by processes that are social, legal, and political, and that can be mapped historically and geographically' (1992, 23; emphasis in the original).
[5] In their discussion of Derrida's thoughts on the relationship between literature and democracy, numerous critics have paid attention to this passage. See Miller (2002b, 63), Culler (2008, 7), Wills (2008, 17) or Attridge (2010, 46).
[6] See Royle's insightful discussion of these ideas in relation to transgression and the breaking free of rules (2003, 45).

any question, to suspect all dogmatism, to analyse every presupposition' (Derrida 1995a, 28).[7] Similarly, they are not to be considered responsible for their characters' actions, words or thoughts (28). Another vital implication – which is the one this book is particularly concerned with – is rather related to our acts of interpretation of literary works and to our very understanding of the practice of literary criticism. The Derridean conception of the literary work as governed by the unconditional secret entails assuming that, as put by Miller, 'the whole meaning of the works in question' may turn on 'what is forever hidden from the reader's knowledge' (2002a, 40). It also implies accepting that all we have is 'the surface of a textual manifestation' whose meanings remain '*locked away* [*au secret*]' (Derrida 1995a, 29; emphasis in the original). This constitutes an essential dimension of what Attridge has called 'the singularity of literature', which we experience as we respond to a literary work as not 'wholly knowable, yielding all its meanings up in one go' (2004, 77). Through our engagement with literary works, then, we discover new ways of knowing but also new ways of not-knowing (Attridge 2015, 258).

The link between secrecy, community, democracy and literature is, then, inseparable in Derrida's thought, an interrelation that this volume, taken as a whole, attests to. In the case of those chapters particularly concerned with secrecy as manifested in specific features of narrative form or with the role of secrets in the development of narrative sequence, they can be seen as supplementing Derrida's approach to the secret in literature. As Derek Attridge points out in the first chapter of this volume, Derrida's discussions of secrecy and literature are very much focused on meaning – 'what is primarily at issue is the unanswerability of the questions raised by the content of the work' (29) – whereas he has rarely addressed the specificity of formal properties of literary texts. Here precisely lies the value of Attridge's contribution to this book, and with it, to literary criticism inspired by Derridean thought: his dealing with the question of 'what the relevance of the Derridean secret might be to the singular event of form' (30).

In *Literature as Conduct*, Miller claims that the explanations we may give to secrets in literature more or less correspond to the prevailing modes of explaining literary texts today: textual or linguistic, psychoanalytic and cultural (2005, 75). These explanations or critical frameworks are certainly present in this volume, in order to respond to the different types of secrets – linguistic, psychic, social or political – to be found in the fictional works selected; 'conditional secrets' that may end up being known. Critical tools, however, may fail – Miller notes – in the face of an 'undecidable' reading situation, in which 'the text is overdetermined', as it 'offers several determinable explanations that are incompatible' (2005, 75), a failure which also takes place when the text gives no explanation at all. This tension between revelation and concealment, veiling and unveiling, traverses the critical readings included in this book, thus showing that this is a tension characterizing literature itself.

---

[7] This 'irresponsibility' on the part of writers should not be seen as some kind of escapism or relegation of writers to an acontextual realm empty of obligations or duties. On the contrary, as Derrida is careful to note, '[t]his duty of irresponsibility, of refusing to reply for one's thought or writing to constituted powers, is perhaps the highest form of responsibility. To whom, to what? That's the whole question of the future or the event promised by or to such an experience, what I was just calling the democracy to come' (Derrida and Attridge, 1992, 38).

The remaining parts of this introduction – named after the three sections into which the volume is divided – go on to explore the meaningful ways in which the concepts of secrecy and community can be brought into dialogue in our approach to literary texts, pointing to the specific contribution of each of the chapters included in the volume. The focus is on twenty-first-century English fiction, embracing writers with very diverse backgrounds, thus providing a comprehensive view of the different national, ethnic and racial communities out of which contemporary English narrative emerges: Ali Smith (Scottish), Naomi Booth (English), Toni Morrison (African American), Alice Munro (Canadian), Zoë Wicomb (South African-Scottish), Jhumpa Lahiri (South-Asian American), Witi Ihimaera (Māori New Zealander), Hilary Mantel (English), Jeanette Winterson (English), Ian Holding (Zimbabwean), Jonathan Franzen (American) and Viet Thanh Nguyen (Vietnamese American). The essays contained in this volume, however, invite us to reassess the relationship between writer, literary work and community, with the secret emerging as that which disrupts an approach to this relationship as based upon mere 'belonging' or identity politics.

As suggested by Nicholas Royle in Chapter 2, the responsibilities of the writer as a 'citizen of the world' in the twenty-first century are urgent and endless: responsibilities towards issues of family and society, individual and social justice, human rights, capitalism, marketization, climate crisis and environmental destruction. At the same time, these responsibilities – Royle is careful to note – do not turn the writer into some 'community representative' (46), or as put by the writer J. M. Coetzee, into 'a herald of community' (1992, 341). In reply to Miller's provoking enquiry in his Foreword into the sense of 'and' in our title and echoing Derrida's words on 'the secret *of* literature and secrecy *in* literature' (2008, 121; emphasis in the original), we intend to approach the relationship between our two main concepts as what actually constitutes a *non*relation, the 'impossible filiation' (Derrida 2008, 117) of the secret *of* community and secrecy *in* community.

Secrecy, literary form and the community of readers

Along the history of literary criticism, theorists and critics, in their attempt to elucidate the specific nature of literature and literary interpretation, have pointed to the presence in literary texts of an enigmatic, secret or obscure dimension of some kind, a dimension they have often approached as built upon a dialectic between the concealment and the revelation of meaning.[8] Frank Kermode, in *The Genesis of Secrecy: On the Interpretation*

---

[8] In *A Theory of Literary Production*, Pierre Macherey argued that 'the speech of the book' is accompanied by 'a certain silence' and 'a certain absence, without which it would not exist' (1989, 85). Roland Barthes, on his part, established 'the hermeneutic code' – related to the creation and interpretation of the enigma – as one of the five codes involved in the construction of any literary text (1974, 19). Umberto Eco has pointed to the long-lasting concern in Western thought with secret knowledge and secret truth: 'truth becomes identified with what is not said or what is said obscurely and must be understood beyond or beneath the surface of a text' (1992, 30). We may also think of Wolfgang Iser's famous criticism of the idea that 'meaning, as a buried secret, should be accessible to and reducible by the tools of referential analysis' (1978, 5), in which he was implicitly pointing to the surface-depth model that has dominated traditional understandings of reading and meaning – and hence of the secret in literature.

of Narrative, was one of the first literary critics to make a systematic analysis of the relationship between literature – narrative in particular – and secrecy, linking it with the problem of interpretation: 'In all the works of interpretation there are insiders and outsiders' (1979, xi). The former has 'immediate access to the mystery', whereas the latter are 'excluded from the elect who mistrust or despise their unauthorized divinations' (ibid.). Although Kermode's particular concern is with the Gospels, more specifically, with parables conceived as 'riddles' or 'dark sayings' (23), he expands this argument about biblical exegesis in order to point to the 'obscurity' that characterizes all narrative: 'the enigmatic and exclusive character of narrative ... its property of banishing interpreters from its secret places' (33-4).[9]

In his essay, 'Secrets and Narrative Sequence', Kermode defines narrative as the result of two processes: the first one is related to the presentation of the fable, and hence to sequentiality, tending towards 'clarity' and 'propriety'; the second one rather tends 'toward secrecy' and 'distortions which cover secrets' (1980, 86), secrets being conceived as those elements 'indifferent or even hostile to sequentiality' (87). In Chapter 3 of this book, Paula Martín-Salván shows the potential that Kermode's thoughts may have for the analysis of a novel such as Toni Morrison's *Love* (2003), in which she identifies an accumulation of textual fragments and details that working 'in a sort of purloined letter device' (56) – like 'marine debris' (ibid.) – are put before the reader's eyes, yet resist to be incorporated into a lineal narrative sequence.

Similarly to Kermode, Matei Calinescu, as pointed out above, has paid attention to the role that secrets play in the sequential structure of narrative, together with the importance that secrets may have for fictional characters, the way they stimulate the reader's inquisitiveness and the possible intertextual dimension of textual concealment (1994, 448–9). Calinescu also differentiates between the 'linear reader' – not caring for 'intricate allusions' and hence secrets – and the 'critical rereader', who in their hunting for 'intertextual clues' and 'distortions' plays 'the game of reading or reading for the secret' (448). This idea of 'rereading' is developed at length in the eponymous book, in which Calinescu analyses the secret messages and codes that may be meant to exclude readers from the text, together with the different psychological, social and communicational implications of secrecy (1993, 227).

In her chapter on Alice Munro's *Too Much Happiness* (2009), Díaz Dueñas shows how Munro's stories invite readers to become 'rereaders', to read between the lines to uncover something hidden (Calinescu 1993, 243). And this is so because Munro's fiction often hinges on subtle and indirect clues that may be missed on a first or superficial reading, and that hint at the secrets surrounding characters' lives and development throughout the story. In particular, Díaz Dueñas focuses on how Munro uses secrets to construct non-conventional female characters that defy stereotypical representations of femininity and to prevent the reader from judging these characters from an ethical point of view. Díaz Dueñas also points to the interrelation between

---

[9] See López (2019) for an analysis – drawing on Kermode's ideas – of the oracular dimension of Chigozie Obioma's *The Fishermen* (2015), together with the importance of parables and prophecies in this novel.

suspense, surprise and the workings of secrecy, and in doing so, she follows Michael Toolan, who has approached narrative suspense and surprise as related to those moments in which the reader's understanding fails, defining narrative secrets and surprises as 'partially foreseeable but unforeseen facts' (2004, 205).

Similarly to Toolan, other critics in recent narrative theory have tried to give an account of the dynamics characterizing that which cannot and will not be represented in fiction, providing different taxonomies and definitions. That is the case of Robyn R. Warhol, who, taking her cue from Gerald Prince's definition of 'the *disnarrated*' – 'those passages in a narrative that consider what did not or does not happen' (quoted in Warhol 2005, 220) – establishes the category of 'the *unnarrated*'[10] to refer to 'those passages that explicitly do not tell what is supposed to have happened, foregrounding the narrator's refusal to narrate' (221; emphasis in the original).[11] We must also refer to *Real Mysteries: Narrative and The Unknowable*, in which H. Porter Abbott focuses on the unknowable as an experience on the part of the reader in his or her encounter with narrative – 'the experience of the palpable unknown' (2013, 12) – paying attention to what he calls 'intentionally induced states of unknowing' (9).[12]

In his analysis of the unknowable, Abbott draws on James Phelan's concept of 'the stubborn', which Phelan employs in his chapter on Toni Morrison's *Beloved* (1987), included in *Narrative as Rhetoric*. Phelan approaches the character of Beloved as eluding a final and comprehensive explanation on the part of the critic and hence as an instance of what he calls the 'recalcitrance' in literature, material that resists the critic's explanatory schema. For Phelan, literary obstacles to understanding and explanation result in two kinds of reading experience: 'The *difficult* is recalcitrance that yields to our explanatory efforts, while the *stubborn* is recalcitrance that will not yield' (1996, 178; emphasis in the original).

Phelan also deals with literary recalcitrance in his chapter on Joseph Conrad's 'The Secret Sharer' (1909), a literary text that powerfully evokes the paradoxical relationship of secrecy and community,[13] having at its centre what indeed constitutes a community of secrecy: the one constituted by the captain and Leggatt. Phelan is interested in how secrets affect the authorial audience's ethical involvement in the captain's story, focusing on the captain's secret protection of Leggatt and on what he sees as the secret of the

---

[10] See Martín-Salván (2020) for an analysis of the unnarrated in Colson Whitehead's *The Underground Railroad* (2016) as neoslave narrative.

[11] Warhol sees the disnarrated and the unnarrated as belonging to the larger category of 'the unnarratable', whose main possible forms are 'the *subnarratable*' (what 'needn't be told'); 'the *supranarratable*' (what 'can't be told'); 'the *antinarratable*' (what 'shouldn't be told'); and 'the *paranarratable*' (what 'wouldn't be told') (2005, 222; emphasis in the original).

[12] Abbott sees these 'states of unknowing' (2013, 9) as manifested in three main forms: the 'cognitive sublime' (23) as related to the unimaginable unknown; the mystery of affective states in relation to narrative syntax and the syntax of narrative; and finally, the presence of narrative gaps and unreadable minds in otherwise realist works.

[13] In this book on community in Joseph Conrad, also inspired by Nancy's thought, Yamamoto devotes one chapter to this story (2017). In the captain's act of welcoming Leggatt, Yamamoto identifies a gesture of unconditional hospitality, so that the resulting community is one of 'strange fraternity' (1, *passim*), which entails the undermining of the individual subject and the surrender of the 'I' to the other (6).

captain's and Leggatt's homosexual attraction. In this chapter and other writings, Phelan has offered an illuminating insight into the relationship between ethical judgement and narrative progression, a relationship that, as Martín-Salván's chapter shows, may be deeply affected by the workings of secrecy. Thus, Martín-Salván effectively draws on Phelan's thoughts in *Experiencing Fiction* (2007) in order to show how secrecy works as delayed disclosure in Morrison's *Love*, altering narrative sequence and calling for a readjustment of the reader's ethical judgement of characters.

In *Others*, Miller also pays attention to secrets in Conrad's 'The Secret Sharer'.[14] Reading the story as one of testing and testimony, Miller points to a central question that remains unanswered: the question as to why the captain decided to hide the fugitive murderer Leggatt (2001a, 166). Miller also mentions other facts that the reader of this story cannot verify or know: whether Leggatt is telling the truth in his version of the murder or how the narrator came to be captain of this ship (152). These are examples of what Miller, following Derrida, calls 'the true secret', which, 'if there is such a thing, cannot be revealed' (151–2).

In order to develop this notion of the secret, Miller refers to *Given Time*, one of the main texts to understand Derrida's conception of the essential relationship between literature and the secret. In *Given Time*, Derrida turns to Baudelaire's story 'Counterfeit Money' ('La Fausse Monnaie', 1869), in which the narrator, after having watched his friend give money to a beggar, is told by him that it was actually a counterfeit coin. Derrida goes on, then, to make a series of hypotheses about why the friend said '[i]t was the counterfeit coin' (1992, 149), and about his real thoughts and intentions. At the end of the day, however, the character takes the secret with him: 'the readability of the text is structured by the unreadability of the secret, that is, by the inaccessibility of a certain intentional meaning or of a wanting-to-say in the consciousness of the characters' (152). The interest, then, of Baudelaire's story 'comes from the enigma constructed out of this crypt which gives to be read that which will remain *eternally* unreadable, *absolutely* indecipherable, even refusing itself to any promise of deciphering or hermeneutic' (ibid.; emphasis in the original). In this way, the secret tells us something essential about literature, just as literature tells us something essential about the secret: what both have in common is 'the essential superficiality of their phenomenality' (153).[15]

Attridge defines Derrida's 'absolute secret' as 'not a matter of concealing something that could be revealed or communicated, but of the apprehension of something that can never be known' (2010, 44). As he explains in Chapter 1 of this volume, '[t]his is secrecy without concealment or possible revelation; it is at once absolute and highly productive' (28). In his chapter, Attridge explores the relationship between this

---

[14] Both Abbott (2013, 12) and Phelan (1996, 213, n. 9) are careful to distinguish their positions from the semantic undecidability they see in deconstructive critics such as Miller and Paul de Man. Though they certainly endorse different critical positions, we believe that it is possible to bring them into dialogue, as Martín-Salván successfully does in her chapter on Morrison.

[15] Kronick (1999), Michaud (2002), Almond (2003), Segal (2008) and Danta (2013) provide insightful discussions of Derrida's conception of the relationship between literature and the secret.

Derridean secrecy and ergodic texts, i.e. works whose formal arrangement challenges continuous, linear reading, focusing on the specific case of Ali Smith's *How to Be Both* (2015). The contribution of non-linear formal features – such as images – to the literary operation cannot be seen as one of conveying mere content to the reader. Instead, Attridge analyses how they contribute to the *experience* of meaning, to the *act-event* through which the reader actively engages with the literary text. In this event, these formal features effectively function like the Derridean secret – a secret on the surface – whose meanings remain undecidable but also inexhaustible.

Nicholas Royle is also inspired by the Derridean secret in order to develop his concept of 'cryptaesthetic resistance',[16] which, in Chapter 2 of this volume, he identifies in novels that 'demand but distract our attention. They seduce but elude. . . . they resist being read even as they open themselves to all the adventures of mind-reading' (44). Royle links his concept of 'cryptaesthetic resistance' with that of 'protective mimicry', which he borrows from biology in order to develop a suggestive theory of the novel. For Royle, the novel as literary form, in order to be read and recognized as such, has to mimic, has to resemble. At the same time, the novel loves to hide and elude, which is what constitutes its 'cryptaesthetic resistance': its capacity 'to immunize itself against being simply received, assimilated, appropriated' (ibid.). Royle exemplifies his ideas through an astute reading of Naomi Booth's *Sealed* (2017), in which he identifies an uncanny literal manifestation of protective mimicry and of what Derrida calls autoimmunity – a body, person or community destroying itself through the very act aimed at protecting itself – a concept to which I will return below.

In her focus on Zoë Wicomb in Chapter 5 of this book, Liani Lochner similarly identifies the secret in Wicomb's texts with a resistance to critical appropriation, in particular, a resistance to being appropriated as mere social, autobiographical or ethnographic documents. Lochner sees this tendency as related to the common perception of postcolonial literature as having its meaning in the background of the author and the literary work's socio-cultural and political context. This is a critical interpretation that Wicomb's texts resist as they stage the performative power of language, thus preventing the reader from locating meaning as content or knowledge that can just be taken away from the text.

In her engagement with the secret as performance in Wicomb's *Playing in the Light* (2006) and 'In Search of Tommie' (2009), Lochner substantially draws on Attridge's ideas about the singularity of literature as an event, for which Attridge finds inspiration in Derrida's repeated association of the secret with 'experience' (Attridge 2010, 47). This indeed constitutes another key dimension of the secret as conceived by Derrida, which the French philosopher makes clear in an interview collected in *Points*: 'It is not a thing, some information that I am hiding or that one has to hide or dissimulate; it is rather an experience that does not make itself available to information, that resists information or knowledge' (1995b, 201). The position of what he calls 'non-know*ing*' (ibid.; my emphasis) also runs throughout 'Passions', in which Derrida approaches the literary

---

[16] See also Royle (1991; 2014) for a discussion of the concept of 'cryptaesthetic resistance'.

secret as an active response, a conception that is behind Attridge's illuminating accounts of the reader's creative and hospitable response to the singularity and alterity of literary works as an inventive event that allows for the irruption of the other into the familiar (2004, 79–93; 2015, 111–32). It is also behind Miller's engagement with speech acts in literature as not being able to be subjected to verifiable cognitive knowledge, and demanding, instead, from the reader, a similar performative, inaugural response (2001a, 2001b, 2005).

It is out of this performative response to the secret in literature that a certain kind of community may emerge. As Miller puts it, the inventive response to the other in the literary work 'is truly inaugural, initiatory, even legislative. Like a declaration of independence, it lays down new rules that imply a new "we," a new community, even a new political order. The other invents me, and through what I do invents others, a community' (2002b, 70). In her chapter, Lochner turns to these words by Miller in order to argue how a reading of Wicomb's fiction allows for an experience of alterity that contests identitarian notions of community. Attridge, for his part, relates the secrecy of literary form to literary reading as a communal activity, one in which readers may share that which cannot be shared, the literary secret,[17] a (non)sharing that exemplifies the paradoxical – yet essential – relationship between literature, secrecy and community.

Communities of secrecy

In *Points*, Derrida expresses his discomfort with the concept of community: 'If by community one implies, as is often the case, a harmonious group, consensus, and fundamental agreement beneath the phenomena of discord or war, then I don't believe in it very much and I sense in it as much threat as promise' (1995b, 355). As Caputo clarifies, what Derrida rejects here is a particular conception of community: community conceived as a self-protective and closed collectivity based upon a 'self-affirming, self-protecting, homogenizing' conception of identity (Caputo 1997, 106). And, as pointed out at the beginning of this introduction, it is precisely the concept of the secret, understood as 'not-belonging' in *A Taste for the Secret* (Derrida and Ferraris 2001, 59), that allows Derrida to imagine a different kind of community, one paradoxically grounded on 'separation' and 'isolation' (58), on *not* having anything in common.

In *The Politics of Friendship*, Derrida addresses his preference for such a community; what he calls, quoting Bataille, 'the community of those without community' (2005a, 37), as opposed to 'communal belonging and sharing' (80). The questioning of 'communal belonging' also traverses this book. Contributions by Lochner, Rodríguez-Salas, Pascual Garrido, Marais or Worthington point to their respective writers' critique of identification and homogeneity founded upon what Derrida calls '*the* genealogical

---

[17] The conception of literature – of narrative, in particular – as an act of sharing secrets is one that many critics, from different theoretical frameworks, have formulated. Calinescu refers to the small and sophisticated community of 'secret sharers' (1994, 447) that will respond to secrets in John Updike. Phelan sees Conrad's 'The Secret Sharer' as exemplifying that '[t]o narrate is to tell secrets; to read narrative is to share in them' (1996, 120).

schema' (105; emphasis in the original), i.e. the approbation given to filiation to 'ethnic identity, descent, family, nation, blood and soil, proper name, proper culture and memory' (2002, 91). We see this critique in Wicomb's resistance to her work being read as representative of South African coloured identity (Chapter 5), Jhumpa Lahiri's engagement with the failure of the family as operative community (Chapter 6), Witi Ihimaera's critique of the patriarchal logic and hegemonic masculinity of the traditional Māori community (Chapter 7), Ian Holding's shame at the white Zimbabwean community's failure to engage with the racial other (Chapter 10) and Viet Thanh Nguyen's disruption of hegemonic and excluding narratives of the American nation (Chapter 12).

In their rejection of a communitarian logic based upon sameness and exclusion, we may content that these writers' works contain echoes of what Derrida calls '"relation without relation," "community without community" … "inoperative" community, "unavowable" communism or community' (2005a, 80–1), thus borrowing Jean-Luc Nancy's and Maurice Blanchot's respective terms. It is highly revealing that in his conceptualization of a different kind of community, Derrida should turn to Nancy and Blanchot, as this volume intends to bring these three thinkers into dialogue. Thus, we agree with Morin (2006, n.p.n.) when she argues that, while adopting different strategies, both Nancy and Derrida put 'community under erasure', as they reject the idea of community as an essence or an identifiable totality based on a transcendental signified such as race, birth or gender.

That indeed constitutes Nancy's aim in his critique of what he calls the 'operative' or 'immanent' community – the dreamed, ideal or lost community – characterized by 'its own immanent unity, intimacy, and autonomy' and by 'its organic communion with its own essence' (1991, 9). In the operative community, death is transfigured into a meaningful substance that provides it with its essentialist character, communion or fusion, such as homeland, native soil, blood, nation, family or mystical body (15). The inoperative community, on the contrary, is made up of singularities that expose themselves in the shared recognition of their respective finitude, otherness and death. It is a community of 'interruption, fragmentation, suspension', which cannot be incorporated into any 'social, economic, technical, and institutional' project (31). The singular beings that constitute this community have nothing in common, except their own mortality, through which they recognize the alterity of the other.[18]

Blanchot depicts his 'unavowable community' in similar terms. Drawing on Bataille's notion of the principle of incompleteness at the root of each being, he contends that '[t]he existence of every being … summons the other or a plurality of others…. It therefore summons a finite community' (1988, 6). Also, similarly to Nancy, he establishes the openness of the community in 'my presence for another who absents himself by dying' (9). But whereas Nancy develops his argument on community in mainly ontological terms, Blanchot introduces the concept of 'choice' in his distinction between 'traditional community and elective community' (46). The former is an

---

[18] See Jiménez Heffernan (2013, 18–31) and Rodríguez-Salas, Martín-Salván and López (2018, 12–18) for a detailed discussion on the main attributes of Nancy's inoperative community.

imposition: 'it is *de facto* sociality, or the glorification of the earth, of blood, or even of race' (ibid.; emphasis in the original). The elective community, on the other hand, which he identifies with the community of lovers and the community of friends, 'no longer cares about the forms of tradition or any social agreement' (47). Blanchot describes it as 'the strangeness of that antisocial society, always ready to dissolve itself, formed by *friends* and *couples*' (33; emphasis in the original).

This community of lovers – Blanchot contends – is not characterized by 'a "fusional or communional" understanding', but by an exposure of the lovers' solitude and death (50), by the sharing of what cannot be shared, which Blanchot refers to as 'the sharing of the secret' (19). This secret, though, is not a truth or object that is owned and shared. The secret is that which breaks 'the boundaries of the person and demand[s] to be shared'; it is just the 'sharing' itself that exposes the community (ibid.).

Chapters 6, 7 and 8 by Pascual Garrido, Rodríguez-Salas and Pérez-de-Luque respectively, included in Part Two of the book, draw on Nancy's and Blanchot's ideas in order to trace a tension, in the novels they analyse, between conventional, traditional forms of community founded on sameness and fusion, and bonds between characters characterized by singularity, secrecy and strangeness.[19] Thus, in her engagement with Jhumpa Lahiri's *The Lowland* (2013), dealing with the uprooted, alienated identity of second-generation Bengali-Americans, Pascual Garrido traces the failure of the family as an operative community of complete communion and identification. The sharing of secrets, instead, exposes Lahiri's characters to the alterity and singularity of others, and hence to a different type of community, namely, the inoperative and non-organic communities of friends and lovers.

Rodríguez-Salas, focusing on Witi Ihimaera's *The Uncle's Story* (2000), explores the confrontation between the traditional Māori clan – as an example of operative, immanent community – and the alternative queer group and elective community of lovers. As this novel depicts how the traditional Māori community silences Sam's homosexual identity, Rodríguez-Salas argues that it is possible to see in it what Derrida, in *The Politics of Friendship*, calls the 'classical concept of the secret' (2005a, 35) – different from the one we have traced until now – and upon which the exclusionary character of community conceived as a project of fusion and identification is built. Furthermore, by reading Sam's forbidden diary in terms of the concept of the crypt, mourning and transgenerational trauma – as articulated by Nicolas Abraham and Maria Torok – Rodríguez-Salas's chapter introduces us to another fruitful direction from which to address the secret in literature, one in which psychoanalytic, textual and Derridean approaches converge.[20]

---

[19] Go to Berman (2001) for an illuminating account of community in modernist fiction. Berman draws on Nancy's thoughts on community, especially in relation to the possibility of a political community going beyond the consensual public sphere and opening itself to marginal voices (14–15).

[20] In *The Wolf Man's Magic Word: A Cryptonymy* (1986), Abraham and Torok develop their concept of the crypt – which offers suggestive possibilities for the psychoanalytic and textual reading of secrets and traumas in characters – one with which Derrida also engages in his Foreword to their study. In 'Derrida's Topographies', Miller reads the crypt in Derrida as related to the constant presence in his writings of a 'place that cannot be mapped', a place that 'resists toponymy, topology and topography'

Juan Luis Pérez-de-Luque analyses Jeanette Winterson's *The Daylight Gate* (2012) as offering an example of two communities of secrecy that, in the context of the Pendle Witch Trials (1612), threaten the normativity of the traditional, male community, dominant in seventeenth-century England: the community of lesbian lovers and the community of the secret coven, made up of witches and misfits. Pérez-de-Luque explores the association in Winterson's novel between secrecy and the historical invisibility those social groups have traditionally suffered from, together with the important role of scapegoating – as conceptualized by René Girard – in the regeneration of the order of the immanent operative community.

Together with their attention to the novels' depiction of communities of secrecy, the aforementioned chapters are concerned with questions of textual and narrative secrecy, which, as we have seen, constitute the main focus of the first part of the volume, thus attesting to the dialogue between the different sections and chapters of this book. Pascual Garrido identifies in *The Lowland*, motifs and tropes that endow it with a dimension of 'cryptaesthetic resistance', Rodríguez-Salas analyses Sam's diary in Ihimaera's novel as a spectral and cryptic manuscript and Pérez-de-Luque turns to Barthes's hermeneutic code to explore Winterson's manipulation of secrets throughout her narrative in order to question the distinction between fantasy and historical fiction.

Underlying these readings there is the implicit question of how to speak of the community of secrecy: how to speak of the secret without betraying the secret. As suggested by Derrida, it has to be through 'a certain way of speaking: secret, discreet, discontinuous, aphoristic, just in disjointed time to avow the truth that must be concealed' (2005a, 54). Similarly, Blanchot talks about 'nocturnal communication, that communication which does not avow itself' (1988, 20), whereas Nancy points to the singular, interrupted 'voice' of community, which 'in its way perhaps avows, without saying it, the unavowable, or states without declaring it the secret of the community' (1991, 62).

This discontinuous, secret voice precisely constitutes the concern of the last chapter included in Part Two, Chapter 9, which deals with a very particular kind of community, the community of the living and the dead, as depicted in Hilary Mantel's novel *Beyond Black* (2005). As the agent that allows such a community to emerge, Hannu Poutiainen analyses the 'aporia of avoidance' (158) in which the medium finds herself, as she must speak of a place – the realm of the dead – that she must simultaneously keep secret. As Poutiainen's essay suggests, the 'art of not speaking' and the experience of being haunted by voices is no other than the art and experience of literature itself.

(1994, 6). In *The Shell and the Kernel* (1994), Abraham and Torok develop their idea of the 'transgenerational phantom', an unspeakable, shameful secret silently and unwittingly transmitted – through cryptic language and behaviour – from one family member to another. See Rashkin (1992; 2008) for an insightful application of Abraham and Torok's psychoanalytic poetics of hiding into literary criticism and cultural studies.

Secrecy, postcolonialism and democracy

Keeping with the concern with textual/narrative secrecy and secrets in community that, as we have seen, runs throughout Part One and Two of the volume, the essays contained in Part Three engage with the 'contemporaneity' of a critical analysis focused on secrecy and community, showing the relevance of these concepts when addressing questions related to postcolonialism, nationalism, democracy or the omnipresence of social media and digital information in the contemporary world.

We may add how, in the context of the unprecedented global crisis because of the COVID-19 pandemic – in the midst of which this book has been composed and completed – the concepts of community and the secret have acquired a new and wider significance, as Kim Worthington points out in the final chapter of the book. The immediate social and political consequences of this pandemic – generalized lockdown, social distancing, closure of borders, and in general, stronger and more pervasive forms of governmental control – have entailed a reconceptualization of the relationship between the individual, collectivity, public space and political power. In the long term, the consequences seem to be pointing in the direction of nationalist protectionist movements, greater national self-isolation, closer monitoring of the population and digital surveillance. Such a contemporary global context suggests a reinforcement of closed and exclusionary forms of community.

On the other hand, the high number of conspiracy theories that the pandemic is giving rise to attests to a tension between secrecy and disclosure in the public and political realms that, before the spread of COVID-19, was already 'a defining feature of the contemporary *Zeitgist*' (Boothroyd 2011, 42). In our current era, the pervasiveness of digital communications and social media, the meta-techniques of data analysis and the technocratic control of society, have entailed the complete surrender of private life to a logic of disclosure and transparency, as numerous thinkers have analysed (Birchall 2011; Boothroyd 2011; Han 2005). Such a context, Boothroyd argues, produces a thirst for the disclosure of secrets of all kinds, a phenomenon that has to be seen as related to the emergence of new forms of knowledge and to the control of access to information (2011, 43).

Part Three of the book, then, opens with Mike Marais's chapter, in which this critic brings the concept of community into dialogue with the question of racial reconciliation in the postcolonial context of Zimbabwe. Marais focuses on Ian Holding's novels *Of Beasts and Beings* (2010) and *What Happened to Us* (2018), arguing that Holding's writing, inspired by shame at the white Zimbabwean community's failure to decolonize itself, seeks to imagine a post-racial and hence truly postcolonial community. Drawing on the thinking of Emmanuel Levinas and Judith Butler, Marais argues that such endeavour has to engage with precariousness as a shared human condition. The chapter also pays attention to Holding's use of the confessional mode, which, in order to go beyond the community's codes of recognition, must work as an economic form without expectation of return, in which the confessor becomes other and unrecognizable – indeed secret – to himself and the community he belongs to. Marais's chapter is in implicit dialogue with previous chapters in the book – namely Lochner's (Chapter 5),

Pascual Garrido's (Chapter 6) and Rodríguez-Salas's (Chapter 7) – which also deal with secrecy and community in relation to postcolonial identity. In different ways, all of them question or resist the immanent and identitarian community in a postcolonial context, with the secret working as that which opens the community 'to the difference of the other ... and not yet imagined modes of being' (Durrant 2003, 111).[21]

Jesús Blanco Hidalga's chapter focuses on secrecy as the nexus that articulates Jonathan Franzen's *Purity* (2015) at three levels: the narrative, the psychological and the socio-cultural. As regards the latter, Blanco Hidalga shows how secrets in this novel work as resistance against the totalitarian drive of what Byung-Chul Han has called 'the transparency society' (2015). For Han, transparency works as the 'ideology' and 'neoliberal dispositive' characterizing our 'digital society of control' (viii), one in which 'the secret vanishes in favor of total exhibition and bareness' (25).

Similarly to Han, theorists associated with what Clare Birchall has called 'secrecy studies' (2016, n.p.n.) have carried out a critique of the hegemony of a rhetoric of transparency in contemporary public life, calling attention to the central role of secrets in all forms of human sociability and public life. In doing so, they are fundamentally indebted to Georg Simmel's sociological work on secrecy. In his 1906 seminal study 'The Sociology of Secrecy and of Secret Societies', Simmel defined secrecy as 'a universal sociological form' (1906, 463), pointing to concealment as one of the essential dimensions of all social relationships (15).[22] In Chapter 11, Blanco Hidalga shows the relevance of Simmel's ideas in order to analyse interpersonal relations in Franzen's *Purity*, depicted as dependent upon the sharing of secrets, and hence, upon processes of mutual trust and acts of confession. In his analysis, Blanco Hidalga also turns to Charles Barbour's astute reading of the secret in Derrida. Barbour, by putting Derrida and Simmel into conversation, approaches the former's 'conception of consciousness as a capacity to keep secrets' (2017, 184), so that secrecy emerges as a necessary condition of our relationship with others. These relations, then, for Derrida, implicitly rely on a 'promise, pact or sworn agreement to say what one believes, and to believe that the other is doing the same' (26); what Barbour calls an 'act of faith' (ibid.).

The attention to the social significance of secrets has gone together with an emphasis on their political value. Thus, Birchall identifies transparency as a specifically liberal democratic ideal, according to which 'secrecy comes to be associated with all that is nefarious ... and transparency with all that is noble' (2011, 66). As opposed to this trend, Birchall – turning to Nancy (73, 75), Blanchot (74) and Derrida (76) – urges us to consider '[w]hat forms of politics, ethics, of being-in-common' (60) secrecy allows us to think of. Birchall's refashioning of secrecy 'as that which resists "enclosing" hegemonic discourses' (72) echoes Derrida's identification of 'the loss of the secret' with 'the totalitarianization of democracy' (Derrida and Ferraris 2001, 59). For Derrida, the

---

[21] Durrant approaches community in a postcolonial context from a theoretical perspective close to the one adopted in this book, relating it to the concept of mourning and focusing on the work of the writers J. M. Coetzee, Wilson Harris and Toni Morrison (2003, 111–17).

[22] See May (2017) for an insightful analysis of secrecy and disclosure in Victorian fiction, drawing on both Georg Simmel's and Erving Goffman's ideas.

secret is imbricated in the very nature of democracy, in particular of what he repeatedly calls the 'democracy to come',[23] articulated in the future form and as a 'messianic promise' (1994, 114). For Derrida, democracy always 'remains to come' (2005a, 306); it remains 'indefinitely perfectible' and 'insufficient' (ibid.), perpetually open to the future, to the other and to justice. The secret, understood, as we have seen, as separation, non-belonging and difference, is precisely what keeps democracy open to heterogeneity, allowing it to go 'beyond the homo-fraternal and phallogocentric schema' (ibid.).

As Thomson argues, Derrida's democracy-to-come 'is the experience of the impossibility of a full democracy which compels us here and now to criticize the inadequacy of so-called democracies' (2005, 38). It is precisely this democratic inadequacy that Kim Worthington explores in the last chapter in this book. Worthington turns to Derrida's thoughts on the interrelation between democracy and non-belonging in order to approach refugeeism as the condition of no longer belonging to a lost community or nation and of not-belonging in the place of arrival. The question of hospitality, then – which as Worthington shows, has also figured prominently in Derrida's later work – becomes central, together with the principle of autoimmunity, which, according to Derrida, is at work in every community: 'a principle of self-destruction ruining the principle of self-protection' (2002, 87). Worthington explores these concepts in relation to Viet Thanh Nguyen's *The Refugees* (2017), focusing on how the ghost(s) of the Vietnam War, embodied as former refugees that now find themselves in the United States, contribute to and challenge narratives of (American) democracy.

Worthington analyses how ghosts in *The Refugees* do not entail the revelation and closure of the secret, but rather an opening up to the experience of secrecy as such. Her reading of Nguyen's text as an attempt to apprehend the 'secret in open view', borrowing Attridge's words (2010, 45), connects with previous chapters in the book in which, as pointed out, we find similar approaches to the Derridean secret in literature as one fully exposed and without depth. The significance of secrets in order to understand the nature of democracy and community has brought us back to the consideration of literature as the realm of secrecy par excellence. All in all, if, as argued by Attridge, the 'implications' of Derrida's thoughts on the secret 'still have to be followed through with any comprehensiveness' (2010, 42), this book constitutes an attempt to do so.

References

Abbott, H. Porter. (2013), *Real Mysteries: Narrative and the Unknowable*, Columbus: Ohio University Press.

Abraham, Nicolas and Maria Torok. (1986), *The Wolf Man's Magic Word: A Cryptonymy*, translated by Nicholas Rand, Minneapolis: University of Minnesota Press.

Abraham, Nicolas and Maria Torok. (1994), *The Shell and the Kernel: Renewals of Psychoanalysis*, translated by Nicholas Rand, Chicago: University of Chicago Press.

---

[23] References such as the 'democracy to come' are scattered among Derrida's works since the 1990s. See, for instance, Derrida and Attridge (1992) and Derrida (1994; 2005a; 2005b).

Almond, Ian. (2003), 'Derrida and the Secret of the Non-Secret: On Respiritualising the Profane', *Literature and Theology*, 17 (4): 457–71.
Anderson, Benedict. (2006) (1983), *Imagined Communities: Reflections on the Origin and Spread of Nationalism*, London: Verso, revised edition.
Attridge, Derek. (1992), 'Introduction: Derrida and the Questioning of Literature', in Derek Attridge (ed.), *Acts of Literature*, 1–29, New York: Routledge.
Attridge, Derek. (2004), *The Singularity of Literature*, London: Routledge.
Attridge, Derek. (2010), *Reading and Responsibility: Deconstruction's Traces*, Edinburgh: Edinburgh University Press.
Attridge, Derek. (2015), *The Work of Literature*, Oxford: Oxford University Press.
Barbour, Charles. (2017), *Derrida's Secret: Perjury, Testimony, Oath*, Edinburgh: Edinburgh University Press.
Barthes, Roland. (1974) (1970), *S-Z*, translated by Richard Miller, New York: Hill and Wang.
Bennett, Andrew, and Nicholas Royle. (2004), *An Introduction to Literature, Criticism and Theory*, Harlow: Pearson, Third edition.
Berman, Jessica. (2001), *Modernist Fiction, Cosmopolitanism, and the Politics of Community*, Cambridge: Cambridge University Press.
Birchall, Clare. (2011), 'Transparency, Interrupted: Secrets of the Left', *Theory, Culture and Society*, 28 (7–8): 60–84.
Birchall, Clare. (2016), 'Six Answers to the Question "What is Secrecy Studies?"', *Secrecy and Society*, 1 (1): https://scholarworks.sjsu.edu/secrecyandsociety/vol1/iss1/2.
Blanchot, Maurice. (1988), *The Unavowable Community*, translated by Pierre Joris, New York: Station Hill Press.
Boothroyd, Dave. (2011), 'Off the Record: Levinas, Derrida and the Secret of Responsibility', *Theory, Culture and Society*, 28 (7–8): 41–59.
Calinescu, Matei. (1993), *Rereading*, New Haven: Yale University Press.
Calinescu, Matei. (1994), 'Secrecy in Fiction: Textual and Intertextual Secrets in Hawthorne and Updike', *Poetics Today*, 15 (3): 443–65.
Caputo, John D. (1997), 'Community Without Community', in John D. Caputo (ed.), *Deconstruction in a Nutshell: A Conversation with Jacques Derrida*, 106–24, New York: Fordham University Press.
Coetzee, J. M. (1992), *Doubling the Point: Essays and Interviews*, edited by David Attwell, Cambridge and London: Harvard University Press.
Culler, Jonathan. (2008), 'The Most Interesting Thing in the World', *Diacritics*, 38 (1/2): 7–16.
Danta, Chris. (2013), 'Derrida and the Test of Secrecy', *Angelaki: Journal of the Theoretical Humanities*, 18 (2): 61–75.
Derrida, Jacques. (1992), *Given Time: 1. Counterfeit Money*, translated by Peggy Kamuf, Chicago: Chicago University Press.
Derrida, Jacques. (1994), *Specters of Marx: The State of the Debt, the Work of Mourning, and the New International*, translated by Peggy Kamuf, New York and London: Routledge.
Derrida, Jacques. (1995a), 'Passions: "An Oblique Offering"', in David Wood, John P. Leavey and Ian McLeod (trans.), Thomas Dutoit (ed.), *On the Name*, 3–31, Stanford: Stanford University Press.
Derrida, Jacques. (1995b), *Points. . .: Interviews, 1974–1994*, edited by Elisabeth Weber, translated by Peggy Kamuf, 132–55, Stanford: Stanford University Press.

Derrida, Jacques. (2002), 'Faith and Knowledge: The Two Sources of "Religion" at the Limits of Reason Alone', in Gil Anidjar (ed.), *Acts of Religion*, 42–101, New York and London: Routledge.

Derrida, Jacques. (2005a), *The Politics of Friendship*, translated by George Collins, London and New York: Verso.

Derrida, Jacques. (2005b), *Rogues: Two Essays on Reason*, translated by Pascale-Anne Brault and Michael Naas, Stanford: Stanford University Press.

Derrida, Jacques. (2008), *The Gift of Death (Second Edition) and Literature in Secret*, translated by David Wills, Chicago: University of Chicago Press.

Derrida, Jacques and Derek Attridge. (1992), '"This Strange Institution Called Literature": An Interview with Jacques Derrida', in Derek Attridge (ed.), *Acts of Literature*, 33–75, London and New York: Routledge.

Derrida, Jacques, and Maurizio Ferraris. (2001), *A Taste for the Secret*, edited by Giacomo Donis and David Webb, translated by Giacomo Donis, Cambridge: Polity Press.

Durrant, Sam. (2003), *Postcolonial Narrative and the Work of Mourning: J. M. Coetzee, Wilson Harris, and Toni Morrison*, Albany, NY: State University of New York Press.

Eco, Umberto. (1992), *Interpretation and Overinterpretation*, Cambridge: Cambridge University Press.

Han, Byung-Chul. (2015), *The Transparency Society*, translated by Erik Butler, Stanford: Stanford University Press.

Iser, Wolfgang. (1978) (1976), *The Act of Reading: A Theory of Aesthetic Response*, Baltimore: John Hopkins University Press.

Jiménez Heffernan, Julián. (2013), 'Introduction: Togetherness and its Discontents', in Paula Martín Salván, Gerardo Rodríguez-Salas and Julián Jiménez Heffernan (eds), *Community in Twentieth-Century Fiction*, 1–47, Houndmills: Palgrave Macmillan.

Kermode, Frank. (1979), *The Genesis of Secrecy: On the Interpretation of Narrative*, Cambridge: Harvard University Press.

Kermode, Frank. (1980), 'Secrets and Narrative Sequence', *Critical Inquiry*, 7 (1): 83–101.

Kronick, Joseph G. (1999), *Derrida and the Future of Literature*, Albany: Suny Press.

López, María J. (2019), 'The "Deadly Secret" of the Prophecy: Performative and Parabolic Language in Chigozie Obioma's *The Fishermen*', *Theory Now*, 2 (2): 148–64.

Macherey, Pierre. (1989) (1966), *A Theory of Literary Production*, translated by Geoffrey Wall, London: Routledge.

Martín-Salván, Paula. (2020), 'Narrating the Underground: Structure and the Slave Narrative Tradition in Colson Whitehead's *The Underground Railroad*', *ES Review. Spanish Journal of English Studies*, 41 (Forthcoming).

Martín-Salván, Paula, Gerardo Rodríguez-Salas and Julián Jiménez Heffernan, eds. (2013), *Community in Twentieth-Century Fiction*, Houndmills: Palgrave Macmillan.

May, Leila Silvana. (2017), *Secrecy and Disclosure in Victorian Fiction*, New York: Routledge.

Michaud, Ginette. (2002), 'Literature in Secret: Crossing Derrida and Blanchot', *Angelaki: Journal of the Theoretical Humanities*, 7 (2): 69–90.

Miller, J. Hillis. (1994), 'Derrida's Topographies', *South Atlantic Review*, 59 (1): 1–25.

Miller, J. Hillis. (2001a), *Others*, Princeton: Princeton University Press.

Miller, J. Hillis. (2001b), *Speech Acts in Literature*, Stanford: Stanford University Press.

Miller, J. Hillis. (2002a), *On Literature*, London: Routledge.

Miller, J. Hillis. (2002b), 'Derrida and Literature', in Tom Cohen (ed.), *Jacques Derrida and the Humanities: A Critical Reader*, 58–81, Cambridge: Cambridge University Press.

Miller, J. Hillis. (2005), *Literature as Conduct: Speech Acts in Henry James*, New York: Fordham University Press.

Miller, J. Hillis. (2011), *The Conflagration of Community: Fiction Before and After Auschwitz*, Chicago and London: The University of Chicago Press.

Miller, J. Hillis. (2015), *Communities in Fiction*, New York: Fordham University Press.

Morin, Marie-Even. (2006), 'Putting Community Under Erasure: Derrida and Nancy on the Plurality of Singularities', *Culture Machine*, 8. https://culturemachine.net/community/putting-community-under-erasure/

Nancy, Jean-Luc. (1991), *The Inoperative Community*, translated by Peter Connor, Lisa Garbus, Michael Holland, and Simona Sawhney, Minneapolis: University of Minnesota Press.

Phelan, James. (1996), *Narrative as Rhetoric: Technique, Audiences, Ethics, Ideology*, Columbus: Ohio State University Press.

Phelan, James. (2007), *Experiencing Fiction: Judgments, Progressions, and the Rhetorical Theory of Narrative*, Columbus: Ohio State University Press.

Rashkin, Esther. (1992), *Family Secrets and the Psychoanalysis of Narrative*, Princeton: Princeton University Press.

Rashkin, Esther. (2008), *Unspeakable Secrets and the Psychoanalysis of Culture*, Albany, NY: State University of New York Press.

Rodríguez-Salas, Gerardo, Paula Martín-Salván and María J. López, eds. (2018), *New Perspectives on Community and the Modernist Subject: Finite, Singular, Exposed*, New York: Routledge.

Royle, Nicholas. (1991), *Telepathy and Literature: Essays on the Reading Mind*, Oxford: Blackwell.

Royle, Nicholas. (2003), *Jacques Derrida*, London: Routledge.

Royle, Nicholas. (2014), 'Reading Joseph Conrad: Episodes from the Coast', *Mosaic: A Journal for the Interdisciplinary Study of Literature*, 47 (1): 41–67.

Segal, Alex. (2008), 'Deconstruction, Radical Secrecy, and *The Secret Agent*', *Modern Fiction Studies*, 54 (2): 189–208.

Simmel, Georg. (1906), 'The Sociology of Secrecy and of Secret Societies', *American Journal of Sociology*, 11: 441–98.

Thomson, Alex. (2005), *Deconstruction and Democracy: Derrida's Politics of Friendship*, London and New York: Continuum.

Toolan, Michael. (2004), 'Expectations in the Process of Reading the Long Story: Alice Munro's "The Love of a Good Woman" and Tobias Wolff's "The Barracks Thief"', in Wolfgang Görtschacher and Holger Michael Klein (eds), *Tale, Novella, Short Story: Currents in Short Fiction*, 193–206, Tübingen: Stauffenburg.

Warhol, Robyn R. (2005), 'Neonarrative; or, How to Render the Unnarratable in Realist Fiction and Contemporary Film', in James Phelan and Peter J. Rabinowitz (eds), *A Companion to Narrative Theory*, 220–31, Malden: Blackwell.

Williams, Raymond. (1973), *The Country and the City*, Oxford: Oxford University Press.

Wills, David. (2008), 'Passionate Secrets and Democratic Dissidence', *Diacritics*, 38 (1/2): 17–22, 24–9.

Yamamoto, Kaoru. (2017), *Rethinking Joseph Conrad's Concepts of Community: Strange Fraternity*, London: Bloomsbury.

Part One

Secrecy, literary form and the community of readers

1

Secrecy and community in ergodic texts: Derrida, Ali Smith and the experience of form

Derek Attridge

Modernism and the ergodic novel

Criticism of the novel is concerned, above all, with meaning – and, most often, meaning as a noun, something that can be extracted from the text or something outside the text to which it refers. Character, plot, scene, motive, development, crisis, recognition, reversal and other features of narrative content are the staple ingredients of most accounts of fictional works. Historical, social and political context are exhaustively examined, and even the material constitution of the books in which novels appear gets a great deal of attention. What criticism less often attends to is the *experience* of meaning, how the text does its work of meaning as it is read. (This, to my mind, is a better way to think of literary meaning – treating it, that is, as a verb rather than as a noun.) In either case, when the question of *form* is being addressed in studies of the novel, and when it's not simply being described, it is almost always assumed to have as its sole *raison-d'être* the enhancement of meaning. (By 'form' I mean simply those aspects of the literary work that are not in the business of directly conveying content to the reader, and thus not drawing directly on the semantic dimension of language.) When Samuel Richardson writes *Clarissa* (1748) in the form of letters, it is in order to convey a sense of immediacy and authenticity in the writing; when Charles Dickens switches between first-person and third-person narration in *Bleak House* (1852–3) it is in order to achieve a contrast between subjective and objective views of the world – these, at least, are the kinds of explanation usually given for formal choices.

The use of innovative formal devices in order to enhance the reader's experience of meaning was a significant marker of modernist fiction. Dorothy Richardson's use of stream-of-consciousness narration in *Pilgrimage* (1915–67) captures the movements of Miriam Henderson's mind; the repeating cycle of narrative voices in Virginia Woolf's *The Waves* (1931) represents the fluidity of human awareness; James Joyce, in developing the technique of interior monologue in *Ulysses* (1922), was able to express the constant flux of an individual's inner life with unprecedented immediacy. And many of the novels labelled 'postmodern' or 'late modernist' similarly find inventive ways of extending the fictional use of language in the service of more precise, more intense, or more humorous representations of human experience – think of Eimear McBride's tortured syntax in *A Girl is a Half-formed Thing* (2013) and *The Lesser Bohemians* (2016), the grammatically continuous, spatially punctuated, prose of Mike McCormack's *Solar Bones* (2016), the unstoppable mental chatter of Lucy Ellmann's *Ducks, Newburyport* (2019), and what has been called the 'stream-of-fractured-consciousness' (Leith 2017) of Will Self's Busner trilogy, the novels *Umbrella* (2012), *Shark* (2014) and *Phone* (2017). What is frequently left out of these discussions is the contribution made by these formal features to the reader's experience that *can't* be accounted for in terms of meaning. Although there is wide acceptance of the notion that in literary works form and meaning are inseparable – the romantic idea of 'organic form' remains powerful – it is worth asking whether there are ways in which form may operate on its own to produce pleasure for the reader.

A comparison with music is instructive: an absolute piece of music, without, that is any associated words or narrative, produces its effects on the listener by means of its handling of sonic form. It is a commonplace that these effects are not, finally, translatable into anything that could be called meaning, yet their subtlety and power receives constant testimony. One might say that music operates in secret if secrecy can be thought of as the condition of being outside language and its referential functions. Poetry is more obviously a parallel case, especially when it exploits to the full the possibilities of sound and rhythm. But my suggestion is that a non-semantic potential exists for *all* formal properties of literary works, and in this essay I wish to explore this proposition in relation to one type of novelistic form.

All the novels I have cited, like most novels, invite a continuous, linear reading in which the primary experience of form is as a constant augmentation, or perhaps complication, of meaning. A different mode of semantic enrichment may happen when the visual layout of the page includes elements that ask to be taken in separately, at a moment of the reader's own choosing. Espen J. Aarseth provides a full discussion of this issue, coining the term 'ergodic literature' for texts in which 'nontrivial effort is required to allow the reader to traverse the text'; by contrast, traditional texts, which require only 'eye movement and the periodic or arbitrary turning of pages', are non-ergodic (1997, 1). Ergodic literary productions are one example of multimodality, a phenomenon that is receiving increasing attention in studies not only of literary texts but other art forms and games.[1] It is the issue of the reader's freedom of choice in ergodic texts and its relationship to secrecy that I want to consider in more detail here.

One traditional manifestation of ergodic form is the use of illustrations, from medieval illuminated manuscripts to Laurence Sterne's graphic interpolations in *Tristram Shandy* (1759–67) to the nineteenth-century illustrated novel.[2] More recent

---

[1] See, for example, Page (2010) and Sachs-Hombach and Thon (2019).
[2] There is, of course, a long history of fictional works in which the visual elements are as important as, or more important than, the textual ones, reaching their apogee with the graphic novel in the twentieth century. In Chris Ware's *Building Stories* (2012), the use of images is combined with the further ergodic principle of multiple parts of different shapes and sizes, which are presented in a box and can be read in any order.

examples include W. G. Sebald's frequent use of photographs, Jennifer Egan's PowerPoint chapter in *A Visit from the Goon Squad* (2010), and, in a different mode, the collaboration between the novelist Ivan Vladislavić and the photographer David Goldblatt in *Double Negative/TJ* (2010). Another type of separate formal element is the footnote or endnote, ranging across Issy's contributions to the 'Nightlessons' chapter of Joyce's *Finnegans Wake* (1939), Samuel Beckett's devastating use of the footnote in *Watt* (1953), Flann O'Brien's mock-scholarly apparatus in *The Third Policeman* (1967) and David Foster Wallace's exploitation of the endnote in *Infinite Jest* (1966). There are numerous related examples in what we might call late-modernist writing; B. S. Johnson uses side-notes as running commentary in one section of *Albert Angelo* (1964), Nicholson Baker entertains the reader with lengthy footnotes in *The Mezzanine* (1988) and a further development of visually simultaneous narrative threads occurs in J. M. Coetzee's *Diary of a Bad Year* (2007) with its triple bands of text. Perhaps the fullest exploitation of the text plus notes format is Vladimir Nabokov's *Pale Fire* (1962), which allows the reader a number of different reading experiences, depending on what route is chosen between the poem and its lengthy apparatus.

The readerly choice evident in the inclusion of non-verbal material is also manifest when alternative routes through a novel are provided. *Finnegans Wake* could be said to be an early example of this mode, since the sentence that runs from the end of the book straight back to the beginning might be taken to imply that the reader can start the text at any point. A well-known Spanish example is Julio Cortázar's 1963 *Rayuela*, translated into English as *Hopscotch*, which provides instructions for an alternative ordering of the chapters; and even more extreme are those novels published in boxes with loose leaves or chapters, such as Marc Saporta's *Composition No. 1* of 1962 and B. S. Johnson's *The Unfortunates* of 1969. Other extravagant games with visual layout include Mark Z. Danielewski's *House of Leaves* (2000) with its dizzying array of typefaces and spatial arrangements, footnotes and footnotes to footnotes, index, diagrams and photographs and J. J. Abrams and Doug Dorst's *S.* (2013), a narrative that unfolds in handwritten marginal notes to a printed novel that has every appearance of being a library copy of a 1949 novel called *Ship of Theseus* by one V. M. Straka, complete with loose inserts. In these examples, the reader has multiple choices in sequencing their reading (and, of course, different decisions produce a different book). And when we leave the category of the printed book for electronic media, we find a new universe of multiple plots, readerly choice and visual effects.

I have argued elsewhere that to read a literary work responsibly is a matter of actively exercising interpretation (of language, of referential detail, of generic conventions and so on) and at the same time passively allowing the text to operate upon one – and, if the work is a powerful one, to effect a change in one's mental and perhaps emotional world.[3] The literary work, therefore, is not, to my way of thinking, an object but an *act-event*. Ergodic novels produce an increase in the reader's active engagement by making conscious choices necessary, but this increased activity is only valuable if it contributes

---

[3] See, for instance, Attridge (2017), *passim*.

to the work's effect upon the receptive reader. In all the examples I have cited, it is possible to make a case for the contribution made by the non-linear materials to the text's production of meaning; harder to account for, however, is the experience of non-linearity, and thus of choice, as *itself* as an element in the act-event of reading.

The question I am asking, then, is this: 'Is the enhancement or complication of the semantic dimension the only way in which this aspect of the reader's experience – the freedom to choose a pathway – can contribute to the work's literary operation, or can it make a contribution by functioning independently of meaning?' (A further question, which I shall come to later, is 'Do ergodic devices have a part to play in the literary work's relation to community?')

Baker gives a witty account of some of the pleasures of ergodic form in one of the many extensive footnotes in *The Mezzanine*, a novel that accepts the gauntlet thrown down by Joyce in *Ulysses* by taking place during a single lunch-hour. Footnoting writers such as Gibbon and Boswell, Baker writes,

> liked deciding as they read whether they would bother to consult a certain footnote or not, and whether they would read it in context or read it before the text it hung from, as an hors d'oeuvre. The muscles of the eye, they knew, want vertical itineraries; the rectus externus and internus grow dazed waggling back and forth in the Zs taught in grade school: the footnote functions as a switch, offering the model-railroader's satisfaction of catching the march of thought with a superscripted '1' and routing it, sometimes at length, through abandoned stations and submerged, leaching tunnels.
>
> 1986, 122

Baker claims that the very act of choosing when to read a footnote is pleasurable, and that the 're-routing' that ensues is one of the rewards of this type of text. Linearity can seem like a straitjacket, especially in this era of hypertext; the single-thread narrative can feel like an unnecessarily limited use of the potential resources offered by the form of the book, a condition even more evident in the case of narratives in electronic media.[4] Being able to decide when to look at an illustration or a footnote, which thread to follow in a set of parallel narratives or how to treat spatial arrangements that complicate linearity are all ways in which the reader's freedom is enhanced. Making these choices impacts upon the experience of the novel as a narrative, of course, but the very fact of being given the choice is itself part of the experience that renders a given work singular. And if the ergodic dimension of such texts can be thought of as operating to some extent independently of the text's meanings, constituting no part of the content that could be captured in a paraphrase, it could be said to operate in secret.

---

[4] The invention of the codex form of the book, replacing the papyrus roll, was a move towards non-linear reading, since it allowed for rapid paging back and forth. The search facility on an e-reader enhances this function. And anyone who uses a contents list or an index is engaging in ergodic behaviour.

Derrida and the secret of literature

The connection between literature and secrecy was something that fascinated Jacques Derrida, representing one aspect of his wider concern with the secret. As Nicholas Royle says in his excellent study of Derrida in the Routledge Critical Thinkers series, 'Derrida's notion of the secret might be elaborated in all sorts of directions: it haunts every word, every name' (2003, 126). A similar claim is made by Charles Barbour, in a book-length examination of the subject: '[I]n Derrida, or at any rate in the later Derrida, ... the problem of the secret is not one problem among many; rather, it is integral to nearly everything he has to say, or every topic he discusses' (2017, 20).[5] One of Derrida's most astute philosophical commentators, Michael Naas, notes that '[t]his emphasis on the secret, indeed, this "taste for the secret," was at the center of many of Derrida's reflections during the 1990s', and points out that his seminar of 1991-2 was devoted to the subject (2012, 127).

Three texts by Derrida are particularly relevant to the question of literature and the secret: an essay with the title 'Passions: "An Oblique Offering"' (1995), a text called 'Literature in Secret: An Impossible Filiation' (published with the second English edition of *The Gift of Death*) (2008), and a discussion of Baudelaire's prose poem, 'La fausse monnaie', or 'Counterfeit Money', in the book *Given Time* (1992a).[6] In 'Passions' Derrida confirms his 'taste (probably unconditional) for literature, more precisely for literary writing' – not, he says, that he likes literature in general or for its own sake, but that he 'likes something *about it*, which above all cannot be reduced to some aesthetic quality, to some source of formal pleasure [*jouissance*]' (1995, 27-8; emphasis in the original). He names this quality 'the secret',[7] but we have to understand the word in a particular way, related to but distinguishable from the common-or-garden meaning. Here is part of his explanation:

> [The secret] does not conceal itself. Heterogeneous to the hidden, to the obscure, to the nocturnal, to the invisible, to what can be dissimulated and indeed to what is nonmanifest in general, it cannot be unveiled. It remains inviolable even when one thinks one has revealed it. Not that it hides itself forever in an indecipherable crypt or behind an absolute veil. It simply exceeds the play of veiling/unveiling, dissimulation/revelation, night/day, forgetting/anamnesis, earth/heaven, etc.
>
> Derrida 1995, 26

---

[5] Elsewhere Barbour comments, '[T]he secret is Derrida's secret preoccupation. At least during this period [the last fifteen years of his life], and perhaps in others as well, it secretly informs everything else he has to say' (2017, 24). One of Derrida's books, written with Maurizio Ferraris, is called *A Taste for the Secret* (2001).

[6] The first of these originally appeared in Wood (1992, 5-35). The French originals are to be found in *Passions* (1993), *Donner la mort* (1999) and *Donner le temps: 1. La fausse monnaie* (1991).

[7] Derrida's phrase is 'au lieu du secret': either 'at the place of the secret' or 'in place of the secret'. He thus avoids implying that 'the secret' is something positive waiting to be found.

We must banish, that is, any idea of the secret as a truth that is hidden but could be uncovered. This is not the secrecy explored from a sociological perspective by Georg Simmel in his well-known essay, 'The Sociology of Secrecy and of Secret Societies' (1906); nor is it the secret that seals the identity of the community of insiders as explored in Frank Kermode's *The Genesis of Secrecy* (1979); nor are we necessarily dealing with works that are essentially unknowable, like those admirably discussed by H. Porter Abbott in *Real Mysteries* (2014). This is secrecy without concealment or possible revelation; it is at once absolute and highly productive.

Literature is an exemplary site of the secret in Derrida's sense because there is no way of putting an end to what he calls 'hypotheses ... about the meaning of a text, or the final intentions of an author, whose person is no more represented than nonrepresented by a character or by a narrator, by a poetic or fictional sentence, which detaches itself from its presumed source and thus remains *locked away [au secret]*' (1995, 29; emphasis in the original). In the case of the literary work, he says, 'there is no longer even any sense in making decisions about some secret behind the surface of a textual manifestation' (1995, 29). Derrida's concern with literature – of which he says 'nothing to this day remains as new and as incomprehensible to me, at once very near and very alien' (Derrida 2000, 20) – is closely related to his concern with questions of testimony and perjury; what interests him is not literary genres or matters of form, but the simultaneous openness and closedness of all varieties of fiction, whether in literature or the courtroom or daily life.[8]

We may turn to Derrida's discussion of Baudelaire's 'Counterfeit Money' for an example of the paradoxes of fiction. In this prose poem, the narrator watches a friend give what seems like a generous donation to a beggar, only to be told by the friend that the coin was counterfeit. Derrida points out that there is no-one we can turn to, neither Baudelaire nor any other authority, to establish the truth or falsity of this utterance. Very few readers, it must be said, would experience any doubt about its veracity from the evidence of the text, but Derrida's point is that the true/false distinction is, finally, an *inappropriate* one to appeal to in such a case: what makes fiction fiction is the undecidability of any assertion made within it. As he says in a resonant footnote to 'Passions':

---

[8] Barbour gives a clear explanation of the role of the secret in testimony in his discussion of Derrida's *Demeure*:

> As Derrida puts it, in a paradoxical manner, 'I must be able to keep secret precisely what I testify to' (*Demeure*, 30). Or, to put the matter differently, even though testimony is by definition public or a public act (something I address to some audience or some other), it also relies on something that cannot be communicated or shared. It is, as Derrida says, 'the sharable and unsharable secret of what happened to me', 'both infinitely secret and infinitely public' (43). Moreover, and for the same reason, inasmuch as it is (and must be) conditioned by secrecy, or what no other person can ever intuit or know, testimony is also conditioned by the possibility of perjury and deception, fiction and literature. That is to say, on Derrida's account, such things are not accidental or secondary with respect to testimony. They are not things that only appear when testimony goes badly or when it is appropriated by a bad or less than scrupulous individual. On the contrary, perjury and fiction are absolutely necessary conditions for the possibility of testimonial truth. There is no testimony except in the shadow of deception.
> 2017, 120–1

Something of literature will have begun when it is not possible to decide whether, when I speak of something, I am indeed speaking of something (of the thing itself, this one, for itself) or if I am giving an example, an example of something or an example of the fact that I can speak of something, of my way of speaking of something, of the possibility of speaking in general of something in general, or again of writing these words, etc.

1995, 142–3[9]

The third of Derrida's texts to consider is 'Literature in Secret'. Leaving aside its readings of the binding of Isaac in the Old Testament, Kierkegaard's *Fear and Trembling* and Kafka's letter to his father, I want to highlight the rather extraordinary connection the text makes between the literary and the experience of Abraham on Mount Moriah (the piece's subtitle, 'An Impossible Filiation', acknowledges the extraordinariness of the connection). Derrida sees the relation between Abraham and God as depicted in the biblical story as an example of the secret, in the same sense as applies to literature: 'For the secret of secrecy... does not consist in hiding *something*, in not revealing the truth, but in respecting the absolute singularity, the infinite separation of what binds me or exposes me to the unique, to one as to the other' (2008, 122–3; emphasis in the original). Responsibility to an absolute singularity is both what Abraham undergoes and what constitutes the experience of literature. In both cases, too, what makes this demand is an *event*, as is evident in Derrida's summing up: '[T]he presumed fictive structure of every work exonerates its signatory from responsibility, before political or civic law, for its sense and referent..., while at the same time increasing in inverse proportion, to infinity, responsibility for the singular event constituted by every work (a void and infinite responsibility, like that of Abraham)' (2008, 156). The literary work in Derrida's eyes, then, takes place as a singular event that we can talk about but that we can never finally close down – and it is because we can never close it down that we keep talking about it. Its secret is what calls for a responsible response from its readers, but because the secret is not one that hides a truth, that responsibility never comes to an end.

It will be evident that in finding the secret to be central to the institution of literature, Derrida focuses very much on meaning: what is primarily at issue is the unanswerability of the questions raised by the content of the work. We have already noted that what Derrida likes about literature cannot be reduced to 'some source of formal pleasure' (1995, 28), and he rarely writes explicitly about formal properties.[10]

---

[9] A related comment occurs in 'Literature in Secret':

> Every text that is consigned to public space, that is relatively legible or intelligible, but whose content, sense, referent, signatory, and addressee are not fully determinable realities – realities that are at the same time non-fictive or immune from all fiction, realities that are delivered as such by some intuition, to a determinate judgement – can become a literary object.
>
> Derrida 2008, 131

[10] Attention to form is, however, implicit in much of his writing on literary works; see, for example, his discussion of the syntax of Celan's poem 'Fable' in 'Psyche: Invention of the Other'; of the structure of Blanchot's *récit* 'The Madness of Day' in 'The Law of Genre'; and of play with sound in Mallarmé's poetry in 'Mallarmé' (all collected in Jacques Derrida, *Acts of Literature*, 1992b). See also Attridge 1994, 53–5.

I want to hold on to the notions of 'event' and 'singularity', and ask what the relevance of the Derridean secret might be to the singular event of form. I have argued elsewhere that we need to beware of the static, spatial implications of the term 'form' (Attridge 2017, 150–70) and, if we want to reflect accurately on what happens when a material text becomes, in the event of reading, a work of literature, we need to think of form, like meaning, as something that *happens*. As I have suggested, when there is talk about the experience of form, the most common approach is to consider its contribution to the meaning of the work as it unfolds; but this may be to miss what is most important about it as an element in a literary event. If matters of content, which is what Derrida is mostly interested in, resist the questioning that would result in indisputable answers, so that it makes no sense to ask if the friend's coin was 'really' counterfeit, formal features resist even the *posing* of such questions. For example, Baudelaire's 'Counterfeit Money' is in prose, though it offers itself as a poem: this is a formal feature about which there is much to say – in fact, there is no end to what can be said about it, and the reason for this is, in Derrida's terms, that it too is part of the secret, a secret on the surface, not one that can be uncovered: it is an essential and obvious aspect of the work's singularity; it plays an important part in the reader's experience; and yet it remains irreducible to meaning.

The particular form that constitutes the ergodic text – a formal arrangement that challenges the linear reading we normally expect of a narrative – is one example of this secret operation: over and above its contribution to the content, it takes place every time the work is read as a non-meaningful event – or, to be more precise, as an event whose meanings remain undecidable and inexhaustible.

How to be both: Secrecy and community

I have a copy of the Penguin paperback edition (2015) of Ali Smith's 2014 novel *How to Be Both* in front of me. The cover shows an apparently unposed photograph of two young women in a street; inside the front and back covers are full bleed reproductions of paintings of standing figures, the first a dark-skinned young man in tattered clothes with a rope serving as a belt, the second a richly dressed person of indeterminate gender holding an arrow and a hoop. After the front matter, including a page of epigraphs, comes a page with the single word 'one' and a simple sketch of a security camera. The narrative that follows is an account, largely in free indirect discourse, of the experiences of a teenage girl in contemporary Cambridge. We find ourselves seeing the world through the perceptions and memories of George (the character's preferred version of Georgia), living with her father and her younger brother and mourning the unexpected death of her mother four months earlier.

Particularly vivid among her memories is a visit to Ferrara with her mother and brother to see the frescoes by the fifteenth-century painter Francesco del Cossa in the Palazzo Schifanoia. The trip, we learn, was prompted by George's mother coming across a photo in an art magazine of 'a man standing dressed in ripped white clothes and wearing an old rope as a belt' (Smith 2015, 47), an image to be found in a room in the aforesaid palazzo. If we recognize this description as fitting the image inside the front cover, we may respond to the invitation to page back and look at it: here we have one of the novel's ergodic features, since we are equally free to continue reading. Similarly, when the trio are in the room in the palazzo, George observes 'a young man or a young woman, could be either, dressed in beautiful rich clothes and holding an arrow or a stick and a gold hoop thing' (51); different readers will find out at different times in the reading process that this image is at the back of the book, and can choose when to look at it and how much attention to give it.

Another image that features significantly in George's story is a photograph given to her by her friend Helena, which is described in detail and clearly refers to the image on the book's cover (Smith 2015, 81–2). If we don't know who the two young women are, we learn near the end of George's story that one of them – whom George is said to look like – is the French singer Sylvie Vartan (who is also the author of one of the book's epigraphs); we might notice, too, that the back cover acknowledges the source of the 'Photo of Sylvie Vartan and Françoise Hardy', enabling us to put a name to the other figure as well. (Alternatively, it is not difficult to find the photograph on Google Images.) George also has a photograph of an actress on her wall, whom it is not difficult to identify as Monica Vitti, though George doesn't seem to know her name; in this case, there is no way of seeing the image other than by moving outside the book.

As the sketch on the opening page suggests, one of the themes of this narrative is surveillance: George becomes preoccupied with a woman named Lisa Goliard who appears to have been watching her mother, no doubt because of the latter's political activities (but also perhaps because they were in love). This motif of watching occurs in many variants: for instance, George comes across a pornographic video of child abuse on her iPad and forces herself to watch a few minutes of it as part of her daily schedule (31–5). Late in George's narrative these references multiply: we find her in the National Gallery in London watching people in front of Cossa's painting of St Vincent Ferrer, and (in a final look ahead) being surprised when one of those with an interest in the painting turns out to be Goliard – after which, she becomes in turn the watcher, installed outside Goliard's house.

George's story ends about halfway through the book; it is immediately followed by another page with the single word 'one', but this time with a drawing beneath it of a flower stalk with eyes instead of blossoms. The narrative that follows begins with pages of poetic prose in the first person from which it emerges that the speaker is Cossa himself and that he has travelled (painfully) across time to find himself in what we realize is the same room in the National Gallery where we recently saw George, who is standing in front of the painting of St Vincent and whom he takes at first to be a boy. The account that follows is for the most part devoted to Cossa's reminiscences, from which we learn that she is in fact a woman who passed as a man (a cross-dressing for which there is no historical evidence), and was thus able to pursue a career as a painter – including some of the frescoes in the 'palace of not being bored' (the Palazzo Schifanoia) (Smith 2015, 196 and *passim*).[11] We also learn, among much else, of Cossa's meeting with an 'infidel' worker in ragged clothes who obtains from her a rope to serve as a belt (283–5), perhaps prompting the reader to take another look at the inside of the cover. There is also a reference to Cossa's painting of St Lucia holding a stalk with eyes instead of flowers, which chimes with the drawing at the opening of this section.

The remainder of the section has Cossa reporting on George's actions: she finds herself always in George's presence, though invisible, and we are able to translate her often bemused description of what she sees into the terms already provided by George's narrative: she observes Goliard's arrival in the room and George's pursuit of her, her few minutes watching the porn video on her iPad and her games with her brother. In George's bedroom, Cossa admires the photograph of Vartan and Hardy ('by a great artist surely in its patchwork of light, dark, determination, gentleness' (Smith 2015, 287–8)), encouraging us to shut the book and examine the cover again, and the one of Vitti (which she takes to be an image of St Monica, assuming that 'Vitti' is Latin for 'victims'). She accompanies George again and again on her mission to monitor Goliard's house and to capture Goliard's image on her iPad – here the story moves beyond the end of George's narrative – and witnesses what must be a reunion with Helena. As Cossa watches George and Helena paint eyes on the wall opposite Goliard's house, she feels herself dragged back 'to be / made and / unmade / both' (372).

The ergodic features of this novel clearly contribute to its content: we can appreciate directly the force and beauty of Cossa's painting (to the extent that small photographic reproductions can do this), and are able to substitute image for words when the photograph of Vartan and Hardy is described. But the same result could be achieved by the simple use of Google or the more elaborate strategy of trips to the National Gallery or the Palazzo Schifanoia; what difference does it make that these images form part of the complex structure of the novel, and that the reader has a choice to make in accessing them? It surely increases the reader's enjoyment, enriching the experience of engaging with the text, adding a dimension to the purely verbal material of the narrative, continuing by other means the concern with seeing that persists throughout the book. Attempting to state exactly how this happens runs the risk of reducing the effects once more to matters of content; like all formal events, this one keeps its secret.

Another ergodic feature is implied by the occurrence of *two* section title-pages with the word 'one': the reader is offered the choice of reading Cossa's narrative before George's, which produces a very different reading experience. Read first, Cossa's account of the girl she finds herself watching after her time-travel throws up a number

---

[11] Some early reviewers speculated that Cossa's section of the novel represents George's reconstruction of the painter's life on the grounds that 'the palace of not being bored' echoes George's mother's explanation that 'Palazzo Schifanoia' means 'the palace escaping from boredom' (also cited as possible evidence is Cossa's use of the phrase 'just saying'). However, Cossa refers to another palazzo – probably the Palazzo Belfiore – as 'the palace of beautiful flowers' (Smith 2015, 196 and *passim*). The idiosyncrasies of Cossa's account, such as her spellings 'Francescho' for Francesco and 'Cosmo' for 'Cosima', require another explanation; Derrida might say that it is a secret.

of puzzles: who is this girl? What is this room she finds herself in? Why does she haunt a particular house? We might be able to deduce the identity of a few of the contemporary items Cossa is bemused by, such as George's tablet, before we find confirmation in the other half of the book. Though, admittedly, few readers are likely to read the sections in a different order from that in which they occur in print. *How to Be Both* could be said to continue the line of experimental fiction in which the reader has a choice in the matter of narrative sequence, like the boxed books by Saporta and Johnson. Although the doubleness of the novel's structure is one aspect of its thematic concern with doubles of all kinds – observable in the title, in the gender ambiguities in both sections, in the relation between original and copy, 'before' and 'after'[12]– it is also part of the innovative formal event that is central to the reader's experience. When George's mother poses a moral conundrum (arising from the historical Cossa's request for more pay in a rare surviving letter), George asks 'Past or present? . . . Male or female? It can't be both. It must be one or the other'. Her mother's answer is: 'Who says? Why must it?' (Smith 2015, 8). What the form of the novel allows the reader to experience is this 'bothness', an experience that, though it can be related to the work's meanings, cannot be reduced to them. It is part of the book's secret.

How to Be Both is even more extraordinary, however. I have another copy of the novel before me, which at first looks identical: the same photograph on the cover, the same image inside it, the same front matter, the same single word 'one' – but in this copy, the drawing that accompanies the 'one' is that of the eyes on a stalk instead of the security camera.[13] And what follows is the Cossa section, after which we again find 'one' with the security camera drawing and then George's narrative. Smith arranged for the book to be published in two different versions, but with no indication in any particular copy that this was the case, or which of the versions it was.[14] Instead of a boxed book offering readers a choice, we have two separate books, each of which provides a distinct reading experience (assuming a reading of the two sections in the order in which they are presented). In this way the theme of doubleness is carried through into the material publication process itself.

You might say that Smith has written two novels, and this would be true up to a point, since it is certainly the case that a reading of version one is a very different experience from a reading of version two. The catch is that no-one can read both novels, unless we imagine the second taking place after such a long interval that all memory of the first has been lost.[15] The full scope of the novel's (or novels') achievement is possible only when we consider it as being experienced by a *community*

---

[12] 'But which came first? her mother says. The chicken or the egg? The picture underneath or the picture on the surface?
  The picture below came first, George says. Because it was done first.
  But the first thing we see, her mother said, and most times the only thing we see, is the one on the surface. So does that mean it comes first after all?' (Smith 2015, 103).
[13] Page references in this essay are to the version in which George's section comes first.
[14] The Kindle edition, however, begins with a statement that gives the game away.
[15] The copy I bought happened to begin with Cossa's section; re-reading the novel, I began with George's, and although I registered consciously the differences this made, there was no way I could share the experience of a reader who first read the sections in this order.

of readers – in fact, its singularity as a work of literature can be acknowledged only by means of such a community, since the existence of two different editions only becomes visible when readers compare their books. Readers of version one can have valuable discussions with readers of version two about their respective experiences of the novel, discussions which are likely to deepen the understanding and enjoyment of both. These discussions are never-ending, as with all discussions about literary works as literary works, because of the secrecy that is involved in literary singularity, including the secrecy of form – which is to say form's resistance to being absorbed into questions of content. And I would extrapolate from the singular example of *How To Be Both* to all works in which the secrecy of form operates: only when approached in the light of a community of readers, contrasting experiences, comparing notes, re-reading in the light of the comments of others, can their achievement be properly appreciated and enjoyed. And only when form operates in a way that can be said to be literary is there any point in having such conversations; our appreciation of non-literary texts is not enhanced by discussions of their form. Or, putting it differently, when we find that it is worth having a conversation about a text's form, we are treating it, to this extent, as a literary work.

Derrida's insistence that the secret, as well as being 'the best-shared thing in the world', is the 'sharing of what is not shared' (2001, 58) might seem to contradict this vision of literary reading as a communal activity. But the opposite is true: were the operations of literature wholly transparent, there would be no point in having discussions about them. Everyone who reads literary works with attention and enjoyment encounters their singularity and secrecy in a singular way, and is likely to gain from hearing about the experiences of others. The experience of form, in particular, is a secret that, as Derrida puts it, 'we *speak* of but cannot *say*' (2001, 58; emphasis in the original).[16] In this respect, literature is perhaps paradigmatic of wider communal relationships; as Barbour argues in *Derrida's Secret*, because we cannot see inside one another's heads, 'every relation and every interaction, even the most minimal mode of communication or exchange, relies on an act of faith, or an ungrounded and ultimately ungroundable belief or trust in the other' (2017, 13). The literary work is also a singular, secret other we have to trust, and this trust, as a crucial aspect of the reader's experience, is constitutive of literature, as it is of community.

References

Aarseth, Espen J. (1997), *Cybertext: Perspectives on Ergodic Literature*, Baltimore: Johns Hopkins University Press.

Abbott, H. Porter. (2014), *Real Mysteries: Narrative & the Unknowable*, Columbus: Ohio State University Press.

---

[16] As is often noted, the formal dimension of literary works is the most resistant to translation: this is an example of the untranslatability that gives rise to endless translation.

Attridge, Derek. (1994), 'Le texte comme autre: La forme sans formalisme', in Marie-Louise Mallet (ed.), *Le passage des frontiers: Autour du travail de Jacques Derrida*, 53–5, Paris: Galilée.
Attridge, Derek. (2017), *The Singularity of Literature*, Abingdon: Routledge.
Baker, Nicholson. (1986), *The Mezzanine*, London: Granta.
Barbour, Charles. (2017), *Derrida's Secret: Perjury, Testimony, Oath*, Edinburgh: Edinburgh University Press.
Derrida, Jacques. (1991), *Donner le temps: 1. La fausse monnaie*, Paris: Galilée.
Derrida, Jacques. (1992a), *Given Time: I. Counterfeit Money*, translated by Peggy Kamuf, Chicago: University of Chicago Press.
Derrida, Jacques. (1992b), *Acts of Literature*, edited by Derek Attridge, New York: Routledge.
Derrida, Jacques. (1993), *Passions*, Paris: Galilée.
Derrida, Jacques. (1995), 'Passions: "An Oblique Offering"', in Thomas Dutoit (ed.), David Wood, John P. Leavey and Ian McLeod (trans), *On the Name*, 3–31, Stanford: Stanford University Press.
Derrida, Jacques. (1999), *Donner la mort*, Paris: Galilée.
Derrida, Jacques. (2000), *Demeure: Fiction and Testimony*, translated by Elizabeth Rottenberg, Stanford: Stanford University Press.
Derrida, Jacques. (2008), *The Gift of Death (Second Edition) and Literature in Secret*, translated by David Wills, Chicago: University of Chicago Press.
Derrida, Jacques, and Maurizio Ferraris. (2001), *A Taste for the Secret*, Cambridge: Polity.
Kermode, Frank. (1979), *The Genesis of Secrecy: On the Interpretation of Narrative*, Cambridge: Harvard University Press.
Leith, Sam. (2017), 'What could be saner?', *TLS*, 31 May 2017. Accessed 18 September 2019. https://www.the-tls.co.uk/articles/private/will-self-consciousness/.
Naas, Michael. (2012), *Miracle and Machine: Jacques Derrida and the Two Sources of Religion, Science, and the Media*, New York: Fordham University Press.
Page, Ruth, (ed.) (2010), *New Perspectives on Narrative and Multimodality*, New York: Routledge.
Royle, Nicholas. (2003), *Jacques Derrida*, London: Routledge.
Sachs-Hombach, Klaus, and Jan-Noël Thon, (eds) (2019), 'Multimodal Media', Special issue, *Poetics Today*, 40 (2).
Simmel, Georg. (1906), 'The Sociology of Secrecy and of Secret Societies', *The American Journal of Sociology*, 11 (4): 441–98.
Smith, Ali. (2015) (2014), *How to Be Both*, London: Penguin.
Ware, Chris. (2012), *Building Stories*, New York: Pantheon.
Wood, David, (ed.) (1992), *Derrida: A Critical Reader*, Oxford: Blackwell.

2

Protective mimicry: Reflections on the novel today

Nicholas Royle

This essay is an attempt to explore questions of secrecy and community in English contemporary fiction in terms of protective mimicry. The term 'protective mimicry' derives originally from Henry Walter Bates who spent eleven years (1848–59) studying butterflies and moths in the Brazilian Amazon, becoming fascinated by the ways in which one creature (such as the *Leptalis*) was indistinguishable from another (an *Ithomia*) from a different family. As Peter Forbes describes it in his book *Dazzled and Deceived: Mimicry and Camouflage*:

> Not only did *Leptalis* mimic *Ithomia*, but the *Ithomia* changed its pattern from region to region, and the *Leptalis* which copied it also changed, in order to maintain the mimicry. Bates found many examples of these copycat shadowings during his travels. And it was not just a case of shadow *pairs* of species. In some places, a group of half a dozen or more different species all showed the same wing patterns. Some were not even butterflies at all, but day-flying moths.
>
> Forbes 2009, 13

Protective or Batesian mimicry, then, involves what Forbes calls 'a defenceless creature obtaining relief from predators by assuming the pattern and colouring of one defended in some way, usually by inedibility – that is, by sailing under false colours' (Forbes 2009, 26). 'Sailing under false colours' might at first sight seem an awkward anthropomorphism, but Forbes's study is in part driven by a desire to acknowledge how thoroughly humans also engage in mimicry and deception (he gives sustained attention to matters of war and camouflage). His book foregrounds the non-exceptionalism of the human and an unsettling of the anthropocentric. Against the poignant isolationism of Wallace Stevens's 'It is the human that is the alien, / The human that has no cousin in the moon' ('Less and Less Human, O Savage Spirit', 1997a, 288), we are confronted with what Forbes calls '[o]ne of the most startling findings of molecular biology', namely 'the revelation that all creatures are closer cousins under the skin than we had imagined. The question "Are you a man or a mouse?" can now be answered "Both" – since around 99 per cent of human genes have a mouse equivalent' (Forbes 2009, 4). 'Under the skin': I leave that phrase to hang, you might like to consider it for the time being, as they say in legal discourse, *sisted*.

Dazzled and Deceived is one of several remarkable recent science books (others would include Richard Dawkins's *The Ancestor's Tale* (2004) and Richard O. Prum's *The Evolution of Beauty* (2018)), which both reflect and encourage a new appreciation of literary studies today. It is a curious irony that, at a time when various forces (organized and random, ideological and teletechnological, economic and instrumentalist, etc.) seem bent on reducing, dismissing and even annihilating a sense of the value of literature, and at a time when increasingly few students appear to be drawn towards reading novels, poems and plays or to thinking about the nature of the literary *per se*, science writing itself seems increasingly sensitive to the ways in which literature can illuminate and guide scientific thinking. The writings of Forbes, Dawkins and Prum engage with literature not only in terms of exploring the powers of storytelling, figurative language and innovative forms, but also in relation to what John Keats called 'Negative Capability': we are immersed in a scene of reading and interpretation, involving 'uncertainties, mysteries, doubts, without any irritable reaching after fact & reason' ('Letter to George and Tom Keats', December 1817, Gittings 1970, 43). One way of understanding this space is in terms of what might be called animal secrecy. In 'How to Avoid Speaking', Jacques Derrida queries the 'somewhat naïve philosophy' according to which 'animals are incapable of keeping or even having a secret'. He points towards 'the possibility of a preverbal or simply nonverbal secret – linked, for example, to gestures or to mimicry, and even to other codes and more generally to the unconscious'. At the same time, he suggests a definition of consciousness itself as 'that place in which is retained the singular power not to say what one knows, to keep a secret in the form of representation'. With Keatsian calmness, Derrida then goes on to observe that, in the realm of the secret, 'nonmanifestation is never assured'. Regarding this daunting, haunting double-negative, he adds: 'According to this hypothesis, it would be necessary to reconsider all the boundaries between consciousness and the unconscious, as between man and animal and an enormous system of oppositions' (Derrida 1989a, 17–18).

My concern here might at least initially look like the reverse operation of the literary engagements that enrich the writings of Forbes, Dawkins and Prum, namely the selection and adaptation of biological concepts and vocabulary for a theory of the novel. It is the sort of reversal, in fact, that Forbes's work prompts us to think about when, for example, he refers to mimicry as 'a fantastical tale of visual punning in nature' (Forbes 2009, 4). For it seems to me that a novel can in turn be described as 'a fantastical tale of visual punning', where the visual would have to do not only with what is recounted or represented (places, characters, events, experiences), but also with the words and blanks on the page (the play of the letter, spacing, formal disposition and division of text, homonymy, anaphora, echo and refrain, strange resemblances, repetitions and doublings of all sorts, both 'within' the text and in the intertextual world beguilingly 'outside' it). To construe a novel as a bizarre but deeply complex 'tale of visual punning' cannot be restricted to language and form, but goes with an unbounded deconstruction of anthropocentrism, with acknowledging and elaborating the ways in which mimicry is not limited to 'man' (or 'woman').

Dazzled and Deceived is mostly concerned with the visual, though it includes a fascinating chapter on smell, especially in relation to the work of Maria Rothschild. As

Forbes notes: '[Rothschild] recognized the neglected fact that mimicry does not begin with one species copying another. It begins with an insect evolving the ability to harvest and store toxic chemicals from its food plant' (2009, 198). But Forbes gives little attention to questions of mimicry and sound: butterflies and moths, like mimic octopuses (about which he also writes eloquently: see 236–9), are quiet creatures, at least to the human ear. I would like to suppose that we can all to some degree identify with Timothy Morton's image of people as 'shy, retiring octopuses that squirt out a dissembling ink as they withdraw into the ontological shadows' (Morton 2013, 3–4), but sound, song and music, voice, tone and timbre are just as vital as the visual. The novel, as a work of protective mimicry, is about the ear as much as the eye. Permit me here to pop in an example from the cuckoo. As Jenny York and Nicholas Davies have recently documented, a cuckoo, just in the wake of laying her egg in the host's nest, can mimic the sound of a hawk in order to divert the host's attention at the crucial moment. As their article in *Nature* summarily puts it: 'Female cuckoo calls misdirect host defences towards the wrong enemy' (York and Davies 2017, 1520). We might here recall Derrida's exposition of Aristotle in 'White Mythology': '[n]o internal characteristic distinguishes the atom of animal sound and the letter. Thus, it is only on the basis of the signifying phonic composition, on the basis of meaning and reference, that the human voice should be distinguished from the call of an animal' (1982, 236–7). For Aristotle, as Derrida describes it: '*Mimēsis* is proper to man. Only man imitates properly. Man alone takes pleasure in imitating, man alone learns by imitation' (237).

Go tell the cuckoo. Elsewhere I have tried to develop some of this thinking in terms of *ornithophony*.[1] An example of ornithophony would be Wallace Stevens's great late poem 'Of Mere Being', in which 'A gold-feathered bird / Sings in the palm, without human meaning, / Without human feeling, a foreign song' (Stevens 1997b, 476–7).[2] Another example would be Yeats's great late poem 'Cuchulain Comforted', in which certain shrouds gather around a mortally wounded man: 'They sang, but had nor human tunes nor words, / Though all was done in common as before; / They had changed their throats and had the throats of birds' (1950, 395–6). Stevens and Yeats suggest that poetry, finally, is ornithophonic. Ornithophony is also, I suggest, integral to an understanding of poetic thinking in the novel.

We imitate, we copy, we mimic far more, far more deeply and extensively than we care to admit, perhaps especially to ourselves. William Wordsworth's great Ode, 'Intimations of Immortality from Recollections of Early Childhood' (1984, 297–302), is best known for its affirmation of the wonderfully dreamlike, timeless world of being a young child, but it also speaks of the spooky and invasive power of mimicry and imitation:

Then will he fit his tongue
To dialogues of business, love, or strife;
But it will not be long

---

[1] For a detailed exposition of ornithophony see 'Four Words for Cixous' in my book *Hélène Cixous: Dreamer, Realist, Analyst, Writing* (Royle 2020).
[2] For an excellent reading of this and related poetry, see Wolfe (2018, 317–38).

> Ere this be thrown aside,
> And with new joy and pride
> The little Actor cons another part;
> Filling from time to time his 'humorous stage'
> With all the Persons, down to palsied Age,
> That Life brings with her in her equipage;
> As if his whole vocation
> Were endless imitation.
>
> stanza 7, 97–107

We fit our tongues, as Wordsworth puts it, in accord with the tongues of others, our so-called role models (mother, father, siblings, friends and loved ones, teachers and fellow pupils, managers and fellow workers, celebrities and other public figures, scripts and shows, gestures and rhythms, tonal and musical snatches of all sorts). Each one of us *cons*, gets to know, studies and learns, commits to memory a part, a script for 'dialogues of business, love or strife', one role after another. Wordsworth cons *his* 'con' perhaps first from Shakespeare, whose seven ages of man in *As You Like It* are rehearsed a little in the Ode.

With advancing knowledge of the function and effects of mirror neurons (the apparent basis on which we are able to empathize and mimic) go the insidious effects of *tele-entrapment*.[3] Who would be without a screen? Monetarization has led to – if not in decisive respects disappeared into – monitorization. You can scarcely hear the difference. Surveillance capitalism monitors but it also has us monitoring. We monitor screens, we screen, we monitor we. Our becoming monitorized beings figures as a crucial corollary crisis alongside climate change and climate breakdown. It is in this context that Lydia Liu has foregrounded the 'uncanny valley' as 'a two-way street', the human becoming robotic as much as vice versa (2019). Wordsworth's poem suggests that each of us goes through life as if our 'whole vocation' – our entire calling, and indeed our very voices and other movements of the body to which this voice never simply belongs – 'were endless imitation'; but tele-entrapment and monitorization inscribe themselves within, in the very experience of so-called interiority. In failing to hear what is monitory in this monitoring we risk giving ourselves over to a sort of totalitarian transparental control and relinquishing a sense of the secret.

There is no limitation to imitation, to having one's words haunted by another or others. Wordsworth's lines stagily stage this with the quotation marks he inserts around the words 'humorous stage',[4] a phrase adopted or adapted from Samuel Daniel's

---

[3] For more on tele-entrapment, permit me to refer to *An English Guide to Birdwatching* (Royle 2017, 206 and *passim*).

[4] The quotation is from Samuel Daniel's dedicatory lines to his *Musophilus* (1599): 'I do not here upon this hum'rous Stage, /Bring my transformed Verse, apparelled / With others passions, or with others rage'. Daniel's 'apparelled' in turn echoes back across Wordsworth's poem, to sound retroactively in its opening gambit: 'There was a time when meadow, grove, and stream, / The earth and every common sight, / To me did seem / Apparelled in celestial light, / The glory and the freshness of a dream' (stanza 1, 1–4). It is as if the humorous stage is set from the very start. Firat Karadas, on the other hand, finds additionally in 'humorous stage' an echo of Macbeth's 'Life's but a walking shadow, a poor player / That struts and frets his hour upon the stage, / And then is heard no more' (5.5.24–6). See Karadas (2008, 77n).

Musophilus (1599). We copy, we con. There is an 'order of mimesis', as Christopher Prendergast playfully invokes it in his richly interesting book of that title (1986). Thou shalt mimic. Imitations 'R' Us. More than any of us can acknowledge (and this is one reason why Freud remains such an enlightening thinker in this context), more than we can ever be conscious of, we con a part, we con parts. We con a part and like to suppose this conning is apart from others. But there is something secret to us, of us, in this conning. And at the same time this 'vocation', as Wordsworth calls it, this call or calling is not just about the experience of childhood or growing up, but a matter of every instant, the present in all its strangeness, desire and desperation, expectation and precarity.[5]

A novel, to be a novel, has to mimic. It has to resemble, it has to be identifiable, that is, recognizable as a novel. Derek Attridge remarks: 'Mimesis [becomes literary] when it involves the performance of mimetivity' (2004, 96). 'Mimetivity' is a neologism. It has a gentle suggestion of 'activity' in its tail. Attridge is talking about the way in which literary mimesis involves a sort of acting out, a performing of itself. This corresponds to the workings of literary fiction, as he puts it: 'Literary fiction involves the *performance* of fictionality, occurring as the experience of an event or a series of events whereby the characters and occurrences apparently being referred to are in fact, and without this fact being disguised, brought into being by the language' (2004, 96; emphasis in the original). This description recalls Roland Barthes's notion of readerly disavowal: the reader thinks, as he or she is reading, '*I know these are only words, but all the same …*' (1990, 47). This logic of disavowal might be likened to the experience of keeping a secret from oneself: it is the logic of 'I know this is not true but I am going to carry on behaving as if it is'. All of this is neither here nor there if we're talking about something like consumer fiction, or reading a novel as a way of 'passing the time', as the saying goes; but it involves quite different stakes when we are engaged in thinking about the very nature of literary mimesis as it informs the act of reading, in other words, when we are thinking about the nature of literarity and about how a text (novel or poem) is doing things with words in ways that we can never fully master or control. Here disavowal would be more akin to a sense of some internal other self that needed to be fooled, like the host in the cuckoo's nest. Except that this internal other might just as well be called a community, for it entails a response to more than one voice, indeed to the vocation of a commonality at once already urgent and to come, of voices and cries, human and non-human, alive, dead and not yet born.

Literary mimesis or mimetivity relates to what Derrida calls the secret of literature. In *Given Time* he writes, apropos Baudelaire's prose-poem 'Counterfeit Money', about the 'secret whose possibility assures the possibility of literature', 'the secret kept both as *thing* or as *being*, as *thing thought*, and as *technique*' (1992a, 153; emphasis in the original). He is talking about narrators and characters: 'these fictional characters have no consistency, no depth beyond their literary phenomenon, the absolute inviolability

---

[5] In this context we might consider the figure of the 'English eccentric' and 'eccentric behaviour'. Social media and the internet in general are extraordinary mechanisms of assimilation: imitation, unconscious mimicry, conformity is the law. Like a little-noticed species of butterfly or bird, the 'eccentric' has disappeared. The word no longer features in the contemporary narrative of the contemporary. Eccentricity is extinct.

of the secret they carry depends first of all on the essential superficiality of their phenomenality, on the *too-obvious* of that which they present to view' (ibid.). There is something secret and inviolable, inviolable because entirely superficial or bare: 'This inviolability depends on nothing other than the altogether bare device of being-two-to-speak' ('*Cette inviolabilité ne tient à aucun autre dispositive que ce lui, tout nu, de l'être-deux-à-parler*') (Derrida 1992a, 153; 1991, 194).

I construe this secrecy in terms of the telepathic: there is a being-two-to-speak but also a being-two-to-feel, a being-two-to-think, and so on.[6] Others speak of '*erlebte Rede*' or 'free indirect discourse'. Related further options include 'interior monologue', 'substitutionary narration', 'dual voice' and 'double voicing'. There is something erotic about telepathy that entwines it with the feeling of secrecy, as well as with threat and terror. It makes a quite different call on us than 'free indirect discourse'. Telepathy has resonances and resources that enable a more expansive and productive engagement with the literary work in terms of an uncertainty about where one voice, or source or identity begins and ends, of what is human and what is not human. Telepathy is originally contemporaneous with numerous other tele-phenomena: the word was invented in 1882. But its potential for thinking about the novel seems to me in many ways still to be elaborated. This is not about some sort of mysticism or witchcraft, but rather about the experience of secrecy and strangeness in the world of a literary work. It is about what communicates (in the) distance, at a distance, and is concerned with feeling – feeling as it is shared between a reader and a text, one text and another text, but also as it is shared, for example, with birdsong, or with things. It is about the often eerie and surprising correspondences between texts and what they communicate about themselves and the environment beyond. It is about the prosopopoeia by which the dead and the living speak to one another and to us in a work of fiction, but also about the activation of the perhaps only ever distant or dimly readable feelings of non-human animals. In the unbounded sense I am adumbrating here, telepathy would be a figure for exploring the novel in terms of what Timothy Clark sees as the Anthropocene's 'bizarre kinds of action at a distance, the collapse of safe distinctions between the trivial and the disastrous, and the proliferation of forces that cannot be directly perceived' (2019, 99).

At the outset of his immense book *Mimesis*, first published in English in 1953 bearing the seemingly innocent sub-title *The Representation of Reality in Western Literature*, Erich Auerbach offers his celebrated 'opposition' of Homer (Odysseus's homecoming in Book 19) and the Bible (the sacrifice of Isaac in the Book of Genesis), as a means of highlighting 'the two kinds of style', the two 'basic types' of 'the literary representation of reality in European literature':

> On the one hand fully externalized description, uniform illumination, uninterrupted connection, free expression, all events in the foreground, displaying unmistakable meanings, few elements of historical development and of psychological perspective; on the other hand, certain parts brought into high relief, others left obscure,

---

[6] See, in particular, Royle (2003, 256–76).

abruptness, suggestive influence of the unexpressed, 'background' quality, multiplicity of meanings and the need for interpretation, universal-historical claims, development of the concept of the historically becoming, and preoccupation with the problematic.

Auerbach 1953, 23

Since *Mimesis* was published, a great deal of attention (in both narrative theory and practice) has been given to the non-Homeric 'style' or 'type', in particular to what might, too hastily, be designated as 'internal' or 'internalized' description. At the time Auerbach was writing, the 'secret whose possibility assures the possibility of literature', as Derrida describes it (1992a, 153), seems hardly to have been noticed. Auerbach refers at one point to what 'German criticism has recently come to call *erlebte Rede* (free indirect discourse)' (1953, 213) and thereafter uses the term on just three occasions (472, 485, 535). Unlike the tacitly humanistic, individualizing notion of 'free indirect discourse' – which narrative theorists such as Moshe Ron (1981, 17–39) and Shlomith Rimmon-Kenan (2002, 111–17) abbreviate to 'FID', as if embarrassed and wishing to conceal (but thereby merely further highlighting) its very awkwardness – and which, I would argue, is never simply 'free' or 'indirect' or 'discourse', telepathy exceeds, moves off, keeps sharing and joining up elsewhere. It is not limited to an anthropocentric domain of one human individual and another, or even to what is living or dead. It reads, it spreads distance with feeling. It is inseparable from a theory and practice of irony and the art of veering. And it is inseparable from the nature of protective mimicry and what is – to recall my favourite definition of literature in Derrida – 'cadaverised like the beast playing dead and melding with the foliage' (Derrida 1993a, 306). As he says elsewhere, one can read a so-called literary text

> as a testimony that is said to be serious and authentic, or as an archive, or as a document, or as a symptom – or as a work of literary fiction, indeed the work of a literary fiction that simulates all of [these] positions ... For literature can say anything, accept anything, receive anything, suffer anything, and simulate everything: it can even feign a trap, the way modern armies know how to set false traps; these traps pass themselves off as real traps and trick the machines designed to detect simulations under even the most sophisticated camouflage.
>
> Derrida 2000, 29

Nature loves to hide, says Heraclitus. To repurpose this in the manner of a hermit crab, I would say that the novel loves to hide. The novel today has to mime, imitate and dissimulate, and at the same time it has to meddle with the language and objects of simulation. It has to set itself against any conception of the novel as, in Maurice Blanchot's phrase, 'a system in which the imaginary leads to a *trompe-l'œil*': the novel, in other words, must not lead to some merely deceptive, if aesthetically seductive unity or effect (2001, 248).[7] And as it engages with an affirmation of singularity, life, promise and

---

[7] Blanchot makes this remark in the course of praising novels that don't '[lead] to a *trompe-l'œil*'. In particular, he focuses on the writings of Virginia Woolf, especially *The Waves*.

hope, while constantly playing with death, including the death drive – '[every] organism wishes to die only in its own fashion', as Freud says in 'Beyond the Pleasure Principle' – every novel invites us to read and think about it as a work of protective mimicry (Freud 2001, 39). The novel works with mimicry of all sorts – first and foremost, no doubt, in the dimensions of the visual and auditory. And in order to be singular, it will also seek to protect itself from being read *either* as 'only' a novel, as 'mere' novel, *or* as just 'another novel', like any other novel. Protective mimicry, therefore, as dissimulation of mimicry, including dissimulation of dissimulation. Protective mimicry is thus linked to what I call cryptaesthetic resistance: novels that endure, novels deemed 'valuable', 'powerful' and 'important', are works that demand but distract our attention.[8] They seduce but elude. They anticipate. They see readers coming, they resist being read even as they open themselves to all the adventures of mind-reading. The capacity of the work to immunize itself against being simply received, assimilated, appropriated is intimately linked to the idea of the secret as what does not belong, to the secret as bound up with the signature and idiom, to what is (as Derrida puts it in 'Biodegradables') 'capable of inducing meaning without being exhausted by meaning', to something that is 'incomprehensibly elliptical' and 'secret' (Derrida 1989b, 845).[9]

This is not an argument on behalf of some authorial sovereignty or self-expression or even about the experience of being human. Rather it has to do with what Hélène Cixous calls 'the secret which escapes' (McQuillan 2002, 185–201), or what Derrida refers to as 'a secret of "me" for "me"' (1995a, 134). It is a question of guarding or keeping, but not of something that is one's own, within one's possession or knowledge or control. 'The keeping is always confided to the other; one cannot keep oneself' (Derrida 1995a, 149). I am playing with English here, or English is playing with me – the language that I love but that can never be mine, since no one owns language. Derrida says 'there is a secret of "me" for "me"' [*Il y a le secret de 'moi' pour 'moi'*] (1995a, 149; 1992c, 143). There is, if you will, a 'me'-cyst, a secret cyst, a hollow or cistern or crypt of 'me' in 'me', for 'me'. No novel mimesis without my-'me'-cyst. The novel holds back, keeps in reserve, it *hides* – but not as an act of wilful or conscious mastery on the part of the writer. Which is not to imply that the writer has no responsibility or should not be guided by 'silence, exile and cunning'. But what insists as it resists, what *cysts/sists* (I leave the vocable to be heard, not knowing how to spell it), is perhaps first of all about a disappearing, dissolution, letting be other. It might be tempting to think of the novelist in this context as a kind of chameleon or an on-the-ground, humble, dwarfish lion (to recall the etymological make-up of the word). As Keats says of the 'camelion Poet': 'the poetical Character … is not itself – it has no self – it is everything and nothing … [the poet] has no Identity – he is continually … filling some other Body' ('Letter to Richard Woodhouse', 27 October 1818, Gittings 1970, 157). Or in a non-lacertian register, we might think of the figure of the Marrano, as Derrida describes it

---

[8] For more on cryptaesthetic resistance, permit me to refer to 'Cryptaesthesia: The Case of *Wuthering Heights*', in Royle (1991, 62); and 'Reading Joseph Conrad: Episodes from the Coast', in Royle (2014, 48–50).

[9] Cf. Derrida's discussion of 'this remainder which remains when the thematics is exhausted', in Derrida (1992b, 61).

in *Aporias* – the novelist as Marrano who is 'faithful to a secret that [s/he] has not chosen', someone '[whose] secret keeps the Marrano even before the Marrano keeps it' (Derrida 1993b, 81).[10]

'I didn't expect a kind of Spanish Inquisition ... Nobody expects the Spanish Inquisition.' You may recall the Monty Python sketch, featuring Cardinal Ximinez, Cardinal Biggles and Cardinal Fang. Michael Palin (as Ximinez) explains that the Spanish Inquisition has three, no, four, no, five chief weapons: 'fear' and 'surprise' and 'ruthless efficiency' and 'an almost fanatical devotion to the Pope' and 'nice red uniforms'.[11] In homage to the Flying Circus, I would like to propose a literary inquisition, a sustained and intensive questioning of the novel today, which is to say of both novel-reading and novel-writing. I would like to suggest, not weapons, but five chief concerns for this inquisition:

(1) Language: it is a matter of trying to reckon with how much language uses us as we use it, how much we are caught up in mimicry at every moment, with every word or phrase that comes out of our mouths or hands, how we find ourselves inscribed, installed and stalled in stories we haven't written, in structures in which we do not believe; and then, at the same time, it is a matter of the unforeseeable, of how language can transform what we think, feel and believe, and can lead us to act on that transformation, thanks not least to the possibilities of *as if*, to the magical dimensions of the performative, of 'doing things with words' (J. L. Austin) or what Saint Augustine called 'making the truth';[12]

(2) Dreams: the role and effects of unconscious energies, the dislocation of the supposed masterfulness of the ego, an exploration of what Cixous evokes as 'the Mother unconscious' (1993, 102), immersion in deep text, submarine or subterranean writing, accompanied by the analysis – and more literally perhaps, the undoing – of the privilege accorded to the sovereignty of the ego, the vigilance of consciousness and the presumed values of an identification between rationality and wakefulness, in accounts of reading and writing.

(3) Sex and sexual difference: a pressuring and even dissolution of the boundaries or limits of erotic pleasure (especially in the realm of reading and writing), together with a questioning and unsettling of assumptions of sexual identity, above all of thinking of sexual difference as binary, or as reducible to the logic of *homo-* and *hetero-*; thus, an affirmation of sexuality as innumerable.[13]

---

[10] It is a notable irony that when I delivered an earlier version of this essay as a lecture at the University of Granada in October 2018, some members of the audience wondered what I – or what Derrida – was referring to, since in contemporary Spanish 'marrano' primarily is a term of abuse and means 'pig'.
[11] See *Monty Python's Flying Circus: Just the Words*, written and conceived by Graham Chapman, John Cleese, Terry Gilliam, Eric Idle, Terry Jones and Michael Palin (1990, 192–3).
[12] See Saint Augustine's *Confessions*, in particular the opening of Book X (1991, 179 ff.). Jacques Derrida explores this Augustinian figure (*facere veritatem*) in numerous contexts. In *Given Time*, for example, he observes: 'One can "make the truth" ["*faire la vérité*"] [the expression is Saint Augustine's] only to the extent that the possibility remains forever open of "counterfeiting" it [*la "contrefaire"*]' (Derrida 1992a, 152, n25). Cf. Derrida (1992a, 168).
[13] Cf. Derrida's remarks in 'voice ii' (1995b, 163–4). Here we might think also of his deconstructive meditation on sovereignty and his critical characterization, in *The Beast and the Sovereign*, of Defoe's *Robinson Crusoe* as a space almost entirely of 'men without women and without sex' – 'as though', Derrida suggests, 'there were some secret contract between sovereign euphoria, paradisiacal euphoria, and the absence of women' (Derrida 2011, 54).

(4) The so-called 'animal question': the relationships between human and non-human animals, the responsibilities of the novelist as an animal in the world, the idea that (in Geoffrey Bennington's words) 'there is nothing specifically "human" ... about meaning' (Bennington 1994, 32), the challenge to think, read and write in ways that don't assume a set of anthropocentric spectacles, gloves or listening devices. In an echoing from Auerbach's *Mimesis* we might undertake a new reading, a transposition and transformation of a term that emerges in a particularly beautiful passage of his book, focusing on a text by Antoine de la Sale (*Le Réconfort de Madame du Fresne*) from 1459 about 'a married couple, talking over their troubles at night in bed'. Here Auerbach invokes the notion of 'creatural realism' (Auerbach 1953, 246–50). The English translator, Willard Trask, notes that the original German term *Kreatürliches* is 'a neologism of the 1920s': 'creatural' emphasizes what Auerbach describes as 'man's subjection to suffering and transitoriness' (Auerbach 1953, 246 n1 and 249). I would like to propose a '*creatural mimesis*', in order to refer to ways of writing and reading, seeing and listening, thinking and doing that reckon with a mimetology not confined to the human, and reckon as well with the suffering and transitoriness of other animals. In the wake of writers such as Kafka, Beckett, Kristof, Lispector, Cixous and Coetzee, I see more signs than ever of such a 'creatural mimesis' in contemporary writing.

(5) Justice: the responsibilities of the novel in relation to the world, of the novelist as a 'citizen of the world', whether apparently local or worldwide, the commitments of the novel to seek to engage with issues of family and society, individual and social justice, human rights, capitalism, marketization and climate crisis, even and especially insofar as this responsibility or commitment has to do with what Gilles Deleuze calls 'writing for a people who are missing' (1998, 4). At the same time these responsibilities do not require that the writer pretend or aspire to be some 'community representative'. The novelist is nobody (as Emily Dickinson might say); s/he questions every kind of belonging, and is apart from rather than a part of. This has to do with the logic of what Derrida calls 'don't count me in': this, he says, 'is the condition not only for being singular and other, but also for entering into relation with the singularity and alterity of others' (Derrida 2001, 27).

The novel has to mimic, it has to resemble, but it also has to tremble. And make tremble. Like a butterfly. The novel is like a butterfly, perhaps, along the path that Jacques Lacan solicits us to imagine, when he talks about mimicry in the context of the eye and the gaze in *The Four Fundamental Concepts of Psychoanalysis*, and recounts the dream of Choang-tsu who dreams he is a butterfly. The novel is like the dream to which Lacan alludes, 'a butterfly for nobody' (Lacan 1977, 76).

In his great essay on mimicry, mime and Mallarmé, 'The Double Session', Derrida proposes that 'there is no essence of literature, no truth of literature, no literary-being or being-literary of literature' (1981, 223). Rather there is what Timothy Clark has wittily called 'being in mime' (1986, 1003–21). '*There is* mimicry [*Il y a* une mimique]', Derrida affirms in 'The Double Session'; and 'Mallarmé sets great store by it' (1981, 206; 1972, 234). Thus in Mallarmé, he argues, we encounter 'the differential structure of mimicry or *mimēsis*' but 'no longer any model [or] copy' behind or preceding it. Instead 'we are faced ... with mimicry imitating nothing ... with a double that doubles no simple, a double that nothing anticipates, nothing at least that is not itself already double' (Derrida 1981, 206). There are correspondences here with Derrida's account of the 'hyperrealism' he associates with the writings of Cixous. In Cixous, he suggests, 'we find a vertiginous kind of truth', namely 'the risk ... of an undecidable fakery' (Derrida 2006, 69). As I have been trying to suggest, protective mimicry entails a kind of double writing, a writing that keeps in reserve even as it displays and plays with its mimetics.

In conclusion, I would like to say a few words about a recent novel by Naomi Booth, entitled *Sealed* (2017). Something like the Westinghouse Electric time capsules buried under Flushing Meadows, New York, which Paul K. Saint-Amour discusses in *Tense Future* (Saint-Amour 2015, 180–2), *Sealed* is a book that rings true, eerily, terribly, without the need for any leaps of faith or quirky demands on credulity: if someone 500 years from now found this narrative buried in the desertified terrain in which it is set, he or she might have no reason to suppose that it is not an autobiographical account. At the same time, it compels us to think about it rather as Derrida suggests we approach *Robinson Crusoe*, that is to say 'not so much [as] an autobiographical fiction as the fiction of an autobiography' (Derrida 2011, 88). This is how *Sealed* begins:

> We came out here to begin again. We came out here for the clear air and a fresh start. No one said to us: beware of fresh starts. No one said to us: god knows what will begin.
>
> Pete found the house online. Mountain View. We'd only seen pictures, but it looked so good – a whole house, the kind you can only dream of in the city, with scrubbed wooden floors, a bright, enamel kitchen, a verandah with views across the valley – that we took the risk, put down the deposit sight unseen. The drive out took longer than we thought and, by the time we arrived, the van was already parked-up in the driveway. The sun was going down, though it was still light enough, just, to see. I sat in the passenger seat for a while as Pete helped the removal men. The front of the house was pretty in an implausible way, like a house in a picture-book or a holiday brochure: a white chalet, edged with dark-leafed, tropical plants. Behind the house I could see the outline of the mountains in the distance, graying in the dusk, and, nearer-by, lights glimmering in the valley bottom. We never had asked why the house was suddenly vacant or why the rent was so cheap. It's best not to pry, Pete says, it's best not to worry. It'll be nothing, he says: a redundancy, a divorce, a clean, old-fashioned death.
>
> By the time I get out of the car the blokes have already started carrying our boxes into the house. Pete has turned on the lights inside and I dawdle in front of the porch. The plants look weird: it's been a while since I've seen anything this lush. I touch the leaves to check that they're real and they're waxy and cool like synthetic matter, but they tear through when I push with my nail. The blooms are enormous – frilly and faintly obscene. I can hear my mother's voice in my head, naming them for me: gardenia, hibiscus. Angel Ivy. Their fragrance follows me, sweet and morbid on the cooling evening air.

> When I get inside Pete grabs my hand, pulls me into the living-room and points to a large box. 'Here,' he says, 'you can sit on this until we get the chairs out.'
> 'I've been sitting all day,' I say, 'I want to look around.'
> 'Not while all this is going on,' he says, 'I don't want anyone to bump our bump.' He leans down and kisses my swollen stomach.
>
> Booth 2017, 3–4

The narrator is pregnant, as we discover with this final, faintly ominous reference to the 'bump' and, with her boyfriend Pete, has moved out of the city to somewhere (we can gradually infer) in the Blue Mountain region of Australia. Already within these half a dozen short paragraphs we confront a curiously unnerving *re-marking* of presentation and representation, an unsettling of 'reality-effects'. The tone seems matter-of-fact, confiding, direct. It is difficult not to empathize with a pregnant woman telling her story. At the same time, little details, twists of phrase and turns of syntax throw shadows over any clear distinction between the real and the virtual, the implausible or the fictional: 'Pete found the house online'; they'd 'only seen pictures'; it's 'the kind you can only dream of'; it 'was pretty in an implausible way, like a house in a picture-book or a holiday brochure'; the narrator has to 'touch the leaves to check they're real' and damages them with her nail in the process. The passage offers striking instances of how explicit references to the virtual, to pictorial or visual representation, to the implausible or the unreal, can intensify a sense of what is real, rather than undercut or efface it.

This is how the novel begins, I suggested, but already there is more going on than meets the eye ('sight unseen', to echo the strange sort of estate-agent idiom that crops up in the second paragraph). Before this beginning there is the title, as well as a dedication (to two women, identified only by their forenames), and an epigraph from the Book of Job: 'Thy hands fashioned and made me; and now thou dost turn about and destroy me … Didst thou not pour me out like milk and curdle me like cheese? …' (Job 10: 8–11). The novel is sealed: the title promises (or threatens) that something is already sealed. God is destroying Job in a bizarre present tense that the discourse of the novel appears to mimic from this beginning which is, of course – like any other 'begin[ning] again' – no beginning.

Roger Caillois, whose work on mimicry inspired Lacan (among others), writes apropos 'the detective novel as game' that 'the story opens on a rigged set' (1983, 4). Every novel can be construed as detective fiction in this regard. But the visual image of stage and set tends to deflect attention from the auditory. Booth's *Sealed* is also an extraordinary work of listening. As Jean-Luc Nancy has observed, 'listening strains toward a present sense beyond sound' (2007, 6). It has to do with a present that comes 'in waves on a swell, not in a point on a line; it is a time that opens up, that is hollowed out, that is enlarged or ramified, that envelops or separates, that becomes or is turned into a loop, that stretches out or contracts, and so on' (13). We might think of the novel as a strange acoustic territory or (to play a little, in a perfectly serious way, on the author's name) audiobooth. We could spend a long time immersed in the sound-waves and resonances and effects of this audiobooth, the more-than-one-voice that pervades – here for instance, in this opening passage, not only in the literal inscription of the 'we', but also in the consistent deployment of common idioms or colloquialisms with a hint of irony, the embedding of the voice of Pete and the voice of the narrator's mother, together with the implicit sense (confirmed later by the narrator's identification as Alice) that the 'I' of the text is not the same as the author.

Anaphora generates unease: 'we came out here ... we came out here ... no one said ... no one said....' Any sense of 'fresh start' is already hollowed out. What is 'said' is an evacuation and spectralization of speech: it is what *no one said*. What no one said ('beware of fresh starts' and 'god knows what will begin') resonates as piercingly as the voice of the narratorial 'we' ('We came out here to begin again ...'). The text will go on to repeat this phrase 'fresh start' several times, emptying out its sense, leaving the reader sensing that the phrase was from the beginning a cliché, mere mimicry, no fresh start of any sort. And the lower-case 'g' for 'god' ('god knows what will begin') silently undoes any Biblical propriety (if Job ever offered any reassurance in that respect). There is no God in *Sealed*. The narrator (shifted in the second paragraph from 'we' to 'I') knows how it will go on. There is secret knowledge. In the present tense in which this narrative duplicitously unfolds, the end is already known. There are, as always in a novel, elements of narrative clairvoyance and narrative clairaudience. But there is also a secrecy in what is not known, in what is promised or threatened, in the to-come of reading, in the mysterious feelings and communications (some human, others not) that interweave and seal up this claustrophobic narrative and its edgy, uncertain inhabitants.

As Derrida says of the language of the crypt in the work of Nicolas Abraham and Maria Torok: 'A certain foreign body is here working over our household words' (1986, xxv). If we cannot already get scents of it in this opening passage of Booth's novel, we are invited to think about it just a page later when the narrator says: 'Pete says it's like repeating the same word over and over to try to learn it, until the word becomes just sound: and then the sound becomes a kind of hex, a weird noise that conjures something darkly different' (Booth 2017, 5). There's nothing supernatural or mystical about this hexical-lexical aspect of Booth's novel, any more than there is about the notions of telepathy, performative magic, narratorial clairvoyance or clairaudience as I've tried to sketch them in this essay.

'Our skin is a hex on us now' (Booth 2017, 17), the narrator announces. The end is beginning. *Sealed* has been classified as a pre-apocalyptic horror novel. It might just as readily (and just as reductively) be categorized as cli-fi, or speculative fiction, or a dystopian novel, or a novel about being buried alive, or a novel about giving birth and becoming a mother. It adopts and inhabits, it mimics and proliferates genres, tones, idioms, assuming them like so many layers or skins. *Sealed* takes up the idea of what Derrida neologistically calls auto-immunity, incorporating and exfoliating it with the sealing of its signature. *Sealed* gives uncannily literal form to the notion of a body (that of a person but also a community) destroying itself through the act of seeking to protect itself. Booth calls it *cutis*. As one scientific expert, an unnamed professor in tropical medicine, is observed to observe, cutis is 'similar in mechanism to an auto-immune disease: a potentially deadly, mis-directed defence response'. The skin begins 'acting in aberrant ways, knitting together in disastrous patterns'. The skin seems to be 'attempting to protect the body from dangerous environmental pollutants, sealing the body off in the process' (Booth 2017, 36). The full name of the disease is later given as '*Cutis Sigillatis*, or the "skin-sealing syndrome"' (47).

Cutis is the cut of Booth's signature as well as the name for the protective mimicry of this skin-apocalypse. And it is not just about humans. As if enacting or re-enacting the logic of Australian immunologist Peter Doherty's *Their Fate is Our Fate: How Birds Foretell Threats to Our Health and Our World* (2012), the narrator's first deadly encounter with cutis is with a small bird fluttering, flurrying madly in the yard. Booth's text here adds a further layer to the sense of 'sealed': along with 'closed up' and 'signed' (and related motifs of pregnancy, live burial and signature), there is the homophone 'seeled' that refers to the stitching up of the eyelids of a hawk or other bird. The narrator describes the little creature:

> There's skin covering the eyes, making the dark grey, giving them the consistency of scuffed suede. The bird makes one more turn towards me, and then it's so close that I get a really good look and then I'm sure of it: the bird can't open its eyes. The eyelid skin makes a dome, fused over the place where the bright little eyes should be. It makes me think of baby birds, the thin, orange skin that covers the glowing blue bulbs of their eyes if they hatch prematurely. This bird's skin is thick and over-developed. Its eyes look reptilian: dry and powdery. And there's no sign of anything below the skin, no latent flinch towards opening. The bird's eyes have been completely sealed over.
>
> Booth 2017, 28

A true understatement: Booth's novel gets *under the skin*. It is *apparently* a novel, an *apparent* novel. It looks for all the world like one. And at the same time it is unlike any other. *Sealed* is (to borrow Derrida's arresting formulation in *The Beast and the Sovereign*) 'living dead, buried alive and swallowed up alive': it lives the 'finitude' of 'its beautiful death' (2011, 130). This finitude is of what he calls *survivance* – a survivance whose *sur-* is 'without superiority, without height, altitude or highness, and thus without supremacy or sovereignty' (131). Even as it explores the 'infinite anxiety' around the panic of what Derrida horrifyingly evokes as 'a baby who would be born without coming into the world' (2011, 265–66), Naomi Booth's book awaits the resuscitation of 'a breath of living reading' (131). In its miming of a ruinous, apocalyptic protectiveness (ironically in accord with all the 'protected' brands of food and drink that recurrently feature in the narrative), *Sealed* is a terrifying, dazzling and also, finally, strangely affirmative, messianic text about what Derrida calls 'literature's secret, the infinite power to keep undecidable and thus forever sealed the secret of what it says' (2006, 18). I leave you to read.

References

Attridge, Derek. (2004), *The Singularity of Literature*, London: Routledge.
Auerbach, Erich. (1953) (1946), *Mimesis: The Representation of Reality in Western Literature*, translated by Willard R. Trask, Princeton: Princeton University Press.

Barthes, Roland. (1990), *The Pleasure of the Text*, translated by Richard Miller, Oxford: Blackwell.
Bennington, Geoffrey. (1994), *Legislations: The Politics of Deconstruction*, London: Verso.
Blanchot, Maurice. (2001), 'Time and the Novel', in Charlotte Mandell (trans), *Faux Pas*, 248–51, Stanford: Stanford University Press.
Booth, Naomi. (2017), *Sealed*, Liverpool: Dead Ink Books. (The author would like to express his warm gratitude to Naomi Booth for permission to quote at length here.)
Caillois, Roger. (1983) (1941), 'The Detective Novel as Game', in Glenn W. Most and William W. Stowe (eds), William W. Stowe (trans), *The Poetics of Murder: Detective Fiction and Literary Theory*, 1–12, New York: Harcourt Brace Jovanovich.
Chapman, Graham, John Cleese, Terry Gilliam, Eric Idle, Terry Jones and Michael Palin. (1990), *Monty Python's Flying Circus: Just the Words*, Vol. 1, London: Methuen.
Cixous, Hélène. (1993), *Three Steps on the Ladder of Writing*, Sarah Cornell and Susan Sellers (trans), New York: Columbia University Press.
Clark, Timothy. (1986), 'Being in Mime: Heidegger and Derrida on the Ontology of Literary Language', *Modern Language Notes*, 101: 1003–21.
Clark, Timothy. (2019), *The Value of Ecocriticism*, Cambridge: Cambridge University Press.
Dawkins, Richard. (2004), *The Ancestor's Tale: A Pilgrimage to the Dawn of Life*, London: Weidenfeld and Nicolson.
Deleuze, Gilles. (1998), 'Literature and Life', in Daniel W. Smith and Michael A. Greco (trans), *Essays Critical and Clinical*, 1–6, London: Verso.
Derrida, Jacques. (1972), *La dissemination*, Paris: Éditions du Seuil.
Derrida, Jacques. (1981), 'The Double Session', in Barbara Johnson (trans), *Dissemination*, 173–285, Chicago: Chicago University Press.
Derrida, Jacques. (1982), 'White Mythology: Metaphor in the Text of Philosophy', in Alan Bass (trans), *Margins of Philosophy*, 207–72, Chicago: Chicago University Press.
Derrida, Jacques. (1986), 'Fors: The Anglish Words of Nicolas Abraham and Maria Torok', in Nicolas Abraham and Maria Torok, Barbara Johnson (trans), *The Wolf Man's Magic Word: A Cryptonymy*, xi–xlviii, Minneapolis: University of Minnesota Press.
Derrida, Jacques. (1989a), 'How to Avoid Speaking: Denials', in Stanford Budick and Wolfgang Iser (eds), Ken Frieden (trans), *Languages of the Unsayable: The Play of Negativity in Literature and Literary Theory*, 3–70, New York: Columbia University Press.
Derrida, Jacques. (1989b), 'Biodegradables Seven Diary Fragments', translated by Peggy Kamuf, *Critical Inquiry*, 15 (4): 812–73.
Derrida, Jacques. (1991), *Donner le temps*, Paris: Galilée.
Derrida, Jacques. (1992a), *Given Time: I. Counterfeit Money*, translated by Peggy Kamuf, London: Chicago University Press.
Derrida, Jacques. (1992b), 'This Strange Institution Called Literature: An Interview with Jacques Derrida', in Derek Attridge (ed.), Geoffrey Bennington and Rachel Bowlby (trans), *Acts of Literature*, 33–75, London and New York: Routledge.
Derrida, Jacques. (1992c), 'Dialangues', in Elisabeth Weber (ed.), *Points de suspension: Entretiens*, 141–65. Paris: Galilée.
Derrida, Jacques. (1993a), 'Circumfession', in Geoffrey Bennington and Jacques Derrida, Geoffrey Bennington (trans), *Jacques Derrida*, Chicago: Chicago University Press.
Derrida, Jacques. (1993b), *Aporias: Dying — awaiting (one another at) the 'limits of truth'*, translated by Thomas Dutoit, Stanford: Stanford University Press.

Derrida, Jacques. (1995a), 'Dialanguages', in Elisabeth Weber (ed.), Peggy Kamuf (trans), *Points . . .: Interviews, 1974–1994*, 132–55, Stanford: Stanford University Press.
Derrida, Jacques. (1995b), 'Voice ii', in Elisabeth Weber (ed.), Verena Conley (trans), *Points. . .: Interviews, 1974–1994*, 167–81, London: Routledge.
Derrida, Jacques. (2000), *Demeure: Fiction and Testimony*, translated by Elizabeth Rottenberg, Stanford: Stanford University Press.
Derrida, Jacques. (2001), '"I Have a Taste for the Secret," Jacques Derrida in Conversation with Maurizio Ferraris and Giorgio Vattimo', in Derrida and Ferraris (eds), Giacomo Donis (trans), *A Taste for the Secret*, 1–92, Cambridge: Polity.
Derrida, Jacques. (2006), *Geneses, Genealogies, Genres and Genius: The Secrets of the Archive*, translated by Beverley Bie Brahic, Edinburgh: Edinburgh University Press.
Derrida, Jacques. (2011), *The Beast and the Sovereign*, Vol. 2, edited by Michel Lisse, Marie-Louise Mallet and Ginette Michaud, translated by Geoffrey Bennington, Chicago: Chicago University Press.
Forbes, Peter. (2009), *Dazzled and Deceived: Mimicry and Camouflage*, New Haven: Yale University Press.
Freud, Sigmund. (2001), 'Beyond the Pleasure Principle', in James Strachey (ed. and trans) in collaboration with Anna Freud, assisted by Alix Strachey and Alan Tyson, *The Standard Edition of the Complete Psychological Works of Sigmund Freud*, Vol. 18: 1–64, London: Vintage.
Gittings, Robert, ed. (1970), *Letters of John Keats: A Selection*, Oxford: Oxford University Press.
Karadas, Firat. (2008), *Imagination, Metaphor and Mythopoeia in Wordsworth, Shelley and Keats*, Oxford and New York: Peter Lang.
Lacan, Jacques. (1977), *The Four Fundamental Concepts of Psycho-Analysis*, translated by Alan Sheridan, London: Hogarth Press.
Liu, Lydia. (2019), 'The Uncanny in the Digital Machine', Lecture at the University of Sussex, 27 February 2019.
McQuillan, Martin. (2002), '"You Race towards that Secret, which Escapes": An Interview with Hélène Cixous', *Oxford Literary Review* 24; in *Reading Cixous Writing* special issue, edited by Martin McQuillan, 185–201.
Morton, Timothy. (2013), *Hyperobjects: Philosophy and Ecology after the End of the World*, Minneapolis: University of Minnesota Press.
Nancy, Jean-Luc. (2007), *Listening*, translated by Charlotte Mandell, New York: Fordham University Press.
Prendergast, Christopher. (1986), *The Order of Mimesis: Balzac, Stendhal, Nerval, Flaubert*, Cambridge: Cambridge University Press.
Prum, Richard O. (2018), *The Evolution of Beauty: How Darwin's Forgotten Theory of Mate Choice Shapes the Animal World*, New York: Anchor Books.
Rimmon-Kenan, Shlomith. (2002), *Narrative Fiction: Contemporary Poetics*, 2nd edition, London: Routledge.
Ron, Moshe. (1981), 'Free Indirect Discourse, Mimetic Language Games and the Subject of Fiction', *Poetics Today*, 2 (2): 17–39.
Royle, Nicholas. (1991), *Telepathy and Literature: Essays on the Reading Mind*, Oxford: Blackwell.
Royle, Nicholas. (2003), 'The "Telepathy Effect": Notes Toward a Reconsideration of Narrative Fiction', in *The Uncanny*, 256–76, Manchester: Manchester University Press.

Royle, Nicholas. (2014), 'Reading Joseph Conrad: Episodes from the Coast', *Mosaic: A Journal for the Interdisciplinary Study of Literature*, 47 (1): 41-67.

Royle, Nicholas. (2017), *An English Guide to Birdwatching*, Brighton: Myriad.

Royle, Nicholas. (2020), *Hélène Cixous: Dreamer, Realist, Analyst, Writing*, Manchester: Manchester University Press.

Saint-Amour, Paul K. (2015), *Tense Future: Modernism, Total War, Encyclopedic Form*, Oxford: Oxford University Press.

Saint Augustine. (1991), *Confessions*, translated by Henry Chadwick, Oxford: Oxford University.

Stevens, Wallace. (1997a), 'Less and Less Human, O Savage Spirit', in *Collected Poetry and Prose*, 288, New York: Library of America.

Stevens, Wallace. (1997b), 'Of Mere Being', in *Collected Poetry and Prose*, 476-7, New York: Library of America.

Wolfe, Cary. (2018), 'Wallace Stevens's Birds, or, Derrida and Ecological Poetics', in Matthias Fritsch, Philippe Lynes and David Wood (eds), *Eco-Deconstruction: Derrida and Environmental Philosophy*, 317-38, New York: Fordham University Press.

Wordsworth, William. (1984), 'Ode: Intimations of Immortality from Recollections of Early Childhood', in Stephen Gill (ed.), *William Wordsworth: A Critical Edition of The Major Works*, 297-302, Oxford: Oxford University Press.

Yeats, William Butler. (1950), *Collected Poems*, London: Macmillan.

York, Jenny E. and Nicholas B. Davies. (2017), 'Female Cuckoo Calls Misdirect Host Defences Towards the Wrong Enemy', *Nature, Ecology and Evolution* 1 (September): 1520-5.

3

'Where all is known and nothing understood': Narrative sequence and textual secrets in Toni Morrison's *Love*

Paula Martín-Salván

Introduction

Reading Toni Morrison's 2003 novel *Love* is a tidal experience. The reader is rocked between the desire for establishing an ordered sequence of events and the accumulation of textual fragments shoring up against a clear timeline. As Frank Kermode established in the seminal essay 'Secrets and Narrative Sequence' (1980), most readers begin at the level of story, trying to identify as they read the chain of events sequentially (and causally) related (83–4). Texts that are worthy of discussion, he claims, tend to contain narrative elements that do not easily accommodate into such a lineal sequence, but rather 'form associations of their own, non-sequential, secret invitations to interpretation rather than appeals to a consensus' (93). Being able to distinguish between those elements that contribute to a sequence and those that deviate may seem to be the primary task to be carried out by *Love*'s readers.

The story narrated in *Love* involves two old women, Heed and Christine, who live in a decayed house in what was once a popular seashore resort for African Americans. As we read on, we discover these women who have spent their lives hating each other were once best friends, a friendship uprooted when Bill Cosey, Christine's grandfather and owner of the aforementioned resort, chooses Heed as his second wife. This constitutes an original act of violence, which turns the house into a Gothic realm of unhomeliness, as the domestic community founded on this act is haunted by its past.

When it comes to establishing a narrative sequence in *Love*, however, the reader encounters a resistance that may be said to originate in a doubly destabilizing narrative method. *Love* shares Morrison's mastery technique of upsetting conventional categories of linearity and voice by combining multiple narrative stances (either by using distinct narrators or through focalization) with a disarranged sequence of events that need to be placed back together in a (hopefully) complete lineal sequence.

Insisting on the seaside imagery, I would claim that the reading process resembles the act of holding a handful of sand in our hands, trying to separate precious shells from beach litter. As we read, we find it increasingly difficult to figure out which fragments from the narrative will fit into the larger sequence, and which are to remain textual 'secrets', which seaside fragments are to be kept as precious and which ones can be discarded as irrelevant. *Love* contains innumerable examples of such material. There is a constant mention of knives, silver spoons, scars and red dresses in the text, a prominence that suggests continuity at the level of story which, nevertheless, does not amount to anything specific in terms of action or psychology.

The relevance of such indeterminacy is brought to the forefront in the opening of the novel, as the ghostly narrator L., who was once a cook in the Cosey household, establishes a dialectic between *then* and *now* grounded on the opposition between a past time when 'there used to be secrets – some to hold, some to tell' and the present, 'barefaced being the order of the day' (Morrison 2003, 3). The contrast is semantically reinforced in the opening passage as 'quiet', 'discreet' and 'silence' are opposed to 'brazen', 'wide open' and 'spread in public'. L.'s argument points to how this, however, reduces knowledge to the surface level: 'Nowadays silence is looked on as odd and most of my race has forgotten the beauty of meaning much by saying little. Now tongues work all by themselves with no help from the mind' (3). The present, therefore, is a realm 'where all is known and nothing understood' (4). L.'s opening monologue strongly invites a reflexive reading, as it seems to imply this is the reading mechanism we will be trapped in: one in which all the facts are put before our eyes, and yet will leave us unable to understand the events.[1]

My intention, in what follows, is to explore the conflict between narrative sequence and textual secrets in *Love*. I would hypothesize that there are two ways to understand the working of secrecy in the novel. On the one hand, secrecy stands for what is obscured or deliberately delayed in the narration, altering our sense of sequence and affecting the reconstruction of a causal chain, and our ethical judgement on the narrated. On the other hand, secrecy reveals itself in what is put before our eyes but we are not able to identify at first as being relevant to causal sequence, in a sort of purloined letter device.

Therefore, while one part of my argument draws on narratological notions of sequence, causality, delayed disclosure and its effect on ethical judgement, another part of it acknowledges the persistence of surface textual secrets which, like marine debris, stay with us until the end of the reading process, but fail to find their place into a narrative whole.[2] It is here that the value of my contribution lies, since while a lot of the scholarly work on this novel focuses on the ethical conflicts represented (Palladino 2012; Bouson 2008; Vega-González 2005; Wen-Ching 2006), the problem of ethical judgement has rarely been regarded from the perspective of narratology, nor has it been related to the peculiar management of secrets and their disclosure in the text.

My approach to the notion of secrecy is grounded, on this regard, on Jacques Derrida's understanding that literature enacts 'a secret that is at the same time kept and exposed, jealously sealed and open like a purloined letter' (2008, 131). The paradoxical

---

[1] The effect is somewhat confirmed in the perceptions of reviewers such as Michiko Kakutani, who wrote about the characters in the novel: 'Even when all their secrets have been unraveled, it is hard to comprehend why they harbor such homicidal rage toward each other' (2003).

[2] This could be assimilated to what H. Porter Abbott has described in *Real Mysteries* as 'intentionally induced states of unknowing' (2013, 9).

nature of exposed secrets constitutes the core narrative strategy used by Toni Morrison in this novel, in which 'all is known and nothing understood' (Morrison 2003, 4). Equally central to my reading is J. Hillis Miller's consideration that linear terminology dominates our understanding of narrative, in a way that invites us to discard anything that does not fit into a causally organized sequence of events:

> The end of the story is the retrospective revelation of the law of the whole. The law is an underlying 'truth' that ties all together in an inevitable sequence revealing a hitherto hidden figure in the carpet. The image of the line tends always to imply the norm of a single continuous unified structure determined by one external organizing principle.
>
> 1992, 18

Attending to the paradox of literary secrets, I would argue that in Morrison's novel if some revelation is at hand, it surely does not materialize into a single storyline. *Love* offers continuous anticipations of such revelation, and thus of a reconstructed, smooth lineal sequence, only to leave us pondering on the bits and pieces that do not seem to find a place in such a narrative pattern.

Retrospective revelation, sequence and causality

As Jean Wyatt has argued in a brilliant reading of this novel, the narrative structure used by Morrison relies heavily on the strategy of delayed disclosure of relevant information. Wyatt reads this as an attempt on Morrison's part to mirror, at the level of reading experience, the psychological mechanism of *Nachträglichkeit*, which, she claims, the main characters in the novel, Heed and Christine, undergo: 'Narrative displacements reflect the protagonists' temporal disorientation, so that the time of the reading is itself discontinuous' (2007, 95). Thus, the reading process enacts the belated unveiling of information about the characters' past, which contributes to explain their present situation. The mutual hatred they profess is revealed as the consequence of emotional wounds inflicted in a past that has been buried by nearly all involved.

It is not casual, in this regard, that reviewers of *Love* tend to depict it as 'gothic': Kakutani described it as 'a gothic soap opera' (2003, n.p.n.) and Elaine Showalter wrote about it that '[t]heir [Heed and Christine's] relationship is almost gothic in its ferocity and passion, as if they were African-American female versions of Cathy and Heathcliff' (2003, n.p.n.). Indeed, beyond the *topos* of the decaying house, the very narrative structure of the novel may be described as 'gothic', to the extent that the thematic patterns we classify as 'gothic' tend to be articulated through the logics of revelation. The paradigmatic gothic narrative is one in which the emergence of the ghostly or the monstrous in the diegetic present works as a symptom of a past that has been repressed and locked away. In other words, present disturbances in the order of things are indexes of a return of the repressed that need to be exorcized in order to allow for a restoration to the 'normal' timeline. In Buse and Stott's words, 'haunting, by its very structure, implies a deformation of linear temporality' (1999, 1). It is precisely on this connection between the thematics of haunting and the deformation of temporality that narratives of revelation stand as structures in which the present can only make sense with reference to a past that needs to be revealed, unburied and incorporated.

Delayed disclosure emerges, in narratives of revelation, as a necessary device, whereby the secrets from the diegetic past are brought into the diegetic present and, hence, to the readers' attention. It is often the case, in narratives of revelation, that the amount of information about the past that would explain the present is distributed asymmetrically among characters and narrators. Focalization tends to be the mechanism through which writers orient the reader by aligning their (lack of) knowledge with that of characters who share their desire to know. In Morrison's oeuvre, a paradigmatic case is that of *Beloved* (1987), where several characters possess the knowledge about Sethe's family's present situation – including Sethe herself, Baby Suggs, Paul D and Stamp Paid – but one of them is exactly *on the same page* in this regard as the reader: Denver (Sethe's daughter and Beloved's sister). Morrison uses Denver as a focalizer and a catalyst of the readers' confusion about Sethe's past life.

In *Dangerous Freedom*, Philip Page identified in Morrison's early novels the recurrent use of a narrative method he named 'the technique of suspension': 'an image or fact is narrated but not fully explained until the narration circles or spirals back to that same incident, explains it further but still not fully, then circles back again, and so forth' (1995, 33). Page's description refers to the technique used by Morrison in texts such as *Beloved*, in the narration of Sethe's murder of Beloved as it is narrated three times from different perspectives. This spiralling technique, I would claim, is also deployed by Morrison in *Love*. For instance, the friendship between Heed and Christine is revealed to the reader in three narrative 'waves' (2003, 78, 95, 199) that focus on the same incident – their meeting on the beach and their sharing of Christine's ice-cream – returning to it to add additional information.

Unlike other Morrison novels organized around the mechanism of delayed disclosure, however, *Love* is peculiar in its distribution of information among characters and readers. Nearly all the characters in Morrison's *Love* know what has happened in their past from the beginning of the novel (i.e. the diegetic present). The deferral of full disclosure is different in this novel because it affects 1) the *causes* of events, rather than the events themselves, and 2) the reader's judgement of the situation, but not the characters'.

L.'s introductory monologue already establishes the connection between Heed and Christine, their mutual hatred and the fact they live together at the Monarch Street house (Morrison 2003, 9–10). By the end of chapter 3 we also know about Heed's marriage to Bill Cosey (60–1), and at the beginning of chapter 4 (75), intraracial prejudice is established as the apparent cause of Christine's and her mother's hate of Heed. The friendship between Heed and Christine is mentioned for the first time also in chapter 4 (75).

As Jean Wyatt contends (2000, 204 n. 5), the novel misleads us into believing Christine and her mother, May, rejected Heed because of intraracial prejudice, seeing her as a poor black parvenu. This is suggested often in the text, in passages where focalization is on Heed: 'Knowing she had no schooling, no abilities, no proper raising, he chose her anyway while everybody else thought she could be run over' (Morrison 2003, 72–3); 'Both of them, mother and daughter, went wild just thinking about his choice of an Up Beach girl for his bride' (75). May is identified, in the narrative focalized through Heed, as the source of class prejudice against Heed and her family, the Johnsons: 'May, who took pains to snub the whole Johnson brood' (76). J. Brooks Bouson, who claims that intraracial prejudice is the 'dirty little secret' Morrison intends to bring to light in *Love* (2008, 358), argues that this is the rationale explaining the hatred involved in the relationship between May, Christine and Heed. By considering May as the ultimate cause of the rupture in the girls' friendship (361), however, she takes the sections depicting May's class prejudice against Heed at face value, without considering the possibility that May's decisions may be guided by her will to keep her daughter away from the paedophile Bill Cosey, something we are only able to grasp after discovering that Heed was 11, and Christine's girl friend, when she married Bill Cosey. This is further suggested in the passage narrating the changes in the Cosey household after his marriage to Heed, as May transfers Christine's bedroom so that she'll be further away from her grandfather's bedroom: 'she told her it was for her own protection. There were things she shouldn't see or hear or know about' (Morrison 2003, 95). As will be argued, though, we are unable to fully grasp the meaning of these sentences until later in the narration.

This delayed disclosure happens nearly two thirds into the narration. It does not amount to a 'surprise ending', but I would claim the rules for it, as established by James Phelan in *Experiencing Fiction*, apply to this case as well. Specifically, we may observe how the disclosed bit of information sheds new light on previously provided bits of text we may now identify as anticipations or 'clues': 'these signals take on new significance in light of the surprise' (2007a, 108). *Love* exploits as its main narrative technique what Matei Calinescu defines as the 'retrospective logic of rereading' (1993, 18): 'in literature little details, which can easily be overlooked or forgotten, may always turn out to play a huge structural role' (19).

From the moment when Heed's age at the time of marriage is disclosed, a readjustment in the reconstruction of linear, unified sequence takes place for the reader. On the one hand, textual elements that appeared earlier are brought back and reconsidered in light of the new connection established between the date of Heed's marriage and her age at the time. These are mostly references to her size, which for most readers have been discarded as irrelevant or explained away through reference to Heed's physical appearance as an adult as well: her 'hand small as a child's' (Morrison 2003, 25), 'small, baby-smooth' (28) are noticed twice by Junior, the woman she hires as secretary, upon meeting her. Later, when Heed shows her a picture of her wedding day, the narrator describes her as Cosey's 'tiny bride', mentioning how 'Heed was swamped by the oversize wedding gown' (60). Her size is mentioned again in the depiction of how she learned to groom her husband: 'she was so little she had to stand on a stool to reach' (124). Later, we may reread key sentences in a new light, like this one: 'Thoughts of Papa and her together in bed drove the two of them [May and Christine] to more and more meanness' (76). Although the sentence is originally inscribed within a longer passage establishing May's class prejudice against Heed, it is inevitable to reconsider the *causes* of May's contempt when considering the sexual intercourse between her father-in-law and her daughter's prepubescent friend.

On the other hand, as anticipated earlier, the nature of the reconfiguration produced by the disclosure of Heed's age at the moment of marriage affects mostly the causal links we had initially established between the key events in the story. The origin of Heed and Christine's hatred would lie not so much in the social prejudices of the latter, but in how marriage to Cosey breaks their girlhood friendship. The explicit reference to this takes place during a conversation between Junior and Christine, when Junior realizes Heed's age at the moment of marriage by following the logics of a reconstructed chronology: 'Wait a minute ... She said she was married for thirty years and he died twenty-five years ago. So she must have been ... a baby' (131). Although the dialogue form may lead us to think Christine's contribution is relevant to Junior's realization, in fact it is not, since she already had the dates necessary to reach exactly the same conclusion she had reached at that point. And so had the reader. Still, this works as a cue for Christine to elaborate and fully address the issue: 'My grandfather married her when she was eleven. We were best friends. One day we build castles on the beach; next day he sat her in his lap. One day we were playing house under a quilt; next day she slept in his bed. One day we played jacks; the next she was fucking my grandfather' (131–2). The idea that this amounts to full revelation is textually emphasized in the narrative: 'It had been a while since the veil parted to expose a wide plateau of lifeless stone' (132).

However, foreshadowing has been consistently used to anticipate what is now made explicit. The issue of Heed's age at the date of marriage is suggested through the perspective of Cosey's friend, Sandler, on how Cosey 'hoped to end by marrying a girl he could educate to his taste' (110); and also through L.'s references to Heed and Christine taken together: 'It was when the girls got in the picture – Christine and Heed – that things began to fray' (104). A further moment of anticipation happens when Heed's and Cosey's honeymoon is narrated, and we read that while Cosey went out in the evenings, Heed stayed at the hotel with 'coloring books, picture magazines, paper dolls to cut out and clothe' (128).

The return from the honeymoon marks the separation between the two friends, 'her friend's eyes were cold, as though Heed had betrayed her instead of the other way around' (128). It seems clear, from this moment on, that the marriage represents a point of no return in their relationship, as inferred from L.'s narration of it as an act of usurpation of someone else's betrothed: '*he chose a girl already spoken for ... The way I see it, she belonged to Christine and Christine belonged to her*' (105; emphasis in the original).[3] Focalization on Heed allows the reader to identify with her bafflement upon

---

[3] The text repeatedly points to Christine's blaming of Heed as the one responsible for breaking their friendship up. Mellard explains the fact she blames Heed rather than Bill Cosey as part of the narcissistic identification between the two girls, which he proposes and analyses: 'While much of her disaffection is caused by the wrong Bill Cosey commits, Christine nevertheless prefers to believe that her anger and rootlessness are the fault of that innocent child bride who had been her best friend. In identification, so it goes' (2009, 707). He explains how identification turns into narcissistic suicidal aggressiveness between Heed and her (ibid.).

her return from the honeymoon, as she fails to understand why Christine has turned against her, and so do we: 'Wonderful as the honeymoon was, she could hardly wait to get back and tell Christine all about it. Hurt by her reception, she kept her stories to herself' (129). Thus, although we already have the facts concerning the main events of the story, we fail to understand the ultimate cause leading to the moment of rupture. Morrison's narrative strategy creates what Greg Forter has termed 'biphasic textuality' (2007, 279), by planting details whose significance is withheld, so that even if the basic elements of the plot are disclosed quite early, the reader is unable to understand the meaning of the mystery they present (278-9). This technique, as claimed by Forter, 'requires a displacement of emphasis from the question "whodunit?" to the question "why?"' (274), which I would argue represents an ethical turn.

Ethical judgement and narrative reassessment

Although Jean Wyatt's analysis of *Nachträglichkeit* emphasizes how withholding key information from the reader affects their incapacity to understand what is being represented with 'rhetorical and pedagogical' intention (2007, 97), my own interest lies in how, once disclosure has taken place, the added information forces us not only into a mental rearrangement of the narrative sequence, which explains the causal links between events, but also an ethical readjustment. Therefore, the second part of my argument regarding the issue of revelation and sequence in *Love* addresses the connection between narrative causality and ethical judgement. In particular, I draw on James Phelan's work in this field in order to argue how deferred knowledge of the causes producing specific effects in the narrative affects ethical judgement.

In *Experiencing Fiction*, James Phelan argues that narratives 'guide their audiences to particular ethical judgments', to the extent that 'narrative judgments proceed from the inside out rather than the outside in' (2007a, 10). From the perspective of rhetorical ethics, he claims, ethical judgements are inextricably linked to the aesthetic dimension of how the narrative is presented to us. Phelan's perception about the interaction between ethical judgement and narrative progression is crucial for my reading of Morrison's *Love*, in that it paves the way for the rhetorical analysis of how the author manipulates sequence and causality in order to guide readers into specific ethical judgements about the characters, and then subverts them in a shocking way. In his magisterial reading of Edith Wharton's *Roman Fever*, Phelan argues that the logics of a surprise ending entail a process of aesthetic and ethical reconfiguration: 'the author includes material in the progression that can retrospectively be understood as preparing the audience for the surprise' (2007a, 95). Such reconfiguration is the outcome of the author's careful manipulation of the audience through a tight control of disclosure (96), which affects both the range of information and the ethical judgement of the characters.

Phelan's analysis focuses on an example in which disclosure happens both for the audience and for the characters, so that the readers' reconfigurations are fed by the characters'. In *Love*, however, the situation is peculiar: Junior is the only character in the novel who does not know about the chronology of the Cosey family's history. It is precisely this fact that creates the narrative opportunity for another character (Christine) to enlighten her on this matter. Everyone else involved already knows that Heed was a 'child bride'. Although the disclosure of this new piece of information can hardly be said to produce an ethical reconfiguration in Junior's opinion of Heed or Christine,[4] it has devastating effects for the audience's ethical judgements, which are deeply transformed from this point on. Therefore, the audience's reconfigurations do not match those of the characters, which also means that disclosure only happens at the level of discourse and emphasizes the meta-ethical position (Phelan 2007a, 53) into which readers are moved.

The disclosure of Heed's age amounts to the revelation of a secret only to readers, not to the characters themselves, so that 'our sense of completion also includes our final understanding of the ethical relations between characters' (Phelan 2007a, 107). The process of reconfiguration, I contend, is one that involves readers' judgement of characters and a reassessment as to the degree of reliability of the different narrators and focalizers in the novel. It is in the wrongly assumed cause of the friends' rupture that the reader's ethical assumptions about the narrative situation are grounded, so that the disclosure of an alternative causal chain in the text forces a reorientation in the ethical parameters for interpretation. As argued by Palladino, the delayed disclosure of the actual causes of Christine and Heed's mutual hatred 'demands complete reconsideration of the facts' (2012, 348).

J. Brooks Bouson, discussing the withholding and disclosure of information about Heed and Christine in the novel, points to the reading process as one through which 'she forces her readers to assemble and then reassemble the personal histories of her characters and to assess and then reassess her characters and their situations' (2008, 359). Although the first process – to assemble and then reassemble – affects the reconstruction of causality and lineal sequence, the second one – to assess and then reassess – points in the direction of the ethical, for it affects readers' judgement about the value of characters and actions (Phelan 2007a, 9). The reassessment the novel invites, moreover, may be said to spring from a degree of indeterminacy about the place of specific narrative components in the sequence, the impossibility to definitely *assemble* every single textual element into a whole. One may invoke here the Derridean notion of 'iterability' as a fundamental feature of literature, according to which a text never exhausts its interpretive potential, what David Wills calls 'contextual inexhaustibility' (2008, 19).[5]

---

[4] The absence of reaction to it on Junior's part is explained in part by the way in which the narrative 'abandons' her perspective immediately upon its disclosure (Morrison 2003, 132). Thus, while Junior is left alone 'to ponder the thought' (ibid.), the narrative follows Christine into the kitchen, where we witness the still overwhelming effect talking about this has on her: 'Back in the kitchen, Christine began to perspire' (ibid.). From this moment on, the absence of references to this disclosure from Junior's perspective is total, which reinforces the perception that she has not been deeply affected by it.

[5] Note that Phelan also uses the idea of iteration implicit in the prefix re- when claiming that rhetorical ethics involves a process of reconstruction (2007a, 13) of the underlying ethical principles in a narrative, and introduces the term 'reconfiguration'.

I would claim that Morrison's mastery is evinced precisely in her subtle management of narrative progression for the sake of ethical judgement. The reconfigurations in readers' judgement of characters affect our views about Bill Cosey – from big-hearted man to inveterate paedophile – as well as L. (detached witness and occasional narrator or active agent, guilty of intervening in the Coseys' affairs), May (paranoid or clear-minded chronicler of historical change), Christine (envious of Heed for the sake of the money or guilty for her friend's sacrifice as child bride) and Heed (proud beloved wife or victim of abuse under Stockholm syndrome).

It is when assessing the effect of such reversals in judgement that we may consider a further dimension of the ethical in narrative also identified by Phelan: the ethics of storytelling itself (2007a, 12). As we realize we have been manipulated by the narrative's multiple narrators and focalizers, the question as to *why* would Morrison devise such a sophisticated narrative (and ethical) structure comes to the forefront, in our attempt 'to identify the author's implicit ethical principles and apply them to the particular techniques of the telling' (Phelan 2007a, 12).

According to Bouson, for instance, this would be provoked by Morrison's intention to illustrate the ambivalence and coexistence of contradictory emotions, basically revolving around the dichotomy between love and hate on which the novel's plot seems to hinge (2008, 360). Palladino, who also describes the reading process as one requiring *re-assessment* of previously provided information (2012, 336), claims that Morrison's technique 'denies the reader any ethical guidance' as part of a postmodern intention, for 'it denounces the unequivocal assumptions and celebrates revision as a way to involve the reader in the making of a story' (336–7). Both critics associate Morrison's technique (explicitly in Palladino's case) with a postmodern stance towards the ethical, in which no absolute judgements can be made and the relativity of each character's position is emphasized.

Although Bouson identifies a greater agency on Morrison's part in the manipulation of the readers' ethical judgement, Palladino claims that Morrison refuses to offer any textual hints as to the narrator's judgement of characters, so that 'the reader is left to interpret the event, to name what is only shown ... Her narration is deprived of any condemnatory and critical stances, it leaves everything up to the reader' (2012, 336).[6] Her contention is that, because the terms 'paedophilia' and 'abuse' are never explicitly used in the text, the author is refraining from offering ethical guidance, incurring in what Phelan has called 'abdication of authorial responsibility' (2007a, 54).

As I am not entirely persuaded by this argument, I will concentrate on our reconfigurations affecting Bill Cosey and L. as a consequence of delayed disclosure of information in the novel, in order to substantiate my argument that, in *Love*, the manipulation of focalization does offer ethical guidance to the reader. The main event about which we feel we are invited to judge from an ethical perspective is fifty-two-year-old Bill Cosey's marriage to eleven-year-old Heed. That it is her age that determines

---

[6] This is also claimed by James Phelan in his argument on Morrison's *Beloved*: 'Morrison stops short of taking any clear ethical stand on Sethe's rough choice and of guiding her audience to judge it in any definitive way' (2013, 214).

the course of ethical judgement, comes from the fact that it is precisely this detail – and not other potentially reprehensible details such as the fact Cosey paid the Johnsons so as to have them accept the marriage – that is belatedly disclosed and from which ethical reconfigurations ensue.

Both L. and Christine depict Cosey's behaviour as a reprehensible one, thus offering clear ethical guidance that influences the reader's judgement.[7] L., in her monologue at the end of the chapter 'Husband', depicts him as 'a reckless old reprobate' with 'a whim' (Morrison 2003, 137); and Christine, upon revealing to Junior how old Heed was at the moment of marriage, points very directly at the issue of paederasty when drawing the line that places Cosey's behaviour beyond the acceptable: 'There's virgins and there's children' (132). Only in the passages focalized on Heed do we get a view of the situation in which romantic love rather than abuse is perceived. As Heed's ignorance and lack of experience is repeatedly underscored by the rest of the characters (Sandler Gibbons, Junior, Christine, May and L.), we tend to perceive her perspective as unreliable.

The dissonance between Heed's perception and what other characters see is best illustrated in Christine's depiction of her as 'the friend who grinned happily as she was led down the hall to darkness, liquor smell and old-man business' (133). The use of the passive voice – 'as she was led' – emphasizes here again her lack of agency, and offers an uncanny image of total unconsciousness – 'grinned happily' – as to the evil that awaits her, suggested in the image of darkness and adult life ('liquor', 'old man business'). Furthermore, as L. emerges in the narrative as the voice of authority and greater agency over matters, her judgement of Cosey stands out as the ethical compass for the readers.

Perhaps the only character who actively contributes to the idealization of Bill Cosey in the novel is Vida Gibbons, neighbour of Silk and old worker at the Cosey Hotel. Her view is clearly counterbalanced by that of her husband, Sandler. In a passage using Sandler as focalizer, their contrasting views are exposed, with Sandler's implicitly aligning with the view that Heed is a victim in a situation provoked by Cosey:

> Vida, in her tale of wickedness, had not said a word about Bill Cosey. She acted as though Heed had chased and seduced a fifty-two-year-old man, older than her father. *That she had chosen to marry him rather than having been told to* ... They forgave Cosey. Everything. Even to the point of *blaming a child for a grown man's interest in her.*
>
> 147; emphasis added

Vida speaks in the voice of the Silk community, the 'they' implicit in Sandler's observation that '[t]hey forgave Cosey'. Sandler's view on the matter, on the other hand, diverges from commonly held opinion, and it opposes Heed's and Cosey's behaviour in

---

[7] Unlike the narrative situation we find in a text such as Nabokov's *Lolita*, analysed precisely from this perspective by James Phelan (2007b), *Love* does not allow the character to express his views on the matter. Except for the passages where Junior enters into a sort of dialogue with Cosey (or with his portrait), his perspective is never offered in the narrative.

terms of agency and passive acceptance. From Sandler's perspective, Vida's and the community's regard of Heed emerges clearly as a case of victim blaming. It is also from his perspective that Vida's idealization of Bill Cosey is dismissed as unreliable and unrealistic: 'Vida had nothing to say about that, and Sandler didn't want the misery of bringing it up, of tilting his wife's idol with a blow of insight' (148).

Finally, it is in this passage as well that we get some insight into Bill Cosey's own view of the matter, as Sandler reminisces about his conversations with him on the issue of his marriage to Heed:

> Uneasy with other men's sexual confidences ... he remembered Cosey's dream-bitten expression as he rambled on about his first sight of Heed ... Listened to Cosey's rapturous description of his wife, Sandler was *not as repelled as he'd expected to be*, since the picture that emerged from the telling called to his mind not a child but a fashion model.
>
> 148; emphasis added

This is the closest we get to *see* Heed through Cosey's eyes, and realize that what is perceived as paedophilic desire comes through as a distorted representation of Heed (that it is indeed distorted seems to be underscored by the ideas of dreaming and rapture mentioned in Sandler's depiction of Cosey's mental state when reminiscing about Heed as a child).

Our judgement of L., on the other hand, is conditioned by the accumulated knowledge we have about Cosey's history. If the narration had started with L.'s confession of her interference with Cosey's death and will, the effect would probably have been one of estrangement from her. Because she only tells us she killed Cosey and forged the will at the very end of her narration, after evidence on how much misery Cosey's actions had brought to all his female relatives, we deem it nearly an act of poetic justice. Our ethical judgement of the situation is thus conditioned and comes closer to what we identify as the implied author's ethical stance regarding Bill Cosey (Phelan 2007b, 231, 233): that he was not a role model, ideal husband and perfect father, but an abusive patriarch who, as Morrison suggests in the 'foreword' to the novel, placed the satisfaction of his whims above anything else, and ignored the consequences (2003, xi). The idea finds a place in the novel itself, as we read, after learning about Heed's age at the moment of marriage, that 'He was the Big Man who, with no one to stop him, could get away with it and anything else he wanted' (133). The 'it' in this sentence is the marriage itself, but it is the 'anything else he wanted' that suggests the idea that even more illicit behaviours would have gone unnoticed or unpunished in the absence of a greater authority.

The question remains, however, as to the absence of ethical judgement on L.'s actions in the text, something no critic or scholar to date has examined. Let us consider the textual circumstances in which the events are revealed: first, the disclosure is *really* delayed until the penultimate page of the text. No space for focalization on another character is allowed, as L. is the last narrator and focalizer. Thus, it is her perspective alone that we can use as guidance, except for the reference that the woman in red who visits Cosey's tomb – we assume it is Celestial, his life-long secret lover – has 'forgiven me for my solution' (202).

The text leads us to think that L. has never confessed what she did to anyone while alive. As several authors have mentioned (Wen-Ching 2006, 657, 665; Palladino 2012, 337–8; Vega-González 2005, 280), L. appears to narrate her part of the story after death, as a disembodied, ghostly presence. The question as to the validity and effect of a confession after death may be raised, although it is not my intention to shift my attention to the realm of theology. We may conclude, yet, that her very identity as a ghost reinforces the idea that she is now beyond judgement. Finally, L.'s own comments on her actions should be considered, as the text clearly invites positive judgement. First, L. claims that 'There wasn't but one solution' (Morrison 2003, 201), suggesting inevitability. Then, she emphasizes her bravery, 'it took some nerve' (ibid.), and describes it as an act of resistance: 'if properly used, it can save you . . .', 'it's hard to do but I know at least one woman who did. Who stood right . . .' (ibid.). Finally, she claims that her purpose was to keep Heed and Christine together: 'Gave them a reason to stay connected' (ibid.). It is perhaps this statement that most clearly illustrates the impact that delayed disclosure has on ethical judgement, as we can only appreciate the loving intention of L.'s crime after we have witnessed Heed and Christine's mutual confession that their hate was a deformed version of their love for one another.

Marine debris, textual secrets

In a novel that appears to be written through tidal movements, in which words, and the ideas they recall, are brought time and again to the readers' attention, a lot of textual material accumulates during the reading process, waiting to be sorted out into their 'right' places in the narrative sequence. This phenomenon could also be described through Page's notion of Morrison's 'technique of suspension' (1995, 33), in which 'meaning is accreted through repetition and layering and as multiple times are overlaid on each other' (4). Although Page emphasizes how Morrison's style enhances the reader's role in the production of meaning (ibid.), he does not consider how her novels force a kind of reading that is always already a rereading. In *Rereading*, Matei Calinescu brilliantly examines 'compulsively rereadable texts', the ones 'beckoning the reader to revisit them in a renewed search for their hidden, tantalizingly elusive meanings' (1993, 3). Using Borges as a paradigmatic example, Calinescu addresses 'the question of concealed meaning' (14) and how it 'haunts the act of rereading, particularly as it comes to focus on tiny textual details, idiosyncratic formulations, letter combinations, patterns of occurrence of names and dates, and other such matters' (ibid.). Kermode's own method for reading into a text's secrets involves paying attention to words used in idiosyncratic ways or odd positions, and to those used with abnormal sequence (1980, 93), the kind of material we would normally dismiss when looking for sequence, closure and coherence (101).

We may find many instances of such 'tiny textual details' in *Love*. L.'s opening statement that 'I could make a point strong enough to stop a womb – or a knife' (Morrison 2003, 3), which inaugurates a double chain of references to knives and unborn children that runs through the whole text. The initial reference by L. in this passage is explained away in the context of Cosey's funeral, when Christine threatens Heed with a knife, a scene that will be fully narrated much later (73). Yet, many other unrelated references to knives are recurrent in the text: Junior is said to sleep with a knife in her hand, ready to defend herself from anyone who tries to prevent her from escaping home (59); a knife is mentioned in the recalling of a mysterious occurrence, as a woman working at the cannery is said to be poisoned upon having been caught with her neighbour's husband: 'the grappling knife still in her hand' (5). The exchange of poison and knife is again mentioned at the end of the passage (9–10), but this time in reference to Heed and Christine and whether they may have killed each other. Poison is, eventually, the method used by L. to kill Cosey, although the word itself is not used in the fragment referring to how 'foxglove can be quick' (201). On the other hand, the reference to a womb – with child – is also recurrent in the text: 'their hearts where the folded child is tucked' (7). It connects to what the text claims is 'the central question': 'who was "my sweet Cosey child?"' (88) mentioned in Bill Cosey's will. Later, we find out that Heed was pregnant in 1958, a child who was never born, but that Cosey thought was his, when in fact it was Knox Sinclair's (171, 173). The ghost of the unborn child in a way haunts the text.

Other recurrent textual details include multiple references to female characters having scars: Celestial, whose scarred face is mentioned several times (92, 201), Heed (28, 80), and in general, women 'wearing scars like presidential medals' (6).[8] Also, women wearing a red dress, as the one Heed gives to Junior (118), the one Heed wears at Christine's birthday party when she dances with a man in a zoot suit (168), the one Celestial was wearing when Heed and Christine first saw her at the beach (187) and the one worn by the woman who visits Cosey's tomb, whom we assume may be Celestial or her ghost (201). Most mysterious among these textual recurrences is the figure of a woman under water. L. narrates her own birth taking place under a downpour: 'you could say going from womb water straight into rain marked me' (64). This is followed by her depiction of the moment when she met Mr and Mrs Cosey, 'the first time I saw Mr. Cosey he was standing in the sea, holding Julia, his wife, in his arms ... Her eyes were closed, head bobbing; her light blue swimming dress ballooned or flattened out depending on the waves and his strength' (64). When Junior offers to bathe Heed (27), this triggers a memory of the latter's wedding night, which will be recalled again later, as she remembers being 'submerged in water in his arms' (77).[9] Multiple references to the rings Cosey won playing poker (20, 73, 74, 85, 91, 129, 193) or the silver spoon used by Heed and Christine to eat ice-cream on the beach upon their first meeting (22, 78, 85, 91) are also textual recurrences that reinforce the idea that the novel drags textual fragments before its readers time and again.

---

[8] Scars and wounds in female characters are recurrent as well in the rest of Morrison's oeuvre, with Sethe's cherry tree-shaped scarred back in *Beloved* featuring most prominently.

[9] Vega-González discusses the associations between water and female characters through the ideas of fluidity and freedom (2005, 284). More specifically, one cannot fail to notice how Heed's memory of her wedding night is a small-scale replica of the original scene with Cosey's first wife, Julia.

Yet, as we reread *Love* in search of the concealed meaning such details may disclose, we end up buried in marine debris. Kermode's insights into 'the comforts of sequence' (1980, 87) and the textual resistance to full revelation in 'Secrets and Narrative Sequence' are key to understanding the dynamics of Morrison's novel (and probably of her entire oeuvre). Kermode's appeal for a reading that focuses on whatever is out of place, idiosyncratic or abnormally recurrent in a literary text (93), is grounded on his own idiosyncratic understanding of the notion of 'secret'. To him, textual secrets are elements that challenge the notion of narrative sequence by resisting to be incorporated into it. These are elements that tend to be erased from attention in the reading process (92), as they do not fit into the major frameworks of action and psychology as explanatory of sequence (98). He proposes a model of reading that abandons the pleasure of making all narrative fragments fit into a causally connected sequence, in favour of the inexplicable accumulation of textual oddities:

> The secrets to which these words and ideas are an index have no direct relation to the main business of the plot ... But they form associations of their own, nonsequential, secret invitations to interpretation rather than appeals to consensus. They inhabit a misty world in which relationships are not arranged according to some agreed system but remain occult or of questionable shape.
>
> 93

Critical readings of Morrison's *Love*, including the one offered in the preceding section, tend to be invested efforts to systematize and arrange textual elements into a causally determined sequence. The novel's temporal structure, I would contend, invites such a method of interpretation. As Bouson states, 'Morrison forces readers to continually construct and re-construct the personal histories of her characters as she reveals secrets within secrets within secrets in narrating their stories' (2008, 363). It does not escape most commentators, however, that a lot of the textual material included in *Love* remains in that 'misty world' (Kermode 1980, 93) of unmotivated recurrence. Thus, Kakutani describes it as 'a deliberately elliptical narrative, intended to create an aura of mystery while withholding from the reader certain crucial secrets about the characters' pasts' (2003, n.p.n.); Carden contends that the novel ends 'with no map for resolution of the questions it raises' (2011, 143), while Palladino claims that 'L.'s ambivalence allows for the text to escape signification' (2012, 343) and later concludes that 'its narration, providing the reader with simultaneous presentations and re-presentations of the story, problematizes accounts of knowledge' (349).[10]

'Reading for the secret', as Calinescu would call it (1993, 243), confronts the reader with the impossibility of incorporating all idiosyncratic textual fragments into the complete narrative sequence which, in Miller's terms, reveals 'the law of the whole'

---

[10] See also Vega-González (2005, 275–6).

(1992, 18). Morrison's narratives persistently challenge readers by placing them in such a situation, inviting them to read for the secret, then forcing them into the realization that textual secrets, like marine debris, cannot be fully absorbed. Eventually, the text proves to be written according to the logics identified in L.'s initial monologue: everything is on the surface, everything is said, but cannot be fully grasped, incorporated or comprehended, 'all is known and nothing understood' (Morrison 2003, 4). This is pure Derridean undecidability, a threat to conventional interpretation, in that it exposes the impossibility of 'making decisions about some secret behind the surface of a textual manifestation' (Derrida 1995, 29). The narrative is 'barefaced', as L. claims is 'the order of the day' (3). Yet, as Derrida argues, the superficiality of the textual phenomenality cannot be penetrated, and this is what constitutes 'the absolute inviolability of the secret they carry' (Derrida 1992, 153).

Thus, this novel hinges on the double meaning of the secret that was outlined at the beginning of this essay, by invoking a narrative orientation towards the past as the site where secrets may be located and, we assume, explain the present in terms of causal sequence. Simultaneously, it points to the irretrievability of total transparency bringing characters together in a community founded on revealed truth. *Love*, we may conclude, illustrates a pattern familiar to any reader of Morrison, one in which revelation works as a major structuring device, but never offers the comforts of a completely unified sequence. Often arranged as communal efforts to retrieve a sense of wholeness from the past, her texts insist on the idea that community may exist not *in spite of* a certain opacity, but precisely *because of* such opacity.

References

Abbott, H. Porter. (2013), *Real Mysteries: Narrative and the Unknowable*, Columbus: Ohio State University Press.
Bouson, J. Brooks. (2008), 'Uncovering "the Beloved" in the Warring and Lawless Women in Toni Morrison's *Love*', *The Midwest Quarterly*, 49 (4): 358–73.
Buse, Peter and Andrew Stott, eds. (1999), *Ghosts: Deconstruction, Psychoanalysis, History*, Houndmills: Macmillan Press.
Calinescu, Matei. (1993), *Rereading*, New Haven: Yale University Press.
Carden, Mary Paniccia. (2011), '"Trying to find a place when the streets don't go there": Fatherhood, Family, and American Racial Politics in Toni Morrison's *Love*', *African American Review*, 44 (1–2): 131–47.
Derrida, Jacques. (1992), *Given Time: I. Counterfeit Money*, translated by Peggy Kamuf, Chicago: University of Chicago Press.
Derrida, Jacques. (1995), 'Passions: "An Oblique Offering"', in Thomas Dutoit (ed.), David Wood, John P. Leavey and Ian McLeod (trans), *On the Name*, 3–31, Stanford: Stanford University Press.
Derrida, Jacques. (2008), *The Gift of Death (Second Edition) and Literature in Secret*, David Wills (trans), Chicago: University of Chicago Press.
Forter, Greg. (2007), 'Freud, Faulkner, Caruth: Trauma and the Politics of Literary Form', *Narrative*, 15 (3): 259–85.

Kakutani, Michiko. (2003), 'Family Secrets, Feuding Women', *The New York Times*, 3 October 2003, accessed 7 May 2020, https://nyti.ms/2FT1dC9.
Kermode, Frank. (1980), 'Secrets and Narrative Sequence', *Critical Inquiry*, 7 (1): 83–101.
Mellard, James M. (2009), '"Families make the best enemies": Paradoxes of Narcissistic Identification in Toni Morrison's *Love*', *African American Review*, 43 (4): 699–712.
Miller, J. Hillis. (1992), *Ariadne's Thread: Story Lines*, New Haven: Yale University Press.
Morrison, Toni. (1997) (1987), *Beloved*, London: Vintage.
Morrison, Toni. (2003), *Love*, London: Chatto & Windus.
Page, Philip. (1995), *Dangerous Freedom: Fusion and Fragmentation in Toni Morrison's Novels*, Jackson: University Press of Mississippi.
Palladino, Mariangela. (2012), 'Aphrodite's Faces: Toni Morrison's *Love* and Ethics', *Modern Fiction Studies*, 58 (2): 334–52.
Phelan, James. (2007a), *Experiencing Fiction: Judgments, Progressions, and the Rhetorical Theory of Narrative*, Columbus: Ohio State University Press.
Phelan, James. (2007b), 'Estranging Unreliability, Bonding Unreliability, and the Ethics of "*Lolita*"', *Narrative*, 15 (2): 222–38.
Phelan, James. (2013), 'Sethe's Choice and Morrison's Ethical Challenge', in *Reading the American Novel 1920–2010*, 213–35, Malden: Wiley-Blackwell.
Showalter, Elaine. (2003), 'Review: *Love* by Toni Morrison. A Tangled Web', *The Guardian*, 29 November 2003, accessed 7 May 2020. https://www.theguardian.com/books/2003/nov/29/fiction.tonimorrison.
Vega-González, Susana. (2005), 'Toni Morrison's *Love* and the Trickster Paradigm', *Revista Alicantina de Estudios Ingleses*, 18: 275–89.
Wen-Ching, Ho. (2006), '"I'll Tell" – The Function and Meaning of L in Toni Morrison's *Love*', *EurAmerica*, 36 (4): 651–75.
Wills, David. (2008), 'Passionate Secrets and Democratic Dissidence', *Diacritics*, 38 (1/2): 17–22, 24–29.
Wyatt, Jean. (2007), *Love and Narrative Form in Toni Morrison's Later Novels*, Athens: University of Georgia Press.

4

Challenging stereotypes of femininity through secrets in Alice Munro's fiction

Mercedes Díaz Dueñas

Introduction

Alice Munro's fiction relies highly on secrecy as a strategy to disclose extraordinary life experiences behind seemingly ordinary people, a mechanism she has described as that of making 'the mysterious touchable' and the 'touchable mysterious' (1974, 33). This chapter analyses the interrelation between this use of secrecy and the challenge to traditional representations of femininity, which can be seen in the way Munro's fiction shuns criticism against women who do not conform to pre-established models, endorsing understanding and forgiveness for unexpected behaviours that make survival possible. With the help of examples from three stories contained in her collection *Too Much Happiness* (2009), this analysis will reveal how secrets serve two purposes in her fiction: on the one hand, they contribute to the construction of the narrative sequence and, on the other hand, as pointed out above, they undermine stereotypical preconceptions of femininity. In order to address this twofold effect of the operating of the secret within Munro's short stories, this chapter relies fundamentally on narrative theory and feminist concerns.

Narrative and secrecy

Within narrative theory, authors such as Matei Calinescu (1993, 1994), Frank Kermode (1980) and Michael Toolan (2002, 2004, 2013) have addressed the relationship between the secret and the construction of narrative. In addition, James Phelan and Peter J. Rabinowitz (2013) have dealt with the field of narrative ethics, exploring the intersections between storytelling and moral values, and focusing on the important role played by the narrator.

Studying the function of secrets in narratives, Calinescu (1994) explains that the dynamics of concealment and disclosure work in different ways. First of all, the very structure of narrative is analogous to the structure of hiding / disclosing a secret or a series of secrets. Secondly, readers of narrative texts are made privy to events that have a secret dimension. In addition, narrative information is withheld, hidden and finally revealed (or not revealed) at specific stages of the narration so as to stimulate the reader's inquisitiveness (Calinescu 1994, 448). Abbott identifies precisely this procedure as '[o]ne of Alice Munro's signature gifts as a writer of short stories', i.e. 'the efficiency with which she builds to a moment of insight that allows us at one and the same time to see a character anew and to see that there is more we can't see' (2008, 455). Lastly, textual concealment may acquire an intertextual dimension (Calinescu 1994, 449). As will be shown in the present study of Alice Munro's fiction, very often the secrets that are withheld or revealed are related to women's relationships with the community they belong to, contributing to the construction of their identities as non-stereotypical. In this sense, Munro's works can be interpreted as what Calinescu has termed 'skilful manipulations of the possibilities offered by the concealment / disclosure of meaning' (1994, 448), being concerned as a writer 'with all that is knowable and unknowable' (Struthers 2000, 295).

On the other hand, Frank Kermode notes how readers first pay attention to the story, i.e. 'events sequentially related' (1980, 83), and explore the conflict between narrative sequence and the operating of secrets in it. Further, building on Kermode's (1980) and Sternberg's (1985) theories, Michael Toolan refines the model by distinguishing between narrative secrets, surprises, suspense and gaps: 'Narrative gaps and secrets are empty or "underfilled" cells in a matrix of the story's characters and events. Or they are cells which *appear* to be empty, but accumulating indications and traces make us suspect that they may and perhaps should be filled' (2002, 416; emphasis in the original). Toolan explains that 'the essence of narrative surprise is that a reader experiences a new development as unforeseen but, upon reflection, foreseeable' (2004, 194), which entails that 'it "fits" the larger structure of narrative conditions and developments in the entire story' (ibid.). He also points to the textual clues that will prompt an array of hypothetical answers from the reader. Usually, the decisive one is not disclosed until the secret is revealed, but 'in a thoroughgoing narrative secret it is *never* conclusively disclosed' (Toolan 2002, 416; emphasis in the original). When this is the case, readers are invited to reflect more deeply on certain aspects of the story and to make decisions about the most plausible interpretations.[1] This paper focuses on the instances where secrets in Munro's stories invite readers to think about female characters as unique individuals who do not conform to stereotypical representations of women.

In this respect, it is highly relevant to keep in mind the emphasis James Phelan and Peter J. Rabinowitz (2013) put on the ethical relationships that underlay the act of telling. Their insights into the importance of the author's decisions about the structural arrangement of the telling and its consequences (155–6) are certainly relevant to the present analysis. As they suggest, choices such as the type of narrator and the use of dialogue, among others, are the basis for 'the ethical dimension of the implied author's communication to the audience' (2013, 156). In this respect, the choice of narrators and

---

[1] Related to this indeterminacy is Munro's open-ended narrative structures, which as Heller highlights, have received abundant critical attention (2005, 70).

the way in which speech and thought are presented in Munro's stories – central for the narrative creation of suspense, surprise and secrecy – will also have ethical consequences for the interpretation of her characters' behaviour.

All the previous aspects are necessarily connected to readers' expectations and their interpretation of the literary text. Toolan points out that 'the text's prospections cumulatively and serially guide the reader to expect the story currently being read to continue and terminate in one way rather than others' (2008, 105). Accordingly, readers develop certain expectations about the characters' fates in these stories. In addition, Calinescu distinguishes between two types of readers: 'a first-time and (probably) one-time, curious linear reader, who doesn't care for intricate allusions ... and a critical rereader, who ... takes up the author's challenge and is willing to play the game of reading or rereading for the secret' (1994, 448). In Munro's stories, both types of readers will be surprised by her way of making the ordinary extraordinary, but the careful rereader will find pleasure in discovering, and sometimes frustration at having overlooked the secrets and surprises created by her narrative. The present analysis takes up Munro's challenge and focuses on how some of these secrets contribute to flouting readers' expectations, particularly in regard to her female characters.

Alice Munro, feminism and beyond

Although Alice Munro shuns feminist labels, feminist theoretical frameworks have been applied to her work since the 1980s.[2] Nonetheless, critics have at the same time made allowances for her particular relationship with feminism. For example, Adrian Hunter states that feminism 'largely fails this test in Munro's writing when it requisitions the female subject for its own political purposes' (2004, 228). Yet, he acknowledges that 'Munro's use of the interrogative story form, and her cultivation of its "minor" status, is the key to understanding the challenge to "traditional structures of meaning and knowledge"' (222).

Maria Löschnigg writes about 'Munro's implicit feminism' (2016, 61) and makes the following relevant point, borrowing Hunter's words:

> Munro's work is characterized, above all, by multiplicity, polyphony, digression and indeterminacy, which indicate the coexistence of equivalent discourses rather than the replacement of one dominant discourse by another. She thus questions predominant patriarchal structures mostly by means of her 'use of the interrogative short story form.' She employs this relativist mode in order to counter fixed ideologies of any kind, including feminism, and 'in order to reveal how these culturally powerful narrational models fall short of the private life stories of women.'
> 60

---

[2] See, for instance, Barbara Godard (1984), Lorna Irvine (1986), Beverly Rasporich (1990), Smaro Kamboureli (1987), Helen Hoy (1991), Magdalene Redekop (1992), Pam Houston (1992), Gayle Elliott (1996) and Ailsa Cox (2004).

This chapter endorses the corroboration made by critics such as Hunter and Löschnigg that although Munro does not place a feminist agenda upfront, her stories pose stimulating questions about the portrayal and development of female characters. Many of the analyses mentioned above have attempted to explain how female identity is constructed and interrogated in her work. However, the role of the secret has not yet been investigated in relationship with this topic.

Munro's stories highlight the human tendency to judge appropriate social and moral behaviour following generalization and stereotype rather than considering individual circumstances. In this sense, Deborah Heller has studied how the stories in Munro's *Friend of My Youth* (1990) are about characters who deviate from the roles expected of them within their fictional world and/or 'from the roles readers may expect them to play in predictable plots' (2005, 70).

The type of multifaceted characterization that often appears in her stories commonly emerges from an equally unsettling backdrop. This fact has been addressed, among others, by Alisa Cox, who has defined Munro's short story aesthetic as 'based in a fluid, ongoing reality which ultimately escapes representation' (2016, 278). Very frequently, as W. R. Martin already remarked in 1982, Munro brings together the paradoxes and contradictions of her characters to illuminate the complex wholeness of existence. Nonetheless, while exploring the complexities of life, she does not repeat traditional approaches to ageing, mortality and the material body (Martin 1982, n.p.n), nor Ailsa she adhere to conventional beliefs of attributing 'development to individuals, regions, or humanity as a whole' (McGill 2016, 136). Moving beyond strictly feminist approaches, the present chapter furthers the exploration of those complex representations of reality and characters, consistently discarding stereotypical representations of female characters, whose singularity she always highlights, through narrative constructions that rely on the use of the secret both in thematic and structural terms.

'Dimensions'

'Dimensions', the story that opens the collection *Too Much Happiness* (Munro 2010, 1–31), is a perfect example of how a narrative may be built by withholding information about what has happened to its protagonist, Doree, gradually releasing important details, which allow the reader to piece together her tragedy. Cox affirms that in this story 'Munro avoids sensationalism and underplays the kind of suspense and dramatic tension expected in conventional crime fiction' (2016, 279). Nonetheless, the story is incredibly effective, probably because it makes use of the four categories Calinescu analyses when describing the functioning of secrets in narratives, as mentioned above: firstly, the narrative hides and then discloses a series of secrets about the protagonist's family; secondly, it makes readers privy to events that have a secret dimension regarding the protagonist's relationship with her abusive husband; thirdly, narrative information is withheld, hidden and finally not revealed to stimulate the reader's inquisitiveness and afterthoughts regarding why those events took place and about the role of both protagonists; and finally, there are intertextual allusions that anticipate some of the secrets revealed throughout the story.

The story is written in the third person and focalizes on the point of view of the protagonist, Doree. The opening presents her as 'a chambermaid at the Blue Spruce Inn' (Munro 2010, 1). The reader learns that she is young, happy with her work and that she is not willing to take her older colleague's advice to train for a better job. The reader's predictions may be that she is an ordinary, somewhat introverted young person, and the expectations about extraordinary events in her life are probably quite low. The attentive reader's suspicions, however, may be raised by the sentence ending the second paragraph: 'She didn't want to have to talk to people' (1). The suspense is further increased when the reader learns that '[n]one of the people she worked with knew what had happened' (2), that her picture had been in the paper, that she had changed her appearance, used her second name (Fleur) and worked now in a different town. However, what had really happened is withheld and the reader's attention is diverted to the bus trip that she is on. In fact, the nonlinear chronology in the narration as well as the change of spatial background deter readers from thinking further about Doree's situation.

The next hidden clue is a very subtle one. It relies on the use of an idiom, which contains a key reference for the development of the story, but is most probably missed on a first reading:

> Mrs. Sands, whom she [Doree] saw on Monday afternoons, spoke of moving on, though she always said that it would take time, that things should not be hurried. She told Doree that she was doing fine, that she was gradually discovering her own strength.
> 'I know those words have been done to death,' she said. 'But they are still true.'
> She blushed at what she heard herself say – 'death' – but did not make it worse by apologizing.
>
> 3

Although Mrs Sands is never described as a psychiatrist or psychologist, the reader easily gathers that this is her job and that Doree is attending weekly sessions with her. The text, as can be seen in the quotation above, may lead to a first interpretation that Doree suffers from some mental disorder or depression, from which she is gradually recovering. Likewise, there is an indirect indication that the problem is related to a death, as Mrs Sands blushes when she realizes the inappropriate choice of words in her use of the idiom 'do something to death'.

Once the main characters of 'Dimensions' are introduced (Doree, her husband Lloyd, their three kids and Mrs Sands), the phrase 'the familiar impediment, that was like a hammer hitting her in the belly' (8) works as a euphemistic expression that makes the reader wonder what is amiss. The fact that the name of Doree's husband is initially omitted, presenting him only as 'he', is also a way of keeping his identity secret for a while. Towards the end of the story, the reader may establish a parallelism between the initial concealment of Lloyd's name and the way he did not show his true colours initially. However, no further explanation is provided because the story continues with a flashback that traces some important moments in the life of the couple.

At first, it seems Lloyd and Doree's relationship had been perfect, because there is complicity between them; he comforts her after her mother's death and they share a particular countryside lifestyle, but gradually it becomes evident to her (and to the reader) that he is abusing her. She needs plenty of time and the counterpoint of her neighbour Maggie, who acts as a foil, to realize that her husband makes her accept certain rules (such as not taking contraception pills or not bottle-feeding their children) that she needs to keep secret from other people surrounding her: 'Maggie was an outsider, not even somebody Doree felt comfortable with. It was Lloyd said that, and he was right. The truth of things between them, the bond, was not something that anybody else could understand and it was not anybody else's business. If Doree could watch her own loyalty it would be all right' (12). The sentence '[i]t was Lloyd said that, and he was right' is particularly revealing of how Doree is controlled by her husband. The less careful reader might interpret this sentence as stemming from a third-person intrusive narrator taking Lloyd's stance. However, the careful rereader clearly discovers that the second part of the sentence is really free direct speech, revealing how far Doree has internalized Lloyd's opinions and accepted that she needs to side with him, which implies keeping their life and his rules secret from the people surrounding them.

The traditional role of the loving, complacent wife, who adopts her husband's opinions without even realizing she does so, is further reinforced by the idea of loyalty. When Doree collapses and seeks help from Maggie, the same notion swirls in the protagonist's head: 'No matter how worn out she got with him, he was still the closest person in the world to her, and she felt that everything would collapse if she were to bring herself to tell someone *exactly how he was*, if she were to be entirely disloyal' (14; emphasis added). This thought, which had been expressed in a conditional form at the end of the previous quotation ('If Doree could watch her own loyalty it would be all right' (12)), turns out to be premonitory, since it foreshadows the tragedy that is to befall: her husband kills their children while she is at Maggie's house and he sentences that she brought it all on herself (15). The only clues the reader gathers about the husband's mental instability are precisely the fact that Doree needs to hide her husband's real character, i.e. 'exactly how he was' (14), and the passing reference to death at the beginning of the story that goes unnoticed at a first reading. However, there is no further explanation in the story about why the husband decides to kill the children. It seems that he is unable to cope with what he may have interpreted as losing control over his young wife, when she walks to their neighbour, exasperated by his behaviour.

Suspicion might be awakened in the type of reader 'who hunts for intertextual clues, telling distortions, and hidden parodic commentaries' (Calinescu 1994, 448), when Lloyd nicknames their neighbour Maggie, who becomes Doree's friend, 'Lezzie'. Using the fourth type of textual concealment described by Calinescu, the intertextual dimension (1994, 448–9), Munro allows for connections with her previous story in the collection: 'Runaway'.[3] As Bigot remarks, 'Lezzie strikes a very disturbing visual echo

---

[3] 'Runaway' was first published in *The New Yorker* in August 2003 and later included in her 2006 collection *Runaway*. It bears thematic resemblances with 'Dimensions' in that both address passionate relationships that entrap women and that unleash some kind of violence.

with the name of the horse in "Runaway," Lizzie, and hence with the name of the axe murderer Lizzie Borden. The visual echo draws a connection between the stories but also heralds the murder of the children' (2017, 101).

It is not until the second third of the story that the reader fully discovers that the relationship is based on a domineering husband and a scared and subjugated wife, when their neighbour Maggie asks, '[i]s everything all right with you? I mean in your marriage? You're happy?' (Munro 2010, 11). The narrator offers then an account through free indirect thought presentation of how Doree perceives her husband at that moment and her feelings towards his behaviour:

> Doree said yes, without hesitation. After that she was more careful about what she said. She saw that there were things that she was used to that another person might not understand. Lloyd had a certain way of looking at things: that was just how he was. ... And sometimes Lloyd did make the enemies into jokes, just as if he was laughing at himself. She was even allowed to laugh with him, as long as she wasn't the one who started the laughing.
>
> Ibid.

At this point in the narration there is a shift: the reader is made aware that the protagonist's husband is not the kind, protective person one might have assumed initially, but nothing anticipates the brutal murder he is about to commit. From then onwards, this ordinary but attractive chap is described as an aberrant being, but without presenting moral judgements.

In spite of his cruelty, Doree does not break free of that secret dependency on her husband. Lloyd manages to keep it alive, although he is interned in an institution. He sends her a letter informing her that he can see their children and that they are in a different dimension.[4] Although Doree thinks he is crazy, 'she still held on to what he'd written, like a secret' (27). She only seems able to disengage herself from him at the end of the story, when she manages to save the life of a boy who has suffered a traffic accident. At this point she interrupts her trip to see him at the institution where he is secluded and the story ends.

There is no comment on Doree's feelings of regret for having left the house, thus leaving her children with their father, although, after such a traumatic experience, it might be an unavoidable thought to consider that if she had stayed at home, her husband would not have killed their children. The thought that she made a mistake storming out of the house might have become especially poignant, since the incident that made her abandon the house was a silly argument about a can of spaghetti (17). However, that part of the traumatic experience is not explored and there is not even a

---

[4] I have argued elsewhere (2019) the importance of what Semino and Short have labelled 'Writing Presentation' category (2004, 16, 98–113) in the analysis of Alice Munro's fiction. It has proved particularly convenient in the analysis of the short story 'Corrie', because it has facilitated the foregrounding of particularly significant passages in the development of the relationship between the two protagonists, which is marked by this type of discourse presentation. Similar conclusions might be reached in this story, since Lloyd's letter is the only purportedly unmediated access the reader has to his words and thoughts.

hint that she blames herself for that decision. This might be regarded as one of the secrets or gaps in the story that are never revealed.

All in all, the story is deeply disturbing, because it seems to convey that the unavoidable outcome of not keeping loyalty (and secrecy about certain aspects of their relationship) to her husband was necessarily this tragedy. In fact, when the third-person narrator reviews towards the end of the story Doree's thoughts about the beginning of her relationship with her husband, the following words are used: 'she had felt no guilt, only a sense of destiny, submission. She had felt that she was put on earth for no reason other than to be with him and to try to understand him' (28). This type of focalization does not contribute to providing a clear morale and neither does it seem to pass judgement on either the husband or the wife, but portrays very clearly that this type of relationship situates women in a no-win situation, where there is no graceful way out.

Nonetheless, Doree emerges as a survivor rather than as a victim; she is able to do good to others, to save the life of a boy whom she did not know and to redeem herself. Contrary to the expectations that may have been created in the reader at first, in the end, the comparison with gold that her name suggests comes to shine, and the stereotype of the young, vulnerable, manipulated woman, who lacks autonomy and agency, is contested.[5] The use of the secret contributes to this effect both thematically and in terms of narrative structure. On the one hand, the secret of the abusive nature of the relationship between the protagonist and her husband is gradually revealed, not presenting her as a victim from the beginning. On the other hand, focalization from Doree's point of view allows for only a partial characterization of her husband, so that the final killing of the children will strike the reader as a surprise. Finally, the reasons why the husband commits the murder are never satisfactorily revealed, unless the generic category of madness is accepted as an explanation, just as the reader is never told whether Doree feels guilty or not. These are all narrative gaps that prevent the reader from judging these characters from an ethical point of view.

'Free Radicals'

Pondering on the implications of secrets, Toolan writes that it is frequent to 'think that telling a secret will vanquish it, but [we] may find on the contrary that its disclosure brings disaster' (2013, 206). Much to the contrary, the story 'Free Radicals' is an outstanding instance of how creating a secret narrative allows a woman to survive (Munro 2010, 116–37). It deploys the most extraordinary confidants: a murderer / burglar and one of his victims. In the fashion of Scheherazade, Nita saves her life by making up a story. After her husband's death, a man breaks into her house and threatens her. While demanding food, he tells her that he has murdered his sister and parents. His

---

[5] This does not necessarily mean that the story ends on a happy note, since as Cox notes survival 'does not necessarily mean full recovery', neither for the boy, nor for her (2013, 287).

sharing of this secret with her seems to lead necessarily to her sacrifice, because no witness of the crimes he has just confessed can be expected to continue living.

In this story, Munro uses some of the techniques deployed in 'Dimensions', such as the use of a third-person narrator, focalization through the main female character and a selection of lexical items that hide references to future key developments in the story, which go almost unnoticed at first reading. The third-person narrator, after setting the backdrop for the story, gives way to the first sentence in direct speech: 'How was I to know he'd steal my thunder?' (Munro 2010, 117). The idiom 'to steal (one's) thunder' means to get the attention that another person has been receiving for something they have accomplished or announced. Here Nita's husband's death diverts people's attention from her cancer diagnosis. The use of this idiom to begin the narrative makes the reader believe that the story will deal with the situation of disease, loss and grief of a woman (a widow now) during old age. What is relevant, however, is that the idiom contains the word 'steal', a concept that will be vital later in the story. It is one of the clues that is left for the attentive reader or 'rereader', the one that reads for the hidden treasure to savour (Calinescu 1993, 262).

In fact, the first seven pages deal with Nita's situation after her husband's death and her memories of how their relationship started. Another clue of what is to befall later is the way in which she phrases the need to enter her dead husband's study, as described in the initial pages of the story: 'One of these days she would have to enter. She thought of it as *invading*' (120; emphasis added). Although in a first reading, this passage will be taken as referring to Nita's feelings about her late husband's study room, it anticipates the turn the story will take a couple of pages later: a man will *invade* her home. In the next paragraph, a further detail contributes to the cumulative effect of clues, when she recalls her husband's mocking of her habit to bolt the cellar door on the kitchen side (121).

Then Munro 2010, there is a sudden turn of events as a man appears in the house, entering under the pretence that he has to look at the fuse box. Very quickly it becomes clear that his intentions are criminal, but the tension is built up by his demanding first something to eat and then to be listened to. Nita plays nonchalant to the point of not inquiring about his story, whereas he clearly wants to tell her about what he has done. The reader learns so from the narrator's report through indirect thought presentation: 'She knew he wanted her to ask what had he done. She was also sure that the less she knew the better for her' (127). There is suspense, as it seems that the reader will not find out, but the intruder insists on imposing his narrative, which he finally reveals: feeling that his parents were unfair in their treatment of his disabled sister and himself, he has shot the three of them.

At this moment the story presents what Toolan has described as 'one of Munro's enduring interests: the unpredictable ways in which we choose to tell our secrets to one person and not to another, and the complex reasons, sometimes hidden even from ourselves, why we do so' (2013, 197). Nita quickly realizes the burden of the secret the intruder has shared with her. Until this moment, she had been trying to keep calm thinking that the cancer she is suffering is already an impending death sentence. These thoughts that the reader is made aware of, but not the intruder, lose their strength at this point and just as the term 'free radicals' she was trying to remember comes to her mind, a strategy for saving her life materializes. She decides to trade secrets and makes up a story to tell him, according to which she is also a murderer, having poisoned her husband's lover. As the reader knows, ironically, her role in reality had not been that of the affronted wife, but that of the lover. This use of irony allows for an additional feeling of complicity with the reader and reinforces Nita's position of power.

Although the third-person narrator makes the reader privy to this exchange of secrets, the rest of the characters in the story are intentionally excluded from the secret. That is the case of the police officers who visit Nita in the resolution of the story. They report to her that a thief and murderer has totalled her late husband's car. She does not reveal at any point that the criminal had been in her house and that she had managed to get rid of him on her own. Indeed, Nita had been strong and creative enough to convince the assaulter that she herself had murdered her late husband's lover, thus saving her life through this story, without the help of the clueless authorities or anybody else. The intruder leaves just menacing her: 'You just remember a word outta you and there'll be a word outta me.' (137). This image is very much in opposition to the stereotype of the old, lonely, sick and vulnerable lady that the reader might have expected initially. In this instance, a story turns a presumably helpless woman in mourning and suffering from cancer into a powerful and clever survivor. Probably, to some extent this is possible because of what Cox describes as a 'certain existential freedom [that] derives from both the social exile of old age and the lack of investment in a long-term future' (Munro 2010, 2013, 288).

As in the previously analysed story, 'Dimensions', the choice of third-person narrator focalizing on the protagonist, and the thematic, idiomatic and structural use of the secret make this reversal of the perception of the female character possible. Although the third-person narrator allows the reader to learn how the people surrounding the protagonist sympathize with her on account of her age, her recent widowhood and her illness, the secrets shared with the reader, but not with the rest of the characters, construct a much more complex, ingenious and powerful old female character.

'Child's Play'

In contrast to 'Dimensions' and 'Free Radicals', 'Child's Play' (Munro 2010, 188–224) deploys a first-person narrator, which has different implications for the construction of the narrative secrets and the relationship between the reader and the main character-narrator. It is probably one of Munro's most shocking and surprising stories, because of the ways in which the secret contributes to shaping the narrative. The architecture of this story deploys two sets of clues or indicators that operate in opposite directions and counter each other systematically: one set seems to direct the 'first-time and (probably) one-time, curious linear reader' (Calinescu 1994, 448) to follow the development of a friendship between two girls from their childhood to the last moments of one of them. As in the first story analysed here, 'Dimensions', the use of a non-linear chronology diverts the readers' attention at crucial moments in the narrative, not allowing them to dwell for too long on the clues that might have revealed the final surprise. The other set of hints invites the 'critical rereader' (ibid.) to discover and connect the secrets encoded in the narrative that build up the final surprise.

The story revolves around three girls, Marlene, Charlene and Verna, and is built on the terrible secret (that Marlene and Charlene drowned Verna) shared by the two former girls, kept for a lifetime and not revealed to the reader until the end of the story. The mood of the story changes dramatically from the beginning (where a melancholic view of female complicity, even sorority, is offered) to the resolution (where the reader is made aware of the cruelty of the two children and their rejection of those who are different). Moreover, it debunks stereotypical conceptions of the candour of children and the solidarity among girls, while it turns the familiar appalling and makes the appalling incidental. Because of the first-person narration, the reader does not learn until the very end of the story that the narrator and her friend are not ordinary girls with exciting childhood memories, but are murderers. It allows the suspense to increase gradually, making the final surprise more powerful.

'Child's Play' opens with Marlene's first-person narration, recalling her parents' reaction to some unspecified tragic incident that involved someone described as 'her . . . The poor thing' (188). Similar to the previously analysed stories, which offer at first sight ordinary and conventional situations, some lexical items work as a warning signal that will probably be overlooked in an initial reading. A stunning understatement, or alternatively a wonderful play on polysemy, hits the attentive rereader in the next sentence, when the narrator mentions the 'foibles' of her 'distant infantile state' (ibid.). The phrasing calls attention onto itself because of the formal and almost archaic expression, with which the narrator seems to search the greatest possible detachment from that distant childhood. However, it is the term 'foible' that offers wider ground for interpretation: in its first meaning it makes reference to a 'minor weakness or failing of character' (*Collins English Dictionary*). Indeed, the story's ending reveals the narrator should have been made accountable for much more than minor weaknesses. On the other hand, the second meaning of 'foible' is the 'weaker section of a sword blade, from the middle to the tip' (*Collins English Dictionary*). In fact, metaphorically, the weakest point of the narrator's life is her childhood, as she confesses at the end of the story.

Immediately after this passage, an extremely powerful sentence, 'Every year, when you're a child, you become a different person' (188), introduces the paragraph that ends in a sentence that contains a very enthralling foreshadowing of what is to happen:

> For a long while the past drops away from you easily and it would seem automatically, properly. Its scenes don't vanish so much as become irrelevant. And then there's a switchback, what's been all over and done with sprouting up fresh, wanting attention, even wanting you to do something about it, though it's plain there is not on this earth a thing to be done.
>
> 188–9

Semantically, the use of the verbs 'drops away' and 'sprouting up', which easily evoke collocations with water, start knitting a net of hints to the outcome of the story. However, the relevance of this statement will most probably go unnoticed at first reading, because, without further explanation, the narration jumps to a flashback that introduces the reader to the narrator's arrival at a summer camp. Marlene, the narrator, meets Charlene at that summer camp, where they are dubbed 'twins' because of their common features, such as their appearance and their rhyming names. They immediately take to each other and ground their friendship on a mutual distaste, mistrust and rejection of a girl called Verna, who seems to have some mental disability. Marlene, probably with the intention of captivating Charlene, exaggerates her dislike of Verna and presents her as a stalker and a freak. Marlene and Charlene develop and nurture those feelings towards Verna, escalating to absolute cruelty. Ultimately, Marlene and Charlene drown Verna without anyone noticing. However, that outcome is not revealed until the end of the story, after the reader learns how, on her deathbed after many years, Charlene makes a last effort to get in touch with her former friend and accomplice, because she wants Marlene to fetch a priest called Father Hofstrader from Guelph, but no explanations about her reasons are provided.

Little does the first-time reader expect that what is calling for attention from the past is remorse for a murder. However, the 'critical rereader' (Calinescu 1994, 448) will continue finding more lexical clues that anticipate what the story is really about. In this sense, the word 'special' also carries a great importance. In the summer camp, children with special needs, such as Verna, were called 'Specials' (201). When years later Charlene writes to Marlene to congratulate her on a professional achievement, she ends her letter with the sentence 'I always suspected you might do something special' (209). Marlene comments that although the word 'special' gave her 'a small jolt' (ibid.) when she thought of it later, she believes Charlene did not mean anything by it. This can be interpreted as a metanarrative comment about the reaction of 'critical rereader[s]' (Calinescu 1994, 448), who will experience a similar response, when noticing the regular intervals at which the word 'special' appears in the story. This reoccurrence calls attention to the expression itself and also links Marlene, Charlene and Verna.

Furthermore, when the narrator is describing her aversion for Verna, the victim in the story, making the reader empathize with her, a very telling adjective appears: 'Children of course are *monstrously* conventional, repelled at once by whatever is off-centre, out of whack, unmanageable' (195; emphasis added). Although the adjective may appear as a hyperbole on first reading, the reader later discovers that it describes precisely that monstrous dimension of children that the story addresses.

In addition, there are hints that may be misleading, upholding the interpretation of the story as focusing on a friendship rooted in the coming-of-age period of the protagonists' lives and helping to keep the secret of the two girls' crime until the last two pages of the story. Early on, there is a paragraph consisting of just one sentence, which reads as follows: 'There has to be great *trust*, of course, but that *trust* can be established at once, in an *instant*' (192; emphasis added). With hindsight, that 'instant' can be interpreted as the moment when Marlene and Charlene drown Verna, and the repetition of the word 'trust' points towards the secret that unites the two accomplices. However, in a first reading, it seems to simply allude to the kind of intimate relationship established between girls, who become friends, thus connecting with the notion of sorority.

Indeed, the first part of the story invites this interpretation on the part of the reader, as the narrator recalls how her friendship with Charlene started, how they explored all the things they had in common and also those they did not share. Immediately after, Marlene makes this tendency to explore points in common extensive to adult women, although she admits that being 'an anthropologist by training' (192) she has 'observed but never taken part in these female exchanges. Not truly' (193). There is no explanation at this point why she does not engage in this type of female confidence that she describes as usual. It is noteworthy that the last sentence in the quotation 'Not truly' again points to the secret she is hiding.

Not only the reader, but also other characters, will be misled into interpreting that Marlene and Charlene's friendship follows stereotypes of female bonding. This can be seen, for example, in the comments of Charlene's husband that the narrator reproduces: 'He [Charlene's husband] knew how much she [Charlene] valued me [Marlene] and now at the end of her life she seemed very keen to see me. She had asked him to get hold of me. It may be that childhood memories mean the most, he said' (213). Similarly, the nurse in charge of taking care of Charlene at the hospital is even further off track. She points to a still more intimate bond between the two women, based on the fact that the patient has asked her, and not her own husband, to hand a note to Marlene: 'Did she scent something illicit, a women's *secret*, an old love?' (214; emphasis added). If readers follow the nurse's suggestion, they will be as misled as the nurse and their surprise at the end of the story will be much greater.

Just a paragraph before the resolution, the reader might get some notion that the whole story partakes in the confessional genre: 'Was I not tempted, during all this palaver? Not once? You'd think that I might *break* open, be wise *to break open*, glimpsing that vast though tricky forgiveness. But no. It's not for me. What's done is done. Flocks of angels, tears of blood, notwithstanding' (220; emphasis added). There is a parallelism between this passage and the one from page 192, commented above, as both of them repeat terms that indirectly allude to the secret shared by Marlene and Charlene and its consequences (in this paragraph, 'break open', in the paragraph above, 'trust'). These passages are foregrounded by appearing as individual paragraphs set apart from the narrative flow. Again, the attentive reader may realize that these foregrounded excerpts contain relevant information about the outcome (or rather the origin in chronological terms) of the story, which constitutes the secret that Marlene and Charlene have kept hidden during all their lives.

When the final revelation arrives, it is remarkable that the crime is never really condemned. Instead, the narrator offers a tentative explanation or justification:

Charlene and I kept our eyes on each other, rather than looking down at what our hands were doing. Her eyes were wide and gleeful, as I suppose mine were too. I don't think we felt wicked, triumphing in our wickedness. More as if we were doing just what was – amazingly – demanded of us, as if this was the absolute high point, the culmination, in our lives, of our being ourselves.

222

Shockingly, although in a cautious way, the crime is presented as an utter accomplishment, a feat, an essential part of the girls' being. The female protagonist emerges once more as a survivor, who seems to make a pledge for forgiveness by presenting her behaviour as the only possibility under her circumstances.

First-time readers, who may have let a vision of ideal childhood adventures and sorority build in their minds as the story progressed, will have to deal with this final confession. In addition, they will have to come to terms not only with an absolute lack of condemnation of the terrible crime, but also with its justification. It is precisely the choice of the first-person narrator and the finally revealed confessional mood that make this lack of denunciation possible. The 'critical rereader' (Calinescu 1994, 448) will be invited to connect the dots that had been hidden in the story and reflect on the complexity of life from childhood to old age.

Conclusions

As has been shown in the analysis of secrets in three stories from *Too Much Happiness* (2010), this paper argues that Alice Munro's skilful manipulation of secrets not only captivates the reader, but also singles out individual women who challenge conventional models of femininity. It is common for her stories to foreshadow relevant future events in such a subtle manner that these hints may remain unnoticed on a first reading. The information about these events is gradually released, unlocking secrets for the reader and inviting a critical rereading and an attentive appreciation of her narrative craft. This technique also allows Munro to eschew a moral judgement of her female characters, defying all forms of simplification, while frequently cheating readers' expectations.

Instead of constructing stories that judge her characters or cast them into pre-existing models of femininity, she creates protagonists that emerge as survivors in diverse ways. This analysis has shown that these women are able to survive the domination of abusive men ('Dimensions'), to stand up to criminals breaking into their house ('Free Radicals') and even to carry the burden of a murder committed during childhood ('Child's Play'). In addition, the study of these stories has exposed that these characters are too multifaceted and elusive to be simplified or easily categorized in traditional terms.

Alice Munro's mature writing reflects the culmination of her lifelong career. This maturity, a lifetime of experiences and of creating stories, seems to make moral judgement according to traditional models of behaviour superfluous. The acceptance of the complexity of human existence appears in its place. Although it is not exclusive to her last two collections of stories, this tendency to shun judgement appears more evident than ever. Instead, her plea is for forgiveness of behaviours that do not follow ordinary and generally accepted patterns. As the narrator in the title story from *Dear Life* reflects, '[w]e say of some things that they can't be forgiven, or that we will never forgive ourselves. But we do – we do it all the time' (Munro 2013, 319). It could be argued that this is the best confirmation of Edward 'Said's view that there is something radical, even transgressive, in the writings of old age' (quoted in Cox 2013, 289–90).

References

Abbott Cox, Ailsa. (2004), *Alice Munro*, Tavistock: Northcote.
Abbot, H. Porter. (2008), 'Unreadable Minds and the Captive Reader', *Style*, 42 (4): 448–67.
Bigot, Corinne. (2017), 'Life and Death, Lines of Flight, Patterns of Entrapment and Survival in Alice Munro's "Dimensions" and "Runaway"', in Oriana Palusci (ed.), *Alice Munro and the Anatomy of the Short Story*, 97–110, Newcastle Upon Tyne: Cambridge Scholars.
Calinescu, Matei. (1993), *Rereading*, New Haven: Yale University Press.
Calinescu, Matei. (1994), 'Secrecy in Fiction: Textual and Intertextual Secrets in Hawthorne and Updike', *Poetics Today*, 15 (3): 443–65.
Collins English Dictionary – Complete and Unabridged, 12th edition 2014, accessed 2 April 2020. https://www.thefreedictionary.com/foibles.
Cox, Ailsa. (2013), '"Age Could Be Her Ally": Late Style in Alice Munro's *Too Much Happiness*', in Charles E. May (ed.), *Critical Insights: Alice Munro*, 276–90, Massachusetts: Salem Press.
Cox, Ailsa. (2016), '"Rage and Admiration": Grotesque Humour in *Dear Life*', in Robert Thacker (ed.), *Alice Munro: Hateship, Friendship, Courtship, Loveship, Marriage: Runaway, Dear Life*, 184–202, London and New York: Bloomsbury.
Díaz Dueñas, Mercedes. (2019), 'Understanding the Secrets in Alice Munro's "Corrie" through Speech, Writing and Thought Presentation Analysis', in Miguel Ángel Martínez-Cabeza, Rafael J. Pascual, Belén Soria, and Rocío G. Sumillera (eds), *The Study of Style*, 111–24, Granada: Editorial Universidad de Granada.
Elliott, Gayle. (1996), '"A Different Tack": Feminist Meta-Narrative in Alice Munro's "Friend of My Youth"', *Journal of Modern Literature*, 20 (1): 75–84.
Godard, Barbara. (1984), 'Heirs of the Living Body: Alice Munro and the Question of a Female Aesthetic', in Judith Miller (ed.), *The Art of Alice Munro: Saying the Unsayable*, 43–71, Waterloo, Ontario: University of Waterloo Press.
Heller, Deborah. (2005), *Literary Sisterhoods: Imagining Women Artists*, Montreal: McGill-Queen's University Press.
Houston, Pam. (1992), 'A Hopeful Sign: The Making of Metonymic Meaning in Munro's "Meneseteung"', *Kenyon Review*, 14 (4): 79–92.
Hoy, Helen. (1991), 'Unforgettable, Indigestible Messages', *Journal of Canadian Studies*, 26 (1): 5–26.
Hunter, Adrian. (2004), 'Story into History: Alice Munro's Minor Literature', *English*, 53: 219–38.
Irvine, Lorna. (1986), *Sub/Version*, Toronto: ECW Press.
Kamboureli, Smaro. (1987), 'The Body as Audience and Performance in the Writing of Alice Munro', in Shirley Neuman and Smaro Kamboureli (eds), *A Mazing Space: Writing Canadian Women Writing*, 31–8, Edmonton: Longspoon/NeWest.
Löschnigg, Maria. (2016), '"Oranges and Apples." Alice Munro's Undogmatic Feminism', in David Staines (ed.), *The Cambridge Companion to Alice Munro*, 60–78, Cambridge: Cambridge University Press.
McGill, Robert. (2016), 'Alice Munro and Personal Development', in David Staines (ed.), *The Cambridge Companion to Alice Munro*, 136–53, Cambridge: Cambridge University Press.
Martin, Walter Rintoul. (1982), 'The Strange and the Familiar in Alice Munro', *Studies in Canadian Literature/Études en littérature canadienne*, 7 (2), accessed 2 March 2018, https://journals.lib.unb.ca/index.php/SCL/article/view/7985.

Munro, Alice. (1974), 'Everything Here is Touchable and Mysterious', *Weekend Magazine*, 11 May: 33.
Munro, Alice. (2010) (2009), *Too Much Happiness*, London: Vintage.
Munro, Alice. (2013) (2012), *Dear Life*, New York: Vintage.
Phelan, James and Peter J. Rabinowitz. (2013), *Narrative Ethics*, BRILL, accessed 22 January 2020, http://ebookcentral.proquest.com/lib/ugr/detail.action?docID=1581545.
Rasporich, Beverly. (1990), *Dances of the Sexes: Art and Gender in the Fiction of Alice Munro*, Alberta, Canada: The University of Alberta Press.
Redekop, Magdalene. (1992), *Mothers and Other Clowns: The Stories of Alice Munro*, London and New York: Routledge.
Said, Edward. (2006), *On Late Style: Music and Literature against the Grain*, New York: Pantheon.
Semino, Elena and Mick Short. (2004), *Corpus Stylistics: Speech, Writing, and Thought Presentation in a Corpus of English Writing*, New York: Routledge.
Struthers, J. R. (Tim.) (2000), 'Alice Munro', in Erin C. Fallon, R. C. Feddersen, James Kurtzleben, Maurice A. Lee, and Susan Rochette-Crawley (eds), *Reader's Companion to the Short Story in English*, 288–98, New York: Routledge.
Toolan, Michael. (2002), 'Narrative Secrets in Alice Munro's Stories', in Szilvia Csábi and Judit Zerkowitz (eds), *Textual Secrets: the Message of the Medium*, 413–18, Martonvásár: Akadëmiai Nyomda.
Toolan, Michael. (2004), 'Expectations in the Process of Reading the Long Story: Alice Munro's "The Love of a Good Woman" and Tobias Wolff's "The Barracks Thief"', in Wolfgang Görtschacher, and Holger Michael Klein (eds), *Tale, Novella, Short Story: Currents in Short Fiction*, 193–206, Tübingen: Stauffenburg.
Toolan, Michael. (2008), 'Narrative Progression in the Short Story: First Steps in a Corpus Stylistic Approach', *Narrative*, 16 May (2): 105–20.
Toolan, Michael. (2013), 'The Complex Tangle of Secrets in Alice Munro's *Open Secrets*', in Charles E. May (ed.), *Critical Insights: Alice Munro*, 195–211, Ipswich, Massachusetts: Salem Press.

5

Zoë Wicomb and the secrets of the canon

Liani Lochner

Reading and the canon

In an interview given in 1990, about three years after the publication of her first short story collection, *You Can't Get Lost in Cape Town* (1987), the South African writer Zoë Wicomb voiced her objection to readings that saw in this work's protagonist, Frieda Shenton, a thinly veiled version of the author herself. Although Frieda, like Wicomb, is from a small community in the Little Namaqualand, attends school in Cape Town and the University of the Western Cape, and eventually furthers her education in England, readers' failure to notice the literary strategy of resurrecting Frieda's mother who is deceased at the beginning of the narrative in the last short story, 'A Trip to the Gifberge', was, for Wicomb (1993), indicative of the reception of black women writers at the time: 'whether they write in the third person or not, they're always received as if it is autobiographical, almost as if we're incapable of artifice, incapable of fictionalising ... It's as if all that is expected of us is the authentic experience' (93).[1] Wicomb's comments speak to the reception of postcolonial literature that finds its meaning – what it is *about* – in the background of the author and the novel's socio-cultural and political context, turning its interpretation into acts of ethnography or biography. This reading of the postcolonial work as a social document treats the text as 'transparent' (Wicomb 1996, 47),[2] a surface that the reader can penetrate to gain in-depth knowledge of the author's world, its interpretation irrevocably intertwined with the dominant narratives on the history of the place and the people depicted; it is a literature without secrets.

Wicomb's concerns hinge on the notion of the reader's expectation of black, female writers as purveyors of cultural knowledge, an instrumentalization of the postcolonial text that suggests an unidirectional relationship between the reader, text (and thus author)

---

[1] Wicomb still seems to be on guard against such interpretations of her works: the protagonist of her latest novel, *October* (2014b), is, like Wicomb, a coloured South African academic originally from the Little Namaqualand, who is now attached to a Glasgow university. At an author reading of *October* in 2015, however, Wicomb was careful to mention her grandchildren before introducing this work as a novel about childlessness. (The event was *The Language of Literature – Attridge at 70*, an international conference celebrating Derek Attridge's contribution to literary studies, held at the University of York on 22–24 May 2015.)

[2] In Wicomb's words, '[t]he structure of the black text has been repressed and treated as if it were transparent' (1996, 47).

and context; the writing is asked 'to explain the society that it comes from' (Wicomb 1993, 93). This, it can be argued, is the unintentional consequence of the postcolonial project's valorization of voice and agency, the ability of the postcolonial subject to speak for herself and also for a previously marginalized community.[3] The standard of authenticity welds this writing to its immediate socio-cultural and political contexts, denies the universality of the postcolonial text and fixes it on the margins of the canon. Put differently, and in terms of the relationship between reading and knowing that this chapter examines, this reception values the work for the knowledge it yields about the context(s) it purportedly depicts over how the structures of writing complicate the reader's ability to know; however, in considering both the content and the form of postcolonial literature, we can make a claim for how this writing expands the notion of the literary itself.

As I will argue through a close reading of Wicomb's short story 'In Search of Tommie' (2009) and with reference to her novel *Playing in the Light* (2006), her writing puts particular pressure on the notion of the postcolonial author as a placeholder for the kind of knowledge the literary text is thought to yield. Keenly aware of the historically embedded categories and concepts the reader brings to the work of literature, including ideas about the author's supposed knowledge of the context itself, Wicomb repeatedly *stages* authorship to link the reader and the writer in the ongoing processes of meaning-making; in doing so, she subverts attempts to authenticate the work through the author's biography and reveals the supposed knowing of the context as created in the mutually implicated events of writing and reading.

Questioning the nature of reading and interpretation itself has been, since its founding, part of postcolonial studies' challenge to the canon's hidden biases. In one of the first texts of the field, *The Empire Writes Back* (1989, with a second edition in 2002), a work published around the same time as Wicomb's collection, Bill Ashcroft, Gareth Griffiths and Helen Tiffin argue that the very idea of canonicity contains a set of implicit suppositions: 'A canon is not a body of texts *per se*, but rather a set of reading practices (the enactment of innumerable individual and community assumptions, for example about genre, about literature, and even about writing)' (2002, 186; emphasis in the original). Thus, the authors called for a radical re-examination of the criteria of value used to select texts for inclusion, and for 'the reconstruction of the so-called canonical texts through alternative reading practices' (187).[4] Chinua Achebe's critique of Joseph

---

[3] To support this claim, it will suffice to refer briefly to two founding texts of postcolonial literary criticism, namely Said's *Orientalism* (1978) and Spivak's 'Can the Subaltern Speak?' (1988). Said uses as one of his epigraphs a quotation from Marx's *The Eighteenth Brumaire of Louis Bonaparte*: 'They cannot represent themselves; they must be represented' (qtd. in Said 1978, epigraph). Both Said and Spivak interrogate the structures of power that mute colonial subjects and construct them as objects of knowledge within colonial discourse.

[4] In relation to this point, Wicomb claims that:

> [t]here is absolutely nothing you can do about the reception of your work – no point in even thinking about it. But institutions can and do play a powerful role in undermining the canon. Never before have teachers produced such defiant syllabuses, or have such outré works been studied at universities. Not only a question of resisting the canon, but of teaching young people to think for themselves what they consider to be good and why they do so.
>
> 2002b, 189

Conrad's *A Heart of Darkness* (2016) and Edward Said's of Jane Austen's *Mansfield Park* (1993) are probably two of the most well-known examples of the 'suspicious reading' of colonial-era texts for their ideological prejudices and historical erasures. Readings of postcolonial literature, on the other hand – and this is the reception to which Wicomb points – have been informed by the desire of the postcolonial project to subvert the silencing of the colonial subject constructed as a stereotyped, essentialist other by colonial discourse. Postcolonial literature's counter has thus been, as Seán Burke formulates it, 'a defence of the specificity of the subject, the grounding of the text in the irreducible personal and cultural experience of its author ... a reassertion of the subject in his/her particularity' (2000, xxviii). Influenced by the work of Barbara Harlow and others,[5] scholarly practice has tended to focus on postcolonial writing as literatures of resistance that give us access to the voices of those who were silenced by colonialism and who bear the brunt of neo-colonialism, the hallmark of which is neoliberal globalization marked by inequality and migration. It is crucial that this critical work continues, but my concern in this chapter is with how this situated reception of postcolonial literature, which privileges its reading as responses to culturally specific experiences of domination and violence to which the author is supposedly privy, grants the postcolonial writer and her work authority to speak only about sectional, politicized interests. This kind of allegorical reading maintains the idea that the 'most valid epistemology' (Wilm 2017, 220)[6] is found in postcolonial literature's content rather than its formal structures. Read as oppositional literature, postcolonial literature is given a 'critical function' (Derrida 1992, 38).[7] However, to claim that this writing can challenge dominant ideologies and dogmas through direct exhortation or empirical evidence is, as Derrida states in an interview with Attridge, to 'limit literature by fixing a mission for it, a single mission. This would be to finalize literature, to assign it a meaning, a program

---

Wicomb's observation speaks to changes within the academic community about the regimes of value used to evaluate literature. As I will argue in this chapter, however, reconsidering the value of a certain kind of postcolonial writing can come about only as a response to a call from the work itself; it is not the result of the application of a certain schema or reading practice.

[5] See Elleke Boehmer's *Postcolonial Poetics: Twenty-First-Century Critical Readings* (especially the first chapter, 'Postcolonial Poetics: A Score for Reading', 2019, 1–17).

[6] In 'The J. M. Coetzee Archive and the Archive in J. M. Coetzee', Jan Wilm warns scholars against the temptation to reinstall 'a very limiting notion of authorial intention' by viewing the material in Coetzee's personal archive at the Harry Ransom Centre at the University of Texas, Austin, 'because it has been private for so long', as more authoritative than his published works: 'Such scholarship ... may revert to traditions of criticism such as biographical, Marxist, Freudian, Lacanian, and Ricoeurian approaches, that found meaning in the secret, the hidden, the suppressed ... The most valid epistemology, as this belief holds, never stays on the surface, never in the light, it never focuses on what is *there*' (2017, 219–20; emphasis in the original). It should be noted, however, that Wilm's use of the word 'secret' here refers to that which was not previously known, whereas this chapter engages with a different notion of the secret, as related to alterity and otherness. See also *Beyond the Ancient Quarrel: Literature, Philosophy, and J. M. Coetzee* (2017), edited by Patrick Hayes and Jan Wilm.

[7] Derrida discusses this phrase after noting that he was one of the signatories to a document affirming literature's 'critical function' (1992, 38) after the Ayatollah Khomeini's call for Rushdie's death. Derrida, however, resists the instrumentalization of literature in the service of identity politics and defends the 'irresponsibility' of the author, 'of refusing to reply for one's thought or writing to constituted powers', as related to his notion of the 'democracy to-come' (ibid.).

and a *regulating ideal*, whereas it could also have other essential functions, or even have no function, no usefulness outside itself' (1992, 38; my emphasis). In responding to postcolonial literature only as an expression of material resistance, we turn it into a social document, a 'regulating ideal' that, in effect, denies its literariness.

If we respond to literature *as literature*, Attridge argues in *The Singularity of Literature* – as forms of writing distinctly different from others such as journalism, the latter a discourse with information as its aim – we gain insight into the 'fundamental processes whereby language works upon us and upon the world' (2004, 130). Literary form, he argues, produces 'a suspension of linguistic instrumentality, a blocking of the aesthetic urge to separate form from content and to assign content alone to the domain of ethics and politics' (119). 'Hospitable reading' (2015, 305) in Attridge's formulation, means being open to this performance of language that can result in a radical reshaping of the reader's understanding of the context that is depicted and of the nature of literary representation itself. Elleke Boehmer's *Postcolonial Poetics: Twenty-first-Century Critical Readings* brings this renewed attention to form to bear on postcolonial literature and calls it a 'postcolonial poetics'; this approach examines the content of the form and asks 'how writing as *writing*, and as *received* by readers, gives insights into aspects of our postcolonial world' (2019, 2; emphasis in the original).[8] Expanding Boehmer's notion of a 'postcolonial poetics', I draw on Derek Attridge's theory of the singularity of literature, a conceptualization of literariness that hinges to a great extent on the idea of the secret, to question the nature of the knowledge gained through reading the postcolonial text. Reformulating Ashcroft, Griffiths and Tiffin's 'reading practice' as a 'reading experience', I will argue, invites a re-examination of postcolonial literature's peripheral position in the canon.

To formulate his definition of the singularity of the literary work 'not as an attribute but as an event' (2011, 47) in *Reading and Responsibility: Deconstruction's Traces*, Attridge develops Derrida's notion of the secret. In 'Passions', Derrida writes of 'a secret without content, without content separable from its performance experience' (quoted in Attridge 2011, 47); in the *Points* interview, he claims the secret 'is not a thing, some information that I am hiding or that one has to hide or dissimulate; it is rather an experience that does not make itself available to information, that resists information or knowledge' (quoted in Attridge 2011, 47). The event of literature, then, 'happens, each time it is read or listened to, so that it is not a matter of surface and depth but a movement of meaning and of feeling that has to be repeated to be apprehended again' (ibid.). In other words, and as applied to postcolonial texts, the reading of a work of literature entails an experience of the performative power of language that prevents the reader from easily transcending its form (surface) and locating meaning only in its content (depth). Moreover, lived through as a temporal event, this reading results not in a form of knowledge that can be taken away from the text, but rather an experience

---

[8] Although both Attridge and Boehmer are concerned with form, their approaches are different: Boehmer draws on relevance theory in linguistics, and Attridge's work is an extended engagement with the ethics of Derrida and Levinas. In *Postcolonial Poetics*, Boehmer does not address Attridge's work extensively, but there seems to be a general indebtedness to the latter's conceptualization of the literary.

of knowing (or not knowing). What does restoring this notion of literariness and the secret to the reading of postcolonial literature mean for its interpretation as an authentic depiction of an experience of cultural domination?

'[N]o matter how relentless the analyser', Attridge argues, 'the literary work is secret because it is singular: it cannot be exhaustively analysed in terms of general codes and conventions' (2011, 46). The postcolonial work, when responded to as literature, cannot fully be known, even if the reader is thoroughly informed about the cultural context depicted. It is thus significant that Wicomb's South African critics – prominent scholars cited in this chapter such as Attridge (2005a), Dorothy Driver (2010a; 2010b) and Andrew van der Vlies (2010; 2011; 2017; 2018), amongst others – have repeatedly noted that her oeuvre is characterized by formal invention that puts pressure on the reader's attempts to finalize its meanings. Reading from within the culture, these scholars should, according to the conventional approach to postcolonial literature in the Western imaginary, have unique access to the cultural knowledge represented in her texts. Her work, however, as Andrew van der Vlies points out, consistently undermines 'totalizing racial categories', cultural identities, and 'official histories' (2018, 11), and thus is not easily subsumed in the dominant narratives on apartheid and post-apartheid South Africa that have framed the reception of its literatures internationally. This does not mean that her work lacks cultural specificity – as Attridge asserts, for example, 'we cannot forget, once we are aware of them, Wicomb's own Griqua origins' (2005a, 159) – but her representation of this community sits uneasily with the notion of cultural identity.[9] This is perhaps the reason why Wicomb is not known particularly as a postcolonial writer, despite so clearly fitting the criteria, writing as a black female writer from and about a country that has experienced the double colonization of British imperialism and apartheid's white hegemony. The very literariness of her work, which evidences traces of the Derridean undecidable, the secret that invites attentive reading, means that she is not recognizable as a postcolonial writer who trades in narratives of authenticity.[10] The formal inventiveness of her work demands a hospitable reading that is open to a reshaping of the expectations of black women's writing.

This chapter thus identifies Wicomb as an author of literary writing that makes a particular demand on both the reader and on the cultural field from which it emerges.[11]

---

[9] Both her work as a critic (as Van der Vlies's edited collection of her essays including an incisive interview underscores) and as a writer (cf. the criticism of, amongst others, the scholars mentioned above), is marked by cosmopolitanism, the notion of the translocal, and a highly critical engagement with authority and authorial responsibility. See *Zoë Wicomb: Race, Nation, Translation* (2018), edited by van der Vlies, and *Zoë Wicomb and the Translocal: Writing Scotland and South Africa* (2017), edited by Kai Easton and Derek Attridge.

[10] Wicomb is also a famously self-effacing author, who publishes with not-for-profit presses and rarely gives interviews. Responses to her works are marked by the repeated claim that she should be more well-known than she is.

[11] Literature, as a cultural product, is situated within a specific historical and cultural context, but is not contained by it; it is always available for reading in contexts very distant from its time and place of origin. This has to do with the structure of a text, 'its iterability', according to Derrida, 'which both puts down roots in the unity of a context and immediately opens this non-saturable context onto a recontextualization' (1992, 63).

What we respond to in a literary work, Attridge argues in *The Work of Literature*, 'can be described in terms of an independent trio of properties, *singularity*, *alterity* or *otherness*, and *invention*' (2017, 252; emphasis in the original):

> that the work that comes into being in our performance of it strikes us with its difference from all other works, its singularity; by its challenge – great or small – to the norms and habits by which we comprehend the world, its otherness; and by the sense that its coming into being as we experience is an opening onto new possibilities of creativity in thinking, feeling, and knowing, its inventiveness. In responding fully to the work, therefore, we are changed – perhaps only momentarily, perhaps permanently – as we adjust our own frames of understanding, our own habits of feeling, our own ways of knowing to allow us to perceive what is before us in its singularity.
>
> 252–3

The reader's encounter with the secret of literature is an experience of alterity, a confrontation with that which they do not know or could not know, because it has been occluded by the cultural order in an effort 'to maintain its capacities and configurations, its value systems and hierarchies of importance'. These 'fresh possibilities', the otherness that the literary text introduces, thus transcend the normative horizon set by the existing cultural order, even if it is always in relation to it (Attridge 2004, 30). Zoë Wicomb's work, in the reading put forward here, introduces new ways of thinking about the relationship between authentic knowledge, postcolonial authorship and authority, and the nature of knowing the postcolonial world through reading its literature. The reading experience, I will argue, imaginatively dislocates the reader from the presumed outsider view of another culture or group that has lived through a form of domination from which standpoint this community is inevitably seen as a cohesive whole. Rather, Wicomb's staging of authorship confronts the reader with writing that can only ever yield a knowledge traversed by secrets, by experiences of not knowing that transcend the dominant discourses on the world depicted. This potentially forges a different kind of reader who can create new communities beyond the identity politics of the time.

Otherness and the universal reader

The authority granted to literature as yielding insights into real-world contexts or conditions informs almost all reading. Seen as a repository for cultural values, literature is a form of narrative that mediates between individual experience and social totality. Literary writing thus, as Derrida argues in *Of Grammatology*, 'almost always and almost everywhere' lends itself to a '*transcendent* reading' (1976, 160; emphasis in the original);[12] that is, we locate the meaning of the work in the context. And, as Fredric

---

[12] For an extended discussion on the notion of transcendent reading, see Attridge's interview with Derrida, 'This Strange Institution Called Literature', collected in *Acts of Literature* (1992, 43–8).

Jameson (1982) cautions us, the individual's approach to the text is informed by their political unconscious – a notion Attridge expands to include the 'embodiment in a single individual of widespread cultural norms and modes of behaviour' and calls an 'idioculture' (2004, 21–2); interpretation itself is thus 'an essentially allegorical act' (Jameson 1982, 10), as we draw on existing structures and frameworks of knowledge to make sense of a text, including our conception of the role of literature in society. For Ian Watt, the genre of the novel itself, born in the eighteenth century, as he postulates in his seminal work, *The Rise of the Novel: Studies in Defoe, Richardson and Fielding*, is characterized by an emphasis on realism, human truths and its attempts 'to portray all the varieties of human experience', unlike the old-fashioned romances (1963, 11). According to Watt, authors such as Defoe and Richardson revolutionized our understanding of what literature is, basing their plots not on 'mythology, history, and legend' but on 'a belief in the individual apprehension of reality through the senses' (14). Watt's account does not offer a comprehensive picture of the landscape of eighteenth-century fiction, but the kind of literary realism that he identifies as a feature of this new genre foregrounds a view of the individual as a knowing subject that, arguably, still provides literary study in the West with a powerful template to think about authorship. It is significant that one of Watt's examples is Daniel Defoe's *Robinson Crusoe: The Life and Adventures of Robinson Crusoe, of York, Mariner ... Written by Himself* (1719), a seemingly autobiographical account of one man's encounter with the new world, which not only drew on the popularity of travel narratives as a way to gain knowledge of faraway lands at the time,[13] but also linked this knowledge to the authority of the writer as an experiencing consciousness. Arguably, it is this authority that postcolonial studies draw on when it argues for the agency of the silenced other, for the ability of *Robinson Crusoe*'s man Friday, as it were, to represent himself.[14] The problem is not only the fixing of the colonizer–other relationship in the canonical text, in Helen Tiffin's well-known argument in 'Post-Colonial Literatures and Counter-Discourse' (1987), but that what postcolonial literature knows is still inextricably tied to Friday as the figure of the postcolonial writer. Thus, while Robinson Crusoe's is the universal experience and encounter with otherness, Friday, as the suppressed voice of the other, speaks only for that colonized, racialized subject.

Wicomb's objections to the reductive expectation of black women writers as authors only of autobiographies cited at the beginning of this chapter were raised in the charged

---

[13] See the *Cambridge Companion to Robinson Crusoe*, edited by John Richetti, specifically Eve Tavor Bannet's chapter, 'Robinson Crusoe and Travel Writing: The Transatlantic World' (2018, 128–41).
[14] For Dennis Todd (2018, 144), Britain's indifference to the impact of the imperial project on colonized peoples is 'captured in that chilling image in J. M. Coetzee's postcolonial retelling of the Crusoe story in his novel, *Foe*: Friday's tongue has been cut out, robbing him of the capacity to tell his own story, to articulate his own identity, or to vindicate his own culture'. Todd's reading of Coetzee's *Foe* can be used here as an example of the 'instrumental reading' in Attridge and Wilm's formulation. It is never confirmed in Coetzee's novel that Friday's tongue has been removed; rather, it is one of the unknowable elements in the novel and reflects, more broadly, Coetzee's concern with the impossibility of knowing those who are rendered other within a particular normative framework and the ethical anxieties of representing the other in the very language through which they are excluded. See Attridge's *J. M. Coetzee and the Ethics of Reading: Literature in the Event* (2005b).

context of the demise of the apartheid state and against the backdrop of the identity politics that marked the emergence of postcolonial literature as a field of academic inquiry. Her concerns, however, continue to resonate beyond these contexts, as even a cursory overview of the networks of representation in which postcolonial literature circulates reveals: writers note expectations that black or female writers will 'naturally and properly' write from 'personal experience ... which translates as writers of colour writing about racism, female writers writing about sexism, and female writers of colour writing about racism and sexism' (Clark 2018), or that, based on templates inherited from the classical traditions, women can speak 'to their own sectional interests, but not speak for men or the community as a whole' (Beard 2017, 16). The institutional positioning and international marketing of postcolonial literature are similar to what the philosopher Julian Baggini identifies in the supposed universalism of Western philosophy, which means that studying comparative philosophy is left 'to people working in anthropology or cultural studies' under the assumption that it 'might help us to understand the intellectual cultures of India, China or the Muslim world, but not the human condition' (2018, n.p.n.). These examples suggest the dominance of a Western epistemological framework and the idea that normative reading always takes place across cultures or gender – that is, the female or black writer is the *other* to the universal reader who is, then, implicitly and typically constructed as white and male.

These readerly expectations of difference and authority are reinscribed by the international marketing of postcolonial literature. As Juliet Gardiner argues, while critical theory (thinkers such as Barthes, Foucault, Derrida) has taught us not to think of the 'historical concrete individual ... as the expressive subject of his or her text',[15] 'the [postcolonial] author has been commodified in particular ways that recuperate the biographical subject and reify authorial intention' (2000, 256). Several critics have pointed to postcolonial authors' complicated and compromised relation to being turned into spokespersons for their cultures informed by reductive narratives on their experiences of colonialism as one they both critique and indulge (and even profit from). Drawing on Graham Huggan's work in *The Postcolonial Exotic: Marketing the Margins* (2001),[16] Sarah Brouillette claims, '[t]he postcolonial author has emerged as a profoundly complicit and compromised figure whose authority rests, however, uncomfortably, in the nature of this connection to the specificity of a given political location' (2011, 3–4). For Wicomb, this has meant being received as an authority on coloured identity: '[I]t may be hard to believe', she tells her interviewers, 'but I honestly

---

[15] As J. Hillis Miller remarks, 'the assumption that the narrator of a novel, for example, must not be identified with the author, however tempting and plausible that identification may be, is the most commonplace of assumptions in literary criticism these days' (2002, 65).

[16] The 'postcolonial exotic', as coined by Huggan, 'marks the intersection between contending regimes of value': 'postcolonialism', which is anti-colonial and challenges 'imperial epistemologies' and 'institutional structures', and 'postcoloniality', that 'capitalises' on 'ideas of cultural otherness' and the worldwide marketing of 'culturally "othered" artifacts and goods' (2001, 68). Ideas of the construction of otherness, the resistance to this construction, and the other rendered as exotic still ask the postcolonial text to answer for its contexts. Moreover, they maintain a relationship between the reader and the author of the postcolonial work that is formed and informed by an expectation of authentic knowledge.

did not know that *You Can't Get Lost in Cape Town* was crucially about coloured identity, not until a critic pointed that out – nobody after all was talking about coloureds in the 80s, the very label had been rejected in the period of resistance' (2002b, 184). Although Wicomb acknowledges the validity of this interpretation – 'they are, of course, right' (2010, 26) – she also identifies a critical practice that recuperates the work for identity politics similar to the dominant mode of reading I have described thus far in this chapter when she asserts, 'in another era in which identity isn't a fashionable topic, one might well have settled on other aspects of the work' (ibid.).

The positing of a universal Western reader who relates to the female postcolonial author and her work only as a cultural other – and grants her authority to speak for this context – is challenged by the reader's encounter with the secret of the work of literature. Wicomb's staging of authorship, as I will illustrate through a brief overview of critics' responses to *Playing in the Light*, foregrounds the acts of writing and reading as experiences of not-knowing that undermine the authority that is granted both to the postcolonial author and to the prevailing understanding of the contexts depicted. The secret thus collapses the incommensurable reading communities implied in Huggan's postcolonial exotic and by Jameson's putative ignorant American reader who feels inadequate in comparison to the 'ideal reader' who is from and will better understand this 'alien' cultural context and thus resorts to a reading explained by already-existing narrative expectations of what the work of the cultural, racial or gendered other is about (Jameson 1986, 66).[17]

I am wary of suggesting a causal link between Wicomb's concerns expressed very early in her career and their fictional representation in a creative work published in 2006 (in paperback in 2008), as it seemingly reinforces the very autobiographical reading this chapter resists. However, it is significant that the reception of *You Can't Get Lost in Cape Town* (1987) that she notes with some disbelief in these interviews, namely that this is an autobiographical exploration of coloured identity, makes its way into *Playing in the Light*, a novel set against the backdrop of the Truth and Reconciliation Commission hearings of the mid-1990s. Indeed, it is possible to read this novel as a particularly literary response to the treatment of the text of a black woman's writing as 'transparent'. *Playing in the Light* is a story of racial passing in which Marion Campbell, raised as white, discovers that her coloured parents became play-whites after the Population Registration Act came into effect in apartheid South Africa. Marion's confrontation with this family secret is not presented as a movement between two distinct identities or communities, from a white to a coloured South African; its revelation results in the questioning and shifting of her self-definition. As María J. López's recent essay on the novel convincingly argues, in Marion's attempts to read the traces of the archive to come to grips with this newly discovered identity as a coloured South African, she encounters only enigmatic, undecipherable signs 'that cannot be endowed with meaning' (2019, 711), which present 'identity-making and representation as an ever-open performative process' (710).

Significant for my argument here is the novel's revelation, in its last pages, of Brenda McKay, a coloured employee who accompanies Marion in her uncovering of the story

---

[17] It is Neil Lazarus (2011) who, in defence of Jameson's much-maligned argument, identifies Jameson's American reader as an ideological construct with which to critique the 'schooled' problematic of reading across cultural difference.

of her parents, as the possible narrator (even author) of the novel we have just read. *Playing in the Light* offers Marion's story as narrated by a third-person omniscient narrator. As Dirk Klopper claims, the 'narrative voice speaks as if from inside [Marion's] consciousness. It is an immanent voice, intimately hers, tracking her thoughts and feelings, conjuring up her memories, recording her responses' (2011, 149–50). Extended sections are focalized through her father, John Campbell, accounting how he and his wife, Helen, came to transgress apartheid's racial classifications. When Brenda reveals to Marion that John has divulged his past to her, and this is the story that she wants to write, 'the story that should be written' (Wicomb 2008, 217), Marion responds vehemently: 'Why don't you write your own fucking story?' Brenda's response, in wording that echoes Wicomb's cited comment at the beginning of this chapter, is telling: 'I know it's a rhetorical question, but let me answer all the same. Writing my own story, I know, what someone like me is supposed to do, what we all do, they say, whether we know it or not' (ibid.). As both van der Vlies (2010, 593–8) and David Hoegberg (2018, 494–500) argue, referencing the novel's allusion to Toni Morrison's *Playing in the Dark*, this artifice positions Brenda as a potential 'subject' of this narrative rather than as an 'object' representing a coloured identity that Marion has difficulty negotiating. She is both the narrator and a character in her own story. This overt fictionalizing, however, keeps the text's secret: the reader is unable to know whether Brenda is indeed the narrator and cannot reach definitive conclusions about the narrative as filtered through her consciousness and politics. As various critics' responses to this revelation of Brenda's potential authorship towards the end of the text show, the reader is impelled to revisit their interpretation of Marion's story, not from the point of view of her consciousness, but as mediated through the writing of another.[18]

Wicomb's *Playing in the Light*, then, collapses a unidirectional relationship between the reader and the text, and the idea that the authority of interpretation resides only on the part of the narrator or the implied author. It is in acknowledging the reader's performance by the language of the postcolonial text that we can understand how literariness can trouble expectations of authentic reading. The encounter with the secret is not the result of a particular demand the reader makes of the text – a suspicious reading to reveal the hidden meanings of the text – but a hospitable response to a call that comes from the text itself. As I will show through a reading of Wicomb's 'In Search of Tommie', the hospitable reader is performed not only into questioning the authority of authorial representation but also the nature of knowing that results from reading.[19]

---

[18] Hoegberg, for example, draws on van der Vlies's commentary and performs a 'systematic rereading of the novel's allusions' (2018, 485), especially Brenda's intertextual references to T.S. Eliot's 'The Love Song of J. Alfred Prufrock' and the work of the South African poet, C. Louis Leipoldt (494–500). According to Hoegberg, 'both the range and strategic complexity of [Brenda's] uses of texts' evince her 'ambition to resist this imposed writerly identity of simplicity and directness' (494).

[19] Wicomb's repeated staging of female authorship includes protagonists such as the already-mentioned Frieda Shenton, the unnamed narrator of *David's Story* (2002a) and Mercia Murray in *October* (2014b), and, as discussed, the implied, but not confirmed, narrator of *Playing in the Light*, Brenda McKay. Making the supposed author of the text a character in the text subverts readers' expectations of the knowledge they will gain about so-called coloured identity, Griqua nationalism, female guerrillas in the anti-apartheid struggle, and racial passing.

Knowledge and the autobiographical author

As there can be no inventiveness without a reader, the literary emerges only in a particular relationship between the reader and the text (which includes the act-event of writing). Derrida claims the impossibility of an essentialist definition of literature: 'Literarity is not a natural essence, an intrinsic property of the text': 'there is no text which is literary *in itself*' (1992, 44; emphasis in the original). Literature has no universal characteristics but is that which arises in a reading that acknowledges both its language, or form and its context.[20] The enjoyment the reader experiences from responding to a text as literature, Attridge argues in *The Singularity of Literature*, does not come from any knowledge we acquire, but 'from the experience of an event of referring, from a staging of referentiality'. In being engaged by the work, we take pleasure in a particular use of language, in 'the *performance* of fictionality', through our awareness that the characters and events being referred to 'are in fact, and without this fact being disguised, brought into being by the language' (2004, 96; emphasis in the original). In Wicomb's short story, 'In Search of Tommie', knowledge is not represented as a noun, as something that can be taken away from the text, but as knowing, as a verb, as the text both stages and engages the reader's affective desire for meaning.

Wicomb's works often announce the theoretical framework with which the novel performs an aesthetic engagement; as Driver argues, theory is not incidental to Wicomb's work, but should be seen as a form of intertextuality (2010b, 150). Thus, in *David's Story*, David's amanuensis announces her valuing of 'meaning in the margin, or absence as an aspect of writing' (Wicomb 2002a, 2), and in 'Art Work', Letty is exasperated with the 'nonsense' Leo talks with his friends 'about the coordinates of space and time' (2014a, 2). In *October* (2014b), it is not incidental that the academic Mercia Murray embarks on a memoir at the same time as she is working on a monograph on postcolonial memory. The reading put forward in this chapter suggests that Wicomb's 'In Search of Tommie' stages and subverts readerly expectations of autobiography through the insertion of the female author figure.

Driver, interpreting the interweaving of the personal and the historical in Wicomb's short story collection, *The One That Got Away* (2009),[21] claims that 'as the figure of the biographical author enters the text, scattering clues for anyone with any research initiative to see (or perhaps to avoid as decoys), so too does she proclaim the author as necessarily produced by that text' (2010a, 536). In 'In Search of Tommie', one of Wicomb's female author figures appears in the character of the androgynously named Chris Hallam who is described, by a character looking at a photograph on the dust jacket of her novel, as 'a slim woman, with short, frizzy hair, and big, strong features' (Wicomb 2009, 52). Based on this description, van der Vlies (2017, 137) identifies

---

[20] In Miller's words, '[t]he essence of literature, if it can be said to have an essence, is not something that descends from on high, from some supernatural realm. It is "produced" by occasions of writing and reading that are historically embedded "acts"' (2002, 63).

[21] As 'In Search of Tommie' was initially intended for inclusion in this collection, Driver's interpretation can be extended to this short story.

Hallam as a cipher for Wicomb herself, a reading supported by any of Wicomb's books' dust jackets, and one that is invited by her propensity to include biographical details in her works. But, of course, this could be the description of a myriad of women in the real world – or Wicomb or no one, for that matter, as Chris Hallam, as far as the reader can know, exists only on the page. As J. Hillis Miller states, explaining Derrida's notion of literature's secret in 'Derrida and Literature', '[a]ll hypotheses about the meaning of a text are permitted not because the reader can make it mean anything he or she likes but because there is in principle no access to the secret originary ground that might verify one of them' (2002, 73). Hallam, Driver's remark reminds us, exists only as a literary phenomenon, and the surface of the text resists penetration towards any secret depth. After all, as Attridge asserts, '[a] work of art states what it states, presents what it presents, no more, no less; and it refuses to say anything further, no matter how hard we press it' (2017, 256).

So, why is the reader invited to detect Wicomb – without verification – in the text? Although van der Vlies is careful to maintain the notion of the author figure as a cipher – thus a site for multiple interpretations – others, such as Chantal J. Zabus (2013) definitively locate Hallam, a fictional female author, in Wicomb's biography. Hallam's 'fictionalized autobiography', Zabus writes, 'ghosts that of Zoë Wicomb, who often writes of passing and whose character in *Playing in the Light* ... is a white woman who comes to the realization that she is the daughter of Coloured parents' (2013, 215). Although this claim contains some puzzling assertions – that Wicomb 'often' writes of play-whites or that Hallam's story or Marion Campbell's in *Playing in the Light* in any way mirrors Wicomb's own – Zabus's reading, which transcends the text by locating its meaning in the author's supposed biography, is one that is staged in Wicomb's short story.

The story, 'In Search of Tommie', is focalized mostly through TS, a young black South African man who reads Hallam's book, in which she gives an account of growing up black in an English town, her Venda father having abandoned her and her mother for a family in Africa, with a 'tingling sense of recognition' (Wicomb 2009, 52). TS knows 'instinctively' – because 'how else could one know such a thing' (51), the text claims – that this is his father, Tommie, who abandoned them to have an English family after being 'ensnared' by an English woman (52). This is what his mother keeps telling him. Even though he knows Tommie only through his mother's stories, he immediately claims kinship with Hallam, convinced that this English woman is his half-sister. He ignores his friend Joe's warning that Hallam's story is 'a fictionalised autobiography, something about its postmodernness' (53). Zabus cites the notion of a 'fictionalised autobiography', but like TS, her interpretation focuses only on the text's possible autobiographical meanings (that is, its content) and not on its performative qualities (that is, the fictionalization of the author's knowledge). Although TS supposes that this postmodernness 'accounted for the jumping about of the story, the fact that he was not always sure of what was going on' (Wicomb 2009, 53), he still reads it as a work of realism, not only ignoring its artifice, but also ascribing authorial intention. He is convinced that Hallam's intention in writing the story was to discover 'her own African roots. Why else would she have written the book?' (53). If literature, as Miller argues in his reading of Derrida's work, 'depends on the possibility of detaching language from its firm embeddedness in a social or biographical context and allowing it to play freely as fiction' (2002, 60), then T S's reading of Hallam's text negates its literariness.

Hallam, who responds to T S's invitation to meet the family while in Cape Town for a book fair, is surprised at their refusal to engage in any form of dialogue: they 'offer no information and ask no questions'; 'they have no interest in what she knows of her father ... they don't ask; they do not require her to say anything' (Wicomb 2009, 53). In fact, her biological father left when she was three, and she has never even seen as much as a photograph of him. However, when T S finally offers his mother's own remaining photograph of the missing father – with Joe still pointing out that there is no family resemblance and Hallam's intent left in doubt – she yields to T S's interpretation and declares her recognition of the man in the photograph as the missing Tommie: 'It is as if she has walked on to a stage to deliver learnt lines from a surrealist script. Whatever will she say next?' (55).

It is tempting to read 'In Search of Tommie' as Wicomb's skewering of the reader in search of biographical details (in other words, Wicomb is Hallam and the reader is TS who has turned the story into an autobiography), but then, doing so would be to map the story onto her own expressed objections to being read autobiographically. It would also be missing the short story's intertextual reference to T. S. Eliot, which as van der Vlies argues, 'insists on the connection of all narratives that presume any measure of authority to all others, which might complicate such authority (or any pretense at originality)' (2018, 17). Moreover, it would be to ignore T S's affective motivations for dismissing the story's artifice, its textual strategies for representation.

Wicomb's 'In Search of Tommie' thus seems to enact what Rita Felski calls the literary text's performance of 'a metacommentary on the traps of interpretation, a canny reading of its own possible readings, a knowing anticipation and exposure of all possible hermeneutic blunders' (2009, 29).[22] And similarly, Wicomb might as well be one of the authors Sarah Brouillette has in mind when she draws on Graham Huggan to claim that 'postcolonial literature evinces a complicated process of indulging, resisting and critiquing its imagined consumption, and will distinguish between readers worthy of applause and those in need of some re-education' (2011, viii). Both of these commentaries on literary interpretation, however, stay within the realm of knowledge – of reading the text correctly or of being in the know with regards to the work of literature's cultural contexts. Wicomb's complex textuality, I argue, performs the reader into recognizing their own interpretive needs and strategies. In Gourgouris's formulation, '[o]ne gains a sense of knowing something other than the knowledge that comes from the words one has read, a knowledge that alters not only one's relation to those words but also the relation to one's sense of self as a "knowing subject"' (quoted in Attridge 2017, 255). T S's search for his father, the man who authored him as it were,

---

[22] In her essay 'After Suspicion', Felski's own notion of neo-phenomenology suggests an approach beyond this, paying attention to 'the stylistic and narrative devices that shape aesthetic experience' (2009, 31).

is mirrored in his attempts to locate the author behind the character in Hallam's story, which, in turn, is reflected in the reader's search for Wicomb in the text. On the one hand, the reader is invited to judge TS as a particularly inept one, approaching Chris Hallam's novel as an autobiographical work, ignoring his own motivations for treating the text as transparent or even the author's ability to know and to convey that knowledge through language in the novel form. Within the short story already, TS's interpretations are seemingly undermined when the focalization shifts to Hallam: she does not know what her father looks like, and she has no burning desire 'to meet her African relations' (Wicomb 2009, 54). The reader is also given no insight into why she wrote the book, but only that she got around to writing it after the death of the man, not her biological father, who raised her and whom she calls Dad. Within the parameters of the story-world itself, there is no originary ground, as the titular sought-for Tommie is as absent from the text as he was from TS's life (not to mention that his death before the events of the short story marks a permanent absence). Like the unnamed absent father in Chris Hallam's novel, Tommie exists only as a character in TS's mother's stories, a cipher on whom they can project their longing and anger.

The reader becomes aware of this only through Wicomb's apparent doubling into an *autre*biographical self, to use Coetzee's term from *Doubling the Point* (1992, 394). Hallam's apparent physical resemblance to Wicomb makes it impossible for the reader to maintain a critical distance from the text, a position from which to evaluate TS's reading; rather, the reader is implicated, with the author, in a co-constructive imaginative engagement with the meaning of the story. As Driver notes regarding Wicomb's project, '[i]f any notion of authority persists in Wicomb's writing, it resides only provisionally in the act of reading; the writer continually hands authority over to the reader, having educated the reader, as it were, through irony and paradox' (2010a, 538). 'In Search of Tommie', however, also leads to a questioning of this readerly authority itself. Although the text keeps its secrets – the reader neither *knows* whether Wicomb is really describing herself or even intending the reader to recognize her in the description, nor does the story confirm that Hallam is indeed Tommie's daughter – the reader's interpretative drive (the end goal of all reading), similar to the dying Tommie's affective needs, seeks the closure of meaning. 'In Search of Tommie' thus performs the reader into questioning her own desires and abilities to know.

Conclusion

Unlike the supposed universal male Western reader and the exoticism that according to Huggan and Brouillette characterizes the circulation of the postcolonial text, Wicomb's reading communities do not stand outside of the text, even if they are foreign to its contexts, and the possible knowledge her texts yield is created in the mutually implicated events of writing and reading. In a field of literary study and a popular reception that is so marked by the desire for knowledge, Wicomb's writing, especially in her staging of an encounter with the autobiographical author, performs the reader into questioning the limitations put on the meanings of the text in search of authentic representation through the biography of the writer. Like TS does to Hallam, the author and the text have no choice but to yield to this interpretation. But if this experience changes the reader – and as this is always a singular experience, it is a claim I can make only of myself as reader – it is not, as Attridge points out, because 'we've added to our store of knowledge, it's because, in gaining access to the work's alterity, singularity, and inventiveness, we've discovered new ways of knowing (and perhaps new ways of not-knowing)' (2017, 258).

This inventiveness of the literary work – its singularity – is what, for Attridge, determines its longevity, its ability to invite hospitable readings and an experience of alterity across cultures and across time. Ashcroft, Griffiths and Tiffin remind us of the assumptions of value that determine the selection of texts for inclusion in the canon; ironically, the very cultural specificity that gives the postcolonial text its symbolic value (Huggan 2001) – in anglophone postcolonial literature, an authentic knowledge of experiences of domination – excludes it from an 'ideologically and institutionally buttressed category of literature' that has 'its roots in the universalist ideology of English culturalism' (Ashcroft, Griffiths and Tiffin 2002, 209). Attridge's redefinition of the universality of the literary, as tied to the notion of the secret, however, gives us a way to transcend implicit judgements of value informed by ideas of culture, race and gender. The traditional explanation for the longevity of works considered canonical, Attridge asserts, 'is that certain writers explore universal human themes with consummate skill, so that their works are timeless, available to anyone who can appreciate good art. The question of context falls away, on the assumption that such works transcend both the conditions of their creation and the conditions of particular readings' (2017, 199); in this understanding of canonicity, the postcolonial text that is so irrevocably tied to its contexts cannot be considered universal. But even works not from the postcolonial world that address human universals never achieve canonicity, as Attridge points out. The secret, however, means that some works of literature are inventive not only in their own cultural context, but also in contexts beyond their own. Although literature 'is not a transhistorical and transcultural category but an institution and a practice with historical and geographical determinants and limits' (Attridge 2005b, 9 f14), the secret opens the possibility of introducing alterity into these cultural contexts and institutional practices. Recognizing a postcolonial poetics at work in postcolonial literature means, then, a renewed contestation of its peripheral position in the canon.

Ashcroft, Griffiths and Tiffin argue that '[r]eading practices ... [that] are resident in institutional structures, such as education curricula and publishing networks' (2002, 186) uphold and inform the canon and ideas of canonicity. The reading *experience* as an event of not-knowing – an encounter with the secret – invites a re-orientation in our approach to postcolonial literatures as forms of authentic knowledge. But more importantly, it asks us to reconsider the very points of departure of Western epistemologies and ways of constructing alien cultures or experiences as other. The literary event, thus, although exploding normative conceptions of community based on identity, can also be community forming. As Miller puts it, the encounter with the secret, with alterity, 'is the invention of the world because it is truly inaugural, initiatory, even legislative. Like a declaration of independence, it lays down new rules that imply a new "we," a new community, even a new political order. The other invents me, and through what I do invents others, a community' (2002, 70). This invention is neither the result of the agency of 'a we or a community of researchers in the usual sense, working according to the rules', nor is its effect a community that can be identified in advance (ibid.). Hospitable reading, as Attridge tells us in *The Work of Literature* (2017, 280–305), can have communal, political and ethical effects without reducing the literary work to a manifesto or social document: although the experience of otherness is always singular – no two readers will respond in the same way to a work – it is through the individual reader that otherness can enter the cultural field. The engagement with Wicomb's *Playing in the Light* and 'In Search of Tommie' recounted here was a response to a call that came from these works themselves, a demand on the individual reader to acknowledge and relinquish conventional strategies for meaning-making that reduce the complexities of being part of and representing a community to the closures of identity. The transformative potential of this for the academic community, the 'new community' or 'new political order' in Miller's parlance (2002, 70) that can be inaugurated, lies not in contesting the canon's schemes of value by adding postcolonial literature to the curriculum, but in giving an account of reading as a potential experience of alterity that always contests identitarian notions of community.

References

Achebe, Chinua. (2016), 'An Image of Africa: Racism in Conrad's "*Heart of Darkness*"', *The Massachusetts Review*, 57 (1): 14–27.

Ashcroft, Bill, Gareth Griffiths and Helen Tiffin. (2002), *The Empire Writes Back: Theory and Practice in Post-colonial Literatures*, 2nd edition, London: Routledge.

Attridge, Derek. (2004), *The Singularity of Literature*, London and New York: Routledge.

Attridge, Derek. (2005a), 'Zoë Wicomb's Home Truths: Place, Genealogy, and Identity in *David's Story*', *Journal of Postcolonial Writing*, 41 (2): 156–65.

Attridge, Derek. (2005b), *J. M. Coetzee and the Ethics of Reading: Literature in the Event*, Chicago: University of Chicago Press.

Attridge, Derek. (2011), *Reading and Responsibility: Deconstruction's Traces*, Edinburgh: Edinburgh University Press.

Attridge, Derek. (2017), *The Work of Literature*, Oxford: Oxford University Press.

Baggini, Julian. (2018), 'About Time: Why Western Philosophy Can Only Teach Us so Much', *The Guardian*, 25 September 2018, www.theguardian.com/news/2018/sep/25/about-time-why-western-philosophy-can-only-teach-us-so-much, accessed 27 September 2018.

Bannet, Eve Tavor. (2018), 'Robinson Crusoe and Travel Writing: The Transatlantic World', in John Richetti (ed.), *The Cambridge Companion to Robinson Crusoe*, 128–41, Cambridge: Cambridge University Press.

Beard, Mary. (2017), *Women and Power: A Manifesto*, New York: Liveright.

Boehmer, Elleke. (2019), *Postcolonial Poetics: 21st-Century Critical Readings*, London: Palgrave Macmillan.

Brouillette, Sarah. (2011), *Postcolonial Writers in the Global Literary Marketplace*, London: Palgrave Macmillan.
Burke, Seán. (2000), 'Introduction', in *Authorship: From Plato to the Postmodern: A Reader*, xv–xxx, Edinburgh: Edinburgh University Press.
Clark, Alex. (2018), 'New Elizabethans / The Best British and Irish Novelists Today', *TLS*, 5, September 2018, https://www.the-tls.co.uk/articles/public/best-british-and-irish-novelists-today/, accessed 24 September 2018.
Coetzee, J. M. (1992), 'Retrospect', in David Attwell (ed.). *Doubling the Point: Essays and Interviews*, 389–95, Harvard, MA: Harvard University Press.
Derrida, Jacques. (1976), *Of Grammatology*, translated by Gayatri Chakravorty Spivak, Baltimore, MD: Johns Hopkins University Press.
Derrida, Jacques. (1992), '"This Strange Institution Called Literature": An Interview with Jacques Derrida', in Derek Attridge (ed.), *Acts of Literature*, 33–75, London and New York: Routledge.
Driver, Dorothy. (2010a), 'The Struggle Over the Sign: Writing and History in Zoë Wicomb's Art', *Journal of Southern African Studies*, 36 (3): 523–42.
Driver, Dorothy. (2010b), 'Review of *The One That Got Away*, by Zoë Wicomb', *English in Africa*, 37 (2): 145–52.
Easton, Kai, and Derek Attridge, eds. (2017), *Zoë Wicomb and the Translocal: Writing Scotland and South Africa*, London and New York: Routledge.
Felski, Rita. (2009), 'After Suspicion', *Profession*: 28–35.
Gardiner, Juliet. (2000), 'Recuperating the Author: Consuming Fictions of the 1990s', *The Papers of the Bibliographical Society of America*, 94 (2): 255–74.
Hayes, Patrick, and Jan Wilm, eds. (2017), *Beyond the Ancient Quarrel: Literature, Philosophy, and J. M. Coetzee*, Oxford: Oxford University Press.
Hoegberg, David. (2018), 'Building New Selves: Identity, "Passing," and Intertextuality in Zoë Wicomb's *Playing in the Light*', *Safundi*, 19 (4): 482–501.
Huggan, Graham. (2001), *The Postcolonial Exotic: Marketing the Margins*, London and New York: Routledge.
Jameson, Fredric. (1982), *The Political Unconscious: Narrative as a Socially Symbolic Act*, Ithaca, NY: Cornell University Press.
Jameson, Fredric. (1986), 'Third-World Literature in the Era of Multinational Capitalism', *Social Text* 15: 65–88.
Klopper, Dirk. (2011), 'The Place of Nostalgia in Zoë Wicomb's *Playing in the Light*', *Current Writing*, 23 (2): 147–56.
Lazarus, Neil. (2011), *The Postcolonial Unconscious*, Cambridge: Cambridge University Press.
López, María J. (2019), '"Moving in 'a Forest of Hieroglyphs'": Enigmatic and Mutable Signs of Identity in Zoë Wicomb's *Playing in the Light*', *Journal of Postcolonial Writing*, 55 (5): 710–22.
Miller, J. Hillis. (2002), 'Derrida and Literature', in Tom Cohen (ed.), *Jacques Derrida and the Humanities: A Critical Reader*, 58–81, Cambridge: Cambridge University Press.
Said, Edward W. (1978), *Orientalism*, New York: Vintage.
Said, Edward W. (1993), 'Jane Austen and Empire', in *Culture and Imperialism*, 80–97, New York: Alfred A. Knopf.
Spivak, Gayatri Chakravorty. (2006) (1988). 'Can the Subaltern Speak?', in Bill Ashcroft, Gareth Griffiths and Helen Tiffin (eds), *The Post-colonial Studies Reader*, 28–37, London and New York: Routledge.

Tiffin, Helen. (1987), 'Post-Colonial Literatures and Counter-Discourse', *Kunapipi*, 9 (3): 17–34.
Todd, Dennis. (2018), 'Robinson Crusoe and Colonialism', in John Richetti (ed.), *The Cambridge Companion to Robinson Crusoe*, 142–56, Cambridge: Cambridge University Press, Kindle edition.
van der Vlies, Andrew. (2010), 'The Archive, the Spectral, and Narrative Responsibility in Zoë Wicomb's *Playing in the Light*', *Journal of Southern African Studies*, 36 (3): 583–98.
van der Vlies, Andrew. (2011), 'Zoë Wicomb's Queer Cosmopolitanisms', *Safundi: The Journal of South African and American Studies*, 12 (3–4): 425–44.
van der Vlies, Andrew. (2017), *Present Imperfect: Contemporary South African Writing*, Oxford: Oxford University Press.
van der Vlies, Andrew. (2018), 'Zoë Wicomb's South African Essays: Intertextual Ethics, Translative Possibilities, and the Claims of Discursive Variety', in Andrew van der Vlies (ed.), *Zoë Wicomb: Race, Nation, Translation*, 3–33, New Haven, CT: Yale University Press.
Watt, Ian. (1963), *The Rise of the Novel: Studies in Defoe, Richardson and Fielding*, London: Penguin.
Wicomb, Zoë. (1987), *You Can't Get Lost in Cape Town*, New York: The Feminist Press.
Wicomb, Zoë. (1993), 'Zoë Wicomb Interviewed by Eva Hunter – Cape Town, 5 June 1990', in Eva Hunter and Craig MacKenzie (eds), *Between the Lines II: Interviews with Nadine Gordimer, Menan du Plessis, Zoë Wicomb, Lauretta Ngcobo*, 79–96, Grahamstown: National English Literary Museum.
Wicomb, Zoë. (1996), 'To Hear the Variety of Discourses', in M.J. Daymond (ed.), *Writing, Theory and Criticism (1990–1994)*, 45–55, New York: Garland.
Wicomb, Zoë. (2002a), *David's Story*, New York: The Feminist Press.
Wicomb, Zoë. (2002b), 'Interview with Stephan Meyer and Thomas Oliver. Zoë Wicomb Interviewed on Writing and Nation', *Journal of Literary Science/Tydskrif vir Literatuurwetenskap*, 18 (1–2): 182–98.
Wicomb, Zoë. (2008) (2006), *Playing in the Light*, New York: The New Press.
Wicomb, Zoë. (2009), 'In Search of Tommie', *Wasafiri*, 24 (3): 51–5.
Wicomb, Zoë. (2010), 'Washing Dirty Linen in Public: An Interview with Zoë Wicomb', in Ewald Mengel, Michela Borzaga and Karin Orantes (eds), *Trauma, Memory, and Narrative in South Africa: Interviews*, 19–29, Amsterdam: Rodopi.
Wicomb, Zoë. (2014a), 'Art Work', *Gutter: The Magazine of New Scottish Writing*, 10: 1–12.
Wicomb, Zoë. (2014b), *October*, New York: The New Press.
Wilm, Jan. (2017), 'The J. M. Coetzee Archive and the Archive in J. M. Coetzee', in Patrick Hayes and Jan Wilm (eds), *Beyond the Ancient Quarrel: Literature, Philosophy, and J. M. Coetzee*, 215–31, Oxford: Oxford University Press.
Zabus, Chantal J. (2013), *Out in Africa: Same-Sex Desire in Sub-Saharan Literatures and Cultures*, Melton, UK: James Currey (Boydell & Brewer).

Part Two

Communities of secrecy

6

Cryptaesthetic resistance and community in Jhumpa Lahiri's *The Lowland*

María Luisa Pascual Garrido

Introduction

Jhumpa Lahiri's work fictionalizes the experience of members of the Indian diaspora, exploring the consequences of displacement for a generation of Bengalis who moved to the US in the 1960s, as well as the effects on their Bengali-American descendants troubled by issues of self-identity and membership to a community. For this reason, most researchers have addressed Lahiri's fiction from the perspective of postcolonial and diaspora studies, focusing on the predicament of her exilic, hybrid characters and looking into the strategies they adopt to overcome their sense of displacement and not belonging (Dhingra and Cheung 2012; Nair 2015; Paudyal 2015). Although acknowledging the relevance of communitarian and identity issues in Lahiri's work,[1] approached from the perspective provided by postcolonial and diasporic critical discourse, my aim is to go beyond the scope of this existing research, which highlights the alienation and trauma of first-generation diasporic individuals and the troubled sense of identity of second-generation émigrés who inhabit a so-called 'third space' (Bhabha 2004, 55).

In order to add a new perspective to previous studies, I will consider different types of community in Lahiri's second novel, *The Lowland* (2013), drawing on the crucial distinction made by Nancy (1991) between 'operative' and 'inoperative' communities, which is closely related to Blanchot's conception of 'avowable' and 'unavowable' ones (1988). My aim is to illustrate the failure of the organic community of the family, a central concern in Lahiri's fiction, by focusing more specifically on the community of siblings formed by Subhash and Udayan Mitra as a case in point. I contend that in this novel, Lahiri's view of such organic forms of community is conflicting, since against the

---

[1] So far, Jhumpa Lahiri has published two short story collections – *Interpreter of Maladies* (1999) and *Unaccustomed Earth* (2008) – and three novels – *The Namesake* (2003), *The Lowland* (2013) and *Dove mi Trovo* (2018). Having moved to Italy, the writer adopted Italian as an alternative language of publication in 2015, when she published an autobiographical volume, *In Altre Parole*, which has also seen a bilingual edition (Italian/English) by the title *In Other Words* (2017), and *Il Vestito Dei Libri* (2016), also available in English (*The Clothing of Books*, 2017).

characters' longing for harmonious integration into an operative community, there emerges the painful evidence of its failure and absence.[2]

Furthermore, I also intend to analyse secrecy as a constitutive feature of *The Lowland*, thus implementing the communitarian reading of this narrative by relating secrecy and community. It is obvious that secrecy plays a very prominent role in a sequential reading of *The Lowland* (2013), as the novel traces the fate of a Bengali family throughout four generations with a focus on the intimate relationship between two brothers, Subhash and Udayan, and the family secrets concealed from Bela, Udayan's posthumous daughter. Secrets are clearly thematized too, not only because of the family's silencing of Bela's true parentage, but also to Udayan's hiding of his clandestine activities with the Naxalites[3] and of his love affair with Gauri.

Hence, after introducing the idyllic childhood of the siblings in Calcutta, allegedly based on their mutual identification and the indissolubility of family ties, the narrative tells of their separation as Subhash moves to Rhode Island and Udayan remains in Bengal. It then narrates the most significant events in Subhash's life away from India; and finally it provides an account of Bela's troubled existence, raised in America by her mother, Gauri, and her uncle, Subhash. Because of Udayan's untimely death, Gauri reluctantly agrees to marry Subhash, starting a new life together in America, which may somehow appease their common loss. Since Bela's true genealogy is only belatedly revealed to her, she grows up believing the caring Subhash to be her biological father and completely ignorant of Udayan's actual bond to her. The concealment of this family secret undoubtedly helps build up a compelling narrative sequence, evincing that in *The Lowland* secrecy operates quite effectively in this respect.

Yet, I contend that secrecy is even more significant beyond the obvious thematization of secrets and their role in the building of plot, for despite the eventual disclosure of secrets allowing Bela to be reconciled to her past, the text remains somehow cryptic and inscrutable, suggesting that textual secrecy is an essential feature of Lahiri's novel. I will argue this is mainly because of the pervasiveness of such motifs as the lowland, a meaningful place for the community of siblings and the family at large, whose symbolic import cannot be unambiguously established, leaving the narrative open to several interpretations. In order to validate this assertion, I will draw on Royle's notion of 'cryptaesthetic resistance' (2014, 48), which may be defined as the inbuilt opacity that turns literary texts into hermeneutically inexhaustible objects.

---

[2] Blanchot distinguishes between the 'failure' and 'absence' of community, using the second term to refer to a necessary event for community to take place: 'absence belongs to community as its extreme moment or as the ordeal that exposes it to its necessary disappearance' (1988, 15).

[3] The Naxalite movement emerged in 1967 in West Bengal (originally in the town of Naxalbari) led by some members (Charu Mazumdar, Kanu Sanyal and Jangal Santhal) of the Communist Party of India (CPI). The movement, intended to redress the obvious imbalance between the rich landowners and the landless, was conceived as an armed struggle necessary to take away the lands from the landlords and re-distribute the land among the poorest people. By 1971, the Naxalite movement had attracted the attention of youths in urban areas such as Calcutta who engaged in this struggle with violent actions against landlords, shopkeepers, teachers, political leaders and police (Stein and Arnold 2010, 408).

Therefore, after briefly reviewing the concept of operative community as theorized mainly by Nancy, one for which Blanchot uses the term 'avowable', I will first examine the organic community of siblings formed by Subhash and Udayan, and then consider its evolution towards a non-operative form of community. In doing so, I intend to establish a connection between, on the one hand, Lahiri's concern with community in *The Lowland* and, on the other, the role of secrecy in the emergence of inoperative communities as an alternative to distinctly organic and supposedly operative ones such as the family. Although other kinds of community – both operative and inoperative – are portrayed in *The Lowland*, they will not be considered in detail because, as the constant allusions connecting the lowland to the sibling community reveal, it is that specific kind of community that Lahiri seems most interested in exploring as an epitome of the communities articulated on the basis of blood ties. Next, I will identify several facets of secrecy in the novel, namely, the role of secrets in determining the success or failure of community, as well as in generating haunting effects on its members. Above all, I will concentrate on proving the cryptic nature of the text by pointing to the elusiveness of certain motifs, such as the lowland itself and the hollow banyan in *The Lowland*. My contention is that a close reading of the text does not easily yield an unambiguous interpretation of its central tropes, blending fusion and division, visibility and invisibility, and hence that *The Lowland* cannot clearly attest either to the presence or the absence of community. Finally, in order to prove the assertion that *The Lowland* is a text highly resistant to unequivocal interpretation, a comprehensive analysis of its key tropes is offered.

Operative and inoperative communities in Lahiri's fiction

In this chapter, I follow the view shared by Nancy (1991) and Blanchot (1988) that traditional communities such as the family, nation or race, intended to fulfil a need for individual immanence and transcendence within a collectivity, have always done so at the expense of singularity, as is evidenced by a number of historical communities Nancy (1991, 9) and Blanchot (1988, 6–7) mention. As Nancy puts it, the ideal of community has conventionally been based on the 'intimate communication between its members' but also on an 'organic communion with its own essence' (1991, 9). In this sense, that idealized operative community was 'made up principally of the sharing, diffusion, or impregnation of an identity' (ibid.).

Yet, the author further argues that the existence of an ideal community, a *Gemeinschaft* that has been destroyed or lost, is just a convenient myth accepted in the face of unbearable loneliness, for '*community has not taken place*', although we are deluded into believing there is a possibility of its recovery by preserving 'social bonds' (Nancy 1991, 11; emphasis in the original). The assumption that such a utopian community has never existed is hard to assimilate, especially when what is at stake is the most organic and primitive form of community: the family. According to Miller, fiction offers models of community either to uphold or criticize them (2015, 88), and Lahiri's fiction is not an exception in this respect. In fact, her novels and short stories make plain the author's great concern with the failure of the family as community, and so she sets off to explore the possibilities different kinds of community – family or, alternatively, friends and lovers – afford individuals profoundly distressed by their sense of not belonging and the absence of a place where they can properly feel at 'home'.

The troublesome relationship between the singular being and community in Lahiri's fiction is particularly poignant for the second generation of Bengali-Americans, hybrid, transnational beings who find it extremely difficult to fully identify with a single community, whether this is their parents' homeland or America, where they are born, raised and form new attachments. This is a common predicament of Lahiri's protagonists in her two short story collections, *Interpreter of Maladies* (1999) and *Unaccustomed Earth* (2008), and her first novel, *The Namesake* (2003). These second-generation émigrés feel profoundly isolated and distressed, sometimes to the extreme that they are even unable or unwilling to take roots, as it happens with Bela in *The Lowland*.

As I intend to illustrate, Lahiri, a second-generation Bengali-American herself, inscribes the quandary of those without community by engaging her readers with the failure of the organic community of the family. I contend that the pervasiveness of images where presence and absence overlap in *The Lowland*, suggests a hesitant position regarding the myth of the family as an idealized operative community where absolute communion is possible and total identification even desirable. Although in Lahiri's fiction the idea of such an organic community seems appealing at first, her stories also provide evidence of its impracticality. What is highlighted in *The Lowland* as well as in the rest of Lahiri's oeuvre is the manifest separateness of the singular being from the community, a pre-existing community believed to have vanished. As will be shown in this analysis, the lost community is generally symbolized by reference to an idyllic but far removed setting either in time or space.

Yet, according to Nancy, it is that hint of the loss of community that paradoxically allows for community to appear. Therefore, as an alternative to failed organic forms of community, there is the emergence of inoperative ones, which are postulated on seven categories: death, alterity, transcendence, singularity, exteriority, communication and finitude (Jiménez Heffernan 2013, 20). Instead of materializing as communal fusion, which implies a rejection of what is singular for the sake of community, as seems to happen to the Mitra brothers in their early years, the inoperative community emerges when the singular being is confronted with alterity, when facing the death of another singular being and hence his/her absence, thus exposing the being to its own finitude while simultaneously revealing what singular beings have in common: death (Nancy 1991, 15). In *The Lowland*, Subhash's geographical separation from his family as he moves to America just inaugurates this confrontation with community, but Udayan's death will attest its absence as will be discussed below. Thus, the inoperative community exposes alterity, for 'community is what takes place always through others and for others' (ibid.). Furthermore, there cannot be a community 'without the sharing of that first and last event which in everyone ceases to be able to be just that (birth, death)' (Blanchot 1988, 9). This conception of community implies the sharing and exposure of what is common to all beings – our mortality – and hence an interpellation to the other, however fragmentary and interrupted this communication may be. This kind of community, mainly predicated on exposure to and communication with the other, can only be understood as short-lived, happening just as an event because 'communication is the constituent fact of an exposition to an outside that defines singularity ... the presentation of the detachment ... of finitude compearing' (Nancy 1991, 29).

On the other hand, there also seems to be a connection between the failure of the operative community and the withholding of secrets in Lahiri's fiction. As singular beings realize their singularity when disagreeing with others in the community, they start keeping secrets. In contrast, the sharing of secrets, however incomplete, implies opening up to others, separate and different. Therefore, it is that awareness of not being identical and the willingness to approach others that is necessary in order for the inoperative community to emerge when the operative one fails. In Lahiri's work, the failure of the family community is particularly visible when its members decide to hide their insurmountable differences, and suspecting the fallibility of blood ties as the basis for community, they establish new attachments outside the family, in alternative or elective communities of friends and lovers that are inoperative and non-organic. An inoperative community can also develop from a failed operative one, when singular beings become aware of their singularity and make an effort to expose themselves to other singular beings.

The actual dispersion of members of the family abroad also provides excruciating evidence of the breakdown of the organic community and even questions its very existence in Lahiri's work. In *The Lowland*, the failure of community is anticipated even before Subhash's departure to America takes place. Hence, despite claims to an indissoluble intimacy on Subhash's part, who 'had no sense of himself without Udayan' because 'from his earliest memories, at every point, his brother was there' (Lahiri 2013, 7), as the siblings grow older, they disappointingly discover they are in fact two singular beings whose different wishes drive them apart. As a result, Udayan starts leading a secret life, hiding his risky political association with the Naxalites as well as his passionate love for Gauri. Udayan's gradual detachment from his closest relatives casts doubts about the indestructibility of the blood ties that are supposed to hold the family together. Furthermore, having been so close in childhood, Subhash experiences Udayan's aloofness as an unbearable loss even before he actually leaves India. Likewise, Subhash's intention to leave Calcutta is deeply regretted by Udayan, who plainly states: 'You're the other side of me, Subhash. It's without you that I'm nothing' (37). Several years later, Udayan's parents and his young wife Gauri will witness his execution in the lowland, an event that forces them to face his death as an irrefutable proof of the ongoing disintegration of the Mitra family. This tragic episode is a turning point in the lives of each one of its members, who remain since then literally and metaphorically disconnected from each other, attesting to the failure of the community.

In *A Taste for the Secret*, Derrida states that '[b]elonging – the fact of avowing one's belonging, of putting in common – be it family, nation, tongue – spells the loss of the secret' (Derrida and Ferraris 2001, 59). Seen in this light, secrecy would then be incompatible with the very idea of an operative or organic community, which is conventionally articulated by tropes of unity, fusion and identification. In such a community, communion removes any possibility of secrecy since everything is already shared and, hence, common.

However, the concealment of secrets from other members of the family is recurrent throughout Lahiri's fiction and also becomes a prominent issue in *The Lowland*, where the author seems to be contesting the utopian belief in operative communities based on an unconditional identification with the family. Although in these narratives members of the older generation, particularly mothers, view the family as a working community capable of granting a powerful sense of belonging and self-identity, members of younger generations look beyond the family to the formation of short-lived, elective communities, by sharing secrets with strangers, friends and lovers and exposing themselves to an alterity beyond the self.

The community of siblings

Although family relationships in general are addressed in *The Lowland*, it is certainly the intimate relationship between the two brothers that Lahiri explores in more depth. Applying the distinction between operative and non-operative communities discussed above, Rodríguez-Salas has deftly analysed the community of siblings in Katherine Mansfield's autobiographical and fictional writings, concluding that the writer manages to 'combine traits of both operative and inoperative communitarian impulses' in order to transform the organic view of community (2016, 67), based on an idealization of sibling intimacy through tropes of mystical unity and fusion, into an inorganic one that does not operate 'death into a substance' (70) and comes to admit the unworking of community by death.

The 'binary or dual community of siblings', to use Rodríguez-Salas' term (2016, 65), formed by Subhash and Udayan, is also initially conceived as being clearly operative and organic, as the brothers seem 'to crave the immanence of a shared community', but turns into an inoperative one, for it is through the shared awareness of the brothers' separation and ultimately 'through death that the community reveals itself' (ibid.). I contend that Lahiri also works with two alternative models of community when exploring the sibling community in this novel, as she highlights the existence of two opposite communitarian drives through a choice of mystifying tropes that simultaneously evoke union and separation, identity and difference, thus underscoring the difficulty of thinking community beyond dominant habits of thought.

In this regard, Nancy has interestingly remarked that 'fraternity' has for a long time designated 'community' as 'the model of the family and of love', a utopian conception that underlies the motto of the Republic of France (Nancy 1991, 9). However, as the author argues in a more recent essay, such a community has lost much of its former appeal as it is thought to have inherited the negative connotations of the familial, 'when the family is no longer a powerful reference' (Nancy and Clift 2013, 119). Pointing out the Christian, patriarchal and sentimental undertones implicit in the concept of fraternity, Nancy and Clift advocate a much needed reconceptualization of the community of siblings beyond the reductive idea of 'absolute identification' among members of the same family, which operates exclusively on the basis of a common blood line, that is, 'by way of the transmission of the seed' (120). Quite on the contrary, it is the process of nursing or nurturing (literal or symbolic), the sharing of 'the external discontinuous and mediated gift of a nutritional substance' that actually generates sibling intimacy through a process of 'incorporation' (121). What results from rethinking family ties in such terms is a new model of the family community and, consequently, of the community of siblings 'that is ... only the combination of chance (an encounter) and an embrace (desire)' (122). By the same token, such an understanding of the family implies acknowledging the existence of a variety of non-traditional familial configurations different from the traditional model that requires the identification and communion of its members with its substance.

Although Lahiri seems at first to yield to this powerful myth of community by associating the siblings with the fusion of the two ponds in the flooded lowland ('the ponds would rise so that the embankment built between them could not be seen' (Lahiri 2013, 3)), it could also be contended that the author is implicitly questioning the validity of the organic community, or at least, insinuating that we may be deceived into believing that there is a community – a single pool. Yet, what the watery surface of the lowland hides is in fact not the presence of one, but of two separate bodies of water, which stand for two separate or singular beings, suggesting division rather than unity. This ambiguity as to the actual nature of the lowland and of the bond that unites the siblings is underpinned throughout the narrative by the reiteration of a number of motifs where presence and absence, fusion and separation, coalesce.

The first chapters of the book definitely reinforce the idea that the existence of the community of siblings hinges on their being permanently together, 'not [losing] sight of one another', with an insistence on an astonishing physical resemblance that causes one to be 'perpetually confused with the other ... their voices [being] nearly indistinguishable', and to appear as if 'they were mirror images' (Lahiri 2013, 12-3). However, as time goes by, the siblings' growing rivalry and their need to assert their singularity will become patent in their determination to take separate paths so as to be able to pursue their individual goals: Subhash starts an academic career as a biologist in the United States while Udayan takes a modest teaching position in India, an undercover for his political activism. It is worth noticing that Subhash eventually leaves India 'not only for the sake of his education but also ... to take a step Udayan never would. In the end this was what had motivated him' (48). Furthermore, the experience of being radically different, evoked by the periodical disconnection of the two ponds in the lowland as the dry season comes, will be more poignantly underlined by the physical distance that ultimately keeps the two brothers apart when Subhash moves to Rhode Island. That geographical separation will definitely compel the brothers to confront the absence of community.

Thus, once settled in Rhode Island, Subhash believes he is 'drifting far from his point of origin' because there he feels 'that some part of him was missing, [that] he desired a companion' (Lahiri 2013, 48). Therefore, the siblings will start exchanging a few letters in a gesture that betrays their nostalgia for what they believe to be a lost community, their wish to remain somehow connected: '[Subhash] felt their loyalty to one another, their affection, stretched halfway across the world. Stretched to the breaking point by all that now stood between them, but at the same time refusing to break' (52). As

Blanchot states, 'community, in its very failure, is linked to a certain kind of writing' (1988, 12), and those letters, which necessarily leave many things unsaid, constitute an effort to share the interrupted myth of community. Their writing is the sort of fragmented communication that typically characterizes the inoperative community, as the brothers start writing to each other because they become aware of the absence of the other. As Nancy claims, 'communication is the constitutive fact of an exposition to the outside that defines singularity ... Communication is the presentation of the detachment (or retrenchment) of this distinction that is not individuation, but finitude compearing' (1991, 29). Therefore, however mystifying and unreliable, the letters Subhash and Udayan exchange indicate a wish to approach the other, to share the secret of community, the awareness that there is no such thing as an operative community. The letters must hence be regarded as an attempt to open up to alterity, to communicate on the part of both siblings, signalling the emergence of the inoperative community that imposes complete silence after Udayan's death.

On his return to India to honour his dead sibling, it is Subhash's confrontation with Udayan's death that ultimately induces him to try to communicate with Gauri, a complete stranger to him, to share with her their common loss, since his attempts at connecting with his parents are totally frustrated by their rejection to share their pain. The parents' absolute denial to expose themselves, to communicate with their son, makes plain the very failure of the family as a community, and will lead Subhash to search for alternative communities throughout his life, perhaps intuiting that community is not a matter of absolute identification and fusion, but of coming together even for a brief moment.

Secrets and cryptaesthetic resistance in *The Lowland*

In order to tackle the way secrecy and concealment work in *The Lowland*, I will also rely, as anticipated above, on the Derridean conception of the secret, which Nicholas Royle has further developed through the notion of 'cryptaesthetic resistance' (Royle 1991; 2014).[4] Despite the apparent transparency of Lahiri's narrative style, *The Lowland* actually requires 'a reading or countersignature that responds to what is elliptical, oblique, hidden away even in the obvious' (Royle 2014, 48-9). This is because of the existence of a tight network of paradoxical images and tropes, like the lowland and its merging ponds, which render the text 'capable of inducing meaning without being exhausted by meaning, incomprehensibly elliptical, secret', as Derrida (1989, 845) would put it. Consequently, the text itself should be viewed as 'a crypt – of itself, always in otherness' (Royle 1991, 62).

---

[4] In *Telepathy and Literature: Essays on the Reading Mind*, Royle offers a suggestive analysis of Emily Brontë's *Wuthering Heights* as a text that offers 'cryptaesthetic resistance' (1991, 61). The author also explains the nuances of the term 'cryptaesthesia', which etymologically 'pertains to the perception ("aesthesis") of what is hidden ("crypto-")' (60).

Given the complementary dimensions of secrecy underlying the concept of cryptaesthetic resistance, it seems necessary to first ascertain each one of them before proceeding with the analysis. Royle first relates the crypaesthetic to 'the capacity of a literary work variously to combine the cryptic and the aesthetic, secrecy and the senses, hiddenness and beauty' (2014, 48). Thus understood, the literary work calls attention to certain textual features and devices by making them conspicuous, while diverting the attention from others which, without being less relevant, might nevertheless engage the curious reader in a game with forms of blindness and insight to scrutinize the text further. In Lahiri's novel, the topographical feature chosen to entitle it, the lowland, is remarkable in this respect because of its misleading insignificance. Although the lowland seems a commonplace setting, it is patent that the place has an inconsistent quality as it may be both visible and invisible, depending on its seasonal flooding, and that it has the power to hide and to reveal whatever lurks beneath. Hence, the lowland is presented as an unfathomable place, whose uncanny nature makes the reader speculate, on the one hand, about the significance of the topography and, on the other, about the true implications of the title of this novel. Other recurrent but seemingly unremarkable motifs in the narrative such as the repeated allusions to doubles and ghosts or to traces left by Udayan, also call for a careful examination. Paying attention to these details may grant greater insight into the deepest but less obvious connections suggested by *The Lowland*/the lowland.

Secondly, from a psychoanalytical perspective, the cryptaesthetic is also closely related to the theory of the crypt as 'a figure of impossible or refused mourning and of transgenerational haunting' (Royle 2014, 49), as developed by Abraham and Torok in *The Shell and the Kernel* (1994). The haunting effect of family secrets undoubtedly deserves attention in Lahiri's fiction, since there are usually traumas repressed by older members of the family that distress younger generations very deeply. From this perspective, Bela's complete detachment from her parents and her pathological avoidance of home could be interpreted as ensuing from the silencing of Udayan's violent death and paternity – which is encrypted in Bela without her being aware of the import of such a disturbing legacy. As Abraham and Torok claim, the phantom haunting the children of a family hiding secrets represents 'the interpersonal and transgenerational consequences of silence' and concerns 'the unwitting reception of someone else's secret' (1994, 168).

Finally, the cryptaesthetic dimension must be associated with such formal aspects as the narrative strategies employed and 'the ways in which a literary work might be said to see its reader coming' (Royle 2014, 49). This entails the power of literary texts to generate 'magical or telepathic thinking', making readers believe that complete omniscience in a third-person narrative is plausible. The narrators' capacity to offer multiple perspectives as well as to choose to convey or omit crucial details of the story certainly explain why, despite the ultimate disclosure of secrets, texts unavoidably leave their readers somehow in the dark, thus creating a crypt.

In the next section I aim to identify the first dimension of the cryptaesthetic by examining the lowland of the title, which I believe to be most significant to articulate the problematic notion of community in this novel and to relate community and secrecy, leaving the other two aspects – transgenerational haunting and magical or telepathic thinking – outside the scope of the present analysis. Together with the lowland, I will also analyse several other motifs as crypts that inscribe the secrets of *The Lowland*.

The lowland: An undecidable topography

The novel opens with a descriptive one-page long passage entirely devoted to the lowland:

> Once, within this enclave, there were two ponds, oblong, side by side. Behind them was a lowland spanning a few acres.
>
> After the monsoon the ponds would rise so that the embankment built between them could not be seen. The lowland also filled with rain, three or four feet deep, the water remaining for a portion of the year.
>
> The flooded plain was thick with water hyacinth. The floating weed grew aggressively. Its leaves caused the surface to appear solid. Green in contrast to the blue of the sky.
>
> Simple huts stood here and there along the periphery. The poor waded in to forage for what was edible. In autumn egrets arrived, their white feathers darkened by the city's soot, waiting motionless for their prey.
>
> In the humid climate of Calcutta, evaporation was slow. But eventually the sun burned off most of the floodwater exposing damp ground again.
>
> So many times Subhash and Udayan had walked across the lowland.
>
> Lahiri 2013, 3

Although occupying a marginal position in the opening description of the lowland, it is remarkable that Lahiri should have chosen the word 'enclave' in the very first line of the narrative to set this landmark. The word goes almost unnoticed in a first reading, since attention is quickly focused on the changing details of the lowland, leaving its adjacent area unattended. According to the *Merriam Webster Dictionary*, 'enclave' designates 'a portion of territory surrounded by a larger territory whose inhabitants are culturally or ethnically distinct' or else 'a place or group that is different in character from those surrounding it'. The entry also offers an etymological note explaining that 'English speakers borrowed "enclave" from the French in the nineteenth century. The French noun derives in turn from the Middle French verb *enclaver*, meaning to "enclose." *Enclaver* itself can be traced to the Latin prefix *in-* and the Latin noun *clavis*, meaning "key."' Therefore, if we were to embark on a cryptonymic analysis of the word, this would indicate that 'enclave' points to the need to find the key to open and lay bare the secrets hidden or 'enclosed' in the lowland. The lowland could thus be interpreted as a crypt where secrets are buried or concealed.

The fact that the 'lowland' is not capitalized indicates that the noun does not designate a concrete location on the map, or a place already destined for a specific use by the city planners of Calcutta. The adverbial 'once' traces back the existence of this topographical feature to a lost moment in history. For a long time the lowland seemed to have been communal ground where 'the poor waded in to forage for what was edible', 'egrets arrived', 'certain creatures laid eggs' and which 'Subhash and Udayan used as a shortcut' on their way to play football (Lahiri 2013, 3). It is plain that when Subhash and Udayan first set foot on it, the lowland still remains an unclaimed and untainted spot only recognizable as a distinct landmark by whoever lives in its vicinity.

The place also lacks a definite extension since it 'spanned a few acres', and its precise limits within the 'enclave' become elusive too; the plain is only visible intermittently, depending on the season. Every year the rains hide the lowland during the monsoon, transforming it into a lagoon with shifting physical boundaries. Therefore, the space is ambiguously described as a stretch of 'damp ground' that may also be 'filled with rain, three or four feet deep' and materialize as 'a flooded plain' (Lahiri 2013, 3). The lowland is definitely presented as an uncanny place whose surface may appear as either solid or liquid, a fact that underlines its unreliable nature.

Despite the apparent irrelevance of a place which, for lack of a better name, is simply identified as 'the lowland', the emotional significance of this landmark becomes patent as the narrative steadily unfolds. By virtue of its association with the happiest memories of the siblings' childhood, the lowland is viewed as an unspoiled spot of paradisiacal connotations, where community was feasible. Nonetheless, since Udayan's shooting takes place there, changing forever the lives of those who had an attachment to him, the lowland will – since then – stand as the place of division too, as death entails a definite separation from community.

Furthermore, as the third-person narrative voice focalizes on each one of Udayan's relatives, it is clear that they ascribe new and contradictory meanings to the lowland. As has been already noticed, the place is identified as the site of both origin and communion, and conversely, of partition and dissolution caused by death. Seen in this light, the lowland can only be regarded as an aporetic symbol of community and the ties that hold it together, a cryptic trope that resists unambiguous interpretation. But, in addition, the lowland also stands as an inscrutable site given its eerie topography, the perfect place for concealment and secrecy, offering great potential to hide as well as to reveal. This is manifest when Udayan tries to escape the police and literally hides by diving into the flooded lowland, only to be caught as he resurfaces to breathe again. Yet, the place itself stands as the site of concealment in a figurative sense too, since Udayan's secret participation in terrorist actions may be hidden there, avoiding being exposed. Hence, when Udayan considers the dangerous effects of engaging in subversive political activism, he immediately thinks of the lowland as a refuge: 'Behind the water hyacinth, in the floodwater of the lowland: this is where, if the neighborhood was raided, Udayan had told her [Gauri] he would hide' (Lahiri 2013, 121–2). It is certainly in that very place where he finally hides from his chasers: 'He entered the section where the water hyacinth was thickest, taking one step, then another, the water receiving him until his body was concealed' (398–9). In this respect, the lowland operates here as a sort of crypt that hides Udayan's body, enabling him to disappear. Therefore, this place symbolically withholds the truth about Udayan's secret life since by submerging in the waters of the flooded plain, Udayan is figuratively veiling the shameful terrorist act he has committed. That secret will never be revealed to his relatives and will thus remain encrypted in the lowland. Finally, the lowland also conceals the truth about Udayan's final demise, since his corpse is never returned to his family for a proper cremation ceremony.

A final characteristic of the lowland must also be considered to shed some light on its topographical and tropological inconsistencies. I am referring to the steady transformation of the lowland, which adds to the difficulties of extricating meaning from this feature of the landscape. The uncertainty that community may have existed, suggested by the draughts and floods that cyclically cover and expose a once idyllic site, is also underscored by a simultaneous process of transformation of the lowland caused by human intervention. As years go by, the pristine waters of the lowland are gradually spoiled by a slow but steady accumulation of debris, so that it becomes increasingly more difficult for Udayan's relatives to recognize it as the hospitable and pleasant place it used to be: 'Bijoli watches as the two ponds in front of the house, and the track of lowland behind them, are clogged with waste. Old clothes, rags, newspapers ... The water that remains has been reduced to a green well in the center' (Lahiri 2013, 213). Despite its ostensible degradation, Udayan's mother continues visiting the lowland where her son's memorial stone was erected, pointlessly speaking to her dead son and unable to accept his absence.

Yet, it is Gauri's return to Calcutta thirty years after Udayan's death that reveals a complete erasure of the lowland: new buildings set up there have completely obliterated any trace of it. This utter alteration of the place may hint at the fact that the idealized community of the family and, in particular, of the intimate community formed by Subhash and Udayan, may have never existed except as a mirage. Gauri cannot find a single remnant of the lowland despite the fact that 'she had forgotten no detail. The color and the shape of the ponds clear in her mind. But the details were no longer there. Both ponds were gone. New homes filled up an area that had once been watery, open. Walking a bit farther, she saw that the lowland was also gone' (Lahiri 2013, 382–3).

The vanishing of the lowland – and of the operative community it evokes – is foreshadowed from the beginning with the numerous motifs Lahiri intersperses in the narrative where categorical oppositions between presence and absence, visibility and invisibility, fusion and separation, are clearly blurred. In addition to the topographical inconsistency of the place that stands for community, an ontological uncertainty is also underscored by several characters who seem to be playing hide and seek, raising constant doubts among their relatives about their actual presence. That is the case of a young Udayan always frightening his mother as 'he hid compulsively, under the bed, behind the doors, in the crate where winter quilts were stored' (Lahiri 2013, 11), a habit that still keeps worrying his parents when he is an adult: '[h]e travelled out of the city, he did not specify where ... They did not hear from him while he was gone. No letter, no way to know if he was alive or dead' (37). After Udayan's death, Gauri, missing Udayan and overwhelmed by the responsibility of raising her child, also gets into the habit of leaving her little daughter Bela unattended for hours on end and then returning unexpectedly, confusing her daughter about her actual presence, and prefiguring Gauri's final desertion of Bela. Finally, an adult Bela is usually absent from her family home for long periods of time, just to return quite unpredictably as if emerging from a hiding place.

In line with the paradoxical coalescence of presence and absence suggested by the peculiar topography of the lowland and the appearance and disappearance of some characters, there are also a number of material traces Udayan leaves behind, which also insinuate there is no clear-cut boundary between what is real and imaginary. An example is Udayan's photo, whose sight shocks and confounds Subhash on his return to Calcutta to honour his dead brother: 'In spite of the picture that hung in his parents' new room, … he could not believe that Udayan was nowhere. But here was the proof' (Lahiri 2013, 108). The memorial stone erected in the lowland can also be counted among such remnants, but it is Bela, Udayan's posthumous daughter, above all the rest, that must be reckoned as trace left by Udayan. She is an undeniable proof of his existence but paradoxically of his absence too, since it is for her sake and because of Udayan's death that Subhash and Gauri get married. Accordingly, Bela is seen by Subhash and Gauri, the two beings most intimately connected to Udayan, as the living proof of Udayan having been once there: '[Gauri] felt as if she contained a ghost, as Udayan was. The child was a version of him, in that it was both present and absent. Both within her and remote' (147).

Therefore, those vestiges of Udayan are just disconcerting evidence of his having existed but tend to disturbingly confuse his relatives as to his actual presence/absence. The truth is that the memory of Udayan haunts those who loved him, such as Gauri who at first sees a double of Udayan in Subhash: 'The same height, a similar build. Counterparts, companions, though she had never seen them together. Subhash was a milder version' (Lahiri 2013, 145). This is emphasized by Gauri's secret acknowledgement that '[s]he had married Subhash as a way of staying connected to Udayan' (156), although to no avail. A similar wish to reunite with Udayan brings Subhash to marry Gauri and to raise his stepdaughter, for Subhash sees in Bela a reincarnation of his dead brother.

It could then be argued that the uncanniness of the lowland, with its shifting appearance, its coming and going out of sight, is reinforced by the constant disappearance and return of Udayan and other family members, revealing the spectral quality of both the lowland and of the operative community it stands for. Accordingly, the lowland, once viewed as a place of union and pleasant memories for the siblings and the family at large, acquires poignant connotations after Udayan's death since it underlines his absence and the definite collapse of the organic community of the family. In this regard, community may be said to work on a trope of undecidability, whose ambiguous symbol, the lowland, equally asserts and denies the possibility and the impossibility of the working or operative community having existed.

Another interesting motif evoking the lost community is to be found in the following passage of *The Lowland*, corresponding to an apparently insignificant episode during Subhash and Bela's visit to Calcutta after the death of Subhash's father:

> They stopped under an enormous banyan. Her father explained that it was a tree that began life attached to another, sprouting from its crown. The mass of twisted strands, hanging down like ropes, were aerial roots surrounding the host. Over time they coalesced, forming additional trunks, encircling a hollow core if the host happened to die. Posing her before the tree, her father took her picture.
>
> Lahiri 2013, 248

The solid presence of the banyan, the national tree of India, goes by as an irrelevant detail in the narrative. However, the existence of a hollow core 'left by the host' hints once again at the tropological undecidability of traces in *The Lowland*. In line with the interpretation of previous motifs, this image could again be taken to state the presence and the absence of community – the family community and the community of siblings.

Conclusion

Lahiri's text does not openly posit the absence and/or failure of the family as a community but articulates by means of the undecidability of its central tropes the author's hesitancy to attest to and uncritically believe in the existence of truly working communities based on blood ties. What makes the interpretation of the lowland and other motifs evasive is the fact that both point to this paradoxical nature of community by merging within a single space presence and absence, visibility and invisibility, truth and secrecy. The family community represented by *The Lowland* is shattered to pieces when Udayan is killed, but as long as the lowland remains visible, even in a distorted form, it also holds the possibility of its re-enactment.

Consequently, it remains unclear how the lowland as a symbol of community should be finally interpreted, since its ambiguity could well endorse the view that community never existed by emphasizing the emptiness of the space of the lowland when the waters evaporate, or else, posit its existence and survival by means of the flooding waters that fill in the space and endow it with life of its own, insinuating a possibility of rebirth and renewal by the cyclical nature of the monsoon that affects the lowland. Returning to the opening scene of the novel, it must be borne in mind that it is in the lowland where '[c]ertain creatures laid eggs that were able to endure the dry season. Others *survived by burying themselves* in mud, simulating death, *waiting for the return of the rain*' (Lahiri 2013, 3; emphasis added). Does this imply that community is latent there only to be reborn? Does this suggest that community may well emerge again at some point in the future? Probably so, but this reading of *The Lowland* leaves no definite statement as to the past or the future of community. The text is cryptic and hence it will not disclose all its secrets.

As I have tried to evince, the lowland should be read as a crypt, a self-contradicting trope, resistant to complete interpretation, where the notions of presence and absence coalesce because of an equivocal topography. I have argued that the unsteady nature of the lowland, with alternating periods of visibility and invisibility, its potential to disclose and to hide, metaphorically suggests the precariousness of a community where singular beings may attain the sense of transcendence and belonging Lahiri's characters seek in the lowland/*The Lowland*.

Furthermore, the elusive nature of the lowland as a physical space figuratively points to the impossibility of fixing meaning, of fully interpreting the material signs, since what is hidden is only partially revealed, offering a limited and shifting view of the place and what it hides. The enclave where the lowland is set holds the key to its final interpretation, but in the case of the lowland/*The Lowland* meaning is inexhaustible. Furthermore, place and family are so intimately interconnected by key incidents in the Mitra family history that it raises the question of whether the family is a working community, fulfilling that wish for transcendence of singular beings, or on the contrary, a community asserting its collapse. The inoperative community thus appears as the communication of that interrupted myth. Accordingly, it may be stated that in *The Lowland,* Lahiri is contesting the widely accepted view that the family is an organic community, suggesting that such an obstinate belief may just be a convenient fiction haunting us generation after generation.

References

Abraham, Nicolas and Maria Torok. (1994), *The Shell and the Kernel*, Vol. 1., edited, translated and with an introduction by Nicholas T. Rand, Chicago: University of Chicago Press.
Bhabha, Homi. (2004), *The Location of Culture*, London: Routledge.
Blanchot, Maurice. (1988), *The Unavowable Community*, New York: Station Hill Press.
Derrida, Jacques. (1989), 'Biodegradables', translated by Peggy Kamuf, *Critical Enquiry,* 15 (4): 812–73.
Derrida, Jacques and Maurizio Ferraris. (2001), *A Taste for the Secret,* edited by Giacomo Donis and David Webb, translated by Giacomo Donis, Cambridge: Polity.
Dhingra, Lavina and Floyd Cheung (eds). (2012), *Naming Jhumpa Lahiri: Canons and Controversies,* Lanham, MD: Lexington.
Jiménez Heffernan, Julián. (2013), 'Introduction: Togetherness and its Discontents', in Paula Martín Salván, Gerardo Rodríguez-Salas and Julián Jiménez Heffernan (eds), *Community in Twentieth-Century Fiction,* 1–47, London: Palgrave Macmillan.
Lahiri, Jhumpa. (1999), *Interpreter of Maladies,* London: Flamingo.
Lahiri, Jhumpa. (2003), *The Namesake,* London: Flamingo.
Lahiri, Jhumpa. (2008), *Unaccustomed Earth,* London: Vintage.
Lahiri, Jhumpa. (2013), *The Lowland,* London: Bloomsbury.
Lahiri, Jhumpa. (2016), *In Other Words,* New York: Alfred Knopf.
Lahiri, Jhumpa. (2017), *The Clothing of Books,* London: Bloomsbury.
Lahiri, Jhumpa. (2018), *Dove mi Trovo*, Milan: Guanda.
Merriam-Webster Unabridged. (2016), accessed 7 May 2019, https://unabridged.merriam-webster.com/.
Miller, J. Hillis. (2015), *Communities in Fiction,* New York: Fordham University Press.
Nair, Chitra Thrivikraman. (2015), 'Politics of In-Between Spaces: Diasporic Travails in Jhumpa Lahiri's Fiction', *Asiatic: IIUM Journal of English language and Literature,* 9 (1) (June): 137–45.
Nancy, Jean-Luc. (1991), *The Inoperative Community*, edited by Peter Connor, Minnesota and Cambridge: University of Minnesota Press.
Nancy, Jean-Luc and Sarah Clift. (2013), 'Fraternity', *Angelaki,* 18 (3): 119–23.
Paudyal, Binod. (2015), 'Breaking the Boundary: Reading Lahiri's *The Lowland* as a Neo-Cosmopolitan Fiction', *South Asian Review,* 36 (3): 15–31.
Rodríguez-Salas, Gerardo. (2016), '"I Am Just As Much Dead As He Is": Community, Finitude and Sibling Intimacy in Katherine Mansfield', *Atlantis,* 38 (2) (December): 63–82.

Royle, Nicholas. (1991), *Telepathy and Literature. Essays on the Reading Mind*, Oxford: Blackwell.

Royle, Nicholas. (2014), 'Reading Joseph Conrad: Episodes from the Coast', *Mosaic,* 47 (1): 41–67.

Stein, Burton and David Arnold. (2010), *A History of India*, 2nd edition, Malden, MA: Wiley-Blackwell.

7

Queering the Māori crypt: Community and secrecy in Witi Ihimaera's *The Uncle's Story*

Gerardo Rodríguez-Salas

Witi Ihimaera was the first Māori writer to publish his narrative in New Zealand in the early 1970s, thus inaugurating the Māori Renaissance. This literary movement, which was the natural outcome of the cultural nationalism in the 1930s and 1940s, asserted 'a separate nationalism within a bicultural nation, one with its own modes of expression, its own history, and its claim to represent a truly postcolonial Aotearoa-New Zealand' (Kennedy 2016, 277). In Ihimaera's fiction, which explores 'a distinctly indigenous political dimension' (Tan 2014, 367), the Māori community is portrayed as an ancient, patriarchal milieu in need of revision to accommodate the subaltern voices of women and sexual dissidence, as exemplified in novels such as *The Matriarch* (1986), *The Whale Rider* (1987), *Nights in the Gardens of Spain* (1995) and *The Parihaka Woman* (2011). Since, as stated by Otto Heim (1999, n.p.n.), in Ihimaera's work 'secrets loom like skeletons behind virtually every door', community theory with a focus on secrecy offers an apt field from which to explore Ihimaera's ethnic and sexual dissident voces, particularly as depicted in *The Uncle's Story* (2000). Although critics such as Margaret Meklin (2003), Sandra Tawake (2006) and Yanwei Tan (2014) focus on the homosexual identity of the protagonists of this novel (Sam and Michael), the present study adds the notion of secrecy in these characters' personal and public ontological negotiation within the Māori clan.[1]

Witi Ihimaera's *The Uncle's Story* revolves around the secrets of Michael Mahana – a contemporary, Māori, gay narrator – and his uncle, Sam, who fought as a New Zealand soldier in the Vietnam War and becomes a ghostly presence in the book. Behind Sam's hegemonic military masculinity, there was a homosexual identity at odds with his Māori background. This secret is the foundation of others that affect the rest of the characters and keep the novel's suspense until the end. Through his Aunt Pat (Uncle Sam's sister), Michael discovers that his grandfather, Arapeta, attempted to burn Sam's diary, but Pat saved it from the fire and gives it now to Michael. He (along with the readers) discovers that the family members silenced Uncle Sam's homosexuality and

---

[1] For a similar study of secrecy in the context of indigenous Australia, see Gerardo Rodríguez-Salas (2018).

his affair with Cliff Harper – an American soldier in the Vietnam War – and that Sam's father physically abused, ridiculed and banished his son before the latter's accidental death in a car crash. The story is currently repeated in the narrator, whose homosexuality is also condemned by his father. However, Michael joins forces with a lesbian girl from the clan, Roimata, and a very strong gay tribal group is formed that demands a reinvention of arranged marriages for gay couples to have biological children and thus create their own queer version of the Māori clan, a gay genealogy. Ultimately, Sam's story is spread and becomes a foundational myth for the new gay tribe.

Considering the contrast between operative and inoperative communities, in Jean-Luc Nancy's words, the aim of this work is to retrieve in *The Uncle's Story* a hidden Māori space for the gay community that resonates with the theoretical notion of the crypt. Secrecy, mourning and transgenerational trauma will be thus tackled in relation to the conquest of a queer Māori space.

'Their own secret language': Community and secrecy in Uncle Sam's story

Similarly to Jeremy Bentham, some post-phenomenological theorists advocate that 'community is a fiction' (quoted in Etzioni 1996, 156). Jean-Luc Nancy prefers the 'graceless' expressions 'being-in-common', 'being-together' or 'being-with' (2003, 31), while Maurice Blanchot warns against the dangers of the word 'community': its resonance with substance and interiority, its religious connotations or its usage to support the claims of supposed 'ethnicities' (1988, 31). Jacques Derrida, in turn, rejects the term altogether, but actually, in line with Blanchot, what he dislikes is the connotation of fusion and identification implied by the very word (Caputo 1997, 107). All in all, these thinkers put community under erasure because of its essentializing and totalitarian effect.

In a philosophical dialogue that started in the early 1980s, Nancy established a distinction between two types of communities: on the one hand, the 'operative community', immanent and self-enclosed, marked by the communion or fusion of its members and substantiated in the essentialist tropes of nation, religion and/or race; on the other, the 'inoperative community', which breaks down its self-protective walls in a journey to explore and welcome alterity; its aim is communication or 'being-outside-itself' rather than communion or fusion: 'It is not a communion that fuses the *egos* into an *Ego* or a higher *We*. It is the community of *others* ... A community is not a project of fusion' (1991, 15; emphasis in the original). Blanchot makes a similar distinction. He argues that the traditional community is imposed, 'it is *de facto* sociality, or the glorification of the earth, of blood, or even of race' (1988, 46). On the contrary, the 'elective community' is identified with the community of lovers and friends: 'the strangeness of that antisocial society, always ready to dissolve itself, formed by *friends* and *couples*' (1988, 33; emphasis in the original). In opposing social laws and conventions, this community is 'antisocial' and pursues 'the destruction of society' (1988, 48).

The present study will explore the contrast in Ihimaera's novel between what can be seen as the operative Māori community (as an example of an immanent and fusional group) and the elective community of lovers (Sam–Cliff), and the gay clan founded by Michael and Roimata as having the potential to dismantle the conventional clan and open it to alterity through potent sexual dissidence and secrecy. *The Uncle's Story* may be approached from what Derrida calls the 'classical concept of the secret', that is, the secret upon which the exclusive and excluding character of the 'community, solidarity or the sect' is built (2005, 35–6). Alternatively, Nancy links communities' general inclination to secrecy with the '*founding fiction*' of Western myths (1991, 17; emphasis in the original), 'the nostalgia for a communal being' (46) and 'the desire for a work of death' (53). This secret is the foundation of the operative or traditional model, a secret linked to its essence in the form of purity, sacrifice, sacredness or violence.

The traditional Māori community silences Sam's homosexual identity as an example of the classical or mythical secret, which in this particular case guarantees the survival of a patriarchal tribal model. The novel cyclically insists in the foundation myth for the *marae*[2] as evidence for the operative community identified by Nancy. This myth endorses the Māori heterosexual matrix, thus stating that any other sexual union 'transgressed the tapu [or sacred] nature' (Ihimaera 2000, 155) and should be heavily punished, as clarified by Arapeta:

> In traditional times, son, people like you never existed ... They would have taken you outside, gutted you and left your head on a post for the birds to eat. Men like you abuse the sperm which is given to man for only one purpose. The very sperm that died inside my mates when they were killed on the battlefield. The sperm that is for the procreation of children. Don't you know that the sperm is sacred? ... You are an affront to your iwi. You are an affront to all that I and my Māori Battalion mates fought for ... Your ancestors are crying in their graves. Can you hear them, son? You are supposed to be a warrior. Instead, you are a woman. You deny yourself the rights, the mana, the sacredness of man. You also deny yourself all those privileges that come to a son born of rank. I am ashamed of you. I am disgusted with you ... I love you, son, but I have to give you your punishment.
>
> 257–8

Arapeta stands for the fusional logistics of the Māori clan and sacrifices family ties to the tribe's general communion. He is reported to have burnt Sam's diary and torn out the page with his son's birth details, thus effectively erasing homosexuality from the clan. Since Sam is presented as the perpetrator of sacrilege, he is compared with the infernal serpent and with Milton's Satan in *Paradise Lost* (Ihimaera 2000, 161, 261), while Arapeta stands for the saviour of his marae by heavily punishing his own son and

---

[2] The *marae* is the communal or sacred Māori space for religious and social purposes.

founding the classical secret on violence.³ Arapeta whips Sam, pisses on him, wishes his death, exiles and banishes him and, when his son is brought back home dead after an unfortunate accident, his body is 'put in an unconsecrated ground' (260–2, 301) as a way to preserve the mystical purity of the clan.

Arapeta epitomizes the essentialist tropes that Derrida theorizes in his *Politics of Friendship* as 'communal belonging and sharing'; namely, 'religion, family, ethnic groups, nations, homeland, country, state' (2005, 80). Arapeta's defence of a patriarchal logic in the Māori clan brings forth the notion of fraternity, discussed by Derrida in this essay, where he presents the history of friendship as associated with 'the family and the androcentric ethnic group', with a 'homo-fraternal and phallogocentric schema' (234, 306). Arapeta's fraternity is deeply ingrained in hegemonic masculinity and violence, which he promotes in his son. When Sam was born, Arapeta read his poking as fighting, so the 'proud father' boxed with his newborn son and bought him a pair of boxing gloves when he was two (Ihimaera 2000, 138). As a renowned patriarch, Arapeta boasts and promotes masculinity in the young men of the marae and entices them to go to war: 'He began to speak and his authority hushed the world. He ceased being a man and, instead, became a God incarnate. No wonder men followed him into battle' (39); 'All his life Sam had heard the old stories of the Māori Battalion's exploits. At every retelling the stories had become more epic – and Sam and his generation had diminished at every telling' (41); 'Fight for the honour of your tribe! Fight until there is no enemy left standing! Go to battle! Go! Go! Go!' (42). Even when war is a death penalty for soldiers, Arapeta links it to manhood and pride, and only Sam realizes that this masculinity is actually performative: 'Sam gestured at the marae and the huge crowd. "Does everything have to be a big production number?"' (37); '"Don't include me in this circus," said Sam. "This is Dad's show. It's got nothing to do with me. He's the man in the middle of the ring. We're just his show ponies"' (39).⁴

However, in spite of this awareness, Sam constantly suffers patriarchal anxiety in the form of nightmares, where his father becomes a monster who devours his identity with connotations of incest and homoeroticism:

> And it was as if Arapeta had been waiting for this very moment when his son was vulnerable and susceptible to attack . . . Disarmed and defenceless, Sam melted into the embrace. 'Dad!' Then he saw the obscene smile on Arapeta's face. Before he could stop him, Arapeta had put his fingers into Sam's mouth, as if to prise it open. Sam started to laugh and push Arapeta away. But Arapeta was strong and now had both hands in Sam's mouth, forcing the jaws wider. With mounting terror, Sam heard his jawbone splinter and crack. Eyes bulging, he felt Arapeta's left hand going

---

³ Using the biblical example of Cain's murder of his brother, Roberto Esposito (2009, 72–6) asserts that a community is invariably linked to a corpse's family blood, which becomes the foundation myth of the community. The one who kills is not a foreigner, but one of the members of the community, and this threat that comes from within substantiates the social group on violence and on this mythical secret. Jeremy Biles (2011), in turn, elaborates this idea of community and sacrificial violence in Bataille and Nancy.

⁴ For a detailed analysis of Sam as the epitome of the Māori warrior, see Michelle Keown (2007, 103–5) and Noah Riseman (2016, 32–44).

down past his tongue, around his tonsils and into his throat. Then the right hand, sliding in. 'Open wide, son, and let Daddy in.' ... And Dad's face was level with his, slick and moist in some unholy kiss.

Ihimaera 2000, 96–7

Arapeta's grotesque masculinity is recurrently questioned in the narrative. In Nancy's and Blanchot's models, death is pivotal in community definitions. The operative community avoids direct confrontation with death through mystical tropes that are fabricated in order to protect the community from death; the inoperative community, however, is marked by a direct confrontation that questions essentialist and mystical models. In Ihimaera, patriotism is displayed as an empty container that mystifies death and is invariably linked to religious inflation. In contrast to the *de facto* sociality represented by Arapeta's glorification of Māori blood, nationalistic values and patriarchy, Sam and Cliff stand for the elective model, the community of lovers who are open to alterity through direct exposure to death. Their romance emerges in the context of the Vietnam War and both of them are confronted to finitude, which makes them reconsider the essentialist values of their respective societies. After the sudden death of his friend Jim and a kid, Sam confronts death right in the eye: '"It could have been me instead of Jim," Sam realised. On this occasion death had brushed Sam by. But he had felt the eddy of wind as death passed' (Ihimaera 2000, 59). Indeed, following the *eros-thanatos* motif, in Māori culture there is an association of homoeroticism with death, as in the following scene where Sam accompanies a dying soldier: 'Sam knelt in front of the soldier and embraced him. The soldier looked deeply at Sam – why should he die – and tears spilled from his eyes ... let his head loll against Sam's chest like a lover. One of his hands found Sam's hei tiki and gripped it' (96). The tragic homoerotic innuendo ('like a lover') is added to the hei tiki, which is the Māori pendant that secretly links Sam and Cliff in their love and eventually exposes them in front of Arapeta's eyes.

The narrative insists on the antisocial and dangerous association of Sam and Cliff as a community of lovers. In line with peripheral voices and forbidden identities, they share a secret, sign language, which can be seen as standing for the singular and apparently inarticulate language theorized by Nancy in his essay 'Myth Interrupted'. Nancy states that this alternative language 'interrupts' the 'founding' (1991, 68) or 'mythic speech', which is 'indissociable from a rite or a cult' (50). Cliff learnt it to communicate with his deaf and dumb brother and Sam as part of the Māori tradition. The suggestion is that traditional communities provide the tools that can be strategically used to establish antisocial associations. This brotherly love that reminds us of patriarchal homosociality leads to secret homoeroticism, 'that secret language that had become their own' (Ihimaera 2000, 163). However, whereas Sam is a victim of the Māori patriarchal background and the ominous symbol of the owl haunts him throughout the novel as fate's punishment for his homosexuality, Cliff openly questions traditional values:

> I'm an American boy through and through. I believe in my country and I would fight to the death for it. But, in my heart of hearts, I think we were wrong to be in Vietnam ... I thought that after Vietnam I'd go back to the States, meet a nice girl, settle down and

get married. I thought I was regular like the other guys: I fucked girls and they loved it. Then you happened to me. Maybe the war does this to people. Changes them.
227

Cliff is more eager to share the secret: 'I don't care. I'm prepared to take the risks. Don't you understand? We were meant to be. We owe it to ourselves to see this thing through' (185). On this occasion Sam replies: 'Oh what the hell ... All right then, yes' (185), and he bravely defies his father after that. Sam and Cliff thus epitomize the community of lovers' antisocial drive.

'Charred': Sam's diary as a haunting crypt

The secrecy or, in Blanchot's words, the unavowability of this community of lovers is exposed in Sam's forbidden diary. This personal writing, I propose, could be read as an example of the psychoanalytic notion of the 'crypt', amply theorized by Nicolas Abraham and Maria Torok, Jacques Derrida and J. Hillis Miller. Derrida participated in several seminars organized during the late 1950s and early 1960s by the Hungarian-French philosopher-psychoanalyst Nicolas Abraham. The topic of the seminars was a reading of Husserlian phenomenology in the light of Sándor Ferenczi's work and Freudian psychoanalysis. After this encounter, Derrida wrote two forewords on this subject, one of them being '*Fors*' in Abraham and Torok's *The Wolf Man's Magic Word: A Cryptonymy*, where concepts such as 'crypt', 'cryptonymy', 'anasemial', 'phantom' and 'transgenerational haunting' were explored.[5]

In '*Fors*', Derrida conceptualizes 'the crypt' in contrast to 'the forum'. Critics such as Wojciech Michera explain that the French noun *for* (plural: *fors*) is an ambiguous word that can be connected with the Latin *forum*, i.e. 'a public square in Rome, the site of court trials' (2014, 198). Michera makes a list of etymological connections (one of them being Latin *foris*, 'outside the door', 'alien' space), and concludes that in French *fors* is an archaic preposition that means: 'without', 'with the exception of', 'while preserving' (ibid.). Derrida thus theorizes the crypt in opposition to the forum:

> Constructing a system of partitions, with their inner and outer surfaces, the cryptic enclave produces a cleft in space, in the assembled system of various places, in the architectonics of the open square within space, itself delimited by a generalised closure in the forum. Within this forum, space where the free circulation and exchange of objects and speeches can occur, the crypt constructs another, more inward forum ... sealed and thus internal to itself, a secret interior within the public square, but, by the same token, outside it, external to the interior. ... Caulked or padded along its inner partition, with cement or concrete on the other side the cryptic safe protects from the outside the very secret of its clandestine inclusion or its internal exclusion.
>
> Derrida 1986, xiv

---

[5] Zoltán Dragon (2005, 254–5) and Wojciech Michera (2014, 197) explain this origin in detail.

Zoltán Dragon clarifies that 'the crypt encloses something or someone (a secret, an unmourned beloved, etc.) *buried alive*. Were it buried dead, it would not haunt, that is there would not be any crypt effects' (2005, 260; emphasis in the original).[6] In addition, J. Hillis Miller discusses Derrida's notion of the crypt in his essay 'Derrida's Topographies' (1994), later included in his book *Topographies* (1995), where leaving aside Abraham and Torok's text, and according to Dragon, Miller takes the concept of the crypt as 'a genuinely Derridean term' (2005, 257). For Miller '[s]omewhere and nowhere in every Derridean topography is a secret place, a crypt whose coordinates cannot be plotted. This place excedes any ordinary topographical placement' (1995, 296–7).

In contrast to Derrida's and Miller's topographic dimension of the crypt, Abraham and Torok define it in linguistic terms. They conclude that 'the tomb's content is unique in that it cannot appear in the light of day as speech. And yet, it is precisely a matter of words. Without question, in the depths of the crypt unspeakable words buried alive are held fast, like owls in ceaseless vigil' (1994, 159–60). Critics such as Dragon (2005, 255) or O'Connor (2011, 113) link this concept of the crypt to the 'anaseme', which, in Abraham's analysis, is 'the unspoken word adjacent to the one that is uttered, always being there but still absent' (Dragon 2005, 255).

In Ihimaera's novel, Sam's diary could be read both as a crypt in the topography of the Māori clan, and as the psychic and linguistic enclave in which Michael's trauma (through Sam) resides. Arapeta believes he has burnt the diary, but Sam's sister kept it for years as a hidden manuscript that is then both there and not there. Trying to locate it will definitely confound Arapeta's mapping protocols. Sam's diary is indeed marked by this cryptic dimension since, as stated by Michael: 'The diary was charred, as if at some time it had been caught in a fire. I fingered through it gently. The slightest motion caused some of its edges to fray and pages to fly like wings in the wind. Some had been burnt right to the spine. Others were missing' (Ihimaera 2000, 34). The cryptonymic analysis of this diary is problematic as Michael will have to infer his uncle's inaccessible traumas through the absent words that were burnt in Arapeta's fire. This manuscript, just like the purloined letter in Edgar Allan Poe's story, stands for an 'enveloped message' that 'prefigures' the missing diary's proper location, 'like a manuscript in a bottle or a story within a story' (Riddel 1979, 123). It becomes an example of Ginette Michaud's spectral manuscript, 'the lost manuscript, forever condemned to err and wander ... an infinite *overture* (and in this *overture*, one must also hear the *opus*, the opening up, the ouvre itself) of a wound' (2002, 83; emphasis in the original).

Even though the novel generally reveals all of the conditional secrets, Sam's incomplete manuscript haunts the readers as a spectral text, as a question never fully answered. Sam becomes the family phantom that haunts the narrative with an unspeakable secret that is only partially revealed, looking for exorcism in the new generation represented by Michael. Indeed, the uncle's story, as inferred but never

---

[6] The crypt is then 'the vault of desire' (Derrida 1986, xvii) or, in Mary O'Connor's words, a 'nostalgic vocation' (2011, 117). These features are central to the understanding of the crypt effect of Sam's diary on Michael, which will be developed in the next section.

proved by Michael, is the *mise en abyme* that takes over the readers' minds, becoming an example of what Esther Rashkin calls 'phantomatic haunting' (2008, 22) – the idea of the phantom whose effects are felt in subsequent generations through the transmission of unspeakable secrets. This idea will be explored in the next section with an analysis of Michael as the receptacle of transgenerational trauma.

'Like looking at a bloody ghost': Michael's transgenerational trauma

As suggested in the previous section, Ihimaera's novel is an apt field to study Abraham and Torok's concept of *cryptophoria* and Derrida's concepts of *hauntology* or *spectropoetics* – the haunting effects of the crypt (Abraham and Torok 1994, lxxii). Michael's reaction to the discovery of his uncle's personal diary and subsequent mourning will be the case study. Dragon states that 'originally the crypt is erected to keep a traumatic knowledge out of the reach of the ego. If the walls of the crypt are torn down, the traumatic secret is set loose ... Nonetheless, the effect of this traumatic secret, the so-called crypt effect, or what later Abraham terms as the phantom effect, reaches and touches the reader' (2005, 262). Indeed, not only is Michael affected by the crypt effect of his uncle's partially lost diary, but so are readers who end up not being revealed the diary's full secrecy. Mary O'Connor distinguishes two types of hauntologies. In Abraham and Torok the phantom's secrets are 'unspeakable' in their 'shame and prohibition', but that does not mean they cannot be spoken; they are meant to be spoken 'so that the phantom and its noxious effects on the living can be exorcized' (2011, 112). In Derrida, on the contrary, the unspeakability of the ghost's secrets 'is not a puzzle to be solved ... the secret is not unspeakable because it is taboo, but because it cannot not (yet) be articulated in the languages available to us' (O'Connor 2001, 112). Derrida then would accept the unreadability of the uncle's journal, which leaves both Michael and the readers in the shadow.

Abraham and Torok introduce two types of mourning, which will be central in the study of Michael. On the one hand, 'introjection', which Torok, quoting Ferenzei, explains as 'a mechanism allowing the extension to the external world of the primitive autoerotic interests, by including these objects of the exterior world in the self-ego' (Abraham and Torok 1986, 112); on the other, 'incorporation', which is when

> [i]nexpressible mourning erects a secret tomb inside the subject. Reconstituted from the memories of words, scenes, and affects, the objectal correlative of the loss is buried alive in the crypt as a full-fledged person, complete with its own topography. The crypt also includes the actual or supposed traumas that made introjection impracticable. A whole world of unconscious fantasy is created, one that leads its own separate and concealed existence.
>
> 1986, 130

In other words, in introjection, upon the death of the other, the ego communes with it, 'introjects the qualities esteemed in the other into itself and continues in a somewhat self-satisfied and complacent way' (Kirby 2006, 466). As clarified by Judith Butler, '[t]his identification is not simply momentary or occasional, but becomes a new structure of identity; in effect, the other becomes part of the Ego through the permanent internalization of the other's attributes' (2004, 58). Introjection might explain why the farewell, although difficult, becomes bearable. In line with the process of communion in operative communities, the result is a mystification of the departed, a metaphorical process of psychic cannibalism where the other is engulfed by the self to avoid pain. In incorporation, which Abraham and Torok consider as a pathological reaction to mourning, the subject does not accept the loss, internalizes the lost other and builds a crypt for them within the psyche. Michera clarifies this process as happening

> when it becomes impossible to replace the lost object with words ... If the subject is incapable of self-satiation with words (metaphors) it embarks upon a more radical activity: it absorbs the imagined *thing*, a fantasy, an object-fetish, isolating it far from the conscious part of the Ego, enclosing it in the crypt. Incorporation is, therefore, a de-metaphorization of the word: by annulling its figurative meanings it preserves the loss of an object as radically unnameable, in this way guarding its secret.
> 2014, 200; emphasis in the original[7]

Even though *The Uncle's Story* gives voice to different characters and each section focuses on one of them, Michael is the general narrative voice, as specified in Part One: 'I, Michael'. Readers feel that Sam's story is not fully grasped and that they are driven by Michael's narration, which adds to Sam's spectral quality. Michael's mourning seems justified by Slavoj Žižek's idea of the presence of the 'living dead' in cultural imagery, according to which 'the deceased returns from the grave to the living to claim an unpaid, symbolic debt' (1992, 23). Michael will become Sam's voice to denounce his uncle's victimization, thus fulfilling the inheritance or transgenerational dimension that Abraham and Torok find in the phantom phenomenon, as specified when they state that '[t]his secret can either be kept knowingly by a parent, or it can be lodged in the crypt of the parent and then inherited as a foreign body within the unconscious of a child: this would cause the inheritor to act as if he / she was "driven by some stranger within"' (1994, 188). This is Michael's case. His family kept Sam's secret away from him. He did not even know about the existence of his Uncle Sam, let alone that he was gay (Ihimaera 2000, 33). This erasure of Sam in the family unleashes hauntology in the new generation represented by Michael, who becomes 'a carrier of his trauma' (Michera 2014, 201).

Michael shows signs of both introjection and incorporation. His close resemblance to Sam is constantly highlighted, so that he is almost presented as a reincarnation.[8]

---

[7] Kirby clarifies this dyad in Derrida: 'Derrida privileges the process of *incorporation*, which classical psychoanalysis has been seen as the pathological response to loss. He does this essentially because incorporation acknowledges the other as other, while the so-called normal process of mourning (introjection) merely assimilates the other into the self in a kind of psychic plagiarism' (2006, 470; emphasis in the original).

[8] Abraham and Torok elaborate the idea of reincarnation in *The Shell and the Kernel* (1994, 141).

As George (Sam's friend) tells Michael: 'Do you realize how much you look like Sam? It's like looking at a bloody ghost' (Ihimaera 2000, 188), and the idea is remarked by Aunt Pat (193). He is so fascinated by his uncle that there seems to be an ontological fusion between both of them, and Michael seems to appropriate Sam's story as his own. His fascination for Sam leads Michael to mystify his uncle's tragic love story throughout the novel, as suggested by his comparison with Tristan and Isolde (335) and with eternal romance (309, 311). However, Michael apparently manages to separate both identities, to respect Sam's otherness as an example of incorporation: 'So long denied knowledge about Uncle Sam, I wanted to do something for him almost as a way of recognising myself' (270). Although Michael covers his own search for identity with a mystic halo because of his infatuation with Sam, he represents a new opportunity beyond the negative homosexual stereotype from the past, epitomized by Sam.[9] He follows his uncle's secrecy model, although the outcome is different and there is a chance for him and the new generation he represents to escape from the prison of classical secrecy. Closely connected with Sam's grotesque nightmare of incest and rape, Michael tells Auntie Pat that as a child he was molested by 'somebody in the tribe', and then reveals to the reader that it was by '[t]wo uncles. Drunk. Coming from a party and stumbling into a room where children slept. Any old bed. Any warm body. Ripping me open like a tin can' (28). The result is another classical secret hidden behind the purity of the Māori community in spite of these dirty and abject origins that need to be erased for the sake of social and moral survival.

Michael's mystification of Sam is his way to avoid transgenerational trauma and it becomes the fuel to ignite the fire of his gay political intervention in the Māori clan. His memory of Sam exemplifies Avery Gordon's perception of 'haunting' as a transformative experience: 'Being haunted draws us affectively, sometimes against our will and always a bit magically, into the structure of feeling of a reality we come to experience, not as knowledge, but as a transformative recognition' (1997, 8). Sam thus stands for Jeffrey Weinstock's idea that 'the ghost is that which interrupts the presentness of the present', that which haunts the surface of official records and 'question[s] the veracity of the authorized version of events' (2004, 5). The revelation of Sam's secret unleashes Michael's exploration of his own identity within his Māori community: 'And now that the lid is off Pandora's Box, I guess whatever is in there, for good or ill, will come flying out' (Ihimaera 2000, 126). The two stories are clearly united in a common identitary purpose: 'Then suddenly it seemed [Uncle Sam] looked past the camera. By

---

[9] In her study *Feeling Backward: Loss and the Politics of Queer History*, Heather Love states that '[t]he history of Western representation is littered with the corpses of gender and sexual deviants. Those who are directly identified with same-sex desire most often end up dead' (2009, 1), and clarifies that '[t]hese feelings are tied to the experience of social exclusion and to the historical "impossibility" of same-sex desire' (4). Love denounces that most texts on homosexuality 'choose isolation, turn toward the past, or choose to live in a present disconnected from any larger historical continuum' (8) and '[g]iven the new opportunities available to *some* gays and lesbians, the temptation to forget ... is stronger than ever' (10; emphasis in the original). Ihimaera confronts this temptation and the new generation represented by Michael uncovers the tragic queer past epitomized by Uncle Sam. Other critics such as Peter Coviello revise this 'unspeakable past' as 'too bleakly stranded' (2013, 1) and linked to abjection.

some trick of light he was looking at me. His eyes drew *me* in. And the past came rushing out' (34; emphasis in the original). As clarified by Michael, '[t]his wasn't just about Uncle Sam. It was also about me' (310). With this transgenerational force, Michael aims for visibility and recognition, which will materialize in a challenging gay community; this will be the focus of the next section.

'Deleted from the text': The queer Māori clan in Michael's story

Once Michael's gay identity is solidly conformed, Sam's spectral manuscript returns in the form of a mighty gay generation, a community opposed to the operative tribal model: 'But if we were lucky, oh, if we were lucky, someone remembered who we were. Someone stopped us from becoming invisible. Expunged from memory. Deleted from the text' (Ihimaera 2000, 322). Michael's proposed model of a gay tribe, however, dangerously resonates with hegemonic masculinity and patriarchal models. His reconstruction of Sam's story partially follows the mythic dimension denounced by Nancy in operative communities. One of Sam's friends, Turei, tells Michael to use his uncle's story strategically to popularize a gay masculinity in the marae:

> You say your uncle was both gay and a soldier? You know, if his story was known, he could become a pretty potent symbol. He would prove that you can be gay – and a warrior. If we could take the message to every marae in the country it would be a breakthrough, because if here's anything our people understand it's the warrior spirit. They may not like what gay Māori men are, but they've always admired bravery and strength.
>
> 294

This revision of Sam's homosexual identity as emulating hegemonic masculinity is clearly problematic in the visibilization of gay models in Māori society, as it condones what critics such as Demetrakis Z. Demetriou call 'internal hegemony' (2001, 341), according to which homosexual masculinity is hierarchically perceived as subservient and inferior to hegemonic masculinity.

In a postcolonial-themed conference in Canada, Michael and Roimata become the academic and political ambassadors of this gay tribe, which demands visibility and a mythical background as valid as the Māori heterosexual matrix: 'Of all the children of gods, my kind – gay, lesbian, transvestite and transsexual – inhabited the lowest and darkest cracks between the Primal Parents. We, now, also wish to walk upright upon this bright strand' (Ihimaera 2000, 343). In the hall of the conference, both Michael and Roimata stand up for their 'small tribe in that hall so filled with history' (344), with a clear allusion to the need to resignify a historical space for them. They display their solidarity with the reference to a dead Māori gay because of AIDS, and how they all go together to the marae as a group, an 'odd tribe' (364), a 'strange tribe' (365), a 'brave gay tribe' (365). In contrast with Sam's banishment and anonymous burial, this united gay group openly claims:

> We are a people. We are a tribe. We bring our dead. If tradition has to be broken, then I will break it. Nobody will stop us from burying our own among the people where they belong. The time for hiding ourselves and our dead is past. The time for burying them in some anonymous cemetery is over.
>
> 365

This gay tribe is inscribed biologically in the Māori clan and, although demonized by tradition, they finally make room for their own space: 'we had been formally welcomed, even if reluctantly, and all the speeches were over' (366). This is precisely the problem for the new model, that it obsessively aims to 'belong' to the operative, traditional clan and ultimately appropriates the Māori standards of the heterosexual matrix as the foundation for this dissident model. The result is an alternative clan that resonates with the essentialism of the old one.

Ethnicity appears in Roimata's debate about Michael's lovers and becomes another example of essentialism. Roimata is described as 'an outspoken Māori activist' (131) because of her university training in Māori studies, women's studies and art history, together with her lesbian identity. After Michael's split with Jason, his former *Pakeha* partner,[10] and his relationship now with Carlos, another white man, Roimata's ethnic essentialism is clear:

> Here I was, thinking of Jason splitting from you would give you the chance to decolonise yourself, regain your sovereignty as a Māori gay man, and what do I find? You've gone colonised yourself again ... All your white lovers! ... And now look at this one, this Carlos. Straight off the white gay assembly line and out of a white gay boy magazine ... but when are you going to go for your mana Māori!
>
> Ihimaera 2000, 277–9[11]

Roimata clarifies how Michael's personal identity riddle is inseparable from a broader political and colonial agenda:

> I only wish, Michael, dear, that you would see that you've been colonised twice over. First, by the Pakeha. Second by the gay Pakeha. Even in the gay world the white majority holds the power, the money, the decision making power – and it is their images which tell you what is desirable, what you should be like and what you shouldn't be like.
>
> 131

In contrast with Roimata's ethnic immanence, Michael opens the door for hybridity in his gay Māori enterprise. Only when Carlos reveals to Roimata that he has Māori blood

---

[10] *Pakeha* is a Māori-language term for New Zealanders of European descent.
[11] In *The Uncle's Story*, Ihimaera clarifies that '[t]he *mana* of a man' is 'his value in Maori culture' (2000, 155; emphasis in the original).

is she pleased because of his Māori ancestry. With Carlos's insertion in the gay tribal project, Michael undergoes both the homosexual visibility and miscegenation that was not possible with Sam and Cliff, and his alternative gay tribe arises apparently as an example of Nancy's inoperative community open to alterity.

However, this new gay tribal model still looks dangerously essentialist and masculinist. After discussing the role of berdaches (American Indian homosexuals), Michael almost proclaims himself a Messiah, thus attaching a mythical quality to his tribe and adopting for himself a visionary role. After all, he seems to have 'introjected' Uncle Sam's mythic quality rather than letting him go. Speaking of berdaches, a colleague affirms that '[t]wins, if one was male and other was female, were particularly favoured by the gods. The male twin specifically, if he became a berdache, was destined . . . to lead the berdache tribe' and Michael reflects: 'Great, so now I was going to become a gay Māori Moses' (Ihimaera 2000, 330). As Yanwei Tan concludes, 'Michael is, therefore, essentially championing a patriarchal mode of struggle that can potentially undermine his own project – as expressed in the notion of a gay tribe – of bringing about a tolerant and nurturing environment for interpersonal relations' (2014, 383).

Not only do they propose visibility but, in creating this queer space in the marae, they do not want to relinquish Māori ancestry: 'The Western model de-privileges any notions that gay men or women might have children. Therefore, the white gay species is the only one that doesn't replicate itself. But our Māori model is a tribal one. It should therefore include the possibility of growing a tribe. Of having children' (Ihimaera 2000, 131). Since arranged marriages are not unusual in the tribe, the gay community strategically uses this custom to both replicate and challenge the Māori family structure. Michael and Roimata will follow the model of Roimata's gay cousin, Tane, and a lesbian girl from the tribe, Leah. Tane provides the key for this new model:

> Marriage should be an option for gay Polinesian men and women. With it we can establish a tribe – a tribe based not just on sexual identity but on family. A tribe must have children to survive. It must also have parents, grandmothers and grandfathers. Even though the children may not be gay by practice, they will be gay by genealogy through their fathers and mothers. When my own children grow up, I want them to think of themselves as belonging to a great new gay family, a wonderful new gay tribe.
> 296

However, as noticed by Tan, there is a utopian dimension to this gay tribe, particularly in the 'radical idea' of marriage between gay men and lesbian women for the sake of having children (2014, 296).[12] Michael's project of a gay Māori clan looks promising as an inoperative community, but, as a result of its founder's unresolved mourning and dangerously essentialist and biologistic model, it becomes just a poor imitation of the operative model of the conventional Māori tribe that it aims to supersede.

---

[12] Tan clarifies that this gay tribal model 'has the obvious weakness of showing insufficient consideration for committed same-sex partners who may jealously guard their love, not to mention the implications for the future children' (2014, 378–9).

The 'hollow coffin': Concluding remarks

Witi Ihimaera's *The Uncle's Story* is invariably built on secrecy. Although the novel follows a succession of conditional secrets that are eventually revealed, Sam's diary, personal trauma and hidden homosexual identity resonate with the Derridean notion of the crypt, which can be applied to the role played in the novel by subaltern voices, mainly gay, inside the Māori clan. These voices are safely protected in a place that, according to Miller, 'resists toponymy, topology, and topography … a secret place whose coordinates cannot be plotted' (1995, 296–7). In Ihimaera, the crypt of the gay community is ultimately made visible, following Abraham and Torok's desirable exorcism and visibilization of trauma. This gay clan that was everywhere and nowhere at the same time gives way to a traceable political location inside the heart of the Māori clan. Indeed, precisely because of this ultimate visibility, the promising gay Māori space proves eventually to be another operative alternative, as the prospective community of those who have no community finally makes its way into the traditional space and forces the gay members' belonging by adjusting their dissident identities to patriarchal, heteronormative dimensions. This gay group appropriates arranged marriages and biological reproduction for gay couples, thus replicating Arapeta's vindictive speech that sperm is sacred and the basis for the foundation of an ethnic and gendered community, a biological gay genealogy. Sam and Cliff make the conventional Māori hei tiki the hidden symbol of their homoerotic community of lovers rather than inventing one of their own. Michael is unable to escape introjection and the result is the absolute mystification and canonization of his uncle that not only becomes the hypermasculized foundational myth of the new community, but also leads to his self-perception as a new Māori Messiah for the gay community. Roimata, the other leader of this queer space, proves an ethnic essentialism that will lead the new community to immanence, borders and exclusion.

This upsetting gay clan revolves around Sam's secret identity. The haunting effects of the crypt do not come to an end, as Sam's incomplete manuscript keeps haunting the readers. Metaphorically speaking, Sam's story – which, like his body, was buried in an unsacred place – seems 'erected upon a "hollow coffin" that must be protected even as it is ultimately opened and revealed as the place of just another missing body, another simulacrum of a simulacrum' (Riddel 1979, 130). Sam remains a question mark in Ihimaera's novel. The readers have the impression that his secret life has been disclosed, but with his accidental death and the partially lost manuscript, part of the story was consumed in Arapeta's fire and is blurred in Michael's manipulative narration of events, which is further evidence that Michael needs a sense of closure in his newly constructed operative community. For the readers, the journal remains a riddle. Just as with the purloined letter in Edgar Alan Poe's story, here we have 'the illusion' of the diary 'restored' (Riddel 1979, 141). But, at least, this cryptic, haunting presence does become a transformative experience and a tangible absence that brings along the promise of a politically enforced gay tribe, even when the materialization of this community is ultimately a failure, a mere copy of the model it intended to supersede.

References

Abraham, Nicolas and Maria Torok. (1986), *The Wolf Man's Magic Word: A Cryptonymy*, translated by Nicholas Rand. Minneapolis: University of Minnesota Press.

Abraham, Nicolas and Maria Torok. (1994), *The Shell and the Kernel: Renewals of Psychoanalysis*, translated by Nicholas Rand, Chicago: University of Chicago Press.

Biles, Jeremy. (2011), 'The Remains of God: Bataille/Sacrifice/Community', *Culture, Theory and Critique*, 52 (3): 127–44.

Blanchot, Maurice. (1988) (1983), *The Unavowable Community*, translated by Pierre Joris, Barrytown, New York: Station Hill.

Butler, Judith. (2004), *Precarious Life: The Powers of Mourning and Violence*, London and New York: Verso.

Caputo, John D. (1997), 'Community Without Community', in John D. Caputo (ed.), *Deconstruction in a Nutshell: A Conversation with Jacques Derrida*, 106–24, New York: Fordham University Press.

Coviello, Peter. (2013), 'Introduction: The Unspeakable Past', in *Tomorrow's Parties: Sex and the Untimely in Nineteenth-Century America*, 1–47, New York: New York University Press.

Demetriou, Demetrakis Z. (2001), 'Connell's Concept of Hegemonic Masculinity: A Critique', *Theory and Society*, 30 (3): 337–61.

Derrida, Jacques. (1986), 'Foreword: *Fors*: The Anglish Words of Nicholas Abraham and Maria Torok', in Nicolas Abraham and Maria Torok (eds), Barbara Johnson (trans), *The Wolf Man's Magic Word: A Crytonymy*, xi–xlviii, Minneapolis: University of Minnesota Press.

Derrida, Jacques. (2005) (1994), *The Politics of Friendship*, translated by George Collins, London and New York: Verso.

Dragon, Zoltán. (2005), 'Derrida's Specter, Abraham's Phantom: Psychoanalysis as the Uncanny Kernel of Deconstruction,' *The AnaChronisT*, 11: 253–69.

Esposito, Roberto. (2009), 'Comunidad y Violencia', translated by Rocío Orsi, *Minerva: Revista del Círculo de Bellas Artes*, 12: 72–6.

Etzioni, Amitai. (1996), 'A Moderate Communitarian Proposal', *Political Theory*, 24 (2): 155–71.

Gordon, Avery. (1997), *Ghostly Matters: Haunting and the Sociological Imagination*, Minneapolis: University of Minnesota Press.

Heim, Otto. (1999), 'Wrestling with the Patriarch', *New Zealand Review of Books Pukapuka Aotearoa*, 1 September 1999, accessed 12 October 2019, https://nzbooks.org.nz/1999/literature/wrestling-with-the-patriarch-otto-heim.

Ihimaera, Witi. (2000), *The Uncle's Story*, Penguin: Auckland.

Kennedy, Melissa. (2016), 'The Māori Renaissance from 1972', in Mark Williams (ed.), *A History of New Zealand Literature*, 277–88, Cambridge: Cambridge University Press.

Keown, Michelle. (2007), *Pacific Islands Writing: The Postcolonial Literatures of Aotearoa/ New Zealand and Oceania*, Oxford: Oxford University Press.

Kirby, Joan. (2006), '"Remembrance of the Future": Derrida on Mourning', *Social Semiotics*, 16 (3): 461–72.

Love, Heather. (2009), *Feeling Backwards: Loss and the Politics of Queer History*, Cambridge, Massachusetts: Harvard University Press.

Meklin, Margaret. (2003), 'A Maori Writer in Two Worlds', *The Gay and Lesbian Review Worldwide*, 10 (1): 30–2.

Michaud, Ginette. (2002), 'Literature in Secret: Crossing Derrida and Blanchot', *Angelaki: Journal of the Theoretical Humanities,* 7 (2): 69–90.
Michera, Wojciech. (2014), 'Image, Crypt, Interpretation', *Konteksty* (special issue): 197–203.
Miller, J. Hillis. (1995), 'Derrida's Topographies', in *Topographies,* 291–315, Stanford, California: Stanford University Press.
Nancy, Jean-Luc. (1991), *The Inoperative Community,* edited and translated by Peter Connor et al., Minneapolis: University of Minnesota Press.
Nancy, Jean-Luc. (2003), 'The Confronted Community', *Postcolonial Studies,* 6 (1): 23–36.
O'Connor, Mary. (2011), 'Canopy of the Upturned Eye: Writing on Derrida's Crypt', *Mosaic,* 44 (4): 109–23.
Rashkin, Esther. (2008), 'Introduction: Vexed Encounters: Psychoanalysis, Cultural Studies, and the Politics of Close Reading', In *Unspeakable Secrets and the Psychoanalysis of Culture,* 1–24, New York: State University of New York.
Riddel, Joseph N. (1979), 'The "Crypt" of Edgar Poe', *Boundary 2,* 7 (3): 117–44.
Riseman, Noah. (2016), 'Elite Indigenous Masculinity in Textual Representations of Aboriginal Service in the Vietnam War', *Journal of Australian Studies,* 40 (1): 32–44.
Rodríguez-Salas, Gerardo. (2018), 'Tasmania's Cupboard: Indigenous and Convict Australia in Carmel Bird's Writing', *Journal of Language, Literature and Culture,* 65 (3): 169–86.
Tan, Yanwei. (2014), 'Recognition, Political and Interpersonal: Gay Tribalism in Witi Ihimaera's *The Uncle's Story*', *Modern Fiction Studies,* 60 (2): 366–86.
Tawake, Sandra. (2006), 'Cultural Rhetoric in Coming-out Narratives: Witi Ihimaera's *The Uncle's Story*', *World Englishes,* 25 (3–4): 373–80.
Weinstock, Jeffrey Andrew, ed. (2004), *Spectral America: Phantoms and the National Imagination,* Wisconsin: University of Wisconsin Press.
Žižek, Slavoj. (1992), *Looking Awry: An Introduction to Jacques Lacan through Popular Culture,* Cambridge, MA: MIT Press.

8

Secrecy, invisibility and community in Jeanette Winterson's *The Daylight Gate*

Juan L. Pérez-de-Luque

Introduction

The goal of the present chapter is to explore the different levels of secrecy and community to be found in Jeanette Winterson's *The Daylight Gate* (2012). In the numerous existing studies on this writer, critics have pointed out the main characteristics and concerns to be found in Winterson's writings. Obsessive motifs such as love, mothers or religion, or the concern with literary historiography are tackled by Onega (2006), López (2007) and Pacheco Costa (2008). In general terms, feminism, gender and queer studies have proven to be fruitful theoretical frameworks to study Winterson's oeuvre, as shown in the works of Rusk (2002), López (2007), Front (2009) and Mingiuc (2011). The last three analyse from that perspective typically postmodern features such as intertextuality, otherness or interrupted narratives. In particular, *The Daylight Gate* has generated several feminist studies, most notably those provided by Van Namen (2013), Lazăr (2014), Antosa (2015) and Kondali (2016). Van Namen (2013) casts light on how non-binary gender identities and non-heteronormative sexualities are depicted as a social threat for men in the novel, and how the protagonist, Alice Nutter, is an independent woman who does not fit the standards of the age. Lazăr (2014) is concerned with the social status and lack of power that women had in the seventeenth century, when the novel takes place, and how the witches in the text challenge that role as they try to find their own mechanisms of power. Antosa (2015), on her part, focuses on the love triangle of the main characters, which also defies the conventions of the time. Kondali, on the other hand, approaches the way in which '[t]he historical novel becomes a way of re-imagining and recasting the official history to incorporate the experiences of women' (2016, 246).

It seems, then, that secrecy and community have been neglected in the existing studies on Winterson, a gap that this essay intends to cover. In this chapter, I plan to put forward how, on the one hand, secrecy is used by the author to provide visibility to traditionally ignored voices. In the case of *The Daylight Gate*, these voices belong mostly to women that, because of their sharing of secret communities (covens and lesbian relationships), threaten the normativity of the traditional, male community. On the other hand, I pay attention to how women in the novel hide important facts from other characters (such as their ability to use magic), and to how Winterson also hides from the reader, until the second part of the novel, the fact that women in her text are actually presented as real witches.

Witchcraft has always been strongly associated with secrecy. Historically, black masses, covens and spells have been dealt with an aura of mystery and occult knowledge, which permeates most of the literary production around that topic. As Luhrmann explains, '[m]agic is steeped in secrecy.... Secret words supposedly open the doors to hidden treasure and remedy manifold ills; they are passed from magician to magician, like possessions, and competing practitioners contest the power of their hidden wares. Fantastic medieval witches held congress under the cover of furtive darkness and the Renaissance magi wrote their texts in garbled code' (1989, 131). The first part of this chapter discusses how Winterson plays with the revelation of secrets inherent in witchcraft, in order to switch from a literary genre – historical fiction – to a different one – fantasy – when the novel, until that moment, had been mainly working according to the parameters of the former. The use of secrecy in the construction of characters and the plot creates an ambiguous piece of fiction; as a result, it is difficult for the reader to know, until the second third of the novel, if some of the characters practise magic or not, that is, if they are real witches. With this game, Winterson gives relevance to voices that have been historically invisible: those of women and misfits. The second part of this chapter will study how the communities present in *The Daylight Gate* are founded on secrecy, and how these collective forms interact with each other and survive just as long as the secret that sticks them together also survives.[1]

My analysis is based on three main theoretical frameworks. Firstly, Roland Barthes's proposal of narrative codes in *S/Z* (originally published in 1970) is suitable to understand how Winterson works with secrets and uses the hermeneutic code – related to the formulation and disclosing of enigmas – in order to hide key information that, when revealed, will radically change the genre of her novel. Secondly, different studies on literary historiography carried out within New Historicism – such as Jackson's ideas on invisibility (2009) and Baker's discussion of the relationship between fantasy and historical fiction (2011) – will allow us to consider how Winterson uses the hermeneutic code in order to create ambiguity around characters and their ability to perfom magic. Finally, the concept of community inspired by Bataille as defined by Blanchot (1988) and Nancy (1991), will provide the suitable tools to approach the configuration and interaction of communities in *The Daylight Gate*. This analysis will also be complemented by Girard's examination of the community's quest for scapegoats in order to relieve communal fears and insecurities (1986).

---

[1] In his discussions of secrecy, Jacques Derrida distinguishes between conditional and unconditional secrets. As Attridge explains (2011, 44), for the French philosopher a conditional secret is a 'common-or-garden secret' that can be revealed. On the contrary, the unconditional secret is the 'absolute' secret 'that can never be known'. The secrets analysed in the present chapter belong to the first category.

Secrecy, invisibility and history

At first sight, *The Daylight Gate* reads as historical fiction,[2] but after the first third of the novel, the genre switches unexpectedly into the fantastic; this change is facilitated by Winterson's masterful use of secrecy. Following Baker, the hypothesis I present is that historical fiction containing fantastic elements pursues a very particular ideological goal, since

> [s]uch a fantastic intrusion ... functions to make visible the cultural dominants represented in the text, clearly defining the space in 'shadows,' the lack, the repressed, before subverting them. And it is in subversion that Jackson (1981, 180) positions the essential function of fantastic literature – in its language, content and structure – to undercut, diffuse and dissolve oppresive cultural orders; orders that create such shadows, such lacks.
>
> 2011, 5

Indeed, through the intrusion of the fantastic into the historical, *The Daylight Gate* offers a historical-ideological reading that transcends mere literary entertainment. The novel fictionalizes the events that led to the Pendle Witches trials, which took place in Lancashire in 1612, echoing the social consequences of the Gunpowder Plot. The text focuses on the lives of Alice Nutter and other protagonists of the trials, mainly the convicted women and men who participated in the black mass, and the people who accused and prosecuted them. In the initial presentation of these events – dealing with the possibility of the supernatural – Winterson follows the conventions of the historical novel. In the introduction, she provides a historical context for the narrated events, making it clear that the places and characters she deals with are real, 'but with necessary speculations and inventions' (Winterson 2012, viii). In this introduction she mentions several historical treatises on witchcraft and sorcery, such as *The Wonderfull Discoverie of Witches in the Countie of Lancashire* (1613), a chronicle of the events taking place in the novel, written by Thomas Potts, or *Daemonology*, one of the key works on witchcraft and demonology written by James I in 1597. As in the case of Susanna Clarke's *Jonathan Strange & Mr. Norrell* (2004) – the text analysed by Baker, which provides an alternative history of nineteenth-century England – the reference to historical figures of greater or lesser importance, but real in the end, reveals 'an effort to pinion the narrative to a "factual" history' (2011, 4).

Within that historical setting, however, Winterson introduces early in the novel hints and secrets that point to an enigmatic dimension that may be approached through Roland Barthes's notion of the 'hermeneutic code':

---

[2] That is, the novel presents some 'connection between reality and truth' (Heller 2011, 89), but with a certain 'necessary anachronism' (Lukács 1962, 61) that 'indicates a fundamental change in the perception of history itself' (Heller 2011, 90). At the same time, Lukács puts forward that the contemporary historical novel focuses not just on relevant historical characters, but on the marginal social strata, dealing 'with the real life of all classes in society' (1962, 294).

> Let us designate as hermeneutic code (HER) all the units whose function it is to articulate in various ways a question, its response, and the variety of chance events which can either formulate the question or delay its answer; or even, constitute an enigma and lead to its solution.... Under the hermeneutic code we list the various (formal) terms by which an enigma can be distinguished, suggested, formulated, held in suspense, and finally disclosed (these terms will not always occur, they will often be repeated; they will not appear in any fixed order).
>
> 1990, 17–19

In relation to the narrative construction of the text, the 'hermeneutic code' may provoke the emergence of a question that may or may not be resolved afterwards. In this way, the author is able to increase interest in a particular point, thus arousing the reader's curiosity and inciting them to continue reading in order to discover the solution to the enigma. Barthes enumerates several elements that configure the hermeneutic code present in a text: there are '*avoided (or suspended) answer[s]*' (1990, 31; emphasis in the original); 'snare[s], set by the discourse for the reader', which evade the truth on purpose (32); 'equivocation[s]', which are a 'mixture of truth and snare' (38); partial answers to the enigma (38); 'false replies', which 'differ from the snare in that error is distinguished as such by the discourse' (42); and 'jamming[s]', when '[t]he discourse declares the enigma it has proposed to be unresolved' (47).

The Daylight Gate begins by situating Lancashire in the wild and dangerous epicentre of northern England: 'Lancashire is the wild part of the untamed'; '[t]he Forest of Pendle used to be a hunting ground, but some say that the hill is the hunter' (Winterson 2012, 1). These initial lines suggest the text's first enigma, as part of the Barthian hermeneutic code. Evading the truth on purpose, Winterson snares the reader, not revealing if the metaphor of the hunter hill hides any kind of supernatural component. According to Antosa, '[f]rom the outset, Winterson weaves a narrative which is ambivalently encoded as real and fantastic, imaginative and horrific' (2015, 160). My argument, however, is that in this first part of the novel, Winterson consciously hides explicit fantastic elements, even if she presents an unknown and equally mysterious scenario. With this Barthian snare, Lancashire and particularly the Pendle Forest are placed on the eyes of the reader as the initial axis of secrecy to be discovered. The need to know more about the place invites the reader to immerse themselves in the reading of *The Daylight Gate*.

None of the events that take place during the first chapters of the novel have any supernatural nature. The female characters, who are called witches, such as Alizon Device or Old Demdike, do not carry out any magical ritual nor show signs of having supernatural abilities. Winterson's narrative presents these people as discordant characters in English society, outcasts who are both feared and hated. At the beginning of the novel, for instance, the pedlar John Law thinks that Alizon Device might own a familiar spirit: 'the Devil had given her a spirit in the shape of a dog she called Fancy' (Winterson 2012, 4). At this point, it is impossible for the reader to know if Alizon has signed an actual pact with the Devil or if it is just something spread by the gossip surrounding the women in the story. The pedlar, a secondary character, provides information about the magical powers of Alizon Device, but this information cannot be contrasted at this point of the novel, thus working as a 'snare' as defined by Barthes (1990, 32), that is, a conscious evasion of the truth. John Law, the first character to appear in the text, hurries on his way back home, reinforcing again the Barthian enigma of the existence (or not) of magic, since '[h]e did not want to step through the light into whatever lay beyond the light' (Winterson 2012, 3). Winterson avoids answering this key enigma, and the result is that, at first, *The Daylight Gate* seems more like a feminist anthropological reading of witchcraft, attempting to explain in a more or less rational way the events that may have occurred in the past. A predominant view in contemporary anthropological and historical readings of witchery is to approach the figure of the witch – and, on fewer occasions, the male sorcerer – as a social scapegoat (Girard 1986; Reineke 1997; Yüzgüller Arsal and Yavuz 2014), challenging the claims of earliest studies such as Margaret Murray's *The Witch-Cult in Western Europe* (1921).[3] The witch is considered as such because she presents elements that differentiate her from the rest of the community (low social class, heretical practices, mental illnesses not diagnosed at the time, practices that denoted a superior intelligence,[4] free thought or expression of discordant femininity or sexuality, among others).[5] The figure of the witch thus becomes the scapegoat to explain bad harvests, human and animal diseases, and misfortunes.

The novel we are dealing with, in its first chapters, also seems to be following this approach to witchcraft. In fact, in some passages, Winterson is especially interested in dismantling any glimmer of fantasy that might slip into the novel, for instance when she refers to the mathematician and astronomer, John Dee: 'He believed he had succeeded in making a tiny phial of the Elixir of Life. Alice did not believe it. In any case, it had not saved the Queen or John Dee. They were both dead now' (Winterson 2012, 6). By using a Barthian 'equivocation', which puts together both truth and a snare (Barthes 1990, 38), Winterson mixes up John Dee's magical background, since the reader will discover later that Dee did not create any Elixir of Life, but he did master the formula of the youth elixir that Alice uses. Something similar occurs when Sarah Device, one of the women who belong to the coven of witches, is abused by two men accusing her of witchcraft. When she is about to be raped, she thinks that '[t]he Dark Gentleman[6] would come for her soon enough. Hadn't Demdike always said so?' (Winterson 2012, 12). The possibility of the Devil saving the woman will never happen

---

[3] Murray claimed that the witches prosecuted during the trials in Europe practised a pagan religion of a strong animist nature. This hypothesis was rejected in the first decades of the twentieth century by most of the historians and scholars.
[4] An illustrative example is Joan Peterson, a woman who prescribed powders and remedies to her neighbours. She was accused of witchcraft for being a 'cunning woman' and she would not accept bribery to swear against another person (Notestein 1911, 214).
[5] See, for example, Horsley's anthropological study on European witchcraft (1979).
[6] The figure of the Dark Man, or a man dressed in black, has been traditionally associated with the Black Sabbath. He is normally considered as the personification of the Devil, and he leads the ceremony or stands as one of its most prominent actors. For more information on this topic, see Miller (2008). The Dark Gentleman appears several times in *The Daylight Gate*, being an evident avatar of Lucifer.

in the story, and the protagonist, Alice Nutter, will be the one who rescues her from the two abusers. Once again, the hermeneutic code is at work here by means of a 'suspended answer' (Barthes 1990, 31), as the author will not reveal the truth at that particular moment. The reader will have to wait to know if the Dark Gentleman is real or just a product of the character's imagination.

What appears to be a process of complete historical rationalization has one of its peak points in the frustrated coven that takes place in the Malkin Tower on Good Friday 1612. The chapter begins with a very negative description of a pilgrimage heading for the tower. It introduces a diverse group of characters, all of them depicted with high degrees of physical and moral degeneration. Shortly afterwards, with the arrival of the protagonist, Alice Nutter, the coven begins. The secret ritual that takes place at the tower includes frenzied chants, the drinking of blood and the respect and devotion of all the people gathered around Alice, who is almost forced to take part on the Black Sabbath and is considered the most powerful witch among them. It is also interesting to note that Alice's appearance is completely opposite to the other members of the witch community. She is a beautiful woman; she looks very young despite her possibly advanced age; she is wealthy and with aristocratic manners, and likes falconry and equestrianism.[7] It is also worth noting that Alice coincides with the profile of a member of the 'sophisticated elite' who practises 'alchemy and astrology' (Horsley 1979, 700), very distant from the lower classes that put into practice a much more animist and wild witchcraft. During the ritual, an interesting discussion takes place, in which several characters affirm that Alice is capable of practising magic, claiming that her beauty is unusual for the age she should be. Alice responds with evasions and a 'sufficiently confusing' answer (Winterson 2012, 30), and when they decide to cut her arm to drink her blood, the following passage becomes particularly relevant:

> Alice was in danger and she knew she had only one chance. She took it. She shouted, 'Get on your knees!' ... Alice Nutter did not hesitate. She pulled open his [James Device's] shirt and scored a triangle in blood opening it out to make a shallow bleeding pentagram on his bare chest. He was trembling with terror.
>
> 31

The protagonist, being accused of having magical powers and harassed in the coven, decides to take control of the ritual. After the group considers her ability to cast spells, something she categorically denies, asserting that 'I cannot make a spell ... I have no magick' (30), Alice, violently and savagely, but totally earthly, escapes from the siege situation, becoming the conductor of the coven. This assertion made by Alice is a clear Barthian 'snare' (Barthes 1990, 32), since as the novel progresses it will be discovered that she is indeed a witch and has gone through numerous magical experiences. But at this point, when Winterson is still playing at making us believe that we are dealing with historical fiction, any hint of magic on Alice's part, which could have been used to get

---

[7] Lazăr examines how the representation of the female body in the novel confronts the 'ugly-therefore-guilty' hag with the 'beautiful-yet-suspicious' sorceress (2014, 1).

her out of the enclosure in the tower, is sharply hidden. In spite of her arcane knowledge, Alice proceeds in a completely mundane way, reaffirming the idea that magic is nothing but alien to the reality of the novel, and that all the rumours are just gossip. This is one of the peak points in *The Daylight Gate*, and Winterson deliberately conceals information so that the ambiguity of the text remains present, and the explanation of witchcraft falls back into the realm of rational events: the hermeneutic game of suspended answers continues. From a Barthian perspective, the snare that Alice performs during the Black Sabbath is particularly relevant, since she could have used her magic to flee from that situation, but she denies over and over again her magical powers. Had she revealed her real nature, the novel would have become a fantasy tale earlier.

The first clearly supernatural happening takes place a few chapters later, and the protagonist is Alice herself. The title of the chapter in question, 'It Begins', settles another enigma, part of the hermeneutic code. The impersonal pronoun 'it' triggers different interpretations and questions of the reader, since the referent of the pronoun is a mystery to be solved: what is it that begins? The chapter in question narrates the appearance of an invisible entity in Alice's living quarters, just as she is reading the procedure to summon a spirit that served Edward Kelley, an alchemist and her former lover. This chapter is the key breaking point in the novel, as from here onwards the tone completely changes, and the novel definitely moves from historical fiction to the fantastic genre, although it still maintains an outstanding historical component. All this takes place through the revelation of a key secret: Alice is indeed a practitioner of magic and, therefore, a witch.

When the reader acquires the knowledge that magic is a reality in the fictional universe of *The Daylight Gate*, they will have to rethink much of the information introduced in the previous chapters, especially everything that concerns the protagonist. The particular moment in which Winterson discloses this secret is, from a diegetic perspective, unusual. The characters have already been introduced, and the historical, non-magical context has been assumed by the reader. The efforts the writer makes at some points, before this moment, to reassert the lack of magic in her fictional universe are outstanding: the whole first third of *The Daylight Gate* is full of Barthian snares, as has been shown in the previous pages. Revealing the magical powers of the witches at the very end of the novel (or even keeping the suspended answer) would have created a completely different effect. Winterson, on the contrary, decides to unveil the fantastic element after we are quite familiarized with the setting and characters, so that from this point onwards the story becomes much darker and gory.

Once the true nature of the novel is discovered, a contrasting effect is produced between the anthropological and social explanation of witchcraft provided in the first chapters of *The Daylight Gate*, and the shock of the fantastic, which questions the veracity of the facts narrated. Winterson places the reader in a situation of scepticism with respect to the historical narrative, since the text moves from the historical genre to fantasy. Although historical novels are grounded on facts, reality is put into question in the fantasy genre. As Groot puts it, 'the historical novel, then, is similar to other forms of novel-writing in that it shares a concern with realism, development of character, authenticity' (2010, 4). The concealment during part of Winterson's novel of its true nature, by means of the hermeneutic code, magnifies the element of fantasy the text contains. The use of the hermeneutic code is what allows the writer to create this effect of destabilization in the novel.

The intrusion of the fantastic in a historical context has an ideological component that is more sharply underlined in the case of *The Daylight Gate*, as this intrusion is done abruptly and unexpectedly and not from the very beginning. In Baker's words,

> As contemporary historical fiction can be witnessed as a dislocation, using the motifs and structures of past literary forms to expose the effacement or 'blindness' that the historical project can produce, so too does fantasy strive to unearth those things that society buries. In both cases there exists a potential range for subversion and examination, undermining and questioning those things taken to be the 'norm,' discovering and rediscovering those dark areas of history unwritten and self unseen.
>
> 2011, 10

As mentioned above, Van Namen (2013), Lazăr (2014), Antosa (2015) and Kondali (2016) have pointed in this direction, providing insightful feminist and queer readings of *The Daylight Gate*, and highlighting the voice given in the novel to historically subaltern groups, mainly lesbians, outcasts and independent women. Such feminist approaches can be fruitfully expanded through Jackson's discussion of the relationship between the fantastic and invisibility:

> An emphasis upon invisibility points to one of the central thematic concerns of the fantastic: problems of vision. In a culture which equates the 'real' with the 'visible' and gives the eye dominance over other sense organs, the un-real is that which is invisible. That which is not seen, or which threatens to be un-seeable, can only have a subversive function in relation to an epistemological and metaphysical system which makes 'I see' synonymous with 'I understand.' Knowledge, comprehension, reason, are established through the power of the *look*, through the '*eye*' and the '*I*' of the human subject whose relation to objects is structured through his field of vision. In fantastic art, objects are not readily appropriated through the look: things slide away from the powerful eye/I which seeks to possess them, thus becoming distorted, disintegrated, partial and lapsing into invisibility.
>
> 2009, 26–7; emphasis in the original

Jackson's idea of invisibility is intimately connected with the notion of secrecy and concealment, which we are dealing with. In the seventeenth century, women were vilified and silenced, victims of a patriarchal system that violated them at will. In the words of Van Namen, '*The Daylight Gate* presents a time where women are subordinated and oppressed. They are subject to torture, rape, and abuse at the hands of men; and women with intelligence and power are regarded with intense suspicion' (2013, 172).

Moreover, in the particular historical context of the novel, we are presented with a group of women who suffer a trial for witchcraft in the midst of a failed revolution that could have completely changed the course of English history, that of the Gunpowder Plot. The historical relevance of both events is not comparable in terms of the critical attention they have received, but it is highly revealing that Winterson especially focuses on the witches, not on the Plot. By introducing the fantastic element, visibility is given to what has been culturally and historically invisible – a witch trial against women and the misadventures of the sorceresses – whereas what has been transmitted as a relevant historical fact, the Gunpowder Plot – a male conspiracy to sink a king – is relegated to invisibility. The attention given to magic brings women – witches – to the foreground, reducing the male murderous plot to a mere backdrop. This attention given to women extends to the novel's general concern with those members of society in a situation of marginality or dispossession – and hence, invisibility – as Alice Nutter herself puts it in a discussion with her lover, Christopher: 'Are you like all other men after all? The poor should have no justice, just as they have no food, no decent shelter, no regular livelihood? Is that how your saviour Jesus treated the poor?' (Winterson 2012, 55).

Coming back to the ideological use of the fantastic within historical fiction, in *The Daylight Gate* history as a discipline is threatened, since the passing from a historically reliable text to a fantastic one creates the idea 'that history can be written and re-written, marginalised or idealised, becoming a political tool and/or a portal to socio-political investigation' (Baker 2011, 1). History thus emerges as something that can be manipulated and narrated following the desires and ideologies of the writer. Or, as Hayden White puts it,

> On the one hand, there are always more facets in the record than the historian can possibly include in his narrative representation of a given segment of the historical process. And so the historian must 'interpret' his data by excluding certain facts from his account as irrelevant to his narrative purpose.... A historical narrative is thus necessarily a mixture of adequately and inadequately explained events, a congeries of established and inferred facts, at once a representation that is an interpretation and an interpretation that passes for an explanation of the whole process mirrored in the narrative.
>
> 1978, 51

If we consider *The Daylight Gate* as a fantastic historical record of the Pendle Witch Trials, Winterson is no more than reporting her own version of the historical events. Characters' magical powers, the presence of the Dark Gentleman or the witch covens will be seen today as fantasy, but considering the fact that witchcraft was something real and part of everyday life in seventeenth-century society, the novel makes us rethink all the processes through which historical reports are created. The average twenty-first-century reader will not believe a word of what Winterson is narrating (and probably she is not expecting us to do so), but her contemporary record of historical events will challenge other historical records. In the words of Kondali, 'historical fiction as a genre has exhibited a tendency to make use of conventions and elements characteristic of other genres, resulting in a form of hybridization. However, contemporary novelists (particularly women writers) frequently depart from the conventions of realistic novel writing to produce alternate historical narratives, such as this novel by Jeannette Winterson' (2016, 250).

The questioning of history by means of the fantastic is a feature present in many other postmodern texts. From Gabriel García Márquez's *One Hundred Years of Solitude* (1967) to Salman Rushdie's *Midnight Children* (1981), or Winterson herself in *The Passion* (1987), the connection has been broadly exploited. Hutcheon coined the concept of 'historiographic metafiction' to refer to this kind of narrative, defining them as 'those well-known and popular novels which are both intensely self-reflexive and yet paradoxically also lay claim to historical events and personages' (1988, 5). Hutcheon rejects that history as a discipline owns the only possible truth, since

> historiographic metafiction refutes the natural or common-sense methods of distinguishing between historical fact and fiction. It refuses the view that only history has a truth claim, both by questioning the ground of that claim in historiography and by asserting that both history and fiction are discourses, human constructs, signifying systems, and both derive their major claim to truth from that identity.
>
> 1988, 93

The Daylight Gate indeed illustrates this constructed nature of both history and fantasy. All in all, it is a novel which, by means of secrecy and fantasy, effectively provides an alternative approach to the figure of the witch. The setting, historical at first, fantastic as the plot unravels, seeks the vindication of women as a subaltern, invisible group during the seventeenth century, prioritizing the plot line of the trials over that of the Gunpowder Plot, which has been significantly more relevant than the Pendle Trials in History Studies. The enigma code is a key resource that Winterson uses in order to perform that vindication. Nevertheless, the relationship between secrecy and fantasy is not only employed in the novel to highlight the role of subaltern groups in history and the invisibility they have suffered from. As analysed in the next section, secrecy also plays a key role in the depiction of the coven and love relationships, the main communities we find in this novel.

Secrecy and community

The secrets that make up *The Daylight Gate* are also important in relation to the different communities present in the novel. In this concern with community, I am following the terms that, inspired by Bataille, were proposed by Blanchot and Nancy. The former differentiates between 'elective' and 'traditional' communities, while the latter distinguishes between 'immanent' and 'inoperative' communities. According to Blanchot, a traditional community 'is imposed on us without our having the liberty of choice in the matter: it is *de facto* sociality, or the glorification or the earth, or the blood, or even of race' (Blanchot 1988, 46). In contrast, he considers that an elective community is so because 'it exists only through a decision that gathers its members around a choice without which it could not have taken place' (46–7). For Nancy (1991), the immanent, operative community is repressive, self-enclosed, strongly opposed to alterity and otherness. The inoperative community, on the contrary, is open to exposure, it is finite and grounded on singularity.

Turning to Winterson's novel, there are two major secrets in Alice's past that determine her identity and development as a character and her relationship with the rest of the characters in *The Daylight Gate*. The first one, as has been already stated, is her magical expertise. Because of that secret, which will haunt her and will ultimately cost her her life, she will engage actively with other characters who also keep secrets. The most relevant one is Elizabeth Southern who, apart from practising black magic, has also had a sentimental relationship with Alice in the past. The love story between these two women is also kept as a fictional secret from all the other characters.

Alice and Elizabeth may be seen as constituting what Blanchot considers a particular case of the elective community, that of the community of lovers (1988, 33). This community is chosen by its members, 'it exists only through a decision that gathers its members around a choice without which it could not have taken place' (46–7), and contrasts with traditional, imposed communities. As lovers, Alice and Elizabeth conform to a community that, in the words of Delanty, 'consists of a withdrawal from society and even the transgression of limits' (2010, 109). Or, as Blanchot puts it, the community of lovers holds a 'secret behind which hides execrable excesses' (1988, 47). In this particular case, the rejection that two lesbian lovers might cause in English society at the beginning of the seventeenth century will trigger the secrecy of the relationship. For the male immanent community, 'lesbian love is a threatening concept in male ideology because men become utterly isolated from this exclusivist "club" and frustration sets in' (Lazăr 2014, 7). As Van Namen points out, 'Alice is the only female character who rejects the limitations of gender. She establishes herself as a person with an identity separate from the restrictive male/female binary' (2013, 173).

As an elective community, the community of lovers is so strong that it transcends death: 'Love is as strong as death' (Winterson 2012, 161). In the words of Blanchot,

> Love, stronger than death. Love which does not suppress death but which oversteps the limit death represents and thus renders it powerless in regard to helping someone else.... Not so as to glorify death by glorifying love, but, perhaps on the contrary, to give to life a transcendency without glory that puts it endlessly at the service of the other.
>
> 1988, 45

As in the case of fantasy, Winterson silences the lesbian relationship to the reader until quite late in the novel. Alice confesses to Christopher Southworth that Old Demdike, one of the hags from the group of misfits, is in reality Elizabeth Southern. This relationship is the reason why Alice protects Old Demdike and provides her with shelter in her own land, and why the protagonist will not escape to France with Christopher Southworth. More, on the contrary, she will try to save Old Demdike/Elizabeth from prison, turning herself in to the authorities to have access to her old lover. Alice does her best to save Elizabeth, moved by the possibility of her lover's death in the gallows. At the end, Elizabeth's soul is taken by the Dark Gentleman before she is taken to public execution. In the case of Alice, her falcon familiar spirit severs her jugular just before she is hung after the trial. None of them will be part of the sacrifice carried out by the traditional community: the two women will not burn at the stake. The community of lovers vanishes, 'always ready to dissolve itself' (Blanchot 1988, 33), but it has been kept in secret until the end. In fact, the only person who will know the secret is Christopher Southworth (and, of course, the reader).

Parallel to this community of lovers runs that of the coven. Whereas in the case of the two lovers what kept them as a secret couple was their lesbian love, here the secret that glues this inoperative community is witchcraft. The group that reunites at the Malkin Tower on Good Friday 1612 is a 'strange, wild, ragged group of men and women' (Winterson 2012, 25). The Black Sabbath has an intended purpose – which will become a secret shared by its members – explained by Elizabeth Device as follows: 'all of us here might free my mother Demdike and my daughter Alizon from Lancaster Castle. I will even free the Chattox if they will help us' (28). The coven is constituted by a community of hags – with the exception of Alice Nutter – who plots how to free some other misfits from a hideous and sickening prison. The secret meeting is interrupted at its climax by the authorities, Roger Nowell, Constable Hargreaves and Tom Peeper, who act as repressive forces of the traditional, male community. As Hargreaves reveals, 'my spies have reported a band of persons travelling through the forest – unknowns – vagrants they could be... or they could be to do with the Good Friday Black Mass that we have suspicions of tomorrow, on Pendle Hill' (Winterson 2012, 22). The use of spies to disclose the meeting reinforces the idea of secrecy that surrounds the gathering, an assembly that might threaten the operative community the authorities control, since as Blanchot puts it forward, the elective community that opposes the traditional community 'has as its ultimate goal the destruction of society... be it in infinitesimal doses' (1988, 48). The witch as an individual might be harmless, but according to René Girard, 'despite her personal insignificance, a witch is engaged in activities that can potentially affect the whole of society' (1986, 17). In fact, the final act of violence and public sacrifice of the witches after the trial restores the order of the immanent operative community. The use of scapegoats, the expelling and destruction of the secret coven, is received with joy and happiness by the society: 'And all the time people were clapping and singing. This was pleasure. This was a holiday' (Winterson 2012, 190). The act of exposing the secret is at the same time a necessary act of social catharsis in which collective violence is admissible, since 'the persecutors are convinced that their violence is justified' (Girard 1986, 6). Roger Nowell explains it to Alice Nutter at a certain point: 'There has to be a sacrifice – don't you understand that?' (Winterson 2012, 152).

Girard explains that the figure of the witch combines many different aberrant abnormalities, both moral and physical, that unleash persecution (1986, 48). In fact, '[i]n any area of existence or behavior abnormality may function as the criterion for selecting those to be persecuted. For example there is such a thing as social abnormality; here the average defines the norm. The further one is from normal social status of whatever kind, the greater the risk of persecution' (18). The group of people gathering at Malkin Tower are both outcasts and physically degenerated, so they are subject to persecution. We find a female character with 'flesh that fell off her as though it were cooked. And her feet stank of dead meat. Today they were wrapped in rags already beginning to ooze' (Winterson 2012, 25). Others were 'getting food from [their] favours given to farmhands' (25). A couple was said to be 'brother and sister though they slept in the same bed' (26), and 'there was the little girl Jennet Device, vicious, miserable, underfed and abused' (26), whose brother 'took her with him to the Dog to pay for his drink. Tom Peeper liked his sexual conquests to be too young to fall pregnant' (26). All the members of the coven are, in a sense, abnormal. Most of them are physically or morally degenerated, and in the case of Alice, she is socially abnormal because of her habits and elevated social class. The coven, as an inoperative community, will act then as a scapegoat for the immanent community that cannot cope with individuals who challenge so powerfully normativity.

Curiously enough, in spite of the fact that the witches are able to use magic, none of them will use it against the members of the immanent community until they start to be harassed and prosecuted. It is only when that happens that Elizabeth Device and Old Mouldheels put a spell on Roger Nowell in order to kill him. As regards Alice, she is perceived by the immanent community as a menace, not for being an outcast as the rest of the members of the coven, but because of the already mentioned features, considered atypical for a woman. As Lazăr explains, Winterson 'foregrounds a society of cruel men that will very quickly attribute evil to women and condemn them to death when they fall out of the norm' (2014, 3). On the other hand, whenever Alice appears in the novel, secrecy is present in some way or another; those who belong to the operative community keep trying to uncover her secrets, and the threats she receives are always connected to those secrets. Roger Nowell, for instance, tells Alice: 'I know more of your past than you imagine' (Winterson 2012, 47), alluding to her relationship with the magician, John Dee. Most of her relationships are based on secrets: her love affair with Elizabeth, her belonging to the coven, her study of magic as an apprentice of John Dee (from where she got the secret dye and the youth elixir) and her affair with Christopher Southworth, who is also an outsider, and who is concealed by Alice as well. The two of them also create a community of lovers that share a secret: Christopher has come back to England to rescue his sister from the trials. Secrecy is also present in Alice's homely spaces. When her dwelling is described, there are constant references to the secret passage that she uses to hide Christopher. First, the reader finds that '[h]e had got into the house after dark and taken the little staircase to her study, and crept through the secret corridor that joined her bedroom' (Winterson 2012, 53). After that, '[s]he had made him get up, taken him down the secret passageway between her bedroom and her study. Locked him in' (85). At the same time, her house in London also has 'secret private rooms' (90) that Christopher uses during his fleeing out of England and that she once used to meet Elizabeth in a private, isolated place. Christopher will get the feeling of 'intruding on another life. A secret life' (156) when he reaches those rooms. And again, Roger Nowell will use Alice's past secrets to attack her. He is aware of Alice collaborating with Christopher (hiding him) after the Gunpowder Plot was dismantled: 'You hid him six years ago when he fled London after the Plot – yes, I know you did so, and it is true I turned a blind eye' (151–2). In relation to this, it is interesting to note that

Alice's association with secrecy creates a link between her and the rest of the women in the novel, all of whom hide secrets from men in one way or another: arcane abilities, secret corridors and rooms in their domestic environments, lesbian relationships or even their real identity, as in the case of Old Demdike/Elizabeth.

The presence of elective communities in the novel – lovers and the coven – can be connected with the previously exposed idea of giving voice through the fantastic to those traditionally kept invisible, namely, women and outsiders in general. It is remarkable that most of the representatives of the operative community are (generally wealthy) men: Roger Potts, Thomas Norwell, their group of minions and several peasants. They personify the repressive power of the traditional community, whose goal is to unravel and disclose all the secrets that the others – women – hide. Christopher, who is the only wealthy man on the outcasts' side, was tortured and castrated after the Gunpowder Plot, so his manly condition is nullified. As Antosa asserts, '[a]s an outcast and an outsider, Christopher stands for a different, positive model of masculinity that includes characteristics of the opposite sex' (2015, 162). This castration, then, 'pushes him to occupy somewhere in between the male and female binary' (Van Namen 2013, 174). At the very end of the novel, Winterson makes it clear that Christopher will also be hunted and eradicated, as another harmful element that threatens the established community, so with his more than likely death, all the different elective communities present in the novel are wiped out, restoring peace among neighbours.

Conclusion

As addressed throughout this chapter, *The Daylight Gate* is a novel that abounds in secrets. Those secrets will not allow the reader to discern, during the first part of the text, if the narration is historical or fantastic. The use of the hermeneutic code as theorized by Barthes, mainly by means of snares and avoided answers, creates a delay in the revelation of one of the key secrets: the fact that witches in this novel do have real magical powers. This revelation gives prominence to the voices of women, witches and outcasts; those traditionally neglected social groups get a central role in the development of historical events, as opposed to the male characters in the story, who mainly become secondary characters. The fantastic genre is thus used to offer an alternative reading of seventeenth-century English historical events, in particular, the Pendle Trials.

Simultaneously, secrets are the articulatory cornerstones on which characters and relationships are founded. Alice Nutter is a character whose identity is entirely built on secrets; as such, she is associated with three different elective communities throughout the novel: a community of lovers with Elizabeth Southern, a second one with Christopher Southworth and, finally, the coven. The communities she belongs to end up disappearing, similarly to Blanchot's point about the volatility of elective communities. The traditional, immanent community is represented in the book by the repressive forces of the authority, mostly male figures. This community cannot tolerate the existence of antisocial communities that threat the social order, no matter if they are made up of witches, lesbian lovers or plotters. Men in the novel will put all their efforts into unveiling the secrets that these elective communities share, in order to make them disappear, nullifying any kind of menace those groups might imply for the status quo. The predatory hunger of the immanent community knows no limits, as it devours any trace of opposition it may find.

References

Antosa, Silvia. (2015), 'In a Queer Gothic Space and Time: Love Triangles in Jeanette Winterson's *The Daylight Gate*', *Altre Modernità*, 13: 152–67, https://doi.org/10.13130/2035-7680/4838.
Attridge, Derek. (2011), *Reading and Responsibility: Deconstruction's Traces*, Edinburgh: Edinburgh University Press.
Baker, Daniel. (2011), 'History as Fantasy: Estranging the Past in *Jonathan Strange and Mr. Norrell*', *Otherness: Essays and Studies*, 2 (1): 1–16.
Barthes, Roland. (1990), *S/Z*, translated by Richard Miller, Oxford: Blackwell.
Blanchot, Maurice. (1988), *The Unavowable Community*, translated by Pierre Joris, New York: Station Hill Press.
Delanty, Gerard. (2010), *Community*, 2nd edition, New York: Routledge.
Front, Sonia. (2009), *Transgressing Boundaries in Jeanette Winterson's Fiction*, Frankfurt: Peter Lang.
Girard, René. (1986), *The Scapegoat*, translated by Yvonne Freccero, Baltimore: John Hopkins University Press.
Groot, Jerome de. (2010), *The Historical Novel*, London: Routledge.
Heller, Agnes. (2011), 'The Contemporary Historical Novel', *Thesis Eleven*, 106 (1): 88–97. https://doi.org/10.1177/0725513611407448
Horsley, Richard A. (1979), 'Who Were the Witches? The Social Roles of the Accused in the European Witch Trials', *The Journal of Interdisciplinary History*, 9 (4): 689–715. https://doi.org/10.2307/203380
Hutcheon, Linda. (1988), *A Poetics of Postmodernism: History, Theory, Fiction*, New York: Routledge.
Jackson, Rosemary. (2009) (1981), *Fantasy: The Literature of Subversion*, New York: Routledge.
Kondali, Ksenija. (2016), 'Revisi(ti)ng History: Jeanette Winterson's *The Daylight Gate* and the Transformation of Historical Novels', *Belgrade BELLS* VIII: 245–60. https://doi.org/10.18485/bells.2016.8.15
Lazăr, Mihaela C. (2014), '"The Indigestible Elements": Witches and Female Identity in Jeanette Winterson's *The Daylight Gate*', *Indian Review of World Literature in English*, 10 (2): 1–9.
López, Gema. (2007), *Seductions in Narrative: Subjectivity and Desire in the Works of Angela Carter and Jeanette Winterson*, Youngstown: Cambria Press.
Luhrmann, Tanya M. (1989), 'The Magic of Secrecy', *Ethos*, 17 (2): 131–65.
Lukács, Georg. (1962), *The Historical Novel*, translated by Hannah Mitchell and Stanley Mitchell, London: Merlin Press.
Miller, Joyce. (2008), 'Men in Black: Appearances of the Devil in Early Modern Scottish Witchcraft Discourse', in Julian Goodare, Lauren Martin and Joyce Miller (eds), *Witchcraft and Belief in Early Modern Scotland*, 144–65, New York: Palgrave MacMillan.

Mingiuc, Andreea. (2011), 'Woman Must Write Woman: Jeanette Winterson and Echoes of French Feminism', *Gender Studies*, 10: 261–72.
Murray, Margaret A. (1921), *The Witch-Cult in Western Europe: A Study in Anthropology*, Oxford: The Clarendon Press.
Nancy, Jean-Luc. (1991), *The Inoperative Community*, translated by Peter Connor, Lisa Garbus, Michael Holland and Simona Sawhney, Minneapolis: University of Minnesota Press.
Notestein, Wallace. (1911), *A History of Witchcraft in England from 1558 to 1718*, Washington: The American Historical Association.
Onega, Susana. (2006), *Jeanette Winterson*, Manchester: Manchester University Press.
Pacheco Costa, Verónica. (2008), *Jeanette Winterson: Literatura y Ciencia*, Sevilla: Arcibel.
Reineke, Martha J. (1997), '"The Devils Are Coming Upon Us:" Myth, History, and the Witch as Scapegoat', in Martha J. Reineke (ed.), *Sacrificed Lives: Kristeva on Women and Violence*, 128–60, Bloomington: Indiana University Press.
Rusk, Lauren. (2002), *The Life Writing of Otherness: Woolf, Baldwin, Kingston, and Winterson*, New York: Routledge.
Van Namen, Kirsten. (2013), 'Fear of the Independent Woman in Jeanette Winterson's *The Daylight Gate*', *The Journal of Supernatural Literature*, 1: 172–80.
White, Hayden. (1978), *Tropics of Discourse: Essays in Cultural Criticism*, Baltimore: Johns Hopkins University Press.
Winterson, Jeanette. (2012), *The Daylight Gate*, London: Hammer.
Yüzgüller Arsal, Serap, and Yavuz, Seda. (2014), 'The Portrait of the "Scapegoat Woman" as Witch', *Synergies Turquie*, 7: 167–78.

9

Novel mediums: The art of not speaking in (and of) Hilary Mantel's *Beyond Black*

Hannu Poutiainen[1]

Introduction

Not a day goes by that Alison Hart – the spirit-seeing, mind-reading, past-haunted and future-telling protagonist of Hilary Mantel's critically acclaimed novel *Beyond Black* (2005) – is not faced with a singular dilemma. She is a medium; her vocation is to serve as a conduit between the world of the living and the world of the dead. This vocation has two sides to it, one a matter of knowledge and the other of social life. The first relates to the revelation of truths: privy to the secrets of the afterlife, her task is to pass them on to the living. The second concerns the possibility of a *socius* – a community – in which both the living and the dead are present: severed from one another by rampant urbanization, they lack a reliable means of communication, and it falls to the medium to bring their respective worlds together. As if her task were to remedy the situation described by Hannah Arendt in *The Human Condition*:

> What makes mass society so difficult to bear is not the number of people involved, or at least not primarily, but the fact that the world between them has lost the power to gather them together, to relate and to separate them. The weirdness of this situation resembles a spiritualistic seance where a number of people gathered around a table might suddenly, through some magic trick, see the table vanish from their midst, so that two people sitting opposite each other were no longer separated but also would be entirely unrelated to each other by anything tangible.
>
> Arendt 1998, 52–3

The world of *Beyond Black* is such a world. There, in the somnolent and solipsistic towns along the London Orbital motorway where Alison plies her trade, what has vanished is the past; and far from vanishing suddenly, as though by some sleight of hand, it has been evaporated by the slower-working magic trick by which the logic of

---

[1] This article is part of a postdoctoral research project funded by the Kone Foundation.

capital – known since Marx to have the ability to make tables disappear[2] – obliterates any collective memory and sense of historical belonging. As Catherine Spooner writes in an insightful essay, *Beyond Black* 'poses the question: what does it mean to be haunted in a culture with no history? If a society has no interest in its personal and collective past, then in what form can that past return?' (2010, 81). It is this indifference to the past that forms the background – at once social, economic and cultural – against which Alison is working. And the adverb 'against' must be taken in two senses at the same time. When the table vanishes, it is not the medium who performs the magic trick; her sleight, however much it may conform to the laws of spectacle, consists in at least partially undoing it. The secret is the table, and in revealing it, she restores, as far as she can, the social bonds – familial, organic, historical – that have been dissolved by the acid touch of capital. It is through her, then, that community re-emerges.

Yet that, though true, is only true by half. For it is also the case that these two sides of the medium's vocation prove nearly irreconcilable. The living come to her to ask questions of their departed loved ones; but what if the truth is hurtful and too destructive to be let out? The dead come to her to send messages to their surviving kin; but what if these messages are too frivolous to merit passing on? It is by means of the secret that she is expected to revive community; but what if the secret is such that community cannot withstand it? And what of the darkest secret of all: that the dead are *dead*, absolutely cut off from any social bond that the living might wish to forge with them? This is brought into full view in the passage that gives the novel its name. Alison is onstage; the audience is asking questions, most of them rather silly, about the world beyond; and as she takes the questions she reflects on the essential and unspeakable non-silliness of what they are being so silly about, of the dead and the place they inhabit:

> People are right to be afraid of ghosts. If you get people who are bad in life – I mean, cruel people, dangerous people – why do you think they're going to be any better after they're dead?
>
> But she would never speak it. Never. Never utter the word 'death,' if she could help it. And even though they needed frightening, even though they deserved frightening, she would never, when she was with her clients, slip a hint or tip a wink about the true nature of the place beyond black.
>
> Mantel 2010, 193–4

There, the novel suggests, is the dilemma. How to avoid speaking of the place beyond black? How, when it is from that place that the dead egress with their messages and pleas? How to speak truly without speaking openly of it? How to let community form around a nucleus of secrecy? To revert to Arendt's simile: How to put the table back without showing it?

---

[2] Speaking of the 'great moment at the beginning of *Capital*', Jacques Derrida asks: 'Is it just chance that he illustrates the principle of his explanation by causing a table to turn? Or rather by recalling the apparition of a turning table?' (1994, 149). Echoing Derrida, one may ask, as a merely phantomatic aside, whether it is 'just chance' that Arendt shuts Marx out of the spiritualistic séance.

The answer: by putting another table in its place. As Colette, Alison's business associate, learns early on in their long tangle of a friendship, the word death almost never slips out; instead, 'Al talked about passing, she talked about spirit, she talked about passing into spirit world; to that eventless realm, neither cold nor hot, neither hilly nor flat, where the dead, each at their own best age and marooned in an eternal afternoon, pass the ages with sod all going on' (Mantel 2010, 43). Her strategy, in other words, is one of substitution, and her very enterprise hinges on the deftness of the switch.

But how, exactly, does she succeed in this? By what means, to what ends, in view of what consequences, with what unforeseen effects? These are the questions – formulated, for reasons I will explain below, with reference to Jacques Derrida's essay 'How to Avoid Speaking: Denials' – to be investigated in the following pages. My approach to these questions will be twofold. Rather than take them in their totality, I will split them into two series that will be progressively wound into one another as the argument develops.[3] The first series is external: it concerns the public-facing aspect of the avoidance. The second series is internal: it concerns the inward effects of what has been avoided. Of these, the first series will be the leading one; the second series will involve itself by degrees in the first. Thus, after setting out the problem of secrecy, I go on to examine how the novel depicts the medium's trade. Then, after investigating the comportment of the medium with respect to her occupation, I will finish by asking what the inner experience of the medium consists of.

Throughout, I will hold the question of community at a remove, observing only that community, however defined, is what the medium is supposed to make. This is for two reasons, one theoretical and the other substantial. The theoretical reason is that, if I am right in supposing that the medium makes community out of secrecy, it follows that the question of secrecy has *logical* priority. The substantial reason is that, if the logically prior question of secrecy is followed consistently, it will result in a transformed conception of what community itself might be.

A note on terminology before I begin. In the language of the novel, the divide between the living and the dead is cast in terms of 'earthside' and 'airside'. The latter is

---

[3] These questions are indissociably bound up with the novel's title. They thus invoke what Jacques Derrida says of another title, Baudelaire's *La Fausse Monnaie*, in *Given Time*. 'As title', Derrida writes, 'it does not form a sentence, it does not say to what it refers, and its referential trait, as well as its referent, remains relatively undetermined' (Derrida 1992, 84). One may say, therefore, that what the novel names, in addition to the place 'beyond black' (and it is essential to note that, since the title refers to a phrase, it is always an open question where one should make the cut: whether, that is, one should speak of the place 'beyond black', of the 'place beyond black', or even of the 'true nature of the place beyond black'), is Alison's desire to avoid speaking of it; thus to read the title correctly is to know that to read is to avoid. Consequently, as Paul de Man says of Keats's *The Fall of Hyperion*, 'it matters a great deal how we read the title, as an exercise not only in semantics, but in what the text actually does to us' (de Man 1986, 16). As to what the title does to us, a suggestion may be found in Derrida's *Aporias*. For Derrida, '*death* is always the name of a secret, since it signs the irreplaceable singularity. It puts forth the public name, the common name of a secret, the common name of the proper name without name. It is therefore always a shibboleth, for the manifest name of a secret is from the beginning a private name' (Derrida 1993, 74; emphasis in the original). My thanks to the editors for indicating the appositeness of this quotation.

also referred to as 'the spirit world' or simply 'spirit'. Those to whom Alison provides her services are variously called 'punters' or 'the trade', whereas those working in the business are called 'mediums', 'psychics' and 'sensitives'.

The medium's dilemma: Withholding the place 'Beyond Black'

The medium's dilemma is that she must speak *from* a place that she must avoid speaking *of*. This latter part of the formulation, as I noted above, is borrowed from Jacques Derrida's essay 'How to Avoid Speaking'. There, Derrida writes:

> Here one is tempted to designate, if not to define, consciousness as that place in which is retained the singular power not to *say* what one knows, to keep a secret in the form of representation. A conscious being is a being capable of lying, of not presenting in a discourse what it nonetheless has an articulated representation of: a being that can avoid speaking. But to be able to lie, a second and already modalized possibility, one must first – a more essential possibility – be able to keep for oneself, by saying to oneself, what one already knows. To keep for oneself is the most incredible and thought-provoking power.
>
> Derrida 2008b, 156; emphasis in the original

In this dual structure we see the root and form of Alison's dilemma. Since secrecy consists of withholding a truth, the place of the secret would be found in consciousness, and it would be from this that consciousness derives its perhaps most unique power. To avoid speaking of the place beyond black, therefore, is to use this 'most incredible and thought-provoking power': not to lie, exactly, but to speak, as Abraham speaks to Isaac, without speaking (Derrida 2008a, 59–61).

Yet the use of this power comes at a cost that can be calculated with syllogistic certainty. Because the truth withheld is that of the 'place beyond black', Alison cannot keep this truth to herself without thereby taking the place beyond black within herself. It is, in other words, not just a place out there that she must not speak of. An *aporia of avoidance*: being able not to speak of it, she retains it as a place within herself.[4] And what is most haunting about this place is that it is coextensive with her consciousness in its totality. Wherever she goes, there the place beyond black is; whatever she sees, there it can be seen; and whatever she says, in whichever

---

[4] This is not unconnected to the problem of the crypt, as addressed by Derrida in 'Fors':

> A fantasy *does not coerce*, it does not impose, as Reality does …, any topographical transformation. In contrast with Reality, the fantasy tends to maintain the order of *topoi*. … Reality is that which would require a change of place, a modification of the topography. … Reality, that about which nothing should ever be known or heard of, would thus be in an essential relation with the secret.
>
> Derrida 1987, xviii; emphasis in the original

In this scheme, the 'place beyond black' would be Reality, and the crypt – that which, being incorporated, is absolutely nonmanifest, hence 'secret' – would be what it situates.

way, it is there to be heard in her words, if not by ordinary people then at least by herself.

And if by herself, then by us, too, who read her mind on the page. From this perspective, the novel might be said to give us a picture, telepathically transmitted, of what takes place in the psychic's mind. And what Catherine Spooner says of Alison's experience would then be true of ours as well: 'For Alison, haunting registers itself physically on the body and its material surroundings, a continuous and distressing disruption of her personal space' (Spooner 2010, 89). Haunted by what haunts her, we would be, to coin a term inspired by Nicholas Royle's thinking of literary telepathy (1991),[5] 'ambiscient', surrounded, as by a diaphanous ether, by what Alison knows, senses and thinks. Like Alison, we would have become 'sensitive', one whose 'senses were arranged in a different way from the senses of most people' (Mantel 2010, 7), able to take every word as either keeping or letting slip the secret that lies at the heart of her dilemma.

What this secret touches upon will be discussed in due course. Here, preliminarily, suffice it to say that the secret is indissolubly bound up with Alison's violent childhood. Growing up in a dilapidated house with an alcoholic mother and a gang of abusive and criminal men, her first encounter with a discarnate spirit occurs at the age of five, when her mother, impatient for a drink and loath to drag little Alison with her, locks her up in the attic with her toy bricks and animals. Mrs McGibbet is the name of this spirit, a sweet little Irish lady with 'blue and round and startled' eyes and a 'cooing voice' (Mantel 2010, 102), a more benevolent presence by far than the crowd of vile characters with ruffianly names – Keith Capstick, Donnie Aitkenside, MacArthur and Nick, Pikey Pete and Bob Fox – one of whom stays with Alison even after he is dead: Morris, a lewd, flatulent, foul-mouthed gnarl of a man, who by some grotesque twist of humour becomes Alison's 'guide' (6), peppering her daily existence with unsage advice and stomach-turning commentary.

But this is only by way of preface. This theme belongs in the second series of questions and will be kept off until later: the external question – how the keeping of the secret relates to those from whom it is kept – must be answered first.

Death and taxes: Mediumship as a profession

The external question is also a question of exteriority: of there being, in the broader world of the novel, an exteriorizing moment where airside secrecy and earthside community coincide without inherent reference to what goes on in Alison's mind. One such detour suggests itself already in the novel's second paragraph:

---

[5] My coinage, however, owes more to the essay 'The "Telepathy Effect": Notes Toward a Reconsideration of Narrative Fiction' (Royle 2003, 256–76), where Royle rebuts 'omniscience' as a critical term, arguing that telepathy is more suggestive of the structure of 'being-two-to-speak' that constitutes the 'essentiality of the literary secret' (266).

> There are nights when you don't want to do it, but you have to do it anyway. Nights when you look down from the stage and see closed stupid faces. Messages from the dead arrive at random. You don't want them and you can't send them back. The dead won't be coaxed and they won't be coerced. But the public has paid its money and it wants results.
>
> Mantel 2010, 1

Even here the dilemma is forming. These troubles belong to Alison by virtue of her power. But they also belong to her by virtue of her profession. An exteriorizing category *par excellence*: like everything else in this world, mediumship is a job, and one may do well or ill at it. Substantially, Alison is doing well, proving her talents by the revelations and reassurances she delivers to her solitude-stricken suburbanites. But financially, she is floundering, which is precisely why she needs someone like Colette, who, carping and disgruntled, coming to share not only the profits of the business and the comforts of an upscale house but also the increasing claustrophobia of coexisting with the dead, moves into Alison's life with all the fine feeling of a pair of forceps.

This mundane note, rich in satirical yield, develops into an important theme. The main intermediary for its elaboration is Colette, whose idea of mediumship is of the uttermost banality.[6] A case in comical point is her early visit to the tax office. As Mantel writes,

> Al hadn't even been registered for VAT, when Colette had come on board as her business brain. As for income tax, her allowances were all over the place. Colette had been to the tax office in person. The official she saw admitted to a complete ignorance of a medium's trade; she was poised to take advantage of it. 'What about her clothes,' she said, 'her stage outfits? Her outfits for meeting her clients. She has to look good, it's a professional obligation.'
>
> 'Not one we recognise, I'm afraid,' the young woman said.
>
> Mantel 2010, 94

There is no advantage to be had: the official will yield no further than to 'pass it up for consideration' and '[t]ake it under advisement' (ibid., 95). A sore defeat, Colette responds to it by undertaking 'to keep a complete record of Al's expenditure on stage outfits' (ibid.). But all of this is to no avail: no more is heard of Alison's taxes.

Stressing the banality of mediumship, such scenes 'in the key of Colette' have the virtue of checking any tendency to romanticize the psychic. But that is not the only task they perform. They also instruct the reader as the narrative progresses towards areas of experience that the cynic is unable to countenance. 'You should know better, Colette', Alison thinks to herself late in the novel, 'but how can you know better? You believe and you half believe, that's the trouble with you. You want the frisson and you want the money, but you don't want to alter your dumb view of the world' (Mantel

---

[6] That Colette's perspective is also a perspective of control is discussed with great perspicacity by Kukkonen and Nielsen (2018, 480).

2010, 322). This last imploration – coming at a point where Colette has glibly joked about certain 'fiends' that constantly hover about – is vitally important. Colette, like the rest of us, lives on what William James called 'an inclined plane of credulity' that 'tips one way in one man, another way in another' (James 1986, 100),[7] and if we, as readers of the novel, do not wish to tip the wrong way, we have to adjust our own plane not by Colette's but by Alison's example.

Yet on this plane, things are far more dangerous, as Alison reminds her audience. It is 1998; Princess Diana has only recently died, and people are eager to hear from her 'in spirit'. Alison is taking questions, first about the prospect of communicating with Diana through a Ouija board, then about what a Ouija board is, and finally about the dangers of – as one woman says – 'Dabbling in that sort of thing'. To which Alison replies:

> 'Oh, yes, dabbling,' Al said. It made her smile, the way the punters used it as a technical term. 'Yes, you don't want to go dabbling. Because you have to consider who would come through. There are some spirits that are, I'm not being rude now, but they are on a very low level. They're only drifting about earthside because they've got nothing better to do. They're like those kids you see on sink estates hanging about parked cars – you don't know if they're going to break in and drive them away or just slash the tyres and scratch the paintwork. But why find out? Just don't go there! Now those sort of kids, you wouldn't ask them in your house, would you? Well, that's what you're doing if you mess about with a Ouija board.'
>
> Mantel 2010, 193

The explanation ends with a warning to the audience. However, since it is immediately after this that Alison meditates on 'the true nature of the place beyond black' (194), it is not impossible to pick up on a second, implied warning, a quaver that betrays the suppression of some further fear. Expressed in terms of a telepathic hypothesis, it is as if the reader were touched, made to tremble,[8] by a secret tremor that splits the voice, giving it a tinge of ontological double-dealing: first a stated, overt, over-the-counter warning to the intradiegetic audience from whom death is withheld; then an implied, secret, underhanded warning to the extradiegetic reader who is exempted from the withholding of death.

It is clear why one should feel thus warned. As Derrida says, the question of how to avoid speaking always harbours the question as to why one should avoid speaking: 'The "how,"' he writes, 'always shelters a "why"' (Derrida 2008b, 154). We know Alison's reason

---

[7] It is perhaps not insignificant that this quotation comes from an essay where James affirms the veracity of certain psychic occurrences involving himself and a medium called Leonora Piper. On James and psychical research, see Algaier (2014).

[8] 'A secret', Derrida says, 'always *makes* you tremble', for example by suggesting 'that violence is going to break out again, that some trauma will insist on being repeated' (Derrida 2008a, 54–5; emphasis in the original). To pick up on this tremor would thus mean being touched by the secret: as Derrida suggests in 'Telepathy', hearing may be a matter of 'touch at a distance – a very old thought, but it takes some archaic to get to the archaic' (Derrida 2007, 236). As I will later suggest, the question of touch is one that touches the very heart of *Beyond Black*.

for the avoidance: she does not want to frighten her clients. We also know the outcome of this avoidance: it is to keep the place beyond black within herself. Knowing this, we ought to know the peril in which we are putting ourselves: to open the book and read on is to give no consideration to 'who would come through' (Mantel 2010, 193).

Making space for what might occur: Mediumship as craft

Hence the twofold importance of the warning: unlike the audience, the medium knows both the 'how' and the 'why' of avoiding to speak. Yet, the distinction between external and internal remains operative. There is, beside the 'how', a 'why' that is strictly professional: a reason for avoidance that pertains to the medium's *craft*.

The theme of craft deepens that of profession. The elaboration of the theme begins early on, in a scene whose purpose is to establish the credentials, both psychic and professional, of our protagonist. Running across twenty-six pages, it would deserve quotation at length, for it is there that Mantel demonstrates her thorough command of the dramaturgy of mediumship: the choreography of its movements, the circuitry of its interlocutions, the management, at the confluence point of earthside and airside, of its flows and drifts and quickenings:

> Look, this is how you do it. Suppose it's a slow night, no one in particular pushing your buttons; only the confused distant chit-chat that comes from the world of the dead. So you're looking around the hall and smiling, saying, 'Look, I want to show you how I do what I do. I want to show you it's nothing scary, it's just, basically, abilities that we all have. Now can I ask, how many of you,' she pauses, looks around, 'how many of you have sometimes felt you're psychic?'
>
> Mantel 2010, 17–18

And from there it goes on from one revelation to another. Health troubles ausculted, life prospects brightened, long-dead children restored *immaterialiter* to their grieving parents: a virtuosic performance. But the medium is not the only virtuoso in the room. For note, in the passage above, the near indistinguishability of voices.[9] It is the narrator speaking as Alison, but an Alison speaking to an addressee that is and is not the audience: speaking, that is, to someone outside but analogous to the audience, in other words to someone like the reader, to a *you* that resembles the reader without being the reader, thus an Alison speaking as the author without being the author. Look, the one who reads is told, this is how you do it. And then the one who reads, reading on, does it.

The impact of this address cannot be underestimated. For the consequence is that Alison is no longer the only one to avoid speaking of the place beyond black: in reading,

---

[9] In her insightful article 'A Word in Your Ear: Mediumship and Subjectivity in Hilary Mantel's *Beyond Black*' (2009), Victoria Stewart relates the question of narrative voice to that of the medium's socio-cultural significance. However, since Stewart makes no mention of the question of the secret, her arguments elide the decisive question of this article: what it is for the voice to reveal and conceal the secret.

we are made to partake of this avoidance. As if the reader, forewarned though they may be, were made unable to avoid *avoiding* speaking of the place beyond black. And this would be because they were reading: dabbling in the book.

But this is a question that belongs to the internal series and must wait a little longer. We are not yet done with the intradiegetic scene, with the verbal and gestural machinery that constitutes the medium's craft. In another of her sociological *aperçus*, Mantel writes:

> Sometimes the punters would ask, 'What's the difference between a clairaudient and an aura reader, a wotsit and a thing?' and Alison would say, 'No great difference, my dear, it's not the instrument you choose that matters, it's not the method, it's not the technique, it's your attunement to a higher reality.' But what she really wanted to do was lean across the table and say, you know what's the difference, the difference between them and me? Most of them can't do it, and I can. And the difference shows, she tells herself, not just in results, but in attitude, in deportment, in some essential seriousness.
>
> Mantel 2010, 172

Here the novel's satirical dimension crosses with the more substantial of its concerns. 'It isn't right', Alison continues, 'to smoke and eat in front of your clients, to blow smoke at them over your crystals' (ibid.). This is because the effect of such deeds, beyond the mere show of disrespect, is to defeat the very purpose of the consultation: to reach out to spirit and receive guidance therefrom. This extends all the way to the face one keeps. Whereas the genuine medium, according to Alison, assents to the imperative that 'you control your face, your expression, every moment you're awake' (ibid.), the purveyor of hackwork is one who lets 'the lines of professional alertness' fade and lets the face fall 'into its customary avaricious folds' (173). And it is precisely to guard herself against such bad practice that Alison 'had made up her mind, in the early days, that the client would not like to see this expression, and so she had invented a smile, complicit and wistful, which she kept cemented to her face between readings' (ibid.). The smile transforms the craft into a veritable art.

But what the *mise en scène* of the smile reveals is that the face is more than the face. Her smile is crafted for the stage, thus a smile that is itself staged, simultaneously sincere and insincere. And yet, in addition to its merely theatrical function, it is also a stage in itself: cemented to her face, the smile traces the boundary between the internal and the external, between the secret that makes and the community that is made. This is because the smile is itself a wound: a cipher for her body, what it hides is the secret of the secret, the traumatic origin and nature of her psychic capacities, an origin as impossible to remember as it is to decipher in the thick scars that run across the back of her thighs.

The scars come to us through Colette's eyes. Alison is packing up for a trip, wearing nothing but a T-shirt, and as she bends over the case Colette comes in; surprised by the sight, she perplexes Alison by asking whether she had done it to herself. 'It had never occurred to her', Mantel writes, 'that she might have inflicted the damage herself.

Perhaps I did, she thought, and I've just forgotten; there is so much I've forgotten, so much that has slipped away from me' (Mantel 2010, 158). Yet this forgetting is complicated by a remembering: 'She remembered Morris saying, we showed you what a blade could do! For the first time she thought, oh, I see now, that was what they taught me; that was the lesson I had' (159). This recollection dissimulates itself at the moment of recollection: as though she had never *realized* the thing she just *thought* she had forgotten.

The smile hides the scar, and the scar, hiding an unreadable past, invents the smile. I will return to this boundary-wound at the final stage of my argument. For now, however, what must hold our attention is the vital lesson that mediumship is indeed an *art*. Because Alison's talents are real, she might, if she so chose, make all her revelations off the cuff. But doing so would thwart her aim. Authenticity gone, there would be no connection, no community, between the client earthside and the spirit airside. Colette, too, realizes this, albeit dimly, when she first comes into contact with Alison, sitting in the audience and having her mind read by this woman who 'seemed to have no spite in her', who 'spoke as if she had her life before her', 'as if her feelings and thoughts could be mended' (Mantel 2010, 75). Reflecting on her 'introduction to the metaphorical side of life', Colette observes that what the medium says is something that 'you were supposed to look at ... all ways up; you were supposed to hear it, understand it, feel all around its psychological dimensions' (75–6). One might add: as one is supposed to do with a novel, for example with this one.

Such, then, would be her art, the *mantike techne* of this novel medium, as made momentarily clear to the spiritually obtuse Colette, who experiences in miniature, as a layperson's version, what Alison feels as a 'strange feeling in her diaphragm, as if her gut were yawning: as if she were *making space for what might occur*' (13; emphasis added). As if, in short, her body were reading.

How to avoid reading: Mediumship as passion

The art of mediumship, then, above and inclusive of its professional and technical aspects, would be an art of community: the skills it draws on, the craft it employs, are used and employed for the purpose of making a vital connection between the living and the dead. It is this purpose that makes mediumship an art; the rest is talent, technique, work.

Yet these are only the externals of the art. Internally, it consists neither in technique nor in craft; though it relies on these elements, they do not constitute it. Nor does this art consist in community, which, as the end for which it is the means, remains outside it. But if not in these, then in what, seen internally rather than externally, can it possibly consist?

This question returns us to where the novel adopts a double voice, speaking at once to two sets of addressees about matters of interpretation, communication and knowledge. Like the intradiegetic audience, the extradiegetic reader is addressed in the medium's words. And yet, unlike the intradiegetic audience, the extradiegetic reader sees through the medium's words into what they conceal. This is what I thematized as the double-dealing of the voice. Addressed to the audience, these words reveal; addressed to the reader, they reveal that to reveal is to conceal; and it is in the voice that this dissimulative revelation takes place.

We already know this voice: it is one that avoids speaking and initiates the reader into this avoidance. We also know how this initiation takes place: it is because the voice avoids speaking of its avoidance that the reader gets drawn into it. Now we are able to identify the place where this avoidance takes place. For it is precisely here, in the revelation of the medium's concealment, that the reader is plunged into 'the space inside her: the arena of combat, the wasteland, the place of civil strife behind her ribs' (Mantel 2010, 2), the place where the art of the medium is made.

This is the point where the internal series of questions must finally be asked. And as they are asked they must be answered. What do the medium's words conceal? That which the medium conceals from her audiences. Why is this not concealed from the reader? Because literature is telepathic. What does this telepathy entail for the reader? That what the medium knows they know too. What does the medium know? The true nature of the place beyond black. What is it to know the true nature of the place beyond black? To take it within oneself as a secret one keeps. Where does this secret come from? It comes from 'literature'. In *Demeure: Fiction and Testimony*, Jacques Derrida writes:

> [A]bove all 'passion' implies the endurance of an indeterminate or undecidable limit where something, some X – for example, literature – must bear or tolerate everything, *suffer everything precisely because it is not itself*, because it has no essence but only functions.... There is no essence or substance of literature: literature is not. It does not exist.... Its passion consists in this – that it receives its determination from something other than itself.... Before coming to writing, literature depends on reading and the right conferred on it by an experience of reading.
>
> Derrida 2000, 28–9; emphasis in the original

The passion of literature is that it depends on something other than itself. No linguistic or discursive event is either 'literary' or 'non-literary'; this is decided in an experience of reading that attends to it as either one or the other. But what is essential to note is that the same is true of reading and for the same reasons. This becomes evident elsewhere, in 'Literature in Secret', where Derrida, meditating on the phrase '*pardon de ne pas vouloir dire*', identifies the reader as one who, faced with the irreducible secrecy of this phrase, 'senses literature coming down the secret path of this secret, a secret that is at the same time kept and exposed, jealously sealed and open like a purloined letter. She has advance sense of [*pressent*] literature' (Derrida 2008a, 131). As though the reader were a medium: telepathic, ambiscient.

The situation is reversed without being annulled. Reading has the right to *confer* upon a discursive event the name of 'literature'. But it does not have the power to *decide* whether 'literature' exists. In the experience of reading, 'literature' is what comes to determine the sense of the reading, the mode in which it attends to what is being read. Reading at once *anticipates* and *suffers* 'literature'. Suffers, because 'literature' is whatever makes reading bear itself, tolerate itself, suffer itself. And it can do this because it is that which comes from the secret, that which comes down the secret path of the secret, such that the reader, in Derrida's words, 'is prey to literature' (Derrida 2008a, 131). To be 'prey to literature' is to be determined in advance by 'literature', not as a mode of language but as the passion proper to reading, as the advance sense that what is to be read comes from the secret.

The preceding analysis of the novel was made on the assumption of a double avoidance. This assumption was that Alison, in speaking to her audiences, and the reader, in participating in Alison's experience, are both enjoined to keep within themselves that which is not to be spoken of: the true nature of the place beyond black. But it is now clear that this is not the only avoidance involved. For there is a further avoidance, an avoidance before the avoidance of speaking, which constitutes the internal aspect of the medium's experience. And what is singular about this avoidance is that it is always already destined to fail. Externally, the medium is one who conceals the secret by a ritualized revelation of it; internally, she is one who cannot avoid suffering everything, bearing everything, tolerating everything that comes to her from spirit. She cannot, in other words, avoid reading, just as the reader cannot avoid reading, in the scars running across the back of her thighs, the signature of the community – if one can call the criminal men of her childhood a 'community' – that haunts her still. Late in the novel, just after Colette bluntly calls her 'retarded as well as fat', Alison is visited by a thought:

> I might be temporarily muddled by the ingress of memory, some seepage from my early life. I feel I was kept in a shed. I feel I was chased there, that I ran in the shed for refuge and hiding place, I feel I was then knocked to the floor, because in the shed someone was waiting for me, a dark shape rising up from the corner, and as I didn't have my scissors on me at the time I couldn't even snip him. I feel that, soon afterwards, I was temporarily inconvenienced by someone putting a lock on the door; and I lay bleeding, alone, on newspapers, in the dark.
>
> Mantel 2010, 317

The scars, we saw Alison remembering, were the scars of her putative 'lesson'. What she remembers now is the 'lesson' itself. Later we learn what it is supposed to 'teach': not to retaliate with scissors against your abusers. However, by this point in the novel, the latter have long since gone airside, where they persist in their malevolent ways – exactly like Morris, who at one point, to Alison's great dismay, finds his old mates and brings them home. These, of course, are the 'fiends' of whom Alison implored Colette not to speak too lightly, but implored in vain, having 'never been able to teach her the art of self-censorship; never been able to make her understand how simple and literal-minded the organisers of spirit world could be. You had to guard the words that came out of your mouth and even the words as they formed up in your mind' (Mantel 2010, 321). That is how deep the avoidance must be; that is how near the fiends are.

But it is not Alison who remembers the substance of the lesson. Mrs McGibbet remembers it on her behalf, materializing for the first time since Alison's childhood. After cautioning Alison not to tell the fiends 'that it was me, McGibbet, that told you nothing at all about it, for I'm in mortal fear of those fiends', she recounts, in an oddly hesitant idiom that negates in order to affirm what it negates, how one day, when all the men are lying in a drunken stupor, she is quite sure she did not see anything, especially not 'a little girl with a pair of scissors in her hand, snipping about a man's private parts' (Mantel 2010, 432). And to this non-seeing she adds the non-hearing of what Morris Warren says to Keith Capstick in the ensuing racket: '[T]oo late I regret my son, for your bollocks are all eaten by the dogs, they cannot sew them back on when they are swallowed ... the little girl herself pays you out for being a dirty bugger' (433).

The dilemma is no longer a dilemma. It is no longer even a passion. It is a wound. And it is this wound, I suggest in conclusion, that the novel names in its title. To read the novel is to be 'prey to literature'. But the 'literature' to which the reader is 'prey' has become more than 'literature' in the institutional sense of the term. As the experience of a secret, 'literature' gives its name to what Alison cannot avoid reading even as she avoids speaking of it. And what she cannot avoid reading is the secret wound that gives its name to 'literature', to this 'work of literary fiction': the 'place beyond black' to which both she and the reader are prey. As Derrida writes,

> This sentence, 'Pardon for not meaning (to say),' simply stays up in the air. Even if it is written in the hardness of a stone, inscribed white on black on the board or confided black on white on an immobile paper surface, captured on the lighted screen (whose appearance, however, is airier or more liquid) of a gently purring computer, the sentence is still 'up in the air.' And being up in the air is what it keeps its secret of, the secret of a secret which is perhaps not one, and which, because of that fact, announces literature.
>
> Derrida 2008a, 132

To mediate is to read, and to read is to suffer haunting: by voices that come into one's ear, by events that take place in one's mind, by ghostly bodies that crowd, swarm, flutter about one's own. Externally, we might say these voices, events and bodies are 'airside' and 'spirit'; internally, we might say they are 'up in the air' and 'literature'; and thus, at the undecidable limit that is the experience of 'reading', we may say that they are at once 'pageside' and 'beyond black', no less 'in us' than they are 'out there'.

Conclusion: Addendum on the 'law of tact'

How to avoid speaking of the place beyond black? The previous pages proposed a double approach to this question. Externally, it was asked how this avoidance relates to those from whom the secret is kept; internally, it was asked what this keeping of the secret entails for the avoidant consciousness. Ultimately, it was suggested that these questions converge at a point where the medium in the novel and the reader of the novel undergo an experience of passion: the place beyond black would be what the medium and the reader alike are made to *suffer*. The 'place beyond black' would be nothing other than a being-made-to-suffer; thus the novel *Beyond Black* would be about avoiding to speak of this being-made-to-suffer.

Such is the conclusion of my argument. Yet the nature of the conclusion prompts a final remark on something that my argument has been elaborately constructed to avoid. In discussing Alison's professional idiom, I have refrained from using the word that best captures its relationship to the secret on the one hand and the audience on the other. This word is *tact*. A discourse that avoids speaking of death, that deals in palliatives rather than harrowing truths, may be said to be an untruthful one. That, at any rate, is how Colette occasionally regards it: 'Uncomfortable truths were smoothed over, before Al let them out to the public; when she conveyed soothing messages, Colette saw, they came not from the medium but from the saleswoman' (Mantel 2010, 151). However, considering the torments that knowing this truth entails, it may also be said to be the most respectful mode of address: it does not impose or force the thought of death upon the addressee. And it would be only right to describe such a discourse as abiding by a *law of tact*. 'Perhaps', Derrida writes in *On Touching*, 'the law is always a law *of tact*.... One cannot imagine what a law would be in general without something like tact: one must touch without touching. In touching, touching is forbidden: do not touch or tamper with the thing itself' (Derrida 2005, 66; emphasis in the original). And yet, Derrida goes on to add, this law 'brings into contact both contradictory orders ... thus exposing them to contamination or contagion' (68). No tactful discourse would be exempt from this contamination. Reading such a discourse, one would not be able to know where or whether it touches on its object, this object being at once the object of the discourse and of the tact, in other words what it must and must not touch upon; thus the reader, owing to the impossibility of knowing whether there has been contact without contact, would not know where or whether one has or has not been touched by this object.

This applies as much to Alison's discourse as to mine. In the novel, this 'object' would be the 'origin' of Alison's 'gift': her traumatizing childhood. Correspondingly, in my reading of the novel, its entire structure has been organized by the touch of this untouchable 'object', obliging the discourse to avoid direct mention where a more tactful course is open: external rather than internal, smile rather than scar, touching without touching.

But now we know that to read the smile is to read the scar. With this knowledge we return to the novel as to an open wound. We are back in the scene where Alison's credentials are established. She is onstage; the first target has just been mind-read; and now Alison is starting to feel out whether there is someone in spirit trying to come through:

> But long before this point Alison has become conscious of a background mutter (at times rising to a roar) situated not there in the hall but towards the back of her skull, behind her ears, resonating privately in the bone. And on this evening, like every other, she fights down the panic we would all feel, trapped with a crowd of dead strangers whose intentions towards us we can't know. She takes a breath, she smiles, and she starts her peculiar form of listening. It is a silent sensory ascent; it is like listening from a stepladder, poised on the top rung; she listens at the end of her nerves, at the limit of her capacities.
>
> Mantel 2010, 19–20

The smile, complicit and wistful, belongs to the audience; the rest, being secret, belongs not to the audience but to the readers, to this community of novel mediums, of which the one who smiles is only the first member.

References

Algaier, Ermine. (2014), 'Epistemic Sensitivity and the Alogical: William James, Psychical Research, and the Radical Empiricist Attitude', *The Pluralist*, 9 (3): 95–109.
Arendt, Hannah. (1998) (1958), *The Human Condition*, Chicago and London: The University of Chicago Press.
de Man, Paul. (1986), *The Resistance to Theory*, Minneapolis and London: University of Minnesota Press.
Derrida, Jacques. (1987), '*Fors*: The Anglish Words of Nicolas Abraham and Maria Torok', in Nicolas Abraham and Maria Torok (eds), Barbara Johnson (trans), *The Wolf Man's Magic Word: A Cryptonymy*, xi–xlviii, Minneapolis: University of Minnesota Press.
Derrida, Jacques. (1992), *Given Time. I: Counterfeit Money*, translated by Peggy Kamuf, Chicago and London: The University of Chicago Press.
Derrida, Jacques. (1993), *Aporias: Dying – Awaiting (One Another At) the 'Limits of Truth'*, translated by Thomas Dutoit, Stanford, California: Stanford University Press.
Derrida, Jacques. (1994), *Specters of Marx: The State of the Debt, the Work of Mourning, and the New International*, translated by Peggy Kamuf, London and New York: Routledge.
Derrida, Jacques. (2000), *Demeure: Fiction and Testimony*, translated by Elizabeth Rottenberg, Stanford, California: Stanford University Press.
Derrida, Jacques. (2005), *On Touching – Jean-Luc Nancy*, translated by Christine Irizarry, Stanford, California: Stanford University Press.
Derrida, Jacques. (2007), *Psyche: Inventions of the Other, Volume I*, edited by Peggy Kamuf and Elizabeth Rottenberg, translated by Peggy Kamuf et al., Stanford, California: Stanford University Press.
Derrida, Jacques. (2008a), *The Gift of Death (Second Edition) and Literature in Secret*, translated by David Wills, Chicago and London: The University of Chicago Press.
Derrida, Jacques. (2008b), *Psyche: Inventions of the Other, Volume II*, edited by Peggy Kamuf and Elizabeth Rottenberg, translated by Peggy Kamuf et al., Stanford, California: Stanford University Press.
James, William. (1986), *Essays in Psychical Research (The Works of William James)*, edited by Frederick H. Burkhardt, Fredson Bowers and Ignas K. Skrupskelis, Cambridge, MA: Harvard University Press.
Kukkonen, Karin and Henrik Skov Nielsen. (2018), 'Fictionality: Cognition and Exceptionality', *Poetics Today*, 39 (3): 473–94.
Mantel, Hilary. (2010) (2005), *Beyond Black*, London: Fourth Estate.
Royle, Nicholas. (1991), *Telepathy and Literature: Essays on the Reading Mind*, Oxford: Blackwell.
Royle, Nicholas. (2003), *The Uncanny*, Manchester: Manchester University Press.
Spooner, Catherine. (2010), '[T]hat Eventless Realm: Hilary Mantel's *Beyond Black* and the Ghosts of the M25', in Lawrence Phillips and Anne Veronica Witchard (eds), *London Gothic: Place, Space, and the Gothic Imagination*, 80–90, London: Continuum.
Stewart, Victoria. (2009), 'A Word in Your Ear: Mediumship and Subjectivity in Hilary Mantel's *Beyond Black*', *Critique*, 50 (3): 293–307.

Part Three

Secrecy, postcolonialism and democracy

10

Shame and the idea of community in Ian Holding's *Of Beasts and Beings* and *What Happened to Us*

Mike Marais

In the context of European expansionism in Africa, race was the principal marker of difference between settler communities and indigenous communities, and determined the differential process through which the former constructed themselves and gained a sense of like-mindedness and commonality. The question that arises in the postcolonial context is whether it is possible for such communities to decolonize themselves by ridding themselves of all vestiges of the colonial relation with its inscription of race as a determiner of difference. As I demonstrate in this chapter, this question, which Timothy Bewes raises in *The Event of Postcolonial Shame* (2011, 192), is one that Ian Holding stages in *Of Beasts and Beings* (2010), and to which he returns in *What Happened to Us* (2018). A further question pondered by these two novels is also one that Bewes asks: 'What would it mean to imagine a literature in which every residue of the colonial relation has been overcome?' And, by extension, '[i]s freedom from the colonial relation possible in a literary work?' (2011, 192).

It is, of course, no coincidence that this white, post-independence, Zimbabwean writer poses such questions in his work. Zimbabwe, in the aftermath of independence in 1980, embarked on a policy of racial reconciliation, with Robert Mugabe pleading for 'a common interest that knows no race, colour or creed', and indicating that such reconciliation would require a decolonization of identity: 'our new nation requires of every one of us to be a new man, with a new mind, a new heart and a new spirit' (quoted in Fisher 2010, 28). The rebirth that Mugabe here imagines is precisely a form of reconciliation that engenders modes of identification that are not predicated on racial difference. Nevertheless, postcolonial reconciliation in Zimbabwe, as Brian Raftopoulos notes, was nothing but 'a formal political hope, ... given the continuing legacy of structural inequality in the sphere of the economy' (2004, xvii). It is especially noteworthy, in the context of Holding's writing, that the majority of white Zimbabweans, although retaining the economic privileges of the colonial period, made little effort to reconcile with their black compatriots. Allison Schute, for instance, refers to the continuance of an 'etiquette of whiteness', a 'custom of social distance with Blacks' (quoted in Raftopoulos 2004, xvi) in the post-independence period. Such separatism is, of course, a clear symptom of the continued racialization of identity in the postcolony.

If, to develop Mugabe's metaphor of rebirth, reconciliation requires that one imagine one's own death in order to be reborn, the white Zimbabwean settler suffered a failure of imagination. As Albert Memmi observes, in a related context, 'it is too much to ask one's imagination to visualize one's own end, even if it be in order to be reborn another; especially if, like the colonizer, one can hardly evaluate such a rebirth' (2003, 84–5).

Holding's fiction, which apart from reviews and a couple of my own essays (Marais 2019a; 2019b) has received scant critical attention, deals directly with the related issues of reconciliation and imagination. In *Of Beasts and Beings* (2010), a disaffected white Zimbabwean teacher, who has distanced himself from the suffering experienced by his black compatriots because of the country's economic inequalities, writes a narrative in which he, through the imagination, places himself in the position of a black man in an African country on the verge of economic collapse. While foraging for food, his character is captured by militia, sold into slavery and subsequently forced to bear a pregnant woman in a barrow on a journey to a distant hospital. *What Happened to Us* (2018), which is set in an affluent suburb in Harare, circa 2013, focuses on its child protagonist's response to the invasion of his family home and the violation of his sister, thereby echoing Holding's first novel, *Unfeeling* (2005), which deals with the trauma experienced by an adolescent who witnesses the murder of his father and rape of his mother by militia who attack their farm in Zimbabwe. The crucial difference, though, is that the narrator of the later novel does not witness the assault of his sister and must therefore try to imagine what has happened to his family.

In this chapter, I show that both *Of Beasts and Beings* and *What Happened to Us* thematize the aloofness and separatism of Zimbabwe's post-independence white community, and therefore the continuance of the colonial relationship in the postcolonial period. At the same time, though, Holding, in these two novels, tries to imagine, from within a context whose structures of identification are part of what Bewes refers to as 'an economy of identity and difference' (2011, 188), a community in which the colonial relation is absent, and which is therefore post-racial and truly postcolonial. In other words, his thematization of his community's failure of imagination is itself an attempt to imagine, from within this very community, what it has been unable to imagine. Holding's writing, quite ironically, attempts to imagine a community that would constitute the end, or death, of the community of which he is a part and from within which he writes. In a sense, he tries to imagine what this community has sought to conceal from itself.

* * *

In both *Of Beasts and Beings* and *What Happened to Us*, the white Zimbabwean community is depicted in terms of its aloofness, separatism and therefore exclusionary nature. For instance, in *What Happened to Us*, the following description of a *braai* or barbeque, while seemingly innocuous, emphasizes, through its use of plural pronouns, the white community's lack of inclusivity:

> [T]here was restored again the sense of comradely unity we all cherished, the inner ties that bound our shrinking community of whites, families coming together,

feasting on a fatty braai, a near continuous flow of beer and white wine, loyal lazing dogs, the darkly restful pool beyond us and above a Friday summer night's distant dotted sprawl over deepest Africa.

Holding 2018, 84–5

The repeated use of plural pronouns, and the explicit indication that their antecedent is the 'shrinking community of whites', along with the context of this gathering, 'deepest Africa', raises the question of what these pronouns exclude. It points to a 'they', 'them', 'their' and thus an outsider, a figure of difference that enables the community's sense of sameness and like-mindedness. In the process, the passage renders ironic the child focalizer's assumption that the 'comradely unity' of the community in question derives from 'inner ties'. Far from being innate and essential, these 'ties' are a function of the linguistic and discursive inscription of racial difference. Moreover, their mere existence exposes not only the continuance of the colonial relation and its economy of identity and difference in the postcolonial period, but also the fact that the community in question is what Nancy would call 'immanent' (1991, 6 and *passim*), a 'project of fusion' (15) and therefore that the totalizing identity that its 'organic communion with its own essence' (9) instantiates leaves no remainder, no semblance of alterity.

In *Of Beasts and Beings* (Holding 2010), the depiction of the white Zimbabwean community's separatism shows how the assignation of cultural forms of difference such as race affect the community's conception of the human by installing distance among people, which, in its turn, enables indifference. The installation of difference masks what Judith Butler, drawing on Emmanuel Levinas's ethics, refers to as the 'vulnerability' or 'precariousness' that all human lives have in common. Precariousness, in Butler's explanation, is a shared condition of human life, since we are all dependent on what is 'outside ourselves, on others, on institutions, and on sustained and sustainable environments' (2009a, 23). By distancing one from some lives, the forms of difference conceal their 'precariousness' and thus common humanity. They efface or deface the 'face' – Levinas's catachrestic figure for vulnerability and 'the extreme precariousness of the other' (1999, 140) – which, as Butler notes, 'communicates what is human' and 'what is injurable' (2004, xviii). Through the inscription of difference, one refuses to see, in Levinas's words, 'the face in the other' and instead responds to the other 'as a force, savage; one identifies the absolute character of the other with his force' (1987, 19). Moreover, this distancing process establishes a normative conception of the human, which, being differentially constructed and distributed, is deeply exclusionary. The 'normatively human' (Butler 2004, xv), in Butler's argument, informs what is deemed familiar, and thus establishes codes of recognition that determine who is produced as a 'recognizable subject' (2009b, xii): that is, 'who counts as a life, who can be read or understood as a living being' and, conversely, 'who lives, or tries to live on the far side of established modes of intelligibility' (iv). In other words, these codes exclude some lives by occluding their precariousness, and accordingly give rise to the anomaly of the human who is less than human. Life, in this understanding, is a concept that is violently produced by the normative operation of power.

Exactly such an exclusionary conception of the human is at work in *Of Beasts and Beings*, in the protagonist Ian's relationship with his servants. What distinguishes this relationship is not the former's overt cruelty or violence in his treatment of the latter, but his distance from them. To be sure, he refers directly to the 'distant aloofness of our master / servant trope' (Holding 2010, 153), and it is this distance that accounts for the indifference and irritation with which he responds to the debilitating leg injury of Tobias, one of his servants. After having described it as a 'mosquito bite' (Holding 2010, 127), he complains as follows: 'going on a trek round town for the sake of an aching leg wasn't one I welcomed' (Holding 2010, 146). From his treatment of him as someone whose life is not pitiable, it is clear that Ian's conception of the human excludes Tobias. Alternatively put, the scope of his sympathetic imagination is limited, and thus predetermined, by his community's normative conception of the human. In its presentation of this relationship, and also in its depiction of Ian's subsequent refusal to help a black man who is wheeling a pregnant woman to hospital in a barrow, the novel makes it clear that the differential process through which notions of the human are constructed involves not only distinguishing humans from 'beasts' – an opposition invoked by its title – but also from other humans. Ian's sympathetic imagination fails in his encounters with black suffering because race, as a marker of difference, conceals from him the precariousness that he shares with these lives. If read in the context of Nancy's argument on immanent communities, his failure of sympathy may be ascribed to his community's conflation of its essence or identity with 'the accomplishment of the essence of humanness' (Nancy 1991, 3).

Significantly, apropos of its meditation on the settler community's conception of the human, the novel depicts the colonial relation as a master–servant relationship. In the Hegelian dialectic of recognition, where humanity is tied to the attainment of self-consciousness and subjectivity, the slave, who is an object or thing, is not yet properly human (Hegel 1977, 111–19), which is why Frantz Fanon, who draws extensively on Hegel's master–slave relationship in his description of the racialized relationship between colonizer and colonized (1967, 216–22), terms black men 'machine-animal-men' (220). In Holding's novel, Ian, having reduced Tobias to a slave, and thus an object, cannot respond to him as a human subject. Since he does not recognize his humanity, he cannot respond sympathetically to his plight.

Initially, Ian is unaware of this failing, and the same is true of Danny, the narrator and protagonist of *What Happened to Us*. Being totally implicated in their community, neither of them realizes that its separatism shapes their response to black people. They do not realize, that is, that they are not autonomous, free agents, but that the community of which they are a part is also a part of them. It follows that selfhood, in both novels, is portrayed as being relational and intersubjective rather than autonomous and self-sufficient. As much is evident from the use of point of view in the following description of a school cricket match in *What Happened to Us*:

> Our parents reclined on the side lines, fanning themselves in the mottled shade of the broad fever trees … The dads glugged cold beers fished from brick cylinders of ice while the moms sipped glasses of chilled white wine, vodka coolers, gin and tonics or mild ciders with a slice of lemon wedged into the bottle

neck. The women chattered and gossiped and we presumed they spoke of idle nothingness. The men talked rugby, business, maybe fishing, definitely the crappy state of the country.

We knew all this from the field even without hearing a word of it, being Friday afternoon during cricket season.

Holding 2018, 77

Although this passage proceeds from the perspective of a first-person focalizer, the 'I' is, in fact, a 'we' and therefore plural and communal. Danny's purview includes not only his team mates on the field, but also their parents on the 'side lines'. What the first-person narration, which is marked by a lack of interiority, provides, is thus not an individual's perspective but a community's. The former is subsumed within the latter. Again to invoke Nancy, the community in question has produced an immanent identity through the exclusion of all that is other than itself.

In both novels, this emphasis on the self's construction by, and ecstatic fusion with, community invests the protagonists' sense of shame on developing an awareness of their complicity in the separatism of their community with a strongly defined communal dimension. In *Of Beasts and Beings*, Ian develops an awareness of what he calls his 'insensitivities' (Holding 2010, 154) in his treatment of black people and confesses to a failure of sympathy with the following words: 'Maybe I'm just ignorant. Maybe the absence of light in my life ...... is the manifestation of my tantamount ignorance to all that surrounds me' (ibid.). What he terms 'my insensitivities', though, are not just his but those of his community, as emerges when his ex-girlfriend confronts him with the circumscribed nature of white life in Zimbabwe, arguing that 'this life we [white Zimbabweans] live here' is 'totally divorced from reality', that it is 'totally unreal' (261). For her, white Zimbabweans, removed as they are from the suffering, hardship and penury that surrounds them, are 'just fuckers on the sideline, bystanders, even worse than that, totally oblivious saprophytes' (262). Ian's 'insensitivities' have been produced by the separatist community that is a part of him, as he acknowledges in his reference to 'the history that constructs me, the attitude I adopt', and in his observation that '[i]t has defined me all along, has made me complicit' (276).

In *What Happened to Us*, the narrator feels complicit in the violation of his sister Rebecca by three black men. Although their motives for the attack are unclear, he suspects that it is a form of retribution for his and his family's racial attitudes and separatism. Indeed, his suspicions in this regard are tacitly endorsed by the novel's allusions to Lucy Lurie's rape by three black men in J. M. Coetzee's *Disgrace*, which David Lurie, her father, ascribes to a 'history of wrong' 'speaking through them' (1999, 156). Holding's novel's invocation of this literary precedent effectively places the violation of Danny's sister in the context of a colonial history that ventriloquizes the actions of individuals by positioning them in a reciprocal economy of retribution and vengeance. Danny's sense of complicity in the violation of Rebecca derives from the fact that he is implicated in maintaining this history's economy of identity and difference in the postcolonial period.

Like David Lurie, in Coetzee's novel, Danny, as I have mentioned, is not physically part of the violation, he does not even witness it, and so cannot claim direct knowledge of what happened to his sister. Despite this, he feels responsible for the attack and even refers directly to 'my guilt' (Holding 2018, 205). Tellingly, though, after using this singular possessive pronoun in this confession, he qualifies it with the plural possessive in the phrase 'our blame' (205). At issue, in both of Holding's novels, then, is not so much a sense of individual guilt as it is a sense of communal shame, which differs from the former in that its focus is not the autonomous individual, but the individual as part of a collective. Shame, as it is here understood, is the response of an individual who becomes aware that they are part of a community that is an integral part of them, and whose practices enable suffering and, indeed, indifference to suffering.

In both novels, the protagonists' sense of shame estranges them from their community and its normative, and therefore differentially constructed, conception of the human. Since they are no longer able to see black people as falling short of the normatively human, and therefore being less than fully human, they are unable to respond indifferently to black suffering. Nevertheless, not being autonomous individuals, they cannot simply dissociate themselves from their community. As Ruth Leys points out, 'guilt concerns *your actions*, or what you do', whereas 'shame concerns *the self*, or who you are' (2007, 130; emphasis in original). I would add, though, that it would be more accurate to say that shame concerns 'who you are' *and* how this affects your actions, 'what you do'. As is evident from Ian's aforementioned admission that the colonial history that 'constructs' him also constructs the 'attitude' that he 'adopts', and from Danny's comment that his 'mind' is haunted by the 'decaying legacy of a dead empire', which 'drives' his 'actions' in the present (Holding 2018, 228), Holding's characters are ashamed not just of their community, but of what they are, and how what they are predisposes them to act in certain ways.

Given that their community is a part of themselves, it follows that, if they are to distance themselves from it, the protagonists of the two novels must also dissociate themselves from themselves. In both texts, an important corollary of the decentring of the normatively human, and concomitant disruption of the codes of recognition that constitute and maintain it, is that the characters become divided from themselves. The disturbance of their community's codes of recognition, and hence of the ways in which they position themselves in relation to others, cannot but disturb their ability to recognize themselves. If they are ashamed of themselves, they must be separated from themselves, which is exactly what Jean-Paul Sartre says of the experience of shame when he describes it as 'a unitary apprehension with three dimensions: "*I* am ashamed of *myself* before the *Other*"' (2003, 313; emphasis in the original). They are establishing their difference from themselves, estranging themselves from themselves, and therefore a part of themselves can no longer be fully recognizable to themselves. In effect, they are both familiar and strange, and therefore becoming uncanny to themselves. To experience shame is to experience the uncanniness of one's self, its divided and mutable nature. As Nicholas Royle points out, the uncanny 'has to do with a sense of ourselves as double, split, at odds with ourselves' (2003, 6). By extension, that which is unfamiliar, or only partly familiar, is 'never fixed, but constantly altering' (5). There is thus a temporal dimension to shame: the self that each of the protagonists is becoming would hardly be recognizable from the perspective of the self that he was, and of which he is now ashamed.

It follows that the *Bildung* that these two characters undergo in their respective novels is quite unlike that of the conventional *Bildungsheld*, which, in accordance with Enlightenment notions of certitude and progress, involves the development of knowledge of self and society in the course of the narrative. Instead of gaining such autonomy, Holding's characters' implication in their community means that their *Bildung*, in placing them at odds with their community, renders them increasingly unknowable to themselves. Furthermore, the *Bildung* that they undergo is indeterminate, incomplete and even ateleological. Their shame initiates a process in which they are becoming estranged from themselves, but never finally become so, and their narratives perform their bifurcation, their unsettled sense that they are not who they had thought they were, and that the familiar is therefore also strange.

In fact, the *Bildung* that the protagonists of the two novels undergo involves an attempt to die which, however, finally proves impossible. When, for instance, the narrator of *What Happened to Us* confesses his guilt for Rebecca's violation, only to qualify it by implicating his community, he is also referring to his attempt to assuage his guilt by engaging in an act of atonement that takes the form of a ritual of self-mortification in which he lacerates his flesh (Holding 2018, 170). The word mortify is, of course, a synonym for shame, and the fact that it derives from the Latin *mortificare*, that is 'put to death', associates Danny's act of self-mortification, which enacts his sense of shame, with a desire to die. If shame inspires the desire to become other than one is, it must require the death of what one is. That is, it requires one to imagine one's own death.

* * *

In *Of Beasts and Beings*, Ian's attempt to imagine his death begins when he tries to overcome the 'ignorance' induced by his race-based separatism by relating to the suffering of black people. His shame obliges him to put himself in the position of a black person and, by experiencing their suffering, come to understand them. Thus, for example, he begins to reflect on the suffering of the man with the pregnant woman in the barrow, whose predicament he had earlier disregarded, and wonders what happened to them, and whether they eventually received help from 'someone else, someone with a little compassion & humanity' (Holding 2010, 266).

In asking himself such questions, Ian has already begun to project himself into the position of these two black people. Clearly, the sympathetic imagination, as it is here understood, has a cognitive dimension. Through it, it is possible to know lives and forms of experience from which one would otherwise be separated. In other words, the novel accords the sympathetic imagination a transcendental capability. To sympathize, in Isobel Armstrong's description of perceptions of this faculty in the eighteenth century, is to understand 'the situation of another person by being able to change places with him in imagination' (1972, 9). In Holding's novel, Ian uses the sympathetic imagination to relate to the lives that his community's normative notion of the human had previously rendered unrecognizable as human subjects. If read in the context of Butler's argument that the norms that render a life recognizable do not exhaust that life, 'that there is a remainder of "life" – suspended and spectral – that limns and haunts every normative instance of life' (2009a, 7), Ian's sympathy is a response to a dimension of the human that exceeds the normatively human and includes the lives that it excludes. It is an attempt to recognize the face that this norm effaces.

As I have already indicated, Ian's newly gained ability to sympathize with black suffering inspires him to write a narrative that is set in an unidentified African country that has been ravaged by war, and which, appropriately enough, traces the vicissitudes of a family that is trying to transport a heavily pregnant woman to hospital in a barrow borne by a slave. He imagines himself in the position of the slave and suffers with him by bearing the pregnant woman to hospital, in this way atoning for his past indifference to black suffering. Ian's imaginative endeavour proceeds along the lines of a Hegelian *Bildung* in which he attempts to pass into his opposite, sublate himself in the process and become the negation of himself or of what he was. At least, this is what is suggested by the dialectical nature of the narrator's relationship to the character he creates, and which is structurally inscribed in the novel by its division into two narratives: the diegetic level in which Ian writes, and the hypodiegetic level, which consists of the slave narrative that he writes.

Significantly, too, in terms of the dialectical overtones of Ian's Hegelian *Bildung*, the ending of the novel metaleptically melds the master narrative with the slave narrative. In it, Ian, who is now accompanied by his slave character, encounters the pregnant woman on the road, takes her to a hospital and leaves her as she is about to give birth to a child. The ending seemingly brings about a dialectical synthesis of master and slave by pairing Ian and his slave character and also by suggesting, with its description of them as 'beings of different yet equal distinctions' (Holding 2010, 292–3), that Ian and the pregnant woman have attained a mutual recognition. In Hegel's dialectic of recognition, only a mutual recognition between self-conscious individuals, an acknowledgement on the part of each of the other's freedom, agency and right to exist, can bring an end to the entire struggle for affirmation (1977, 104–19, 263–94, 355–63; see also Findlay 1977, xvii). Holding's novel concludes with the suggestion of a synthesis of master and slave, and, with it, the recognition of a common humanity. The attendant suggestion is that such a synthesis would destroy the colonial relation and therefore preclude the continuance of colonial history in the postcolonial period. In this regard, Ian and the woman's mutual recognition of each other ostensibly terminates racial difference. When he and the slave encounter the woman, they do not 'even register the colour of her skin' (Holding 2010, 292), the implication being that the colonial relation is no more and that a truly postcolonial condition has been attained through the recognition of a common humanity that had previously been concealed by racial difference.

Nevertheless, the synthesis alluded to in the novel's ending is highly indeterminate. The master narrative and slave narrative never quite morph into a nativity narrative. For instance, the detail that Ian and the slave character leave the woman before her child has been delivered, defers Ian's dialectical rebirth, which means that the novel ends with a promise that has yet to be fulfilled, a potential that is yet to be realized, a dialectic that has yet to be synthesized, and this indeterminacy is further signalled by the fact that the ending is written in the future tense. The dialectical synthesis that it postulates is ineluctably futural.

Moreover, the novel quite self-consciously suggests that it cannot describe this synthesis because it itself is implicated in the colonial history that it wishes to transcend.

For instance, Ian's observation that he and the slave would not notice the colour of the woman's skin, self-evidently distances the narration, and therefore the novel as a whole, from the non-racial state that it attempts to describe. After all, if one were not to notice race, one would not notice that one had not noticed it. Similarly, the narrator's claim that the three would address one another in a language that is without words, and which proceeds through a 'silent transferral of meaning' (Holding 2010, 292), is couched in English, a language with words that are differentially structured, and which, in the colonial period articulated the racial division on which the colonial relation is premised. With these words, the text effectively inscribes distance and difference between itself and the postcolonial relationship that it attempts to describe. In fact, it indicates that it is a negation of that which it describes. It itself is part of what prevents it from presenting the dialectical synthesis towards which it aspires.

Importantly, the sympathetic imagination is partly responsible for this stalled dialectic. Shortly before the ending, Ian reads his manuscript and dismisses as 'nothing more than stereotypes' (Holding 2010, 286) the characters he has created, which implies that, rather than transcending his position and occupying their position, he has merely ventriloquized them from his position, which is itself ventriloquized by colonial history. Instead of enabling him to die by passing into his opposite, by sublating and becoming other than he is, the sympathetic imagination has consolidated his old self by securing his masterful position. The imagination thus fails to bring about the recognition of the lives that have been excluded by the normatively human – which is what is required for Ian to become other than he is – because it proceeds from a position within the frames of recognition that maintain this norm. It is itself a shameful exercise of power, as is connoted by Ian's response to his realization that his narrative is a 'gross misrepresentation' (Holding 2010, 287): 'I sit here in shame' (286). Despite endeavouring in good faith to understand the other through the sympathetic imagination, he reduces them to the same.

Ultimately, then, the novel inscribes an irreducible tension between the imagination's transcendental drive and shame's insistence on the self's irrevocable implication in a culture that positions it. A corollary of this tension is that Ian, who writes because he wants to die (and, in a Foucauldian moment, even accuses the text of killing him [2010, 282]), cannot die because his writing asserts the position in culture that he wishes to vacate. Accordingly, he must continue to write, which means that his *Bildung* is stalled, without term, and that his writing is only ever an endless dying or waiting to die.

Nevertheless, Ian's failure to recognize the lives that are violently excluded by his community's normative operations of power enables the novel itself to take account of them. In presenting his failure to recognize the precariousness of the lives excluded by the normatively human, and thereby inscribing distance between itself and that which it fails to present, the text gestures towards the lives in question. By dividing itself from itself, it points to that which exceeds its representational protocols and the codes of recognition that inform them. In effect, it ironizes its representations and, in doing so, adjures its reader to interrogate their omissions and exclusions rather than slavishly suspending disbelief in them through sympathizing with them.

In this regard, the scene in which Ian reads what he has written holds a mirror to the actual reader's reading of the novel. Significantly, as I have indicated, he dismisses what he has written as 'gross misrepresentations' and 'stereotypes' (287) that conceal, and so efface, the face they were meant to reveal. From this dismissal, it is clear that Ian's reading does not simply dutifully follow what he has written, but breaks with it, interrupts it and follows instead what it has failed to represent. This is to say, his reading follows the face rather than its effacement. He reads beyond what he has written to the lives that his representations have failed to recognize. If, in their engagement with the novel, this scene was to reflect the actual reader's reading practice, they too will read more than they read and hence respond to the lives that the text has failed to present.

My argument, then, is that the novel, in defamiliarizing its representational protocols and thereby alienating its reader, seeks to place them in a relationship without correlation to the lives that it has not recognized. So, although it fails to recognize them, its interruption of itself urges its reader to question and disrupt its representations, and so gain a sense of the presence of the lives that they exclude. Indeed, for Butler, it is precisely through the disruption of representational forms that 'something about the precariousness of life [may] be apprehended' (2004, xviii). In fact, she distinguishes between the recognition and apprehension of precariousness. Like Levinas, who maintains that the face cannot be thematized (see, for example, 1991, 78, 86), she argues that precariousness cannot be recognized, but then goes on to say that the excess of the norms of recognition, the remainder that 'limns and haunts every normative instance of life', may nevertheless be apprehended. Unlike recognition, apprehension, which is not grounded in cognition and is not a form of comprehension, does not recuperate that to which it relates within the same. It is 'not yet recognition' and 'may remain irreducible to recognition' (Butler 2009a, 5). In gesturing beyond itself and thereby adjuring its reader to read more than they read, to read between and beyond the lines, Holding's novel imparts to them an apprehensible sense of the precariousness of the lives that it has excluded.

It is now necessary to refine my claim, in the introduction to this chapter, that Holding attempts to imagine a community that has overcome the colonial relationship. The fact that he stages the failure of this attempt in *Of Beasts and Beings* suggests that he does not so much seek to present a community that includes what the normatively human excludes, as it is to gesture to the possibility of such a community. Indeed, as I shall now demonstrate, even this claim needs to be refined since the kind of community intimated by Holding's writing is itself one that is grounded in an apprehension of precariousness and hence a profound dissatisfaction with its norms of recognition.

* * *

At least, this is certainly the case in *What Happened to Us*, which, although never explicitly attempting to imagine a community predicated on an apprehension of the precarious character of lives excluded by the normatively human, constantly points to just this possibility. In this regard, the novel's use of the confessional mode of writing is significant, since confession always implies a community. Like his self-mortification, the confession that Danny writes proceeds from his sense of guilt for his sister's violation and is a form of atonement. Indeed, the acts of confession and self-mortification are aligned in the novel by the depiction of the latter as a form of writing.

In mortifying himself, Danny inscribes his shame on his body and, in later years, reads the scars of shame like 'a blind man reading braille' (Holding 2018, 226). His confession, which is also an act of shame, succeeds and supplements his self-mortification. Through it, he continues his self-mortification, which is to say, he tries to die. Like Ian, he writes because he wants to become other than he is. He writes because he wants to die.

In itself, this self-estranging dimension of his confession differs from conventional forms of modern confession, which are aimed at reconciling the confessant with community (see Brooks 2000, 2; and Foucault 1978, 61–2). Ordinarily, that is, the confession of guilt reintegrates the confessant into their community, thereby consolidating and maintaining the community in question. As Michel Foucault argues, the confession of guilt is a form of micro-power, 'the effect of a power that constrains us' (1978, 70). In confession, the confessant is interpellated, which is to say produced and reconstituted as a recognizably human subject, thus affirming their community's norms of recognition. By contrast, the self-estranging aspect of Danny's confession is also necessarily his attempt to estrange himself from his community – which, as I have argued, is a part of his self – and, in so doing, to become unrecognizable to his self and therefore to his community. His confession, it follows, attests to the *Bildung* that he undergoes, which may be described as a process of becoming strange to himself.

Not surprisingly, this process inscribes a marked tension in the novel between the experiencing I and the narrating I. Initially, the experiencing I, as I have noted with reference to Danny's focalization of the cricket match in this novel, provides a community perspective, and is therefore plural rather than singular. The I that experiences the events to which the narrating I confesses, accordingly lacks the interiority associated with modern confession, and with it the ability to withhold information from others. Indeed, the so-called 'inward turn' that characterizes modern confession is precisely the ability to keep secrets, or to conceal oneself from others (Brooks 2000, 5, 11). Confession is a rendering public of what has previously been concealed, kept secret, held private and so withheld from community. In *What Happened to Us*, the experiencing I's lack of interiority means that the narrating I cannot confess to such a secret. As I have already established, the guilt to which he confesses, that is, his sense of complicity with his sister's violators, is one that he shares with – rather than withholds from – his community. As Danny puts it, albeit before the attack, his guilt is 'non-specific' (Holding 2018, 24), which, in turn, means that his confession lacks tangible, incriminating content. It is the confession not of an autonomous individual's personal, private guilt, but of his shame at his and his community's complicity in having created and maintained the conditions that have led to Rebecca's violation and suffering.

As such, the *telos* of Danny's confession can hardly be reconciliation with and reintegration into his community, which would stabilize its norms of recognition. The mere fact that he confesses places the confessing I, the narrating I, at odds with both his former, experiencing self and with his community. His shame, that is, inscribes his distance from them, even as it asserts his relation to them. In itself, the self-division performed by Danny's confession means that it, rather than consolidating his community, undermines the differences through which it establishes and conserves itself, and thereby interrupts the norms of recognition that they install. His confession proceeds from his sense of shame at the way in which these norms, concomitant on the separatism of his community, have enabled its indifference to black suffering, which in turn has led to the retributive attack on his sister. Indeed, it proceeds from an awareness that this separatism is part of an economy of identity and difference, which, in its turn, has generated an exchange cycle of retribution, reprisal and vengeance. By extension, Danny's confession is ultimately inspired by, and therefore has its origin in, what exceeds the cultural inscription of difference, that is, the precariousness of all human life, an apprehension of which has the potential to end the cycle of violence produced by the racial antinomies of colonial history. Indeed, his confession enacts the narrating I's desire 'to somehow reach out, make a connection, lay to rest our bitter entwined pasts' (Holding 2018, 228) and 'seek atonement' (229).

Evidently, then, Danny's confession does in fact aspire towards reconciliation with community. However, it seeks not reintegration into the community of which he is a part, but integration into one that is predicated on an apprehension of the precariousness of human life, as opposed to differential constructions of the human. In other words, the confession implies a community, but one that does not yet exist, and which is futural in nature. By the same token, the confessor implied by the confession would have to be part of this community and is therefore also ineluctably futural. It follows too that the implied confessor, from the temporal perspective of the narration, the time of the confession, is wholly unknowable, unrecognizable. Only a confessor from a community that has overcome the colonial relation and the norms of recognition that inform it could grant the absolution and forgiveness which, as in all confession, is the *telos* of Danny's confession.

The absence of the confessor whom it implies necessarily endows Danny's confession with a dimension of secrecy, which means that it seems to hinge on a contradiction of sorts. On the one hand, as with all confessions, it occurs with the expectation of forgiveness and absolution and therefore takes place within an exchange economy. In exchange for speaking the truth, the confessant will be forgiven, and accordingly has an expectation of the confessor, which is to say some form of advance knowledge. The confessant, in asking for forgiveness, and thereby assuming that they are willing and able to grant it, presumes the confessor's position, which is to say recognizes them. It is for this reason that Derrida argues that 'one cannot forgive, ask, or grant forgiveness without this specular identification, without speaking in the other's stead and with the other's voice' (2008, 137). As with sympathy, then, confession involves a form of ventriloquism.

On the other hand, though, Danny's confession is directed at, indeed addressed to, a confessor and to a community that is wholly other and of whom, strictly speaking, he can therefore have no expectation or any form of knowledge. His confession implies a confessor and community that are unknowable and unrecognizable – indeed, secret – from the time of the confession, which is also the time of the colonial relation's economy of identity and difference.

There is, however, no contradiction here since the confession that the novel presents is aneconomic in form. Being futural and absent, the confessor that it implies is only conceived of as a possibility that may or may not be realized, which, in its turn, renders the confession incomplete, irrespective of its teleological drive. The time of confession is the time of unintentional waiting for someone who, if they were to arrive, could and would not be recognizable. In effect, their identity would be a secret. Moreover, Danny's confession is a giving that is finally without expectation of return. Even if he were to be forgiven and integrated into the futural community towards which the novel gestures through his confession, he would have become other to what he is in the time of confession and so unrecognizable to himself, a secret from that self. In a sense, he would have died, gone absent and the self that confesses would therefore not be able to receive the gift of absolution. Somewhat perversely, then, Danny's confession is thus a form of giving that operates outside the reciprocal economy of the gift. It is a giving without expectation of return and therefore inscribes an irreversible movement to the other. In fact, it is an offering of self, a gift of death.

Its aneconomic dimension means that Danny's confession sustains the possibility of forgiveness, despite its aporetic nature in Derrida's argument. In her thoughtful discussion of confession in Ian McEwan's *Atonement*, Kim Worthington argues that the 'impossible possibility of forgiveness' can be kept 'alive' only by an 'unwritten' other (2013, 166). It is just so in Holding's novel where the implied confessor is only ever conceived of as a possibility that has yet to be realized.

In addition, the aneconomic nature of the confession forestalls a return to self, which is usually what characterizes the confession of shame. As Elizabeth Povinelli notes, such confessions, in the context of a history of injustice, allow 'the liberal subject to feel herself or himself to have been unintentionally causing wrong and to be constantly moving to rectify that wrong' (2002, 162). If it enables a return to self, the confession of shame is itself shameful.

Most importantly, in terms of my argument in this chapter, its aneconomic aspect means that Danny's confession, from its time in colonial history, speaks of its relation to a future time that is wholly other. As confession, it addresses the time in which it is received by the other, which means that it contains within itself the time of the other. Before it is received by the other, it is given to them and their time. Crucially, then, it constantly speaks to this other time, addresses it, is directed at it, even though it does not represent it. Its aneconomic nature therefore means that, although it cannot represent the precarious nature of other lives, Danny's confession is nevertheless able to establish a performative relation with precarious life. As a performance, it enacts its relation to an unrepresentable other.

So, while the confession is non-representational in its relation to precarious life, its performative dimension enables the novel to convey to its reader an apprehensible sense of the precariousness of life. In reading it, the reader cannot but be aware that, while the text addresses them, it also addresses a time and condition that exceeds the time of colonial history in which they themselves are located and within which forgiveness is impossible. That is, the text's ambivalent address addresses the reader but also exceeds them by gesturing elsewhere to another, unrepresentable time in which community is grounded in an apprehension of the precariousness of human life and in which forgiveness is therefore possible.

Through the performative nature of Danny's confession, which speaks incessantly of that which it has not presented, the novel estranges itself from itself and the history in which it is implicated. It is this uncanny self-division that enables it to impart a sense of the precarious nature of life. Since it tends constantly towards that which exceeds recognition and its modes of presentation, it gestures throughout to a beyond, an outside, which is already within it. In other words, the novel testifies to a sense of the shared precariousness of life that exceeds culture's differential structures and its frames of recognition.

* * *

In my reading at least, Holding's two novels do not deem it possible to imagine a literature from which all traces of the colonial relationship have been overcome. Nevertheless, they both indicate that it is possible to imagine a literature that negotiates its implication in the frames of recognition embedded in this relationship by gesturing towards the possibility of a community that is premised on an apprehension of the precariousness of life that underlies the cultural inscription of difference. By extension, these two novels do indeed suggest that it is possible for communities to negotiate the colonial relation, if not rid themselves of its every residue. It is necessary, in conclusion, briefly to reflect on the idea of community that they communicate.

As I have demonstrated, Holding's two texts seek to expose the reader to what underlies the difference between insider and outsider through which community establishes itself. Differently put, they relate them to what community's constructions of the outsider, and potential enemy, seek to occlude. Crucially, though, they, at the same time, expose them to that which is also occluded by the sameness that community constructs for itself in positing an outsider. After all, the sameness of community's insiders is premised on the difference of the outsider, and so must itself be a construct. The sameness of the inside and the difference of the outside necessarily work together to conceal the precariousness of human life, thus facilitating and obscuring the differential distribution of precariousness that Butler terms precarity.

Since the precariousness of life questions both difference and sameness, I am sympathetic to but not entirely convinced by arguments that global literature, through its transcendence of national boundaries, imagines the possibility of a global community that, in its inclusivity, excludes exclusion. If the sameness of community is premised on difference, a questioning of difference cannot but question sameness and hence the very possibility of an all-inclusive community. Accordingly, the idea of a global community sits uneasily with the notion of precariousness. For Levinas, sameness is certainly not ontic togetherness: it is rather a concealment of the intersubjective nature of identity, which is grounded in an encounter with the strangeness or radical alterity of the other person that renders them proximate rather than distant. In Levinas's understanding, the other is not just community's outsider, but its insider, one's neighbour. Put differently, the neighbour is a stranger, just as the stranger is a neighbour. From this perspective, ontic togetherness cannot be conceived of as an ecstatic melding of selves. Should community define itself intersubjectively, it would have to predicate itself on a hospitable apprehension of the radical otherness of the other person that would resist the presumptions of recognition and disable the culturally constructed differences that enable its specious sameness.

In the process, such a community would open itself to an order of relationality beyond itself that exceeds the construction of identities and communal fusion, and therefore recognizes, in Nancy's terms, that 'you (are / and / is) (entirely other than) I' (1991, 29). By recognizing the secrecy of the other, the community in question would acknowledge the fundamental secrecy that conditions being together, that enables our relations with others and therefore constitutes the social bond. Rather than engaging in 'a project of fusion', this community would thus assume 'the impossibility of its own immanence' (Nancy 1991, 15).

If, as I have argued, Holding's novels impart to the reader a sense of the precarious character of life, it would follow that they, at best, conceive of the kind of 'unavowable community' of which Maurice Blanchot speaks (1988): that is, one that unworks itself even as it establishes itself, and thereby seeks to render its hospitality to the outsider less conditional. By unworking itself, it would constantly defer the differences through which it constructs itself, thereby defamiliarizing its norms of recognition and rendering itself uncannily familiar and strange. Such a community would therefore only ever be in the process of becoming a community. After all, as Nancy points out, a community that assumes 'the impossibility of its own immanence' is also one that assumes its 'incessant incompletion' (1991, 38). Like the postcolonial community suggested in Holding's novels, such an incipient, inchoate community would be one that waits endlessly for the community that it has yet to become.

References

Armstrong, Isobel. (1972), *Victorian Scrutinies: Reviews of Poetry, 1830–1870*, London: Athlone.
Bewes, Timothy. (2011), *The Event of Postcolonial Shame*, Princeton: Princeton University Press.
Blanchot, Maurice. (1988) (1983), *The Unavowable Community*, translated by Pierre Joris, Barrytown: Station Hill.
Brooks, Peter. (2000), *Troubling Confessions: Speaking Guilt in Law and Literature*, Chicago and London: University of Chicago Press.
Butler, Judith. (2004), *Precarious Life: The Power of Mourning and Violence*, London and New York: Verso.
Butler, Judith. (2009a), *Frames of War: When is Life Grievable?*, London and New York: Verso.
Butler, Judith. (2009b), 'Performativity, Precarity and Sexual Politics', *AIBR: Revista de Antropologia Iberoamericana*, 4 (3): i–xiii.
Coetzee, J. M. (1999), *Disgrace*, London: Secker and Warburg.
Derrida, Jacques. (2008), 'Literature in Secret', in David Wills (trans), *The Gift of Death (Second Edition) and Literature in Secret*, 117–58, Chicago: University of Chicago Press.
Fanon, Frantz. (1967) (1952), *Black Skin, White Masks*, translated by Charles Lam Markmann, London: Pluto.
Findlay, J. N. (1977), 'Foreword', in G. W. F. Hegel, A. V. Miller (trans), *Phenomenology of Spirit*, v–xxx, Oxford: Oxford University Press.
Fisher, J. L. (2010), *Pioneers, Settlers, Aliens, Exiles: The Decolonisation of White Identity in Zimbabwe*, Canberra: ANU E Press.

Foucault, Michel. (1978), *The History of Sexuality*, Vol. 1, translated by Robert Hurley, New York: Pantheon.
Hegel, G. W. F. (1977) (1807), *Phenomenology of Spirit*, translated by A. V. Miller, Oxford: Oxford University Press.
Holding, Ian. (2005), *Unfeeling*, New York: Scribner.
Holding, Ian. (2010), *Of Beasts and Beings*, London: Simon and Schuster.
Holding, Ian. (2018), *What Happened to Us*, Stroud: Little Island.
Levinas, Emmanuel. (1987) (1953), 'Freedom and Command', in Alphonso Lingis (trans), *Collected Philosophical Papers*, 15–23, Dordrecht: Martinus Nijhoff.
Levinas, Emmanuel. (1991) (1961), *Totality and Infinity: An Essay on Exteriority*, translated by Alphonso Lingis, Dordrecht: Kluwer Academic.
Levinas, Emmanuel. (1999) (1995), *Alterity and Transcendence*, translated by Michael B. Smith, London: Athlone.
Leys, Ruth. (2007), *From Guilt to Shame: Auschwitz and After*, Princeton and Oxford: Princeton University Press.
Marais, Michael. (2019a), 'Reconciliation, White Shame, and the Sympathetic Imagination in Ian Holding's *Of Beasts and Beings*', *Research in African Literatures*, 50 (1): 198–212.
Marais, Michael. (2019b), '"A Cry in the Vast Dark": Ian Holding's *What Happened to Us* and the Confession of Shame', *The Journal of Commonwealth Literature*, 14 October 2019, https://journals.sagepub.com/doi/abs/10.1177/0021989419873369.
Memmi, Albert. (2003) (1957), *The Colonizer and the Colonized*, 6th edition, translated by Howard Greenfeld, London: Earthscan.
Nancy, Jean-Luc. (1991), *The Inoperative Community*, edited by Peter Connor and translated by Peter Connor, Lisa Garbus et al., Minneapolis and Oxford: University of Minnesota Press.
Povinelli, Elizabeth A. (2002), *The Cunning of Recognition: Indigenous Alterities and the Making of Australian Multiculturalism*, Durham, NC: Duke University Press.
Raftopoulos, Brian. (2004), 'Introduction: Unreconciled Differences: The Limits of Reconciliation Politics in Zimbabwe', in Brian Raftopoulos and Tyrone Savage (eds), *Zimbabwe: Injustice and Political Reconciliation*, viii–xxii, Cape Town: Institute for Justice and Reconciliation.
Royle, Nicholas. (2003), *The Uncanny*, Manchester: Manchester University Press.
Sartre, Jean-Paul. (2003) (1943), *Being and Nothingness: An Essay on Phenomenological Ontology*, translated by H. E. Barnes, London and New York: Routledge.
Worthington, Kim L. (2013), 'Self-Writing, Forgiveness and Ethics in Ian McEwan's *Atonement*', in C. Holler and M. Klepper (eds), *Rethinking Narrative Identity: Persona and Perspective*, 47–69, Amsterdam: John Benjamins.

11

'Whilst our souls negotiate': Secrets and secrecy in Jonathan Franzen's *Purity*

Jesús Blanco Hidalga

Introduction

In his novels, invariably concerned with the complex and elusive ways in which the social and the individual domains intersect, American novelist Jonathan Franzen shows a distinctive preoccupation with community. More specifically, his fiction often laments what he perceives as a generalized communitarian decay that has accompanied the demise of industrial society (Beck 1992) and the ensuing ascendancy of late capitalism in the United States. However, in his novels, the characters' attempts to tackle social problems, such as corporate malfeasance, environmental damage or overpopulation, tend to backfire or even end in plain disaster. Accordingly, Franzen's novels often stage a retreat from an intractable social sphere into the smaller communities of family and lovers. Certainly, the latter are also portrayed as a turbulent realm, fraught with dysfunctional relationships, suffering and compulsive behaviour, but, in contrast with society at large, the private sphere is not beyond repair. In Franzen's novels, there is always a possibility of redemption within the communities of families and lovers. In this way, unmanageable social conflicts are symbolically resolved, which is, as Fredric Jameson (1981) and Franco Moretti (1987) have argued, the *raison d'être* of the classic novel.

In Franzen's latest novel, *Purity* (2015), the novelist continues to study the ways in which individuals are affected by large socio-cultural trends and, no doubt, there is a good measure of symbolic resolution of social conflict within the private field of the family. However, Franzen's usual exploration of the social, familial and romantic ties that have always been the focus of his novels has gone, so to speak, one level under – and what Franzen has found out is that at the foundations of these bonds there is secrecy.

Indeed, *Purity* is deeply concerned with secrets. The notion of secrecy is the conflicted nexus that articulates Franzen's text at three levels: the narrative, the psychological and the socio-cultural. To begin with, secrets, withheld or shared, are the motor that drives its romance-like plot. Then, secrecy is posited in the novel as a constitutional foundation of the self and a prerequisite of interpersonal relationships, from the social domain at large down to the world of two of the community of lovers. Finally, secrecy, or more precisely, its loss in contemporary culture, is the critical concept that Franzen wields in possibly his most acerbic socio-cultural diatribe yet, this time concerning the effects of the omnipresence of social media and the digital world.

Secrets and narrativity

For the sake of clarity, I shall begin with narratological and generic considerations concerning the narrative role of secrecy in the novel. Concisely, we could say that secrets in *Purity* help Franzen achieve the necessary narrativity to articulate the novel. As is the case with other contemporary novelists, Franzen's inclination towards a realist novel of social analysis has encountered a serious cultural or ideological obstacle, namely an apparently unsurmountable difficulty to think the present in historical terms. According to theorists of realism such as Auerbach (1955) or Lukács (1955), realism requires that the characters' drama should take place in an intelligible social context and be projected against a background of moving history. Over the last decades of the last century, this kind of thought has become increasingly difficult in a cultural environment persuaded by the belief that the world has turned into an overwhelming, inscrutable web of systems, while history in turn has come to an end. The plot of Franzen's early novels – *The Twenty-Seventh City* (1988) and *Strong Motion* (1992), was organized upon conspiracies, which led some critics (e.g. Burn 2008) to ascribe them to the typically postmodernist subgenres of conspiracy novel or systems novel.[1] However, I have argued elsewhere (Blanco Hidalga 2017, 63) that, rather than a token of postmodernist lineage, in *The Twenty-Seventh City* and *Strong Motion* conspiracies were convenient narrative resources with which to generate narratable events in a socio-historical situation perceived as essentially flat and eventless, almost impossible to connect with the characters' biographies. It is significant, to be sure, that secrecy also had a relevant role in those novels, as it is an indispensable condition of conspiracy. In any case, from *Strong Motion* onwards, Franzen has increasingly relied upon other sources of narrativity, namely the time-honoured genres of *Bildungsroman*, melodrama and romance, all of them characterized by vigorously forward-moving narratives. *Bildungsroman* is usually driven by the conflict between the hero's need for self-determination and the demands of socialization. Melodrama, on its part, shows a welcome capacity to generate a sense of memorability out of daily life. Finally, eventful plots and perspectives of salvation typically characterize romance. In this sense, *Purity* can be easily seen as a latter-day romance, and secrecy is the motor that drives its peripeteian plot full of romance-like

---

[1] This distinctively postmodernist genre was defined by Tom LeClair, in his study of DeLillo's narrative *In the Loop* (1987), as a scientifically informed variety of fiction, strongly influenced by the workings of 'the System', which is conceived as an intricate network of systems of all kinds: semiotic, economic, ideological, etc.

situations, such as disguised identities that are eventually disclosed, life-changing coincidences and dramatic changes of fortune. Above all, what characterizes *Purity*'s plot is the fact that its hero's evolution has all the features of a quest, which is, from the beginning, a quest for knowledge.

A glimpse at only part of the novel's tempestuous plot will suffice to show the important role performed by secrets in the narrative. Purity Tyler (Pip, in her aptly Dickensian nickname) is a young graduate who lives in a squat in Oakland, as her insecure job cannot afford her to repay a large student debt. She is also troubled by the fact that her mother, whose real name Pip ignores, refuses to tell her about her family background. It is the case that, for reasons unknown at the beginning of the novel, she left Pip's father after she got pregnant and assumed a new identity before Pip was born. After a series of romantic vicissitudes, Pip ends up working as an intern for The Sunlight Project, a leak-hosting organization led by the charismatic German activist Andreas Wolf, a Julian Assange-like figure devoted to divulging secret misdeeds by corporations and governments. Both Pip and the reader ignore that Wolf knows the truth about Pip's identity. Then the narrative travels back in time to the Democratic Republic of Germany in the 1980s. In that section of the novel, we learn that Andreas Wolf had committed a secret crime: the murder of a Stasi informant, named Horst, who was sexually attacking his teenage stepdaughter, Annagret. Wolf shares this secret with Annagret – his accomplice in the crime – and later with American journalist Tom Aberant. Wolf met Aberant in Berlin after Germany's reunification and convinced the journalist to help him move Horst's corpse to a safer location. Back in the present, Wolf tells Pip his secret in order to win her trust. Rejected by Pip and upset with Aberant, Wolf breaks into the journalist's personal computer and extracts a file containing a lengthy confessional narrative. In this text, Aberant gives an account of his tormented relationship with his wife, Anabel Laird. Laird was a feminist artist heir to one of the richest families in America, who, after her relationship with Aberant had ended, disappeared without leaving a trace. In this way, we get to know that Anabel is none other than Pip's mother. Malevolently, Wolf sends the file to Pip, who thus finally learns of her family origins.[2] After a convenient narrative ellipsis, we see how a well-adjusted Pip, emotionally satisfied and financially secure, organizes a reconciliation meeting for her parents. Salvation has not been just metaphoric for her.

These are only some of the secrets that hover around the novel's chapters. In fact, their presence is felt throughout and a sense of what the characters – and the reader – know or ignore about each other is constant. Secrets in *Purity* perform a function that is different from the traditional concept of suspense, taken as uncertainty as to the outcome of a denouement, be it partial or final. Nor is it the kind of concealed

---

[2] Aberant's text, which is another secret revealed, constitutes a modern-day version of the classic romance *topos* of the found manuscript (McKeon 2002, 57), and sheds light on the narrative by conveying essential biographical information about the characters. In fact, the stolen file performs a double function in the novel. On the one hand, it fulfils the need for knowledge shared by Pip and the reader. On the other, it brings about further events as it prompts Pip to take action leading to her parents' reconciliation.

intertextual allusion for the sophisticated reader described by Calinescu (1994). From a structural point of view, however, the role of secrets in the novel is essential: they create a certain imbalance (*déséquilibre*) in the state of affairs, to use Todorov's term (Todorov 1968, 96), or, as Propp (1968, 34) would put it, a situation of 'lack' that sets the narrative forward.

Pip's unrest at her mother's stubborn withholding of her secret is the starting point of the novel. Her restlessness is the novel's too, and it can be understood in the light of Peter Brooks' analysis of narratives in *Reading for the Plot* (1984). The secret knowledge denied to Pip – and the reader – by her mother produces a state of narratability in the text, which is described by Peter Brooks in erotic terms: 'a tension, a kind of irritation, which demands narration ... a condition of tumescence, appetency, ambition, quest' (Brooks 1984, 103). According to Brooks, desire 'inhabit(s) the language of narration' (55). The critic characterizes this drive following Lacan's interpretation of the concept of desire: 'desire is born of the difference or split between need and demand' (ibid.). From this, we may infer that at the heart of our desire for narrative plots ultimately lies a desire for meaning. Indeed, nothing stimulates desire like a secret, as all secrets imply a promise of reward in the form, precisely, of meaning.[3] In fact, the mere existence of a secret already seems to presuppose the desiring hero of a quest. In this way, Pip is defined by her mother's secret, or, to put it another way, by her desire to know. What is more, this is a desire which the reader, to use René Girard's term, mimetically partakes of. As Jodi Dean explains, 'secrecy generates the very sense of a public it presupposes. The secret designates that which is designed to be known, that which hasn't yet been disclosed. In so doing, it presupposes a subject that desires, discovers and knows, a subject from whom nothing should be withheld' (2002, 10). It is clear that a suspected secret has a powerful, unescapable effect on the people holding the suspicion. Furthermore, the power of a secret lies in the supposition that it exists, rather than in its content. Derrida defined this as the 'secrecy effect': 'Wherever knowledge can only be supposed, wherever, as a result, one knows that supposition cannot give rise to knowledge, wherever no knowledge could ever be disputed, there is the production of a *secrecy effect*, of what we might be able to call a *speculation of the capital secret or on the capital of the secret*' (1994, 245; emphasis in the original).

This implies that, as I discuss below in this article, secrecy is a form of (power) relationship in the first place; and that a secret is always marked by the potentiality of its future disclosure. Eva Horn has argued, apropos of Edgar Allan Poe's *The Purloined Letter*, that '[t]he secret thus indicates a certain "aggregate" state of knowledge, a form of looming latency or potentiality that is more powerful than its actual content. It is the potential for future disclosure that constitutes the power that its holder has over others' (2011, 7). As *Purity* shows, this potential for disclosure can be the motor of a narrative,

---

[3] This drive, as the German thinker Georg Simmel is careful to explain, may arise from a fallacy, namely the typical error 'that everything secret is essential and significant' (Simmel 1906, 465). For Simmel, there is a 'natural impulse to idealization' heightened by phantasy, which distinguishes secrecy 'by a degree of attention that published reality could not command' (466).

as, at the end of the day, the relations between the great keepers of secrets in the novel (especially Anabel Laird and Andreas Wolf) and the rest of the characters are not that different to those established between the narrative itself and the reader.[4] In fact, there is a narrative-like quality in secrecy and its potential disclosure that naturally points at romance. As the German sociologist Georg Simmel argues, secrecy is 'sustained by the consciousness that it might be exploited, and therefore confers power to modify fortunes, to produce surprises, joys and calamities' (1906, 467). What is more, Simmel discerns an evolutionary formula in secrecy that can also be related to certain characteristics of narrative. According to Simmel, 'throughout the form of secrecy there occurs a permanent in-and out-flow of content, in which what is originally open becomes secret, and what was originally concealed throws off its mystery' (ibid.). This is something that can be attributed to many a narrative and it is certainly the case with *Purity*.

Against transparency

If there is an intimate relationship between secrecy and narrativity, according to the German philosopher Byung-Chul Han (2015) there is something about contemporary culture that works against both. For Han, in our time transparency has been fetishized and totalized to constitute what he names 'the transparency society'. Attributing a noxious character to transparency may seem counterintuitive these days, but, according to Han, this merely shows it having become mystified and turned into an ideology, and a totalitarian one at that. For Han, the distinctive cultural operations of our time are hyper communication, acceleration, endless addition and storage. As he says, '[a]ddition is more transparent than narration' (2015, 29), as the latter requires selection and exclusion. In a word, narration requires a measure of negativity, which tends to be banned in a society dominated by positivity. Besides, for Han, transparent space is always semantically impoverished (31).

In the sphere of politics, according to the German philosopher, rather than bringing about increased accountability for governments and corporate power, or extended enfranchisement for the citizens, '[c]ompulsive transparency stabilizes the existing system most effectively' (Han 2015, 7). Again, this may seem at odds with contemporary trends: as Clare Birchall explains, the notion of transparency in politics and government activity has come to be identified as an absolute good in popular political discourse, especially within the radical Left (2011, 1).[5] However, endorsing the current idolization

---

[4] At this point it is interesting to notice that Franzen's narrative use of the secret and his vindication of secrecy as a foundation of social relations and even the self are somewhat at odds with the way in which he, as an omniscient narrator, uses free indirect speech to show the content of the characters' mind, illuminating their most intimate thoughts and motives (with the exception of Anabel and, to a lesser extent, Andreas). We can only speculate as to the effects of a less transparent depiction of the characters' thoughts that would have left more room for ambiguity and, by the same token, a wider potential for interpretation, should Franzen have chosen that way.

[5] Even for Georg Simmel, 'enlightenment which aims at elimination of the element of deception from social life is always of a democratic character' (1906, 447).

of transparency actually implies important risks for the Left. As Birchall argues, '[r]epresentative liberal democracy is deemed "fair" simply by allowing scrutiny rather than with reference to the economic or social policies being scrutinized. And as it is strengthened, other visions of democracy – social, direct or radical democracy – become less viable' (4).

In his manifesto, Han makes a similar point: '[t]ransparency is inherently positive. It does not harbour negativity that might radically question the political economic system as it stands. It is blind to what lies outside the system' (2015, 7). In addition, compulsive transparency ties political action to the most immediate present, preventing any long-term vision. Han observes, admittedly in coincidence with Carl Schmitt, that 'politics is strategic vision. For this reason alone, it inhabits a realm of secrecy. Total transparency cripples it' (6). Certainly, it is easy to notice that acts of real political resistance often require a high degree of secrecy, especially at their initial stage. After all, as Horn explains, following Koselleck, secret societies and lodges were the birthplace of modern political man, as they protected the enlightened opposition to absolutism in the eighteenth century (2011, 9). The end of secrecy amounts then to a depolitization, a transition to a post-political era.

Han's vision is consistent with Franzen's negative view of leakers of the Julian Assange[6] type in *Purity*, against whom he sets the more constructive labour of investigative journalism (a work, Franzen emphasizes, akin to narrative in its being based on Enlightenment-derived principles of research, selection and synthesis). In contrast, the leaker's work is shown to be politically barren or even counterproductive.[7] As journalist Leyla Helou exclaims in the novel:

> The leakers just spew. It takes a journalist to collate and condense and contextualize what they spew. We may not always have the best of motives, but at least we have some investment in civilization ... The leakers are more like savages ... they have this savage naïveté, like the kid who thinks adults are hypocrites for filtering what comes out of their mouths.
>
> Franzen 2015, 493

---

[6] During the writing of this article, British officers arrested Julian Assange in the Ecuadorian embassy in London where he had taken refuge for seven years after the Ecuadorian authorities had withdrawn their protection. He has to serve a one-year sentence for violation of probation in the UK, after which he faces extradition to the United States, where he will confront seventeen charges of espionage, besides the original one of conspiracy to reveal classified information. Independently of our opinion about his politics, strategies and, especially, the way he manoeuvred to avoid the Swedish justice in a case concerning sexual abuse, we should remember that, in the event of his extradition to the United States, Assange – a non-American citizen – could be cumulatively sentenced to up to 180 years of imprisonment. This incarceration, as shown by the case of former intelligence analyst Chelsea Manning, held for years in solitary confinement, is likely to be characterized by inhumane conditions. We should remember that this would be the punishment for divulging true information concerning, among other, the extent of the brutality of US intervention in places such as Iraq and Afghanistan. The consequences for the state of freedom of speech and information around the world are obvious.

[7] The way WikiLeaks' revelations of Hillary Clinton emails may have promoted Donald Trump's election might be one such case.

Indeed, without the analytic and contextualizing efforts of expert journalists, disclosed information becomes mere accumulation: ineffective, vulnerable to a subsequent revelation issued by opposing quarters that may spread opposite views. As Dave Boothroyd points out, democracy cannot be founded on a kind of knowledge that amounts to 'a series of latest disclosures' (2011, 54). In the absence of informational authority, disclosure practices can take the form of an 'information war' in which claims and counterclaims 'are pitched against one another', ultimately becoming meaningless (ibid.). This is the environment where conspiracy theory thrives and fake news proliferates. In *Purity*, Franzen goes to considerable length to show the investigative efforts of the indefatigable Helou concerning major negligence in a US nuclear military base. Helou's work eventually takes the form of a solid, unassailable piece of reportage, which Franzen is obviously intent on presenting as a grounded, delimited and self-contained piece of knowledge about the world in the form of a narrative. Franzen's attempt to restore informational authority to investigative journalism is also an effort to restore a Habermasian public sphere and its Enlightenment values, a move that seems in the last stance another side of his inveterate hostility to postmodernism and its bracketing of cultural, political and epistemological foundations (see for example his 2002 essay 'Mr Difficult'). In contrast with the pessimistic vision of previous work such as *The Twenty-Seventh City* or *Strong Motion*, Franzen seems to assert here not only the necessity, but also the feasibility of enlightening the public. In doing that, Franzen is also legitimating his own position, since what applies to journalism seems also valid for a closely related eighteenth-century invention: the classic novel. Indeed, from its inception this genre was characterized by a distinctive analytic-pedagogical calling: making sense of a rapidly transforming world through the narrative of its characters' life trajectories (see for example Brooks 2005). It is, however, impossible not to notice here that Franzen is defending the guiding principles of classic realism in a novel that is largely a romance.

Franzen shares with Han the view that sees an inherent totalitarian drive in demands of total transparency. In this, Han is certainly not alone. For example, Brooks has analysed Rousseau's desire for a transparent society as an ideal ultimately leading to the revolutionary Reign of Terror (2000, 162). Derrida has also argued in this way: 'For me, the demand that everything be paraded in the public square and that there be no internal forum is a glaring sign of the totalitarianization of democracy' (Derrida and Ferraris 2001, 59). Accordingly, Franzen is careful to attribute a measure of totalitarianism to Wolf's organization, which is aptly dodged by the protagonists by resorting to melodramatic secrecy: since The Sunlight Project requires all internal communications to be public, when Andreas seeks private contact with Pip he gives her a handwritten secret note, to be burned after being read.

Franzen and Han also seem remarkably close in their identification of a totalitarian character in a culture that is completely dominated by social media. This totalitarianism is even more effective because it disguises submission as voluntary participation, while it reaches to every corner of our lives. Han decries the rampant exhibitionism of social media comparing it to an inverted panopticon of sorts. As he argues:

> While occupants of the Benthamian panopticon are aware of the supervisor's constant presence, the inhabitants of the digital panopticon think they are free ...

> The society of control achieves perfection when subjects bare themselves not through outer constraint but through self-generated need, that is, when the fear of having to abandon one's private and intimate sphere yields to the need to put oneself on display without shame.
>
> Han 2015, 46

In *Purity*, Franzen also presents the digital world as totalitarian, drawing an explicit parallelism between socialist Germany, which certainly was a true panopticon state, and contemporary culture:

> Before he'd quit doing interviews, the previous fall, he [Andreas]'d taken to dropping the world *totalitarian* … In fact, he simply meant a system that was impossible to opt out of. You could cooperate with the system or you could oppose it, but the one thing you could never do, whether you were enjoying a secure and pleasant life or sitting in prison, was not to be in relation to it. If you substituted *networks* for *socialism*, you got the internet. Its competing platforms were united in their ambition to define every term of your existence.
>
> Franzen 2015, 447–448; emphasis in the original

The comparison extends to the internet moguls, who the novelist likens to the socialist regime hierarchs:

> Like the old politburos, the new politburo styled itself as the enemy of the elite and the friend of the masses, dedicated to *giving consumers what they wanted*, but to Andreas … it seemed as if the Internet was governed more by fear: the fear of unpopularity and uncoolness, the fear of missing out, the fear of being flamed or forgotten.
>
> 449; emphasis in the original

After the publication of *Purity*, scandals such as the Cambridge Analytica-Facebook affair in early 2018 – concerning the harvesting of data from Facebook users and their subsequent use for political advertising purposes – have added new dimensions to the public's awareness of the oppressive aspects of the push for transparency of contemporary digital culture. For Shoshana Zuboff, the use of the trail of data we generate in our daily activities has enabled contemporary digital enterprises to evolve Han's 'society of control' (Han 2015, 45) into a new and extremely totalitarian form of capitalism that she has called 'surveillance capitalism' (2019). According to Zuboff, unlike older configurations of our mode of production, surveillance capitalism does not feed on labour but rather on every aspect of human experience. As she puts it, 'all aspects of human experience are claimed as raw-material supplies and targeted into behavioral data. Much of this work is accomplished under the banner of "personalization," a camouflage for aggressive extraction operations that mine the depths of everyday life' (Zuboff 2019, 19).

In any case, not only does Franzen present the digital world as totalitarian in *Purity*. He goes even further to identify the Internet's grip on people as death itself, as the ultimate compulsive manifestation of Freud's death drive. Online pornography is the obvious symbol of the compulsive repetition induced by the Internet:

> It was only much later, when the Internet had come to signify *death* to him, that he realized he'd also been glimpsing *death* in online porn. Every compulsion, certainly his own viewing of digital images of sex, which quickly became day-devouringly compulsive, smacked of death in its short-circuiting of the brain, its reduction of personhood to a closed loop of stimulus and response.
>
> Franzen 2015, 465; emphasis in the original

Here the humanist Franzen identifies the dissolution of the border between the private and the public sphere, which he attributes to the Internet, with no less than the end of the individual, now enslaved to the machine. The narrating voice describes it forcefully: 'the characteristic annihilation of the distinction between private and public ... the dissolution of the individual in the mass. The brain reduced by machine to feedback loops, the private personality to a public generality: a person might as well been already dead' (ibid.).

Secrets and mutual trust

Franzen's horror at the processes described above obviously arises from a conception of secrecy as a fundamental dimension of both the self and society. This idea has a forerunner in Georg Simmel. The German thinker observed that in all acts of human interaction, the mutual knowledge of the participants is rather limited in comparison with the vast zones of the other that are left in the shadow. According to Simmel, not only the self but also society are founded upon secrecy, as secrets structure and shape social relations. What we know about other people is always based upon a much larger zone of their being and experience we do not know about. Since a part of the other is always concealed from us, social relations rest on mutual faith. As Simmel argues, 'life rests upon a thousand presuppositions which the individual can never trace back to their origins, and verify; but which he must accept upon faith and belief' (1906, 445). For Simmel, an increasingly credit-based economy, and the 'pursuit of science' whereby scientists confidently rely on their colleagues' findings, are two clear examples of the kind of trust that characterizes modern societies.

Charles Barbour has recently explored Simmel's influence on Derrida, showing that secrecy was a life-long concern for the French philosopher. As Barbour explains, along a considerable number of works Derrida posits secrecy as an essential foundation of the self, indeed the hallmark of the human. Barbour attributes to Derrida the notion that consciousness amounts to the ability to keep secrets (2017, 187), since for him, a basic characteristic of human consciousness is the existence of an inner world concealed from others. This is precisely the idea behind these remarks by Andreas Wolf in *Purity*: 'How do you know that you're a person, distinct from other people? By keeping certain things to yourself. You guard them inside you, because, if you don't, there's no distinction between inside and outside. Secrets are the way you know you even have an inside. A radical exhibitionist is someone who has forfeited his identity' (Franzen 2015, 275). Therefore, to surrender privacy in the way contemporary culture tends to encourage, means to surrender 'the sovereignty of the self', to use Barbour's words apropos of Othello, 'a play about the sovereignty of the self, or the way that each of us, or some element of each of us, remains hidden from all others, or withdrawn in sovereign isolation' (2017, 41).

Derrida concurs with Simmel on the importance of mutual faith for social interaction. In his study of Derrida, Barbour refers to this kind of trust as an 'oath' (2017, 38). As Barbour puts it, for Derrida 'every social relation or interaction relies on a (typically silent or implicit, but nonetheless effective) promise, pact or sworn agreement to say what one believes and to believe that the other is doing the same' (25–6). In other words, that which divides us (the shadow zones in our knowledge of the other) also holds us together by means of an implicit pact.

The importance of mutual trust is central in *Purity*. Towards the end of the novel, for example, Pip tries to help her psychologically troubled housemate, Dreyfus. Confronting his paranoid tendencies, she insists: 'Can you trust me? Everything will be OK if you trust me' (Franzen 2015, 542). However, for the characters in the novel trust is hard to come by. 'Can I trust you' is a question that the novel's characters frequently address to each other. Often tormented by the secrets they carry and trapped in dysfunctional family relationships, they find that sharing a secret is the obvious way of creating a bond of trust between two people. Pip finds it difficult not to be hostile to boys interested in her, partly because 'the only person in the world she trusts is her mother' (10). When Pip first contacts Andreas via email, she (rightly) suspects his manipulative intentions. The way she proposes to build mutual trust is to share secrets: 'But trust goes both ways, right? Shouldn't you also have to trust *me*? Maybe we should tell each other some little thing we're ashamed of. I'll even go first' (61; emphasis in the original). Besides, if shameful secrets can estrange us from the other, as Nathaniel Hawthorne's fiction exemplifies in characters such as Dimmesdale or Wakefield, sharing them is the way to bridge the social gap and regain a sense of belonging.

However, from another point of view, Pip – like other characters in the novel – eventually discovers that to partake in a secret also means to be inevitably entangled. Even more, it often leads to feeling guilty because of secrets perceived as shameful. Then again, for these cases there are the obscure pleasures of confession at hand. As Simmel explains, '[s]ecrecy sets barriers between men, but at the same time offers the seductive temptation to break through the barriers by gossip or confession. This temptation accompanies the psychical life of the secret like an overtone' (1906, 466). In fact, 'the joy of confession' as Simmel puts it, 'may contain [a] sense of power in negative and perverted form, as self-abatement and contrition' (ibid.). In this way, Pip feels increasingly estranged from his hosts in Denver, Tom Aberant and Leyla Helou, until she breaks down and confesses Andreas Wolf had sent her there. In the same way, guilt-ridden Annagret seeks the relief of confession to Andreas's mother, Katya. In contrast, this way of building trust is denied to the world-famous Andreas:

> Imagine the state of distrust in which I move through the world. Revealing anything shameful to anyone I run the risk of exposure, censure, mockery. Everyone should be told about fame before they start pursuing it: you will never trust anyone again... and yet everyone wants to be well-known, it's what the whole world is made of now, this wanting to be well-known.
>
> If I told you, when I was seven years old my mother showed me her genitals, what would you do with that information?
>
> Franzen 2015, 65

In fact, Andreas is not only a global celebrity, but also a fugitive from justice in different countries around the world. Besides, he grew up in a state where anyone could be an informant. This has made him familiar with a certain degree of paranoia. According to Barbour, the faith or trust required by any human interaction both needs and generates suspicion or even paranoia. We need this capacity for suspicion 'to operate in the ambiguous, undecidable zone between trust and doubt', where 'we negotiate the essential secrecy or opacity of our relations, perhaps our experience as such' (Barbour 2017, 170). In any case, Andreas, an inveterate womanizer, only attains real intimacy with teenage Annagret, who shares with him the secret of her being sexually abused by her stepfather. Nevertheless, after Andreas murders him with her help, their fear of being caught and their secret guilt estrange them for years. In time, Andreas will unsuccessfully try to escape his permanent isolation by sharing his secret with Tom Aberant. He will also use this scheme with Pip, with more obvious manipulative purposes.

Confession as aggression

The sharing of secrets is a fundamental concern in *Purity*, a novel that abounds in acts of confession. The first effect of the use of these rhetorical operations in a narrative is that they readily conjure up the illusion of a deep, substantial self for the confessing character. By fore fronting opacity, acts of confession evoke inner recesses of the subject, promoting what Peter Brooks has called 'the metaphor of depth' (2000, 102). However, as Brooks has studied, confession is an extremely complex and ambiguous kind of speech that can serve a variety of obscure purposes. For this critic, acts of confession are 'motivated by inextricable layers of shame, guilt, disgrace, contempt, self-loathing, propitiation and expiation' (36). As Brooks explains while dealing with Rousseau, confession and self-exposure may involve a kind of obscene, 'deviated recognition of self in a wish-fulfilling fiction' (51). This is exemplified in *Purity* by the disturbed Andreas, whom we frequently see struggling with self-loathing through acts of confession – the most dramatic of which leads to his suicide by jumping off a cliff (Franzen 2015, 513). But Franzen is most keen on showing how sharing secrets may become an effective and noxious way of manipulating the other. Sharing secrets can certainly bring people together to form a small community, but secrets may also be, so to speak, weaponized to inflict an unwanted bond on someone, separating them from other communities (the Latin *secretus* means 'to set apart'). As Boothroyd points out, receiving a secret amounts to an encounter with 'an absolute alterity which is "in me" in the form of a secret' (2011, 46). In a way, a shared secret affords the other a way into the self, and when a secret is forced on us, this relation may have the form of an unwanted encroachment. Sexual abuse by her stepfather starts this way for Annagret. In an ominous scene, Horst, an unofficial Stasi informant, tells Annagret that her mother, a nurse who works in a hospital, has become a drug addict and is stealing drugs from work. Horst explains to Annagret that, should her mother's problem be known, she would lose her job, probably go to prison and they would have to leave the comfortable flat which his relations with the Stasi had afforded them:

'So we have to keep it secret.'
'But now I wish I didn't know! Why did I have to know?'
'Because you need to help me keep the secret. Your mother betrayed us by breaking the law. You and I are the family now.'
...
'Oh, I wish you hadn't told me anything.'
'But I did. I had to. And now we have secrets together. Just you and me. Can I trust you?'
Her eyes filled. 'I don't know.'
'Tell me a secret of your own. Then I'll know I can trust you.'
'I don't have any secrets.'
'Then show me something secret. What's the most secret thing you can show me?'

Franzen 2015, 92–3

Secrets forced upon characters by other characters with manipulative intentions are frequent in the novel. Andreas was an illegitimate child who had been adopted by a leading figure of the socialist regime, a circumstance unknown to him. One day, his real father, a former graduate student now living in destitution after being incarcerated, approaches teenage Andreas with reproachful words about his mother, very much like the ghost of Hamlet's father (Franzen 2015, 118). Andreas, on his part, is proficient at the game of using secrets to mess with other people's minds. Most notably, Andreas's confession of his crime, first to Aberant and later to Pip, may be seen, to use Brooks' words, as 'a subtle act of aggression, a demand for self-judgment and counter-confession on the part of the interlocutor, a demand for a kind of common transparency in the assumption of generalized guilt' (Brooks 2000, 165). Unsurprisingly, here the bond inflicted by the reception of confession is experienced by the receivers as contamination and taint. Andreas certainly tries his best at manipulation with Pip, who, as she repeatedly puts it with characteristic frankness, in turn feels her brain churned with a 'wooden spoon':

'I'm going to tell you something that I've only told one other person ever. After you hear it, I want you to think about which one of us has the real power over the other. I'm going to give you the power you say you don't have. Do you want it?'
   'Oh boy. More truth?'

Franzen 2015, 270

Eventually, Pip is spared partly by her distinctive pure heart and unassuming self-reliance (being in that a very American hero), and partly by her keen awareness of the power game involved in Andreas's way of acting. She clearly perceives that secrets can be a source of power over the other. In her encounter with the 'appropriately named' Andreas Wolf (66), she discovers that seduction is a perilous game for the self, as it involves guarding one's secret part of the self while making guesses at the concealed part of the other: 'She worried that she'd said the wrong thing – that he'd seen through her attempt to turn their talk away from love, and was hurt. And so she kissed him' (286). Later on, Pip finds out that secrets may be turned into weapons when Andreas uses the secret of Pip's identity to take revenge on both her and Tom Aberant.

The importance of confessional acts in the novel exceeds psychological considerations. From a narratological point of view, they contribute substantially to the narrativity and the compelling force of the story. Not only do they drive, willingly or not, the characters together, they also include the reader in these small communities of knowledge. They appeal to the voyeuristic inclination inherent in our reading of fiction. *Purity* illustrates how revelations in a narrative can be both rewarding and tantalizing, stimulating us to expect new satisfactions of our curiosity.

'Merger of souls', or, the dangers of too much trust

The most important of the novel's subplots is the one that concerns the troubled love-hate relationship between Pip's parents, Tom Aberant and Anabel Laird, recounted by Tom in a confessional, first-person narrative. Here Franzen takes his exploration of the way secrecy structures our relationship with the other to the domain of the couple's life. As I have explained (Blanco Hidalga 2017, 220), in this part of *Purity*'s narrative, melodramatic situations are taken to new heights of intensity in Franzen's fiction, as the novelist proceeds to invest them with the particular sublimity and transcendence of the Gothic. What Franzen shows in the story of Tom and Anabel is, simply put, what happens when two lovers relinquish secrecy between them. The passionate and politically radical Anabel drags the innocent Tom into a relationship of such intensity it isolates the couple into a small, private world. Anabel relentlessly demands that no secret should exist between the two, and Tom is carried away in an ecstasy of commitment. This is not only a kind of totalitarianism of the private sphere: here the lover's ambition clearly places superhuman demands on their relationship. There is true hubris in their design, as Tom describes their relationship as no less than 'a dissolution of the boundaries of our selves' (Franzen 2015, 379). This aspiration for communion seems specially misguided in the light of recent critiques of the concept of community, such as those provided by Blanchot (1988) or Nancy (1991), who propose a community of singularities based precisely in the non-shareable. From a related perspective, Derrida argues for the respect of secrecy in our relationship with the other: 'For the secret of secrecy ... does not consist in hiding *something*, in not revealing the truth, but in respecting the absolute singularity, the infinite separation of what binds me or exposes me to the unique' (2008, 122–3; emphasis in the original).

There is no direct entrance to the absolute alterity of the other (or, at least, none that is not traumatic). As Derrida explains in *The Gift of Death*, '*tout autre est tout autre*' (82; emphasis in the original). Accordingly, the French philosopher proposes a community based on interpretation or, as he says, 'allegoresis': '[a] community that does not constitute itself on the basis of a contemporaneity of presences but rather through the opening produced by what you have called allegoresis – that is, the interpretation of a text not given, not closed on itself, an interpretation that itself transforms the text' (Derrida and Ferraris 2001, 24).

This kind of community could be conceived then as a sort of open-ended text, a narrative without closure, always in need of interpretation. Here we may recall, with Frank Kermode, that 'narrativity always entails a measure of opacity' (1979, 25). For the critic, all narrative requires interpretation, exegesis and accordingly it implies a certain amount of secrecy. The mere act of subjecting a narrative to interpretation entails investing it with a degree of darkness to be illuminated by its interpreter, be it a critic or lay reader. We have seen that secrets, by their mere presence, create interest and depth. When Tom and Anabel deliberately renounce opacity in their relationship, their community is bound to end in trauma, and their narrative is sure to stall. In Tom's account, his relationship to Anabel resembles the curve of drug addiction. There is the initial rush and excitement: 'All drugs are an escape from the self, and throwing myself away for Anabel, doing something *obviously wrong* to make her feel better, and then reaping the ecstasy of her renewed enthusiasm for me, was my drug' (Franzen 2015, 382; emphasis in the original). Later he describes his feeling after their engagement: 'The ring on her finger had magical powers. I was fucking my *betrothed*, there was a new dimension to the joy of it, an immeasurably deeper chasm into which to throw myself, and no end to the falling' (393; emphasis in the original). Finally, there is the agonizing end: 'Now I was experiencing her psychic pain directly as my own. The heaven of soul-merging was a hell' (399).[8]

After a number of years of disdained secrecy, Tom and Anabel's relationship is completely exhausted, which amounts to saying that their common narrative has stopped, like a stream becoming stagnant in a toxic atmosphere of mutual reproach. In keeping with the parallelism between narrative and human life drawn by Brooks, it is significant that by the end of their marriage, sexual activity has virtually vanished. Not because of typical conjugal ennui, but, as Tom puts it, 'because our souls were merged' (Franzen 2015, 403). This outcome was easy to predict if we have to believe Simmel on marriage and other analogous relationships:

---

[8] Doubt arises here as to whether Franzen really believes in the possibility of such a mystic union. Is Franzen actually positing it or should we attribute it to Tom's naivety or self-interest as a narrator? Be it as it may, there seems to be an evolution in Franzen's narrative in this respect. In his early fiction, the lovers' relationship was the encounter of two solitudes, and failed communication with the other was the norm. In *The Twenty-Seventh City* (1988), Martin Probst and his wife Barbara struggled in their marriage, while in *Strong Motion* (1992), Louis Holland lamented what he perceived as a lack of communion during sexual intercourse with Renée Seitchek. However, a turning point appears at the end of *Freedom* (2010). At the climactic moment of the novel, the melodramatic reconciliation of Walter and Patty Berglund, there is a glimpse at the possibility of communion while the two characters look into each other's eyes (Franzen 2010, 559).

That which we can see through plainly to its last ground shows us therewith with the limit of its attraction, and forbids our phantasy to do its utmost in adding to the reality. For this loss no literal reality can compensate us, because the action of the imagination of which we are deprived is self-activity, which cannot permanently be displaced in value by any receptivity and enjoyment.

Simmel 1906, 461

We could add here that what is true for marriage is also true for narrative, currently starved in our transparency society. Being a moralist at heart, Franzen cannot resist providing an example of the road to follow in love relationships in the last part of the novel. Pip and Jason represent this path, as they show that trust realized in cooperation is compatible with respect for the other's alterity.

Conclusion

The novel ends with Tom and Anabel meeting in the latter's cabin after more than twenty years apart, in a reunion arranged by Pip. The results are unlikely to turn out as Pip desires, and she symbolically closes the cabin's door on her parent's endless argument. The novel thus attains only partial closure, which means that the desire for knowledge that has driven forward the narration – both Pip's and the reader's desire – is only partially satisfied. To his credit, Franzen refuses to smooth out that particular source of negativity in a melodramatic neat closing. This is a finale probably more attuned to a contemporary kind of realism than the Jane Austen-like epilogues of *The Corrections* (2001) and especially *Freedom* (2010). It rather seems an adaptation of the romance form to a cultural environment that has grown wary of neat narrative closure. As befits a romance, the novel does end with the recognition and salvation of its protagonist, who embodies hope for the new generation, brought about mainly by Pip's ability for forgiveness. As the heroes of romances usually are, Pip is vested with a certain symbolic character: she represents the power of secrets to set forward a narrative – both the novel's and her life's – and she becomes Franzen's vehicle to explore the importance of secrets in human relationships. Actually, her instinctive assumption of the need for some degree of opacity in personal relationships, as well as her sceptic look on the digital world, set her as a figure of optimism that to an extent counteracts the sombre view of contemporary culture offered by the novel. However, there is an irreducible element of negativity in the novel's ending, embodied by the recalcitrant incapacity of Tom and Anabel to forgive each other. This may be seen as a statement in the context of what Han calls the 'society of positivity' (2015, 5). In fact, with this ending, Franzen is saving a measure of narrativity that indeed could spawn yet another story. All in all, it seems an appropriate way to close a novel that constitutes a veritable vindication of secrecy in the narrative, the socio-cultural and the interpersonal domains.

References

Auerbach, Erich. (1955) (2003), *Mimesis: The Representation of Reality in Western Literature*, Princeton: Princeton University Press.

Barbour, Charles. (2017), *Derrida's Secret: Perjury, Testimony, Oath*, Edinburgh: Edinburgh University Press.

Beck, Ulrich. (1992), *Risk Society: Towards a New Modernity*, translated by Mark Ritter, London: SAGE.

Birchall, Clare. (2011), 'Transparency, Interrupted: Secrets of the Left', *Theory, Culture and Society*, 28 (7–8): 60–84.

Blanchot, Maurice. (1988), *The Unavowable Community*, translated by Pierre Joris, Barrytown, NY: Station Hill Press.

Blanco Hidalga, Jesús. (2017), *Jonathan Franzen and the Romance of Community: Narratives of Salvation*, New York: Bloomsbury.

Boothroyd, Dave. (2011), 'Off the Record: Levinas, Derrida and the Secret of Responsibility', *Theory, Culture and Society*, 28 (7–8): 41–59.

Brooks, Peter. (2005), *Realist Vision*, New Haven and London: Yale University Press.

Brooks, Peter. (2000), *Troubling Confessions: Speaking Guilt in Law and Literature*, Chicago: The University of Chicago Press.

Brooks, Peter. (1984), *Reading for the Plot: Design and Intention in Narrative*, Oxford: Clarendon Press.

Burn, Stephen J. (2008), *Jonathan Franzen at the End of Postmodernism*, London: Continuum.

Calinescu, Matei. (1994), 'Secrecy in Fiction: Textual and Intertextual Secrets in Hawthorne and Updike', *Poetics Today*, 15 (3): 443–65.

Dean, Jodi. (2002), *Publicity's Secret: How Technoculture Capitalizes on Democracy*, Ithaca, NY: Cornell University Press.

Derrida, Jacques. (2008), *The Gift of Death (Second Edition) and Literature in Secret*, translated by David Wills, Chicago: The University of Chicago Press.

Derrida, Jacques. (1994), '"To Do Justice to Freud": The History of Madness in the Age of Psychoanalysis', *Critical Enquiry*, 2 (2): 227–66.

Derrida, Jacques and Maurizio Ferraris. (2001), *A Taste for the Secret*, translated by Giacomo Donis, Cambridge: Polity Press.

Franzen, Jonathan. (1988) (2010), *The Twenty-Seventh City*, New York: Noonday-Farrar.

Franzen, Jonathan. (1992) (2007), *Strong Motion*, New York: Picador-Farrar.

Franzen, Jonathan. (2001) (2010), *The Corrections*, New York: Picador-Farrar.

Franzen, Jonathan. (2002), 'Mr. Difficult: William Gaddis and the Problem of Hard-to-Read Books', *The New Yorker*, 20 September 2002, accessed 24 November 2011, http://www.newyorker.com/magazine/2002/09/30/mr-difficult.

Franzen, Jonathan. (2010), *Freedom*, London: Fourth Estate.

Franzen, Jonathan. (2015), *Purity*, London: Fourth Estate.

Han, Byung-Chul. (2015), *The Transparency Society*, translated by Erik Butler, Stanford: Stanford University Press.

Horn, Eva. (2011), 'Logics of Political Secrecy', *Theory, Culture and Society*, 28 (7–8): 103–22.

Jameson, Fredric. (1981) (2002), *The Political Unconscious: Narrative as a Socially Symbolic Act*, London and New York: Routledge.

Kermode, Frank. (1979), *The Genesis of Secrecy: On the Interpretation of Narrative*, Cambridge, MA: Harvard University Press.

LeClair, Tom. (1987), *In the Loop: Don DeLillo and the Systems Novel*, Urbana, IL: University of Illinois Press.
Lukács, György. (1955) (2006), *The Meaning of Contemporary Realism*, translated by John and Necke Mander, Monmouth: Merlin Press.
McKeon, Michael. (1987) (2002), *The Origins of the English Novel, 1600–1740*, Baltimore: John Hopkins University Press.
Moretti, Franco. (1987) (2000), *The Way of the World: The Bildungsroman in European Culture*, translated by Albert Sbragia, London and New York: Verso.
Nancy, Jean-Luc. (1991), *The Inoperative Community*, translated by Peter Connor, Lisa Garbus, Michael Holland and Simona Sawhney, Minneapolis: University of Minnesota Press.
Propp, Vladimir Iakovlevich. (1928) (1968), *Morphology of the Folktale*, 2nd edition, translated by Laurence Scott, Austin: University of Texas Press.
Simmel, Georg. (1906), 'The Sociology of Secrecy and of Secret Societies', *American Journal of Sociology*, 11: 441–98.
Todorov, Tzetan. (1968), 'La Grammaire du Récit', *Langages*, 12: 94–102.
Zuboff, Shoshana. (2019), *The Age of Surveillance Capitalism: The Fight for a Human Future at the New Frontier of Power*, London: Profile Books.

12

Conversing with spectres: Secrets and ghosts in Viet Thanh Nguyen's *The Refugees**

Kim L. Worthington

> *To exorcise not in order to chase away the ghosts, but this time to grant them the right, if it means making them come back alive, as* revenants *who would no longer be* revenants, *but as other arrivants to whom a hospitable memory or promise must offer welcome ... out of a concern for* justice.
>
> Derrida 1994, 175; *emphasis in the original*

Secrets – and ghosts – haunt the work of Viet Thanh Nguyen, Pulitzer Prize-winning novelist and award-winning literary critic. They abound, too, in Jacques Derrida's corpus. This essay attempts a productive reading of both writers via a discussion of Nguyen's collection of short stories, *The Refugees* (2017).[1] Many of the stories in *The Refugees* turn on the revelation of secrets by characters or, conversely, on the efforts of characters to keep secrets concealed. In others, ghosts appear, as 'real' entities or in the form of haunting memories – memories not only *of* past events, but ones that signify the compulsive, relentless 'reliving' of these events, which is commonly understood as symptomatic of trauma. My interest, however, is not (only) in the role these traumatic secrets or ghostly figures play in the individual lives of characters or how their 'revelation' is acted out via a range of pathologies that occasionally have dire consequences but are often painfully banal. I argue, rather, that Nguyen's text invites us to consider how the ghost(s) of the Vietnam War, embodied in/as (former) refugees now 'at home' and 'belonging' in America, contribute to and unsettle narratives of (American) democracy.

I begin by paraphrasing Nicolas Abraham: 'What haunts are not the dead, but the gaps left within [the nation] by the secrets of others ... like [strangers] within' (1987,

---

* In memory of my dear friend and colleague Allen Meek who generously read and provided incisive feedback on an early draft of this essay not long before his untimely death in June 2020.

[1] In his essay 'Just Memory', Nguyen distances himself from Derrida's 'utopian arguments about the (im)possible' (2013, 151); however, towards the end of *Nothing Ever Dies* he notes the value of some aspects of Derrida's arguments regarding forgiveness (2016a, 287–8, 290–1).

287, 290).[2] Abraham was an early theorist of (intergenerational) trauma and/as haunting. Derrida contributed a lengthy foreword, titled 'Fors', to Abraham and Maria Torok's radical reworking of Freud's Wolf Man case, *Le Verbier de L'Homme aux Loups* (1976) / *The Wolfman's Magic Word: A Cryptonymy* (1986). If Abraham's (supplemented) comment appears to offer a rather serendipitous yoking, on my part, of the notions of secrecy and haunting, in what follows I hope to show this is not the case. Indeed, this conjunction appears throughout Derrida's corpus, to the extent that 'the secret' and 'the ghost' seem synonymous at times. I am particularly struck by Abraham's description of haunting (transgenerational) secrets as being like strangers within a person (or nation, for my purposes). In 'Fors', Derrida describes the same as 'a parasitic inclusion' (1986, xvi), a particularly resonant phrase if we think ahead to his later work on autoimmunity (especially in relation to democracy). It is also apposite in my discussion here, because refugees are often pejoratively described as 'parasites' living off the 'host' nation (Jeffers 2012, 47–50).

Despite what some have argued is the influence of Abraham and Torok's work on Derrida's thinking, there are significant differences between them. In the former, the phantom 'family secret' remains unsaid because it is shameful and taboo but, if spoken (of), can be uncovered and exorcized. For Derrida, in contrast, 'the ghost and its secrets are unspeakable in a quite different sense', as Colin Davis explains:

> [T]he ghost's secret is not a puzzle to be solved; it is the structural openness or address directed towards the living by the voices of the past or the *not yet formulated possibilities of the future*. ... The ghost pushes at the boundaries of language and thought. The interest here, then, is not in secrets, understood as puzzles to be resolved, but in secrecy.
>
> Davis 2007, 13; emphasis added

This future-focused orientation is crucial and what makes Derrida's haunting, or secrecy, potentially productive. In what follows, I seek to remain alert to the problems inherent in an all-encompassing elision of spectrality/haunting and the affective qualities of trauma as simply negative, for individuals and collectivities. In much of the scholarship characteristic of what Roger Luckhurst refers to as the 'spectral turn' (2000, 527), the appearance of a spectre is akin to being 'possessed' or 'gripped indefinitely by an *anachronistic* event' (Blanco and Peeren 2013, 11; emphasis added). I take seriously María del Pilar Blanco and Esther Peeren's assertion that '[t]he danger of marking all remembering with the affective registers of melancholia is that we may come to understand memory as working solely on the basis of repetition and negativity, rather than on its progressive (future) productivity' (13). This, I argue, applies not only to the

---

[2] In the original, Abraham is writing of transgenerational trauma in which past acts are hidden from descendants: 'What haunts are not the dead, but the gaps left within us by the secrets of others ... the burial of an unspeakable fact ... like a ventriloquist, like a stranger within' (1987, 287, 290). On the influence on Derrida of Abraham's (and Maria Torok's) 'hauntology' and the differences between these, see Blanco and Peeren (2013), Colin Davis (2007; 2005) and Laurie Johnson (2000).

'progressive (future) productivity' of individual memory but also to memories that are collective, not least as they are constitutive of (ostensibly) democratic nations such as the US.

It is imperative to recall that for Derrida the spectre 'is always both *revenant* (invoking what was) and *arrivant* (announcing what will come)' (ibid.). 'Pure hospitality', Derrida asserted in an interview, 'consists in welcoming the *arrivant*, the one who comes' (quoted in Naas 2008, 21). The *arrivant* 'surprises the host – who is not yet a host or an inviting power – enough to call into question, to the point of annihilating or rendering indeterminate, all the distinctive signs of a prior identity, beginning with the very border that delineated a legitimate home and assured lineage, names and language, nations, families and genealogies' (Derrida 1993, 34); it 'affects the very experience of the threshold' (33). My discussion of Nguyen's *The Refugees*, focused primarily on the first story 'Black-Eyed Women' (2017, 1–21), seeks to keep the figure of the *arrivant* in full view. As such, I draw not only on aspects of Derrida's 'hauntology' or 'spectrality' but also on his many comments on (political) secrecy.

Political secrecy: Singularity and democracy (to come)

In the past two decades, especially, the role of political secrecy has attracted growing critical attention, contra to the claims of William Walters and Alex Luscome who, writing in 2017, assert that '[s]ecrecy is a curiously neglected mediator of power knowledge relations' (2017, 7). They acknowledge 'some important interventions' naming 'Vincent, Thompson, Dean, Neocleous and Mearsheimer', for example, but nonetheless assert that 'secrecy, it seems, has yet to be placed at the centre of political studies' (ibid.). Whether or not considerations of secrecy should occupy this 'centre' is a moot point. I note, however, that Walters' and Luscome's list of 'interventions' is rather partial, omitting as it does the work of theorists such as Gary Hall (2007), Eva Horn (2011; 2013), Clare Birchall (2011; 2014) and Chris Danta (2013). Perhaps this omission is because what these latter critics share is an approach to political secrecy via the lens of continental philosophy, notably the work of Derrida. Apart from Horn, however, their work is curiously silent on the ways in which Derrida engages (with) literature in his discussions about secrecy and democracy. Horn offers this:

> Perhaps today fiction is the only (or at least the most lucid) way to speak, as it were, 'openly' about the precise nature of political secrecy without falling into the trap of the secrecy effect. Since fiction does not claim, as history and journalism do, to offer the 'ultimate truth' of an event, it is better suited to analyse and reconstruct the minute workings of political secrecy – its mechanisms more than its content. Fiction offers possible versions of an event ... [A] tale, more than any treatise, can succinctly illuminate the subtle economy of light and dark, inclusion and exclusion, suspicion and power at work in secrecy.
>
> 2011, 118

There is much to consider here, not least the idea that literature might expose the mechanisms of (political) secrecy rather than merely the content of *a* secret (which it might also do, the obvious example being detective literature).

Rarely is the word 'secret' used literally by Derrida to refer to a sharable or communicable *thing* that a person or persons choose(s) to hide or conceal from others. As he asserts, 'the secret of the secret … doesn't consist in hiding *something*, in not revealing the truth of it, but in respecting the absolute uniqueness, the infinite separation of that which ties me or exposes me to the unique, to the one as to the other, to *the One as to the Other*' (2008, 122–3; emphasis in the original). The secret is better understood as a 'technique' (2013, 290) or an 'effect' (245). What matters is 'the *supposition* that there is a secret, not its actual content'; its power 'arises from the mere threat that it may be revealed' (Horn 2011, 109; emphasis in the original). At stake is the idea that the depth of literature is illusory, a semantic *effect*, promising meaning or a resolution that can never be found at a 'centre'. Evoking Frank Kermode in a discussion of Derrida and secrecy, Mark C. Taylor writes '[s]ince the "genesis of secrecy" is always missing, there is nothing to tell. I repeat, there is nothing to tell. The secret is that there is no secret' (1992, 184). Quoting from Derrida's 'Remarks', Derek Attridge suggests that '[t]he literary work is secret because it is singular: it cannot be exhaustively analysed in terms of general codes and conventions, no matter how relentless the analyser' (2010, 46).

For Derrida, secrecy is bound up with questions about democracy. Modern democratic discourses routinely valorize transparency and openness as good, not least because they appear to foster accountability for those with power. As such, 'in modern democracies, secrecy has become the maligned half of a fraught secrecy–transparency dyad' (Kumar, Martin and Bray 2015, 5). Given the high currency of claims about transparency, modern governments often downplay or hide their extensive reliance on 'espionage, secret operations, surveillance and the classification of information' (Horn 2011, 104). Government-sanctioned secrecy is routinely justified via an appeal to state security, resulting in 'an ongoing, often expensive negotiation between the security of the state and the rights of its citizens [to privacy]' (Birchall 2011, 14). It is conventionally democratic to suggest that no one need keep secrets in order to be a member of the state, hence the (moral) value accorded to freedom of expression, of the press, of movement, of coming out of the closet, and so on. At the same time, the individual's right to privacy is considered a cornerstone of liberal democracy. Mark Neocleous writes of a 'fairly simple but well-established claim: that a democratic society is one with an entrenched defense of privacy (preferably in a codified constitution) and one in which the bare minimum of state affairs is carried out in secret' (2002, 85). Birchall makes a similar call and suggests that 'Derrida's work on the secret can help us to think through the problems of a democracy committed to the idea of total transparency'; she argues that 'far from being inimical to each other', transparency and secrecy 'are symbiotic' (2011, 12).

Derrida captures this tension or symbiosis in his assertion that there is '[n]o democracy without respect for singularity or irreducible alterity, but no democracy without "community of friends" (*koina ta philon*), without the calculation of majorities, without identifiable, stabilizable, representable subjects, all equal' (1997, 22; emphasis in the original). 'Tragically irreconcilable', Derrida avers, these 'two laws are irreducible to one another' and constitute what he refers to as the 'wound' of democracy, albeit this keeps open the possibility of an impossible 'democracy to come (*la démocratie à venir*)' (ibid.; emphasis in the original).³ Drawing on the root of the word 'community', in dialogue with Maurizio Ferraris, Derrida offers this pithy summation of the 'secret' of democracy: 'we know in common that we have nothing in common' (2001, 58). Further, he famously acknowledges that he has 'a taste for the secret, it clearly has to do with not-belonging'. He rephrases this idea soon after: 'Belonging – the fact of avowing one's belonging, of *putting in common* – be it family, nation, tongue – spells the loss of the secret' (59; emphasis added).⁴ This is important to my consideration of *The Refugees*. Perhaps nothing better encapsulates refugeeism than the condition of no longer belonging (to a lost 'community of friends', or to 'family, nation and tongue') *and* of 'not-belonging' (in the place of arrival, the host nation). Put another way, what a refugee seeks is hospitality, the word, or rather concept, so central to Derrida's later work; she seeks to be a welcome *arrivant* in the (democratic) nation, rather than be regarded as a (potentially threatening) foreign body, a parasite in the host.

In my reversion to biological metaphors, I gesture towards a term/concept that Derrida used with increasing frequency in his writing: autoimmunity. His most sustained discussion of this occurs in the two essays that comprise his later work *Rogues* (2005), in which he argues, in short, that democracy is threatened internally by the very logic that constitutes it. Democracy is 'a concept that is inadequate to itself, a word hollowed out at its center by a vertiginous semantic abyss that compromises all translations and opens onto all kinds of autoimmune ambivalences and antinomies' (2005, 72). One of these, suggests Michael Naas, is 'that between freedom, the unconditionality and incalculability of freedom, and the measure and calculability of equality' (2008, 134). 'For Derrida', he argues,

> one must continue to negotiate between the calculable and the incalculable, invent new ways of calculating or reasoning between them. Hence individual autonomy, which tends to immunize itself against infection by the other, has as its only chance an autoimmunity that opens it up to its others, even if this autoimmunity threatens to destroy the autonomy of the self through this chance, that is, even if it threatens to destroy the power of an autonomous individual, indeed right down to the power to welcome and receive the absolute singularity of an other.
>
> Ibid.

This autoimmune 'opening up' to others applies not only to individuals, but to the body of individuals that constitute a democratic nation, the *demos*. So, then, it applies to what Naas suggests is the 'autoimmunity of hospitality': 'the necessity ... of welcoming

---

³ On 'democracy to come' see, for example, Derrida (1993; 1994; and, perhaps most fully, 2005).
⁴ J. Hillis Miller asserts that for Derrida, one must resist such forms of belonging, 'including any political belonging, because what [one] really *is* something entirely singular, sui generis. Therefore his most important transactions are extrapolitical responses to the demands made on him by the complete otherness of other singularities' (2008, 216; emphasis in the original).

a guest who threatens to turn the host's immune system against itself, right up to and including the host's very capacity to receive or invite a guest' (ibid.). He continues:

> The host [nation] thus needs the guest, or the *parasite* [the secret, the ghost], to be himself, and yet the *parasite* also threatens not only the life but the very self-identity or ipseity of the host [nation]. This does not mean that the host [nation] cannot or should not choose and select, decide who is to be received and who not; it's just that this choice must be made with the recognition, first, that such a reception is always self-affirming and self-serving, and thus 'hospitable' only in the conditional sense, and that, second, it too is always a risk to the extent that the other who is received is never completely identifiable or known.
>
> 134–5; emphasis added

Unconditional hospitality, or democracy, would require an open invitation to all, even that or those that threaten(s) to destroy it or exercise freedom by voting against it. Protecting against such destruction may involve undermining or resisting the very principles of hospitality/democracy: limiting civil liberty, placing limits on equality or policing borders. Derrida gives several examples of such autoimmunity. One of these was the Algerian government's decision to 'kill democracy rather than let it die' (Czajka 2017, 42) by suspending the 1992 democratic elections to prevent a non-democratic Islamic regime from being voted into power (Derrida notes, too, that the Nazi state came to power via democratic election). Another is the action of the democratically elected American administration's decision, following 9/11, to curtail various democratic freedoms 'in the name of, or under the pretext of, protecting those same freedoms, or else taking measures to suppress information about its intentions in Iraq under the pretext of spreading freedom and openness throughout the Middle East' (Naas 2008, 13). In a not dissimilar way, as I write (April/May 2020), countries worldwide, many democratic, are enacting strict policies that limit personal freedom – not least the freedom of movement – in a bid to deal with the threat posed to their citizens by an invading 'foreigner': the COVID-19 coronavirus. There is growing public discontent with such policies, worldwide, and speculation that the attempted 'cure' of forced stay-at-home orders and business closures are worse that the disease itself (insofar as they threaten livelihoods, mental health, rights of free association, etc.). 'Give me liberty' states a sign held up by anti-lockdown protesters in America in past weeks. Others are overtly biological: 'Sacrifice the weak' and 'Natural immunity'. Preventing the actions and speech of these protestors, chilling as their messages might appear, would be tantamount to denying one of the cornerstones of liberal democracy, the (autoimmune) right to self-critique.[5]

---

[5] In New Zealand, from where I write, there is currently debate about the constitutional legality of a governmentally imposed national 'lockdown' that severely restricts civil liberties (words like 'socialism' and 'totalitarianism' are surfacing) as a means of limiting the spread of COVID-19, despite the remarkable containment of the disease effected by these measures.

There are, of course, many extensive and illuminating discussions of Derrida's thought on the aporia of autoimmunity and its relevance to politics. My purpose here is not to repeat what others have said but, as noted at the start, to suggest some ways in which the ideas I have sketched may enliven a reading of Nguyen's *The Refugees*, and how this, conversely, may perhaps expand further our understanding of the ways in which Derrida's work sheds further light on some of the crucial questions that beleaguer our contemporary world, notably resurgent nationalism, globalization and what has been dubbed 'the refugee crisis'.

Foreign bodies: Ghosts in Nguyen's text

Nguyen's narrator in *The Sympathizer* opens with a gesture towards Ralph Ellison's *Invisible Man*, a novel famously about America's lack of (racial) inclusiveness: 'I am a spy, a sleeper, a spook, a man of two faces' (Nguyen 2015, 1). This might have been spoken by the author himself. Secrets and ghosts haunt the writing of this 'man of two faces' (or places), a (former) refugee from the Vietnam/American War now (long) resident in the US where he arrived with his parents and brother at the age of four. *The Sympathizer* was Nguyen's first published work of fiction, but by no means his first publication. A professor of English, American Studies and Ethnicity at the University of Southern California, his first publications were non-fictional. *Race and Resistance: Literature and Politics in Asian America* (2002) was followed by a series of essays, the content of which makes clear his interest in 'the dead' and how one might remember/represent them (two of the most influential are titled 'Speak of the Dead, Speak of Vietnam' (2006) and 'Just Memory: War and the Ethics of Remembrance' (2013)).[6] The year after the publication of *The Sympathizer*, Nguyen released another critical monograph, *Nothing Ever Dies: Vietnam and the Memory of War*, which begins: 'This is a book on war, memory, and identity. It proceeds from the idea that all wars are fought twice, the first time on the battlefield, the second time in memory' (2016a, 4).

Of *The Sympathizer*, Nguyen says that '[m]any people … characterized [it] as an immigrant story, and me as an immigrant'. He refutes this: 'No. My novel is a war story and I am not an immigrant. I am a refugee who, like many others, has never ceased being a refugee in some corner of my mind' (2016b, n.p.n.). His instance on being acknowledged as a refugee is political:

> Immigrants are more reassuring than refugees because there is an endpoint to their story; however they arrive, whether they are documented or not, their desires for a new life can be absorbed into the American dream or into the European narrative of civilization. … By contrast, *refugees are the zombies of the world*, the

---

[6] In the former he writes of old family photographs as 'universal signs of our place in the world as refugees, found in every household as keepsakes of memory, hallowed signs of our haunting by the past. Photographs are the secular imprints of ghosts' (2006, 8).

undead who rise from dying states to march or *swim toward our borders* in endless waves.

Ibid.; emphasis added

Although *The Refugees* was published in 2017, it predates his earlier publications in conception and the first story in the collection, 'Black-Eyed Women', might be seen as a frame for all his writing to date. According to Nguyen, writing the story took '17 years and something like 50 drafts' (Vongkiatkajorn 2017, n.p.n.). If, as he avers, the second time a war is fought is in memory, then, as Josephine Livingstone suggests, '[t]he ghost is an apt figure for the war that is fought a second time. It is a metonym for the memory of a living person, as well as the vocalizing embodiment of death itself' (2017, n.p.n.). It is also, as Nguyen's above comment makes clear, a metaphor for the undead, the zombie-refugee that swims towards the borders of the state.

The first-person narrator is a thirty-eight-year old Vietnamese (former) refugee, living in California with her mother (we only discover her gender about halfway through the story, a surprisingly unsettling moment for the reader). She works as a ghost writer, penning the memoirs of those who have survived tragedies. At the time when the central events of the story took place, she recalls, she was writing a memoir for the sole survivor of a plane crash, ironically named Victor, which killed his family (he claims to see their ghosts). The narrator notes the irony of her profession for, as we learn, she is not only a 'survivor' herself but also – at least figuratively – a ghost. And by the end of the story she is not simply ventriloquizing for others but writing ghost stories of her own. Thus the 'ghost writer' is a ghost(ly) writer who writes about ghosts. In the narrative present, the ostensible time of writing the story, she recounts the arrival, at their home, of her brother's ghost one night in the recent past. At first, he is only seen by her mother: 'she said he must have disappeared because he was tired. After all he had just completed a journey of thousands of miles across the Pacific' (Nguyen 2017, 4). The surreal suggestion of a ghost who has arduously swum across the world's largest ocean can be dismissed by the reader, at least initially, as the imaginings of the elderly mother who believes in ghosts and avidly tells ghost stories. When the narrator asks her mother how the ghost got to their home, she replies,

> 'He swam.' She gave me a pitying look. 'That's why he was wet.'
> 'He was an excellent swimmer,' I said, humouring her. 'What did he look like?'
> 'Exactly the same.'
> 'It's been twenty-five years. He hasn't changed at all?'
> 'They always look exactly the same as when you last saw them.'
>
> 4–5

The narrator acknowledges that she has tried to forget her older brother, 'but just by turning a corner in the world or in my mind I could run into him, my best friend' (5). She recalls shared events from their 'youth in a haunted country' (Vietnam during the war) and the way he had told her 'ghost stories', proclaiming them to be 'historical accounts from reliable sources' – these being the old 'black-eyed women' who squatted in the village market of their childhood (6).⁷ The narrator also recalls other stories, ones told later by her parents, in America, about the dangers of 'our young countrymen, boys who had learned about violence from growing up in wartime. ... [A]ll of them proof of what my mother said, that *we did not belong here*. In a country where possessions counted for everything, we had no belongings except our stories' (7; emphasis added).

Here, only a third of the way into the story, we have ghosts and memories, history and storytelling, nationhood, (not) belonging(s) – and secrets. At this juncture it is valuable to return to Derrida's work on secrecy and singularity, sketched above, and the figure of the spectre in his writing. As Colin Davis explains, the word 'hauntology' (*hantologie* in the original French) was coined by Derrida in *Specters of Marx* and 'supplants its near-homonym ontology, replacing the priority of being and presence with the figure of the ghost which is neither present nor absent, neither dead nor alive' (2005, 373). Derrida urges the need to 'speak *to the* specter, to speak with it ... especially *to make or to let* a spirit *speak*' (1994, 11; emphasis in the original). Davis elaborates that '[c]onversing with spectres is not undertaken in the expectation that they will reveal some secret, shameful or otherwise. Rather, it may open us up to the experience of secrecy as such,' an experience that 'may undermine what we think we know' (2007, 11).

The narrator in 'Black-Eyed Women' indeed 'convers[es] with' a spectre. When she first meets her ghost-brother some nights after he appeared to her mother (he's still the age at which he died, fifteen, and still wearing the clothes in which he died, although they are faded), she recalls thinking, '[p]erhaps this apparition ... was not a figment of my imagination but a symptom of something wrong, like the cancer that killed my father. ... Panic surged from that bottomless well within myself that I had sealed with concrete' (Nguyen 2017, 9). It is very possible to read the ghost-brother as a manifestation of what Henri F. Ellenberger famously referred to as the 'pathogenic secret' or the disease of the uncanny that is symptomatic of trauma (1993, 341–55). In a trajectory that connects Freud to many contemporary trauma theories, this 'secret' is a memory that cannot be discharged; its meaning cannot be assimilated by an individual into a healing narrative of identity. More, it cannot be articulated directly and manifests in language only 'through ellipsis, indirection and detour, or fragmentation and deformation' (Schwab 2010, 107).

The influential Cathy Caruth describes trauma as a fundamentally 'paradoxical experience' (1991, 417). Roger Luckhurst writes of Caruth's conception of trauma that it is 'somehow ... seared directly into the psyche, almost like a piece of shrapnel, and is not subject to the distortions of subjective memory' (2008, 4). It is 'a crisis of representation, of history and truth, and of narrative time' because '[n]o narrative of trauma can be told in a linear way: it has a time signature that must fracture conventional causality' (5). Geoffrey Hartman elaborates on the 'two contradictory elements' of

---

7 In *Ghosts of War in Vietnam*, Heonik Kwon writes of the 'social vitality' (2008, 3) of ghosts in post-War Vietnam; they 'are a preeminent popular cultural form in Vietnam and also a powerful, effective means of historical reflection and self-expression' (2). Kwon considers the cultural significance of wandering ghosts in addressing memories of the 'American War'. See also Martha and Bruce Lincoln (2015).

trauma: 'One is the traumatic event, registered rather than experienced. It seems to have bypassed perception and consciousness, and falls directly into the psyche. The other is a kind of memory of the event, in the form of a perpetual troping of it by the bypassed or severely split (dissociated) psyche' (1995, 537).

Such (now familiar) theorizing seems all too easily 'placed' on 'Black-Eyed Women' and its 'fractured' temporality: the narrative moves between the present in which the narrator writes, the past in which her brother's ghost arrived, a more distant past of their time on a refugee boat, the even more distant past of the Vietnam War and also the pasts that others recollect in their (ghost) stories. The narrator acknowledges to the ghost-brother that they shared experiences that 'I've tried to forget.... But I can't' (Nguyen 2017, 14). She writes (in the present): 'I had not forgotten our nameless blue boat and it had not forgotten me' (ibid.), and then proceeds to tell her (literal) secret, that about which she has not been able to speak until this moment. As a child of thirteen she, along with her parents and brother, fled Vietnam on a refugee boat that was attacked by pirates. As they rounded up the girls and young women, her brother tried to protect her and was killed by a blow to his head. She was raped in front of her parents. Of this, she recalls, 'I could hear nothing. Even when I screamed I could not hear myself ... The world was muzzled, the way it would be ever afterward with my mother and father and myself, none of us uttering another sound on this matter. Their silence and my own would cut me again and again' (16). The unspeakable is figured as 'the parrot of a question, asking me how I lived and he died' (12). In a comment that seems particularly suggestive here, Gabriele Schwab writes that '[t]rauma attacks and sometimes kills language. In order for trauma to heal, body and self must be reborn and words must be disentangled from the dead bodies they are trying to conceal' (2010, 41). The figuring of trauma as a (psychic) wound is very common in trauma theory. Both the narrator and the ghost-brother are wounded. When he visits his sister, he still has a bruise on his temple 'but the blood was gone' (Nguyen 2017, 8). When he asks, '[d]oes it still hurt for you?' she replies, 'Yes' (ibid.).

If we approach the story through the lens of (Caruthian) trauma theory we might read it as ultimately redemptive, as recounting an act of healing as the narrator lays to rest the ghost of her brother: the family secret, in Abraham's terms, is exorcized. She is eventually 'disentangled from the dead bod[y]' of her brother when she realizes that 'the parrot crouched on [her]shoulder' can be got 'rid of' by 'letting it speak' (Nguyen 2017, 17). When the parrot/she asks the ghost-brother, 'Why did I live and you die?' he answers, '[y]ou died too.... You just don't know it' (ibid.). The ghost writer, then, is herself a ghost – or, at least, a zombie. Following this revelation, the brother-ghost disappears 'for good' having 'said all he wanted to say' (19). The encounter can be read as cathartic, enabling a productive mourning. The narrator subsequently tells her mother 'I haven't said all I wanted to say' (ibid.) and begins writing her own book. It is a book of ghost stories, some told to her by her mother, some recalled as told by her brother who heard them from the 'black-eyed women', and at least one that is her own – the one we are reading. In these terms, then, she is finally able to speak her secret; she is at last able to cry for herself, her brother, her parents and 'all ... those other girls who had vanished and never come back, including myself' (ibid.).

To my mind, this reading is insufficient. It forces the kind of closure that for Derrida, as discussed above, denies the secret – or the secrecy – of the spectre, and of literature. We might be better to approach the story in an attempt to apprehend the 'secret in open view' (Attridge 2010, 45) – which may or may not be a secret at all. As Derrida repeatedly states, while ghosts (*revenants*) arise from the past, they are *arrivants*, too: they haunt in a present that is always becoming the (receding) future. We might do well to focus less on the revelation of a secret from the past in the story (the previously untold account of murder and rape) than on the fact that the narrator's writing functions not to exorcize and silence the ghosts of the past – Vietnamese, American, Vietnamese American, African American, Korean, Japanese, communists or anti-communists – but to 'keep them alive' in the present. So too with Nguyen's stories. His characters are certainly haunted (some transgenerationally) by the Vietnamese past/war, but I would like to suggest that cumulatively the collection is equally concerned with how they, as refugees, haunt America and open questions about the 'secret' of the nation's democracy.

In *Nothing Ever Dies*, Nguyen considers how Vietnam, its war and its dead, are (un)justly remembered and forgotten – in Vietnam, America and elsewhere. The book is a sustained challenge to what he asserts, in an earlier essay titled 'Just Memory', are forms of 'nationalist memory, powerfully exclusionary and powerfully inclusionary' (2013, 152), concerned as these are with 'the forgetting of strategic others – the enemy outside, the minority within, the ideologically disagreeable, as well as civilians, women, children, the disabled, animals, and the environment' (151).[8] In *Nothing Ever Dies*, Nguyen writes of the refugees who settled in the US, especially in Little Saigon in Orange County, California, the setting for several of his stories in *The Refugees*. He scathingly refers to Little Saigon as 'the embodiment of the "American Dream in Vietnamese," where capitalism and free choice reign' in 'a rebuke against communism' (2016a, 40). He continues, 'Little Saigon is an example of American capitalism and democracy operating at a refined level of soft power' (41):

> [A]ccording to the informal terms of the American compact, the more wealth minorities amass, the more property they buy, the more clout they accumulate, and the more visible they become, the more other Americans will positively recognize and remember them. Belonging would substitute for longing; membership would make up for disremembering. This membership in the body politic would be made possible not only by economic success, but also through winning those political and cultural rights of self-representation denied to the exiles and refugees when they lived under communism.
>
> Ibid.

Most importantly, he argues, Little Saigon's inhabitants need(ed) to prove themselves to be 'ideal' refugees, a 'model minority', and to distinguish themselves and their 'strategic hamlet' from 'the sidelined ghetto, barrio, and reservation of the American nightmare'

---

[8] Nguyen acknowledges the influence of Paul Ricoeur's *History, Memory, Forgetting* (2004) at various points (for example 2016a, 73–4, 179, 294–5).

(42) – for 'even in pluralist America, the weak and the defeated find themselves rejected' (44). They needed, thus, to conform to what Yến Lê Espiritu refers to as 'a conventional story of ethnic assimilation', which also means a greater chance of 'financial reward' (Espiritu 2006, 413). Nguyen refers to the US as 'the country that imagines itself as a perpetual innocent' (2016a, 51), strategically forgetting not just its actions during the American War but its loss of that war, too. These facts are erasable not only because the enemy was Communism (with a capital C) and 'capitalism has won in the end' (286), but also because America 'magnanimously' offered tens of thousands anti-communist Vietnamese 'refuge' after the Fall of Saigon. In *Body Counts: The Vietnam War and Militarized Refuge(es)* (2014), Espiritu argues that popular American narratives about the 'rescue' of 'good' (anti-communist) Vietnamese after the war, and the 'refuge' provided to them in the US, not only retrospectively justified America's military presence in Vietnam but also acted to justify later military interventions elsewhere in the world. These narratives reinforce, she suggests, the racialized and militarized projects of the US, through to the present, and defend them in terms of an ideological opposition to the heinous 'other' of communism (or, say, Islam).

Avery Gordon, in *Ghostly Matters*, argues that the trope of the ghost is never simply about an individual's loss or trauma: it 'figure[s] the whole complicated sociality of a determining formation that seems inoperative (like slavery) or invisible (like racially gendered capitalism) but is nonetheless alive and enforced' (1997, 183). The figure of the ghost, she suggests, invites 'not a return to the past but a reckoning with its repression in the present' (ibid.) and what this means for the future. What, then, of the ghostly figures of Vietnamese refugees in the US? Espiritu suggests that instead of producing narratives of traumatized refugees, in which trauma is 'conceptualized only as pain, suffering, and distress, we can read trauma productively as a disruption of the US myth of "rescue and liberation" that enunciates violence and recovery simultaneously' (2006, 421–2). She reminds us that scholars (and filmmakers and novelists) who portray the flight of Vietnamese to the US 'as a matter of desperate individuals fleeing political persecution and/or economic depression ... completely discount the aggressive roles that the US government, military, and corporations have played in generating this exodus in the first place' (422–3). Quoting Nguyen, she asks, '[h]ow would refugees, not as an object of investigation, but as a site of social critique, "articulate the incomprehensible or heretofore unspeakable?"' And, gesturing to Avery Gordon: 'How do we pay attention to what has been rendered ghostly, and write into being the seething presence of things that appear to be not there?' (424).

In a 1990 interview with Elizabeth Weber, Derrida claimed that '[a]ll experience open to the future is prepared or prepares itself to welcome the monstrous *arrivant*' (quoted in Royle 2003, 110). Nicholas Royle elaborates on this by claiming that '[t]he figure of the *arrivant* haunts everything [Derrida] has said about the future', continuing:

> Like the word 'arrive', '*arrivant*' has to do with what comes to the shore (from the Old French *ariver* 'to reach the shore', from the Latin *ad* 'to' *rīpa* 'shore'). ... As

Derrida puts it [in *Specters of Marx*], it is a matter of 'absolute hospitality,' of saying 'yes' or 'come' (or, perhaps, 'be free') to the *arrivant(e)*, in other words to the future that cannot be anticipated. ... The *arrivant* 'surprises the host – who is not yet a host or an inviting power – enough to call into question ... the very border that delineated a legitimate home' [quoting Derrida from *Aporias*], the home-shore or the door and threshold of one's home.

2003, 111; emphasis in the original

'Black-Eyed Women', and *The Refugees* more generally, asks us to reckon with what official memories/narratives of the Vietnam War and its ostensibly compliant residue – (former) refugees living on American soil – repress in the American imagination. It invites us to consider how the legacy of this war continues to haunt transgenerationally (the narrator tells us that often stories come to her, through her mother (Nguyen 2017, 21)),[9] and how this might relate to, and unsettle, America's 'democracy'. Threaded through the story, as in the entire collection, are allusions to multiple ghosts other than the obvious – in 'The Black-Eyed Women' the ghost-brother and narrating 'zombie' sister – who have come 'to the shore'. Consider these 'visitors' to the 'haunted country', Vietnam, for example, who feature in the stories of the eponymous black-eyed women: '[T]he upper half of a Korean lieutenant, launched by a mine into the branches of a rubber tree; a scalped black American floating in the creek not far from his downed helicopter, his eyes and the exposed half-moon of his brain glistening in the water; and a decapitated Japanese pirate groping through cassava shrubbery for his head' (6). The words of the narrator in the final paragraph of the story appear to refer to the mutual haunting of each others' realms by the living and the dead – 'As they haunt our country, so do we haunt theirs' (21) – but the ambiguity introduced by the choice of word 'country' suggests the reciprocal haunting of America and Vietnam.

Unwelcome *arrivant(e)*s, the (in)coming, also call into question the border or 'home-shore' of America in 'Black-Eyed Women' and *The Refugees* more generally. Uninvited, non-ideal minorities are regarded with disdain or pity (but also compassion, at times) by 'legitimate' Vietnamese refugees, who were invited in and allowed to remain on the condition of compliance and assimilation. In 'Black-Eyed Women', the narrator's mother buys the brother-ghost new clothes of which she says, 'he can't be wandering out in the cold ... like a homeless person or some *illegal immigrant*' (Nguyen 2017, 11; emphasis added). The satirical fourth story in the collection, 'The Transplant' (73–97), turns on a hurtful but rather minor deception and an agreement between a Mexican-American and a second-generation Vietnamese refugee to remain silent about the employment of illegal Latino overstayers with 'phantom identities' (95). In the ironically titled 'War Years' (49–72), the fear of appearing non-compliant, of being seen as a communist sympathizer, results in a US-Vietnamese refugee shopkeeper donating money to an anti-communist guerrilla group, despite her belief that it is

---

[9] In 'Just Memory' Nguyen evokes W.G. Sebald's and Marianne Hirsch's terms 'secondhand memories' (sic) and 'postmemory', respectively, when writing of how 'the traumatic experiences underwent by my father and mother were passed on to me' (2013, 144–5).

'extortion' (her husband suggests it is 'hush money' paid to 'make our lives a little easier'; 53).

In these ways, through the portrayal of the singularity of individuals within the US Vietnamese refugee community and the multiplicity of that which haunts them and continues to do transgenerationally, *The Refugees* resists homogenizing narratives of American democratic inclusion. Importantly, the framing story reminds us that the inclusivity implied in the notion that everyone is equal (and free), the premise that underpins the narrative of immigrant assimilation and the American Dream in the US, relies on the notion of a bordered 'home' from which those less free, or less equal, are barred. Hospitality – an invitation to enter – is offered on the condition of assimilation to 'the same', to a 'community of friends' that is premised by the 'calculation of majorities', as Derrida puts it (1997, 22). This is why 'belonging' or 'putting in common [to a people or nation] ... spells the loss of the secret' (Derrida and Ferraris 2001, 59). The 'tragedy' of the demand for or expectation of sameness diminishes or negates the freedom to be equally singular and this aporia haunts (American) democracy and refugee's desires to belong.

The Refugees, gently, persuasively, invites thinking about the exclusions and inclusions democracy requires – and not just that of America, or those that occurred in the past. It encourages consideration of the violent retrenchment into nationalism in current times, in a world which not too long ago vaunted its cosmopolitanism but now, increasingly, denies refuge to those who are, often, the victims of our own democratic projects. Writing of the refusal of France to grant refuge – 'hospitality' – to those displaced after WW2 (an all too prescient situation given the attempts of countries to close their borders in the recent 'refugee crisis'), Derrida says:

> because being at home with oneself (*l'être-soi chez soi* – *l'ipséité même* – the other within oneself) supposes a reception or inclusion of the other which one seeks to appropriate, control, and master according to different modalities of violence, there is a history of hospitality, an always possible perversion of the law of hospitality (which can appear unconditional), and of the laws which come to limit and condition it in its inscription as a law.
>
> Derrida 2001, 17; emphasis in the original

Here then is democracy's secret: its hospitality is always riven by the possible perversion of the very laws that constitute it. Danger and threat do not only exist in the form of the foreigner without, or the ingested parasite (or the virus) that can be expelled or immunized against; danger is also always within, possible as an attack on the 'self' of the nation by democracy itself. Even if we shut our borders to others out of fear of challenging difference, Nguyen suggests, we cannot close out the ghosts that will continue to haunt us. This is a secret that is not a secret at all, for it is in full view: however tightly bolted the door, vast the ocean or high the (Mexican!) wall, ghosts will haunt our democratic narratives and encourage rereading, singular and endlessly open at once: 'At bottom, the specter is the future, it is always to come, it presents itself only as that which could come or come back' asserts Derrida (1994, 48). It is this that opens democracy to the future, but not necessarily a utopian one. We cannot know what secrets 'the spectre' will reveal or withhold but remain alert to its presence, waiting. Nguyen's narrator concludes of his father in the story 'Someone Else Besides You' (2017, 151–80) that 'he was waiting, just like us, for what was to come' (180). Or maybe, as at the start of Derrida's *Specters of Marx*: 'Someone, you or me, comes forward and says: "*I would like to learn to live finally*"' (Derrida 1994, xvii).

References

Abraham, Nicolas. (1987), 'Notes on the Phantom: A Complement to Freud's Metapsychology', translated by Nicholas Rand, *Critical Inquiry*, 13 (2): 287–92.
Attridge, Derek. (2010), *Reading and Responsibility: Deconstruction's Traces*, Edinburgh: Edinburgh University Press.
Birchall, Clare. (2011), 'Introduction to "Secrecy and Transparency": The Politics of Opacity and Openness', *Theory, Culture and Society*, 28 (7–8): 1–19.
Birchall, Clare. (2014), 'Radical Transparency?', *Cultural Studies Critical Methodologies*, 14 (1): 77–88.
Blanco, María del Pilar and Esther Peeren. (2013), 'Introduction: Conceptualizing Spectralities', in María del Pilar Blanco and Esther Peeren (eds), *The Spectralities Reader: Ghosts and Haunting in Contemporary Cultural Theory*, 1–27, New York: Bloomsbury.
Caruth, Cathy. (1991), 'Introduction', *American Imago*, 48 (4): 417–24.
Czajka, Agnes. (2017), *Democracy and Justice: Reading Derrida in Istanbul*, New York and London: Routledge.
Danta, Chris. (2013), 'Derrida and the Test of Secrecy', *Angelaki*, 18 (2): 61–75.
Davis, Colin. (2005), 'Hauntology, Spectres and Phantoms', *French Studies*, 59 (3): 373–9.
Davis, Colin. (2007), *Haunted Subjects: Deconstruction, Psychoanalysis and the Return of the Dead*, Houndmills: Palgrave Macmillan.
Derrida, Jacques. (1986), 'Fors: The Anglish Words of Nicolas Abraham and Maria Torok', in Nicolas Abraham and Maria Torok (eds), Nicholas Rand (trans), *The Wolf Man's Magic Word: A Cryptonymy*, xi–xlviii, Minneapolis: University of Minnesota Press.
Derrida, Jacques. (1993), *Aporias*, translated by Thomas Dutoit, Stanford: Stanford University Press.
Derrida, Jacques. (1994), *Specters of Marx: The State of the Debt, the Work of Mourning, and the New International*, translated by Peggy Kamuf, New York and London: Routledge.
Derrida, Jacques. (1997), *The Politics of Friendship*, translated by George Collins, London and New York: Verso.
Derrida, Jacques. (2001), *On Cosmopolitanism and Forgiveness*, translated by Mark Dooley and Michael Hughes, London and New York: Routledge.
Derrida, Jacques. (2005), *Rogues: Two Essays on Reason*, translated by Pascale-Anne Brault and Michael Naas, Stanford: Stanford University Press.
Derrida, Jacques. (2008), 'Literature in Secret: An Impossible Filiation', *The Gift of Death and Literature in Secret*, 119–58, 2nd edition, translated by David Wills, Chicago: Chicago University Press.
Derrida, Jacques and Maurizio Ferraris. (2001), *A Taste for the Secret*, translated by Giacomo Donis, Cambridge: Polity Press.

Ellenberger, Henri F. (1966) (1993), 'The Pathogenic Secret and Its Therapeutics', in Mark S. Micale (ed.), *Beyond the Unconscious: Essays of Henri F. Ellenberger in the History of Psychiatry*, 341–59, translated by Françoise Dubor and Mark S. Micale, Princeton: Princeton University Press.

Espiritu, Yến Lê. (2006), 'Toward a Critical Refugee Study: The Vietnamese Refugee Subject in US Scholarship', *Journal of Vietnamese Studies*, 1 (1–2): 410–33.

Espiritu, Yến Lê. (2014), *Body Counts: The Vietnam War and Militarized Refuge(es)*, Oakland: University of California Press.

Gordon, Avery F. (1997), *Ghostly Matters: Haunting and the Sociological Imagination*, Minneapolis and London: University of Minnesota Press.

Hall, Gary. (2007), 'The Politics of Secrecy: Cultural Studies and Derrida in the Age of Empire', *Cultural Studies*, 21 (1): 59–81.

Hartman, Geoffrey. (1995), 'On Traumatic Knowledge and Literary Studies', *New Literary History*, 26 (3): 537–63.

Horn, Eva. (2011), 'Logics of Political Secrecy', *Theory, Culture and Society*, 28 (7–8): 103–22.

Horn, Eva. (2013), *The Secret War: Treason, Espionage, and Modern Fiction*, translated by Geoffrey Winthrop-Young, Evanston: Northwestern University Press.

Jeffers, Alison. (2012), *Refugees, Theatre and Crisis: Performing Global Identities*, Houndmills: Palgrave Macmillan.

Johnson, Laurie. (2000), 'Tracing Calculation [Calque Calcul]: Between Nicolas Abraham and Jacques Derrida', *Postmodern Culture*, 10 (3): 1–12.

Kumar, Miiko, Greg Martin and Rebecca Scott Bray. (2015), 'Secrecy, Law and Society', in Greg Martin, Rebecca Scott Bray and Miiko Kumar (eds), *Secrecy, Law and Society*, 1–19, London and New York: Routledge.

Kwon, Heonik. (2008), *Ghosts of War in Vietnam*, Cambridge, MA: Cambridge University Press.

Lincoln, Martha and Bruce Lincoln. (2015), 'Toward a Critical Hauntology: Bare Afterlife and the Ghosts of Ba Chúc', *Comparative Studies in Society and History*, 57 (1): 191–220.

Livingstone, Josephine. (2017), 'Viet Thanh Nguyen's Ghosts', *The New Republic*, 26 July 2017, accessed 18 March 2020, https://newrepublic.com/article/144016/viet-thanh-nguyens-ghosts.

Luckhurst, Roger. (2008), *The Trauma Question*, London and New York: Routledge.

Miller, J. Hillis. (2008), 'Derrida's Politics of Autoimmunity', *Discourse*, 30 (1–2): 208–25.

Naas, Michael. (2008), *Derrida from Now On*, New York: Fordham University Press.

Neocleous, Mark. (2002), 'Privacy, Secrecy, Idiocy', *Social Research: An International Quarterly*, 69 (1): 85–110.

Nguyen, Viet Thanh. (2002), *Race and Resistance: Literature and Politics in Asian America*, Oxford and New York: Oxford University Press.

Nguyen, Viet Thanh. (2006), 'Speak of the Dead, Speak of Vietnam: The Ethics and Aesthetics of Minority Discourse', *CR: The New Centennial Review*, 1 (2): 7–37.

Nguyen, Viet Thanh. (2013), 'Just Memory: War and the Ethics of Remembrance', *American Literary History*, 25 (1): 144–63.

Nguyen, Viet Thanh. (2015), *The Sympathizer*, New York: Grove Press.

Nguyen, Viet Thanh. (2016a), *Nothing Ever Dies: Vietnam and the Memory of War*, Cambridge, MA: Harvard University Press.
Nguyen, Viet Thanh. (2016b), 'The Hidden Scars All Refugees Carry', *The New York Times*, 2 September 2016, accessed 18 March 2020. https://www.nytimes.com/2016/09/03/opinion/the-hidden-scars-all-refugees-carry.html.
Nguyen, Viet Thanh. (2017), *The Refugees*, New York: Grove Press.
Ricoeur, Paul. (2004), *History, Memory, Forgetting*, translated by Kathleen Blamey and David Pellauer, Chicago: University of Chicago Press.
Schwab, Gabriele. (2010), *Haunting Legacies: Violent Histories and Transgenerational Trauma*, New York: Columbia University Press.
Taylor, Mark C. (1992), 'nO nOt nO', in Harold Coward and Toby Foshay (eds), *Derrida and Negative Theology*, 167–98, New York: State University of New York Press.
Vongkiatkajorn, Kanyakrit. (2017), 'Pulitzer Prize-winning Author Viet Thanh Nguyen "Never Stopped Being a Refugee"', *Mother Jones*, January/February 2017, accessed 18 March 2020, https://www.motherjones.com/media/2017/01/viet-thanh-nguyen-refugees-sympathizer-pulitzer-prize-vietnam-war/.
Walters, William and Alex Luscome. (2017), 'Hannah Arendt and the Art of Secrecy; Or, the Fog of Cobra Mist', *International Political Sociology,* 1 (1): 5–20.

Index

Abbott, H. Porter 7, 7 n.12, 8 n.14, 16, 28, 34, 56 n.2, 69, 72
Abraham, Nicolas and Maria Torok 12, 12 n.20, 16, 49, 51, 115, 121, 128–31, 136–7, 169, 207–8, 216, 221–2
alterity (*also* otherness) 2–3, 10–12, 46, 89 n.6, 92–4, 101–2, 110, 112, 114, 124–5, 127, 132, 135, 139, 149, 175, 186, 200, 202–3, 210, 211 n.4
see also the other
Anderson, Benedict 2, 16
Attridge, Derek 4, 8–9, 10, 23–35, 87 n.1, 90–1, 93 n.14, 101, 103
'Introduction: Derrida and the Questioning of Literature' 3 n.4, 17
J. M. Coetzee and the Ethics of Reading 93 n.14, 101–2
Reading and Responsibility 3 n.4, 9, 16–17, 90–1, 102, 140 n.1, 153, 210, 216, 221
The Singularity of Literature 4, 10, 17, 25 n.3, 30, 35, 41, 50, 90, 92–3, 97, 102
The Work of Literature 4, 8, 10, 17, 92, 98–9, 101–2
see also Derrida and Attridge, 'This Strange Institution Called Literature'
autoimmunity (*also* autoimmune) 9, 16, 49, 208, 211–12

Barbour, Charles 15, 17, 27, 27 n.5, 28 n.8, 34–5, 197–9, 204
Barthes, Roland 5 n.8, 13, 17, 41, 51, 94, 140–4, 152–3
Berman, Jessica 12 n.19, 17
Bhabha, Homi K. 107, 121
Bildungsroman 190
Birchall, Clare 14–15, 17, 193–4, 204, 209–10, 221
Blanchot, Maurice 2, 15, 29 n.10, 43, 43 n.7, 51, 127–8, 152

The Unavowable Community 11–13, 17, 107–10, 114, 121, 124, 137, 140, 148–50, 153, 187, 201, 204
Boehmer, Elleke 89 n.5, 90, 90 n.8, 102
Booth, Naomi 5, 47–51
Sealed 9, 47–51
Brooks, Peter 183, 187, 192, 195, 199–200, 202, 204
Butler, Judith 14, 130–1, 137, 175, 179, 182, 186–7

Calinescu, Matei 1, 6, 10 n.17, 17, 59, 66, 68–9, 71–4, 76, 79–80, 82, 84–5, 192, 204
canon (*also* canonical, canonicity) 87–8, 90, 93, 101–2
capitalism (*also* capitalist) 2 n.1, 5, 40, 46, 189, 196, 217–18
Caputo, John D. 3, 10, 17, 124, 137
Coetzee, J. M. 5, 15 n.21, 17, 25, 46, 89 n.6, 93 n.14, 100, 103, 177, 187
colonial (*also* colonialism, neo-colonialism) 88–9, 94, 134, 180–1, 184–5
relation 173–6, 180–2, 184, 186
see also postcolonial
communism (*also* communist) 11, 108 n.3, 217–19
community (*also* communal) 1–2, 5, 9, 14, 46, 49, 55, 64–5, 69, 87–8, 89 n.4, 94–5, 107, 117, 143–4, 155, 164, 166, 173, 179, 181, 220
and hospitality 7 n.13, 16, 186–7, 207, 208, 211–12, 218, 220
inoperative (*also* non-identitarian, unavowable) 2–3, 7 n.13, 10–13, 91, 107–14, 120–1, 124–8, 135, 148–53, 186–7, 201–2
of lovers (*also* of friends) 12, 110–12, 124–8, 136, 148–53, 189–90, 210–11, 220

operative (*also* organic, traditional, identitarian, knowable) 2, 2 n.1, 10–13, 91, 102, 107–12, 118–21, 124–8, 131–3, 139, 148–53, 174–9, 201–2
  of readers 5, 10, 26, 33–4, 41, 69, 88, 92, 95, 100, 102, 169
  and secrecy 1, 4–5, 7, 10, 10 n.17, 12–13, 15, 28, 33–4, 37, 72, 101–2, 108, 111–12, 114–16, 123–8, 139–40, 148–53, 156–7, 159, 163, 169, 199
  of siblings 107–9, 112–16, 120
  see also confession and community; democracy and community; family and community; homosexual (*also* gay, queer) community; postcolonial community
concealment (*also* conceal) 1, 4–6, 8, 13, 15, 27–8, 43, 66, 68, 71–2, 75–6, 108, 112, 114, 116–18, 130, 145–6, 151, 162, 164–6, 174–6, 180, 182–3, 186, 191, 193, 197, 201, 207, 209, 216
confession (*also* confess, confessional, confessor) 14–15, 65–6, 79, 81, 83–4, 149, 177–9, 191, 198
  and community 182–6, 199–201
Conrad, Joseph 7–8, 10 n.17, 89
COVID-19 coronavirus 14, 212
crypt (*also* cryptic) 8, 12–13, 27, 44, 49, 108–9, 114–18, 120, 123–4, 128–31, 136, 158 n.4
  cryptaesthetic resistance 9, 9 n.16, 13, 44, 44 n.8, 107–8, 114–16
Culler, Jonathan 3 n.5, 17

death (*also* dead, deadly, mortality) 11–13, 30, 41–4, 47, 49–50, 65–6, 74–6, 78–9, 89 n.7, 100, 108, 110–12, 114–15, 117–20, 124–7, 129–34, 136, 143, 149, 151–2, 155–7, 159–62, 164, 168, 174, 178–9, 185, 196–7, 207, 213–17, 219
  see also exposure; finitude; singularity
democracy (*also* democratic) 14–16, 193–5, 207–12, 217, 219–20
  to come 3–4, 16, 16 n.23, 89 n.7, 210, 210 n.3
  and community 3–4, 16

Derrida, Jacques (*also* Derridean) 2, 9, 15, 17–18, 23, 27–30, 32 n.11, 35, 45 n.10, 49, 51–2, 62, 69, 90–1, 94, 98–9, 103, 114, 121, 124, 129–31, 136–7, 140 n.1, 169, 185, 187, 197–8, 204, 207–8, 211–13, 215, 217–18, 220–1
  Acts of Literature 29 n.10
  Aporias 45, 157 n.3, 209–10, 219
  The Beast and the Sovereign 45 n.13, 47, 50
  'Biodegradables' 44, 114
  'Circumfession' 43
  On Cosmopolitanism and Forgiveness 220
  Demeure 28, 28 n.8, 43, 165, 167
  'Dialanguages' 44
  La dissemination 46
  'To Do Justice to Freud' 192
  'The Double Session' 46–7
  Donner le temps 27 n.6, 42
  'Faith and Knowledge' 11, 16
  'Fors' 12 n.20, 49, 128, 129 n.6, 158 n.4, 208
  Geneses, Genealogies, Genres and Genius 47, 50
  The Gift of Death 158, 161 n.8, 202
  Given Time 8, 27–8, 41–3, 45 n.12, 69, 157 n.3
  Of Grammatology 92
  'How to Avoid Speaking' 38, 157–8, 161
  'Literature in Secret' 3, 5, 27, 27 n.6, 29, 29 n.9, 56, 165–7, 184, 201, 209–10
  'Passions' 3–4, 9, 27–9, 69, 90
  Points. . . 9–10, 90
  The Politics of Friendship 10–13, 16, 16 n.23, 125–6, 210, 220
  Rogues 16 n.23, 210–11
  Specters of Marx 16, 16 n.23, 207, 156 n.2, 210 n.3, 215, 219, 221
  'Telepathy' 161 n.8
  On Touching 168
  'voice ii' 45 n.13
  'White Mythology' 39
Derrida, Jacques and Derek Attridge, 'This Strange Institution Called Literature' 3, 4 n.7, 16 n.23, 44 n.9, 89–92, 97

Derrida, Jacques and Maurizio Ferraris, *A Taste for the Secret* 2–3, 10, 15, 27 n.5, 34, 46, 111, 195, 202, 211, 220
disclosure (*also* disclose) 1, 14, 15 n.22, 56, 68, 71–2, 74, 78, 108, 115, 120, 136, 140, 142, 145, 150, 152, 191–3, 195
 delayed 8, 56–66
 see also revelation

ergodic texts 9, 23–6, 30–4
ethics (*also* ethical) 15, 90, 90 n.8, 93 n.14, 102, 175, 213
 see also narrative and ethical judgement
exposure (*also* exposition, exposed) 2, 11–12, 16, 29, 56–7, 108 n.2, 110–12, 114, 127–8, 149–50, 165, 168, 175, 186, 199, 201, 210
 see also death; finitude; singularity

family (*also* familial) 5, 37, 46, 58–9, 62, 74, 95, 98–9, 115, 123, 129, 131, 135, 156, 174, 177, 180, 191, 198, 200, 208–9, 213–14, 216
 and community 11–12, 107–14, 118–21, 125–6, 189, 211
 see also community of siblings
Fanon, Frantz 176, 187
femininity (*also* feminine) 6, 71, 84, 143
feminism (*also* feminist) 71, 73–4, 139, 143, 146, 191
finitude (*also* finite) 2, 11, 50, 110–11, 114, 127, 130, 149
 see also death; exposure; singularity
Forter, Greg 61, 69
Foucault, Michel 94, 183, 188
Franzen, Jonathan 5, 189–205
 The Corrections 203
 Freedom 203
 'Mr. Difficult: William Gaddis and the Problem of Hard-to-Read Books' 195
 Purity 15, 189–205
 Strong Motion 190, 195, 202 n.8
 The Twenty-Seventh City 190, 195, 202 n.8
Freud, Sigmund (*also* Freudian) 41, 44, 52, 89 n.6, 128, 197, 208, 215

ghost (*also* ghostly) 16, 56–7, 66–7, 98, 115, 119, 123, 130, 132, 156, 167, 200, 207–8, 212–20
 see also spectre

Han, Byung-Chul 15, 18, 193–6, 203–4
Hegel, G. W. F. (*also* Hegelian) 176, 180, 188
Holding, Ian 5, 11, 14, 173–88
 Of Beasts and Beings 14, 173–88
 Unfeeling 174
 What Happened to Us 14, 173–88
homosexuality (*also* gay, homosexual, queer) 8, 12, 123–5, 127, 131–6, 139, 146
homosexual (*also* gay, queer) community 124, 133–6
hospitality, *see* community and hospitality
hospitable reading 10, 90–1, 96, 101

imagination 144, 174, 176, 179, 181, 203, 215, 219
invisibility (*also* invisible) 27, 32, 109, 115, 118, 120, 133, 139–40, 145–8, 152, 218
 historical 13, 140–1, 147–8, 152
 see also subaltern

Jiménez Heffernan, Julián 2, 2 n.3, 11 n.18, 18, 110, 121

Kermode, Frank 5–6, 18, 28, 35, 55, 66, 68, 70–2, 202, 204, 210

Lahiri, Jhumpa 5, 11, 107–22
 Interpreter of Maladies 107 n.1, 110
 The Lowland 12–13, 107–22
 The Namesake 107 n.1, 110
 Unaccustomed Earth 107 n.1, 110
Levinas, Emmanuel 14, 90 n.8, 175, 182, 186, 188
literary form 1–2, 4, 5, 9–10, 23–6, 28, 29 n.10, 30, 32–4, 38, 49, 73, 88–91, 97, 100, 115, 145–7, 193
 see also narrative form

Macherey, Pierre 5 n.8, 18
Mantel, Hilary 5, 155–69
 Beyond Black 13, 155–69

masculinity 11, 123, 126–7, 133, 152
meaning 39, 46, 56, 59, 61, 73, 81, 87–9,
 91–2, 98, 100, 181, 215
 as event (*also* as experience,
  performance) 9, 23–30, 90, 97, 102
 and secrecy 4–5, 8, 26–9, 33, 44, 66,
  68–9, 72, 89 n.6, 95–6, 98, 114,
  116–18, 120–1, 182–5, 192, 210
Miller, J. Hillis 5, 8 n.14, 18–19, 70, 103,
  121, 128, 138, 222
 Ariadne's Thread 57, 68–9
 Communities in Fiction 2, 2 n.2, 109
 The Conflagration of Community 2 n.2
 'Derrida and Literature' 3 n.5, 10,
  94 n.15, 97 n.20, 98–9, 101–2
 'Derrida's Politics of Autoimmunity'
  211 n.4
 'Derrida's Topographies' 12 n.20, 129,
  136
 Literature as Conduct 4, 10
 On Literature 1, 3–4
 Others 8, 10
 Speech Acts in Literature 10
Morrison, Toni 5–8, 15 n.21, 55–70
 Beloved 7, 58, 63 n.6, 67 n.8
 Love 6, 8, 55–70
mourning 12, 15 n.21, 30, 80, 115, 124,
  129–31, 135, 216
Munro, Alice 5, 71–86
 Dear Life 84
 Too Much Happiness 6, 71–86

Naas, Michael 27, 35, 209, 211–12, 222
Nancy, Jean-Luc 2, 7 n.13, 15, 19, 52, 121,
  138, 154, 188, 205
 'The Confronted Community' 124
 The Inoperative Community 11–13, 107,
  109–12, 114, 124–7, 133, 135, 140,
  148, 175–7, 187, 201
 Listening 48
narrative 1, 5–8, 10 n.17, 13, 15, 23–6,
  30–2, 43, 49, 57–61, 71–4, 78, 80–1,
  84, 92, 99 n.22, 142, 189–93, 201–3
 causality 56–62, 215
 and ethical judgement 6–8, 56, 61–6,
  71–3, 78
 form 4, 7 n.12, 115

sequence 1, 4, 6, 8, 33, 55–61, 66, 68,
 71–2, 108
 see also secrecy (*also* secret) and
  narrative sequence
Nguyen, Viet Thanh 5, 11, 207–23
 'The Hidden Scars All Refugees Carry'
  213–14
 'Just Memory' 207 n.1, 213, 217,
  219 n.9
 Nothing Ever Dies 207 n.1, 213, 217
 Race and Resistance 213
 The Refugees 16, 207–23
 'Speak of the Dead, Speak of Vietnam'
  213
 The Sympathizer 213

the other 2–3, 7 n.13, 10–11, 15–16, 29, 34,
 44, 93–4, 102, 110, 114, 130–1, 149,
 152, 175, 178, 180–1, 184–7,
 197–203, 210–12, 216, 220
otherness, *see* alterity; the other

pandemic *see* COVID-19 coronavirus
Pendle Witch Trials 13, 141, 147, 148,
  151–2
performance (*also* performative) 9–10, 41,
 45, 49, 90, 92, 95–100, 126, 145, 148,
 156, 160, 162, 179, 183, 185, 191,
 191 n.2
 see also meaning as event (*also* as
  experience, performance)
Phelan, James 7–8, 10 n.17, 19, 59, 61–5,
 70–2, 86
politics (*also* political) 3–5, 9–10, 12 n.19,
 14–15, 23, 29, 31, 73, 87–90, 92–6,
 102, 108 n.3, 111, 113, 117, 123,
 132–4, 136, 147, 173, 193–6, 201,
 209–13, 217–18
postcolonial (*also* postcolonialism,
 postcoloniality) 14–15, 88, 88 n.3,
 90, 97, 107, 123, 133, 173–5, 177,
 180–1
 author (*also* writer) 88–9, 91–5
 community 14–15, 174, 182, 186–7
 literature (*also* text, work) 9, 87–91,
  93–4, 96, 99–102
 see also colonial

Index 229

precariousness (*also* precarious) 2 n.2, 14, 120, 175–6, 181–2, 184–7
protective mimicry 9, 37, 39, 43–4, 47, 50

race (*also* racial, racialized, intraracial) 5, 11–12, 14, 56–7, 59, 91, 93, 95–6, 101, 109, 124, 148, 173–7, 179–81, 184, 213, 218
Rashkin, Esther 13 n.20, 19, 130, 138
refugees 16, 207–23
rereading (*also* rereader) 6, 59, 66, 68, 73, 76, 79, 81–2, 84, 96 n.18, 220
  see also community of readers; hospitable reading
responsibility (*also* responsible) 3–5, 25, 29, 44, 46, 60 n.3, 63, 89 n.7, 91 n.9, 118, 178, 181
revelation (*also* reveal) 1, 4–5, 8, 16, 27–9, 37, 56, 61–2, 64–5, 68–9, 71–6, 78–84, 88, 94–6, 108–10, 112, 115, 117–20, 129–30, 132, 134, 136, 140–2, 144–5, 150, 152, 155–6, 160, 162–6, 182, 191 n.2, 194–5, 199, 201, 207, 210, 215–17, 220–1
  retrospective 57–61
  see also disclosure
romance 93, 127, 132, 189–91, 193, 195, 203
Royle, Nicholas 1, 3 n.6, 5, 9, 17, 19, 27, 35, 37–53, 108, 114–15, 122, 159, 169, 178, 188, 218–19

secrecy (*also* secret) and narrative sequence 1, 4, 6, 8, 55–6, 66, 68, 71–2, 108
  see also community and secrecy; concealment; meaning and secrecy
shame (*also* shameful, ashamed) 11, 13 n.20, 14, 118, 125, 130, 173, 177–9, 181, 183–5, 196, 198–9, 208, 215
Simmel, Georg 15, 19, 28, 35, 192–3, 197–8, 202–3, 205
singularity (*also* singular) 2–4, 9–13, 26, 29–31, 34, 38, 43–4, 46, 74, 90–2, 97, 101–2, 109–11, 113–14, 120–1, 127, 149, 155, 157–8, 166, 178, 183, 201, 209–11, 215, 220
  see also death; exposure; finitude
slavery (*also* neoslave narrative) 7 n.10, 174, 176, 180–1, 218
Smith, Ali 5, 23–35
  How to Be Both 9, 23–35
spectre (also spectral, spectrality) 49, 119, 130–1, 179, 207–9, 215–17, 220–1
  spectral manuscript 13, 129, 133
  see also ghost
subaltern 88 n.3, 103, 123, 136, 146, 148
suspense 7, 72–5, 79, 81, 123, 142, 191

telepathy (*also* telepathic, telepathically) 42–3, 49, 115–16, 159, 159 n.5, 161, 165
Toolan, Michael 7, 19, 71–3, 78–9, 86
transparency (*also* transparent) 14–15, 34, 40, 69, 87, 95, 100, 114, 193–7, 200, 203, 210
trauma (*also* traumatic, traumatizing) 77, 107, 115, 129, 136, 161 n.8, 163, 168, 174, 202, 207–8, 215–16, 218–19
  transgenerational 12, 124, 130–3, 208

undecidability (*also* undecidable) 4, 8 n.14, 9, 28, 30, 47, 50, 69, 91, 116, 119–20, 165, 167, 199

Vietnam War 16, 123–4, 127, 207, 213–19

Warhol, Robyn R. 7, 19
Wicomb, Zoë 5, 9–11, 87–104
  'Art Work' 97
  David's Story 96–7
  'To Hear the Variety of Discourses' 87
  October 87 n.1, 96–7
  Playing in the Light 9, 87–104
  'In Search of Tommie' 9, 87–104
  You Can't Get Lost in Cape Town 87, 95
Williams, Raymond 2, 19
Winterson, Jeanette 5, 139–54
  The Daylight Gate 13, 139–54
witchcraft 13, 42, 139–54
  see also Pendle Witch Trials

www.ingramcontent.com/pod-product-compliance
Lightning Source LLC
Chambersburg PA
CBHW072145290426
44111CB00012B/1979